I0868063

Writing Human Rights

Writing Human Rights

The Political Imaginaries of Writers of Color

Crystal Parikh

University of Minnesota Press
Minneapolis
London

The University of Minnesota Press gratefully acknowledges the generous assistance provided for the publication of this book by the Abraham and Rebecca Stein Faculty Publication Fund in the Department of English at New York University.

Portions of chapter 2 were published as "'Come Almost Home': Human Rights and the Return of Minor Subjects," *Journal of Human Rights* 12, no. 1 (2013): 121–37 (www.tandfonline.com). An earlier version of chapter 3 was published as "Writing the Borderline Subject of War in Susan Choi's *The Foreign Student*," *Southern Quarterly* 4, no. 3 (2009): 47–66. An earlier version of chapter 4 was published as "Regular Revolutions: Feminist Travels in Julia Alvarez's *How the García Girls Lost Their Accents* and *In the Time of the Butterflies*," *Journal of Transnational American Studies* 3 (2011): 1–28. Portions of chapter 5 were published as "Being Well: The Right to Health in Asian American Literature," *Amerasia* 39, no. 1 (2013): 33–47.

Published by the University of Minnesota Press
111 Third Avenue South, Suite 290
Minneapolis, MN 55401-2520
http://www.upress.umn.edu

Library of Congress Cataloging-in-Publication Data

Names: Parikh, Crystal, author.
Title: Writing human rights : the political imaginaries of writers of color / Crystal Parikh.
Description: Minneapolis : University of Minnesota Press, 2017. | Includes bibliographical references and index.
Identifiers: LCCN 2016043359 (print) | ISBN 978-0-8166-9705-2 (hc) | ISBN 978-0-8166-9706-9 (pb)
Subjects: LCSH: American literature—Minority authors—History and criticism. | Human rights in literature. | Politics and literature—United States—History.
Classification: LCC PS153.M56 P385 2017 (print) | DDC 810.9/3529—dc23
LC record available at https://lccn.loc.gov/2016043359

For Nikhil

Contents

UN International Bill of Human Rights
Toni Morrison, *Beloved*

Introduction

The U.S. Good Life, the UN World, and the Human Rights Record

> *To get to a place where you could love anything you chose—not to need permission for desire—well now,* that *was freedom.*
>
> —Toni Morrison, *Beloved*

Human rights are easy to dismiss, and they have been regularly cast off, in theory and in practice. Detractors come in all shades of political and critical hue: the realist, the revolutionary, the relativist, the chauvinist. Skeptics not only debate the effectiveness of human rights law and institutions as instruments of deterrence and justice, but also question whether "human rights" actually even *exist* as such. Yet, despite persistent doubt and mistrust, by the dawn of the twenty-first century, human rights had achieved international status as a geopolitical lingua franca. The tremendous growth of human rights discourse in myriad forms of political speech, social struggle, and popular culture is mirrored in the veritable explosion of academic attention, friendly or otherwise, to human rights, which was once under the almost exclusive purview of legal studies, political science, and international relations. Now, scholars in the humanities have increasingly entered the conversation, asking about the aesthetic and cultural renderings of human rights principles, rhetoric, and politics.

Writing Human Rights takes as its premise the idea that human rights provide deeply meaningful methods of political and moral imagining, especially for subjects whose recognition by the state is tenuous, if not altogether foreclosed. Human rights politics and discourse put forward the acutely innovative set of related propositions that all human beings are, despite other social differences, equal with respect to rights and thus have equal claims to these rights, that these rights are natural, not contingent upon the whims of political authority, and that any government's legitimacy depends upon its ability to secure these rights for its subjects.[1] Elaborated in varied legal documents, including national constitutions and the charters of regional and international organizations, with more or less (often less) historical effectivity, human rights principles in themselves convey an ethical vision that has shaped the meaning of modernity as well as real and imagined encounters across the globe.

But while the claims of human rights are universal and timeless in scope, the spatial and historical parameters of *Writing Human Rights* are more carefully delimited. This book treats American literature by writers of color—or what I call "minor literatures"—from the closing years of the Cold War to the early years of the U.S. "war on terror," a period we might designate as the "contemporary."[2] In so doing, this book intervenes in and contributes to the study of human rights and literature by reading the political theory of human rights through the ethical deliberations staged in narratives authored by contemporary American writers of color. Against a strain of American cultural studies that almost entirely reproves norms and rights discourses, *Writing Human Rights* takes seriously the significance and place of political and moral norms, even as it explores the ethical conditions under which new norms, more capacious formulations of rights, and alternative kinds of political community emerge. Rather than discussing human rights norms in the sweeping and monolithic terms that also often characterize their treatment in literary and cultural criticism, I consider the specific principles that have been articulated as individual, and in some cases collective, rights. I do not intend to uniformly and summarily celebrate *nor* dismiss human rights. Instead, the following chapters offer close and dialectical readings of the transnational political subjects, agencies, and communities that minor literatures imagine in order to understand their implications for various human rights documents, as legal texts and aspirational ideals, and vice versa.

Besides reenlivening political aspirations for solidarity and justice, which, as this introduction elaborates, seem to have been abandoned since the end of the Cold War, my survey of American literature through the perspectives of postcolonial, postsocialist, and transnational/diaspora studies in the following chapters serves several related purposes: (1) to conceptualize an ethico-politics of human rights in literature in such a way that they cannot be reduced to the humanitarian "right to intervene" in the affairs of others; (2) to "provincialize" America and the limited and exceptionalist accounts of American political freedoms and cultural goods that have, since the end of the Cold War, predominated global imaginaries of the "good life"; and (3) to signal how literatures so often seen as marginal or provincial salvos in "identity politics" within the United States spiritedly articulate the "planetary" concerns that critics have recently conceived out of older notions of "world literature." In the context of the U.S.-led liberal internationalism and neoliberal transnationalism that I describe in this introduction and chapter 1, human rights discourse has readily been conflated with liberal humanitarianism. As I further describe in chapter 2, such liberal humanitarianism evacuates political subjectivity and social desire from those whom it addresses, ascribing to them instead abject victimhood. The objects of humanitarian campaigns—almost always located elsewhere than the United States—are ones whose (bare) life must be saved and whose personhood must be (re)made to reflect suppositions of the American good life.

In contrast, *Writing Human Rights* probes a duality in the historical conception of human rights by which to elaborate the ethico-politics that minor American literatures engage. On the one hand, the subject of human rights has largely been imagined as a latently American one—always already, that is, American in character and desires. On the other hand, however, human rights are imagined to be that which *others*—other people in other places—need, while Americans always already enjoy an exceptional "good life," not only in terms of material comforts and political freedoms, but in the sense of the good moral life of *bios,* by which Greek philosophy designated the "proper" form of living. This duality is one mediated by a racial dialectic of social vulnerability and national belonging, which renders freedom, justice, and self-determination for persons of color in the United States an ongoing and incomplete political project. The following chapters, then, seek to demonstrate how a human rights *literacy* pairs the minor subjects of American literary studies with decolonization, socialist, and other political struggles in the global South. While racial minorities are by no means the only subjects who might lay claim to human rights, any more than writers of color are the only artists whose works partake in such a cultural politics, it is my contention that the social and historical location of these particular minor subjects proves an indispensable fulcrum for reading the possibilities of human rights against the mandates of possessive individualism, multicultural neoliberalism, and modern state sovereignty.

The human rights method I propose is thus a dialectical critique of idealized American rights, freedoms, and good life that obtains in the human rights record, and minor literatures prove a considerable repository for those forms of being, ways of life, and subjects of rights made otherwise impossible at our current juncture.[3] In the remaining sections of this introduction, I offer a brief historical overview of the international and domestic postwar contexts in which an international human rights regime came to be established, focusing in particular on *Beloved* by Toni Morrison as a watershed novel for fathoming the implications of that past for the present. Ending the introduction with the postsocialist integration of a postcolonial global order, fashioned through neoliberal ideals, I move in chapter 1 to consider how U.S. writers of color, facing a newly burgeoning domestic market for their literary production, took stock of the radically altered landscapes of the late Cold War. This first chapter argues that minor literatures by Ernest Gaines *(A Gathering of Old Men)* and Maxine Hong Kingston *(The Woman Warrior)* preserve and re-member forms of Afro-Asian solidarity organized around the right to self-determination and cultural cooperation, as well as the rights to social security and economic development, that the human rights record, in particular the International Convention on the Elimination of All Forms of Racial Discrimination, makes manifest.

Chapter 2 describes the type of ethical witness that a transnational human rights imaginary enables by considering how minor literatures materialize the "minor subjects" of human rights rendered otherwise impossible within a domestic court of claims. Reading the novels *Dogeaters* by Jessica Hagedorn and *A Gesture Life* by Chang-rae Lee for the fundamental "right to have rights," which the Universal Declaration of Human Rights (UDHR) decrees must be recognized for all human persons, I consider how human rights politics take on a "life of their own," generating subjects that cannot be reduced to either the citizens of liberal states or the victims of authoritarian states saved and ministered to by liberal humanitarianism. Since the production of this political subject depends fundamentally on the characterization of human existence as *embodied vulnerability,* chapter 3 accordingly moves to consider the "right to the security of person," especially as it is formulated in the UN Convention against Torture. By examining how Susan Choi's novel *The Foreign Student* returns to the period of postwar civil rights reform and the institution of the security state during the Korean War, this chapter traces how war and torture "work over" the body in pain to stabilize the border between domestic and foreign, as well as Communist and capitalist, to secure racialized ideals of national identity. At the same time, it probes how critical commitments to "human security" and the security of person in minor literatures open onto alternate horizons of political community.

Since the end of the Cold War, human rights discourse has been not only globalized in scope, but also increasingly "pluralized" in texture, as human rights instruments have come to address the plight of particular groups that are considered in need of distinct care. The second half of *Writing Human Rights* hence explores the subject positions of three such particularized groups—women, the disabled, and children—often chiefly considered in humanitarian imaginaries as objects of abuse and of charitable benevolence, but rarely as active political agents and desirous subjects who make claims in their own names. Chapters 4 and 5 and the conclusion explain how minor literatures construct these subjects in relation to specific (but interrelated) human rights principles—the right to revolution, the right to health, and the right to family—in order to sanction lifeworlds and forms of "good life" other than that endorsed by (neo) liberalism. Drawing on the Convention on the Elimination of All Forms of Discrimination against Women, the Convention on the Rights of Persons with Disabilities, and the Convention on the Rights of the Child, the final chapters of *Writing Human Rights* read narrative fiction by Julia Alvarez (*How the García Girls Lost Their Accents* and *In the Time of the Butterflies*), Jhumpa Lahiri *(Unaccustomed Earth),* Ana Castillo *(So Far from God),* and Aimee Phan *(We Should Never Meet),* all of whom rearticulate the geopolitical common sense of "good life" through their representations of vulnerable but resilient human rights subjects.

As human rights scholars and activists insist, the panoply of human rights is indivisible. In the words of the UN Office of the High Commissioner for Human Rights, the "improvement of one right facilitates advancement of the others." This point became exceedingly clear to me as I worked out a human rights approach in the following chapters. I found how easily I might have addressed a range of human rights norms with respect to any of the texts I consider in this book. For example, a novel such as Morrison's *Beloved,* which I examine below, demonstrates with painstaking precision how inexorably linked are the right to have rights (i.e., standing), the right to security of person, and the right to family for the former slave women and men it depicts. Likewise, in its portrait of life-threatening illness in the midst of civil unrest and international warfare,

Choi's *The Foreign Student* considers how security of person (or bodily integrity)—a right conventionally understood to guard against unlawful detainment and torture—might also more subtly involve the right to health, as well as the right to self-determination. While such interdependency of human rights and human beings is a theoretical crux for the readings I present, it also renders my particular organizational structure and emphases somewhat contingent and the discussion of "good life" with respect to any single author or text necessarily incomplete. My intent throughout has therefore been to suggest the ethico-political possibilities for reading minor literatures, rather than to provide an exhaustive account of "the good life" that they avow.

Finally, as does much scholarship concerning the theory and politics of human rights, I emphasize bodily and social vulnerability throughout the following pages. At the same time, I also bring the insights of feminist and queer studies to bear on a discussion that too often reproduces the very discursive and epistemological objecthood of those whom it addresses. I thus also constantly stress the way in which minor literatures give voice to the complex *desires* of these subjects and how such desires—sexual as well as social—mediate the subject's experiences of vulnerability and agency. On the one hand (and as elaborated in chapters 2 and 3), social institutions and material culture mean to provide protection for vulnerable embodied human beings, that is, to put at least *some* bodies "at ease" with their physical and natural environments. Yet, such security also often "feels" deadening, wherein shifting and unpredictable forms of desire can quickly and profoundly antagonize such protocols of comfort and protection. Desire can thus propel even the most privileged of subjects back into "risky" practices and environments that render them newly vulnerable, and, as my survey of a broad range of texts suggests, this remains true even for those often deemed "deprived" or "disadvantaged." Working across political theories of human rights and social theories of gender and sexuality, my readings in this book offer a characterization of the human as vulnerable, but never a figure of pure lack. Rather, our vulnerability both conditions *and* is a product of the different types of volition that move us in, and into, relations with others, and I employ the phrase "want otherwise" to denote this relation between our exposedness and desire. My hope is that such a method might incite us, in the words of Ann Cvetkovich, "to imagine a political life that would be able to do some justice to the unpredictability of desire."[4]

A Global Nation and the Limits of Self-Determination

Why are human rights that are nominally universal so regularly cast as Western, and especially American, in character and significance? Contemporary international human rights discourse originated with the founding of the United Nations in 1945; the UN Charter established the Commission on Human Rights, which in turn drafted the International Bill of Rights. The political and discursive history of human rights reflects and is embedded within a postwar history where the moral hegemony of political and economic liberalism eventually displaced both fascism and communism. At the same time, liberalism is itself plagued by the contradiction between, on one hand, its theory of natural rights grounded in the individual person and, on the other, its avowal of statist practices and positive law, which derive their legitimacy from the sanction that sovereign power avails to itself. States have thereby extended rhetorical acknowledgment to human rights without providing substantial means of practical enforcement.[5] In its consistent failure to stem atrocities and human rights violations since 1945, the international community does not simply ignore or exhibit indifference to the plight of the vulnerable. Rather, the problem of rightlessness is a structural problem endemic to the modern state system.[6]

As Hannah Arendt famously observed, since the French Revolution, the question of human rights has been entwined with that of national emancipation, such that "only the emancipated sovereignty of the people, of one's own people, seemed to be able to insure them."[7] Thus, although the "rights of man" were supposed to be independent of all governments, "it turned out that the moment human beings lacked their own government and had to fall back upon their minimum rights, no authority was left to protect them and no institution was willing to guarantee them."[8] Consequently, civil or constitutional rights always conceptually (and too often practically) supersede human rights, assuming that "all human beings were citizens of some kind of political community," which, in the modern regime of law and politics, amounts to the sovereign entities of nation states.[9] The seemingly stable totality of the nation-state system renders those excluded from such community an "unfortunate *exception* to an otherwise sane and normal rule," and for that reason the subjects of human rights, Arendt laments, exist as a problem of nonrecognition: "No law exists for them."[10]

Besides being subject to indiscriminate police action, the stateless enjoy whatever liberties or privileges that they *do* only out of *charity* and not as a right, per se.[11] For Arendt, the loss of recognition before the law amounts to a loss of the "right to have rights," rendering the stateless "nothing but human."[12] In this case, human rights need not necessarily be abandoned but instead become, in effect, "a new right to 'human interference' " and, in particular "the right to invasion" enjoyed by other state actors, who choose when, where, and in whose name bare life will be protected.[13] In her conception of the "state of nature," Arendt thus finds not the *source* of human rights, but rather their "destitution."[14] Arendt's vision of any good life is in this way bound up in positive law, by which the sovereign authorizes and cultivates the "rights of man and citizen." Ultimately, as Hope Lewis concisely puts it, the "fundamental irony of the international human rights movement" is "that states, often the most egregious violators of human rights . . . were also to be relied on as the primary and most powerful protectors" of those same rights.[15]

It is nearly impossible to overstate the extent to which the United States managed and exploited, in its own interests, the ideological contradictions inherent in human rights after World War II. In particular, the exigencies of the Cold War overdetermined the historical and political iteration of human rights, marshaling their possible scope and meaning toward achieving U.S. aims in this global conflict from the 1950s through the 1980s. While this version was initially pitched in counterpoint to the fascist regimes of the Axis enemies, by the time the Commission on Human Rights began crafting an international bill of rights, U.S. officials were as interested (if not more so) in the "soft power" that they could wield through the United Nations as they were in any practical implementation of human rights principles on the ground. The State Department crafted its own policy on human rights, largely ignoring social and economic rights, and this became, in turn, a critical precedent for how human rights have been conceived in the United Nations and other international bodies.[16] American liberalism and then neoliberalism—which, as I discuss below, have certainly enjoyed global hegemony since 1989—and their interfaces with the international human rights regime during and after the Cold War have therefore rendered an alternative genealogy of human rights fragmented and scattered in terms of any *political movement*.[17] Great power politics steered almost every aspect of U.S. foreign policy and international engagement during the Cold War and were further compounded by the isolationist tendencies that have perennially held sway (especially among members of the Republican Party) in the U.S. Congress, as well as by a vision of free trade across borders (as, for example, institutionalized in the Bretton Woods charters). As a result, international human rights have been tethered to the U.S. Bill of Rights as a model of individual freedoms, a narrowing of range that I seek to challenge.

The United States remarkably orchestrated a postwar order that at once recognized and granted legitimacy to decolonization movements while also buttressing its own (as well as Western European) geopolitical and economic domination. In order to appreciate the significance and effect of this achievement, we must go well beyond facile notions of American "imperialism" and even "neo-imperialism" and look to a longer history of democratic self-determination and nation building, which in turn profoundly shaped an integrationist vision of a new international order.[18] As Charles Bright and Michael Geyer argue, the American nation has been anomalous with respect to nation-making paradigms. Neither a version of the transformation of ancient societies into modern states (as in France or Britain), nor an example of the "insurgent" nationality consolidated in struggles against these imperial powers, the American nation stands as a "novel political formation":

> Who were its citizens, if people, white and male, from almost everywhere and anywhere constituted the nation? What was its sovereign territory, if the borders were in motion and the state barely in control of a people pushing beyond them? What was the imagined community of the nation if its first principles were the rights of (all) mankind? How could a global nation be also, and at the same time, a sovereign nation?[19]

Bright and Geyer conclude that such a universalizing imaginary has always posed a problem for defining national sovereignty, that is, for "efforts to define a people and territory fit for self-government."[20] Rather, the boundaries of the nation-state have been unstable, and "American civil society . . . has always been more than the United States—reaching, grasping, pushing beyond the territorial confines and evading control. . . . America was always larger, more boundless than the United States, and in this respect always already a global nation."[21]

A conventional perspective on the "Americanization" of the globe after 1945 assumes that U.S. leaders sought increasing geopolitical and economic power in order to secure "the American way of life." This view, however, tends to obscure the extent to which that very imaginary of "American life"—characterized by a corporate-industrial order, free movement across integrated territories of social exchange, and affluent, consumerist lifestyles—was consolidated *through* a Cold War agenda and constructed against the threat of Soviet political and economic programs.[22] American national identity *and* U.S. foreign policy during the Cold War crucially depended upon bringing different territories and peoples under U.S. national influence, fostering affective identifications between Americans and these others, and promoting free trade between them; they depended, in other words, on what Christina Klein calls "the global imaginary of integration."[23] Equating American economic health and national security with access to other regions of the world, but steeped in unwavering conceptions of the nation as the leader of the free world and the victor *over* imperialist forces in World War II, U.S. foreign policy ideologically remapped the nation and its place in the world.

Liberals, beginning with Franklin Delano Roosevelt (following the lead of Woodrow Wilson before him), saw the political and economic future of the United States as inextricably tied to territorial and cultural expansion and crafted an image of the nation as a global power that countered a longer tradition of isolationism.[24] At the same time, this power could not reproduce the imperial character of European or Soviet expansionism. The integrationist worldview—forged through both official political speech and more informal social representations and cultural practices—achieved these dual ends by giving rise to sentimental discourses of equality and tolerance.[25] American expansion and exchange with other peoples of the world were imagined to be reciprocal and symmetrical. As such, winning the decades-long Cold War essentially entailed the campaign to "win hearts and minds" in the decolonizing world by disseminating American ideals of freedom and images of the "American way of life."

The Atlantic Charter, a World War II policy statement agreed upon and issued by Roosevelt and Winston Churchill that served as a blueprint for postwar planning, offered one of the earliest instantiations of this "American global nation." Along with its stipulations that neither the United States nor Britain sought territorial gains at the conclusion of the war and its call for a common postwar disarmament, the Atlantic Charter provided for territorial adjustments "in accord with the wishes of the peoples concerned" and the right to self-determination for "all people." (Additionally, it called for global economic cooperation and advancement of social welfare, including the lowering of trade barriers and the freedom of the seas, as well as "a world free of want and fear," points to which I return in the next chapter.) Reviving a rhetoric first proclaimed in Woodrow Wilson's Fourteen Points policy statement during World War I, the Atlantic Charter's espousal of self-determination seemed to extend the promise of political autonomy and equality for a host of colonized peoples across the globe. As importantly, though (and as I elaborate in chapter 1), anticolonial leaders understood the self-determination pronounced in the charter to constitute *a right,* rather than a "gift," a stance eventually adopted in the International Bill of Rights, although notably absent in the UDHR of 1948.[26]

At the same time, however, the American imaginary of integration tied the rights and freedoms of American citizens to the fates of decolonizing others and, in particular, to the orderly integration of those others into an American global imaginary.[27] A fundamental contradiction (one to which, I argue in this book, contemporary writers repeatedly return) hence underwrote the liberal imaginary of integration. It is that, as Americans understood it, those rights and freedoms being promised to other peoples in other places remained nonetheless the special provenance and manifest destiny of the American citizen.[28] Thus, during and after the Cold War, a cultural pluralist ethos came to express, rather paradoxically, a nationalist superiority that was supposed to be simultaneously universal *and* unique to the United States.[29] The *functional* solution to this quandary rested on harnessing anticolonial aspirations to the limits of the sovereign nation-state form.

In other words, in this era, from the perspective of the great powers, self-determination amounted to the consolidation of an international order organized completely and necessarily around sovereign nation-states that functioned as readily to *limit* political will as to allow for its expression.[30] This entire new world order of "united nations," as John D. Kelly and Martha Kaplan argue, emerged *after* World War II as an alternative to one defined by competing European empires.[31] Throughout the nineteenth century, empires subsumed "nations," which, in turn, were predominantly equated with "races."[32] But in its postwar planning, the United

States viewed a system of formally equal, self-determined nation-states as necessary for global stability. At this moment, then, liberalism began to obscure vestiges of nations-as-races, with nations-as-states, where states would serve as politically neutral containers of lower-level ethnic, racial, and class politics.

The international peace envisaged in this "united nations world" required nation-states to serve as *the* horizon for *all* politics, such that relations *between* states remained peaceful and, in turn, ensured "open economic doors."[33] Of course, if those "doors" had to be more coercively "held open," the United States assigned to itself the policeman's role of doing so.[34] Thus, the "predicament of post-coloniality" consists of "the fact that decolonization as actually experienced was entry into a new world order already tooled for purposes at best differing from the aims of the anticolonial movements, and at times clearly obstructive of them."[35] In this united nations world, American economic and political interests mandated that "all that a political agent in any 'new nation' could rightly aspire to was his or her national interest, and that interest could only, responsibly, be [the] dream of 'being free.'"[36]

For first Wilson and then Roosevelt, the stability of a new international order hinged on what they deemed to be the precarious line between nationalist self-determination and revolutionary "anarchy."[37] Both administrations saw radical or socialist politics as vehicles of dangerous unrest, and they limited support for nationalist movements to those that championed stable states, free of the taint of communism.[38] As American aid and leadership proved essential to the rebuilding of Western Europe, the United States eventually prevailed upon its European allies to abandon ongoing imperial designs in favor of American Cold War interests.[39] But the United States also cast itself as the "senior, wiser adviser, ready to help a junior nation in need of modernization and development."[40] Beyond Europe, the U.S. mission was accomplished by building political and cultural alliances with local elites, in order to gain access to local markets, and providing military aid and training, especially in those nations where leftist campaigns had made inroads, in order to secure the development of emergent states as well as their commitment to U.S. Cold War policies aimed at containing the Soviet bloc.

Certainly organized around U.S. interests, the united nations world nevertheless articulated the imaginary of global integration and the American way of life through the consecration of politically free and formally equal sovereign states.[41] The American self-image as the world's exemplary *post*colony determined the destinies of a multitude of subjects not only in the United States, but across the globe, by placing the idealization and protection of *American* citizenship (rather than those of European liberal traditions or other postcolonial societies) at the center of the new world order. As Odd Arne Westad persuasively puts it: "Victory in World War II was therefore a victory not just for an alliance, but also for the American way of life itself."[42] From World War II (with intimations in World War I) to the current "war on terror," international wars, international trade agreements, and social and cultural exchange remarkably articulate with an American "way of life" that, on a global terrain, becomes identified with "the good life" itself.[43] At the same time, since the late 1960s, the control that the United States has had over a global "American civil society" has been tenuous at best. U.S. executive and congressional leaders have alternately embraced *or* denounced U.S. involvement in "nation building" and securing state sovereignty in other regions of the world, especially where its own economic interests are ambiguous. Instead, transnational institutions—for example, corporations and NGOs—have more regularly taken up the charge of disseminating American ideals, both as economic practices and as conceptions of rights and property.[44] The most commonplace iterations of international human rights have also corresponded to this imagined community whose "first principles were the rights of (all) mankind"—a community ascribed to and claimed by the U.S. nation-state, but one that, as I contend in the following pages, always potentially outpaces it and escapes its control.

Domestic Jurisdiction and Liberal Racial Reform

Within the newly forming United Nations, the "domestic jurisdiction" clause provided the practical mechanism for stabilizing an integrating world order. John Foster Dulles, who served as a U.S. adviser in the creation of the United Nations, as one of the drafters of the UN Charter's Preamble, and later as secretary of state under President Eisenhower, inserted the crucial language that stated: "Nothing contained in the present Charter shall authorize the United Nations to intervene in matters which are essentially within the domestic jurisdiction of any state or shall require the Members to submit such matters to settlement under the present Charter." This clause ensured protection of state sovereignty, thereby effectively limiting the application of human rights principles; scholars and activists alike have identified it as the source of the United Nations' "failure to act" in countless instances of international crimes and atrocities ever since.[45] The clause operationally (if not ideologically) resolved the quandary resulting from, on the one hand, the guarantee of self-determination as state sovereignty and, on the other, the UN Charter and the UDHR's proclamation of inherent, inalienable dignity and rights for all human beings "without distinction of any kind." In insisting that the clause was a non-negotiable precondition for the United States to sign on to the charter, Dulles principally satisfied a congressional Southern bloc worried that UN membership would imperil Jim Crow segregation.[46]

I highlight this particular episode to underscore that, despite leading the charge in the formation of the institution, not only did the United States actively vitiate the practicability of the United Nations—reducing it instead to an organization that maintained great power balance—and its various human rights instruments, but it did so in good part to maintain the legal and social order of white supremacy at home.[47] As Daniel Sargent has argued, a more robust and common sense of human rights—what he calls its "rediscovery"—in the United States thus became possible (to the extent that it did take hold) only *after* the successes of the civil rights movement, the demise of Jim Crow, and the more general expansion of Fourteenth Amendment protections by the Warren Court, all of which "reaffirmed liberal self-confidence . . . that change could be achieved through gradualist methods."[48] Accordingly, the black freedom struggle within the United States was induced to play out as a domestic civil rights movement, even as many of its leaders extended visions of social and economic justice on a global scale.[49] During the war, the NAACP viewed the Atlantic Charter as heralding a radical transformation for racial minorities *in the United States,* and under the leadership of W. E. B. Du Bois, it challenged the domestic jurisdiction clause in 1947 by petitioning the Commission on Human Rights to investigate the conditions of social, political, and economic inequity facing African Americans in the United States.[50] However, U.S. delegates (in considerable agreement with and receiving assistance from "the friend of the Negro," Eleanor Roosevelt) in the United Nations quickly and decisively shut down the appeal, and U.S. commentators disparaged the NAACP for playing into the hands of the Soviet Union, which had sponsored the petition.[51]

As the Cold War unfurled in the second half of the twentieth century, black leaders found themselves entirely subject to this logic of "containment," the strategic principle devised by George Kennan and a fundamental pillar of the Truman Doctrine. As the United States sought to limit the influence of the Soviet Union, first in Eastern Europe and later in Asia, Africa, and Latin America (despite the Soviet Union's skepticism, at least during the 1940s and 1950s, that Communist revolts were even feasible in colonized regions of the world), it began providing military and economic aid in order to, in the words of President Truman, "support free peoples who are resisting attempted subjugation by armed minorities or by outside pressures."[52] By Eisenhower's term in office, the "imaginary of containment," as Klein terms it, not only regarded the Cold War as a zero-sum game, with no room for nonaligned or neutral nations, but "communism" provided a flexible designation for identifying (and caricaturing) struggles thought to be antipathetic to U.S. security and capital's interest.[53] Together, integration and containment amounted to a "dual policy" that provided support for anticolonial leaders and national self-determination, "but only as long as the exercise of that right did not override the ideological predilections of the state."[54] This polarizing political frame thrived as powerfully *within* the United States as in other nations, as Cold War pressures established boundaries on black internationalist perspectives, demanding that African Americans prioritize (American) national unity *over* (transnational) racial solidarity.[55] Black leaders such as Walter White, Roy Wilkins, and Philip Randolph increasingly distanced themselves from radicalism and instead stressed a civil rights platform, while the federal government sought to "contain" the publicity, especially international exposure, available to more voluble critics of American racism, such as Du Bois, Paul Robeson, and Josephine Baker.[56]

At the same time, developments in the Cold War, including the Soviet Union's ready dissemination of images of American racial hierarchy and violence to newly independent nations, convinced many U.S. foreign policy and federal officials of the need for reform in American race relations.[57] The NAACP began to cast racial reform as part of the struggle against Communism, and the Truman administration not only initiated the desegregation of the military, but filed briefs in civil rights cases regarding restrictive covenants, segregation on railroad cars, and school segregation.[58] In all of these instances, the Justice Department stressed the harm done to the nation's international image by segregation and racial discrimination.[59] And yet, even as government officials sought to minimize segregation by portraying it as a localized problem, rather than a national one, groups such as the U.S. Information Agency avidly incorporated racism into a story of national redemption and reform, heralding a "new reconstruction" that was being achieved by a gradual and progressive change that dismantled racial hierarchy.[60]

Concurrently, fearing that racially exclusive immigration restrictions also blemished the image of U.S. democracy abroad, liberals successfully implemented sweeping reforms to immigration law. The 1952 McCarran-Walter Act increased the ceiling on national quotas and did away with the bar to naturalization for Asian immigrants. In 1965, Congress eliminated altogether the system of quotas based on national origins (instituted in the 1920s) that excluded almost all immigration from non-European nations outside the Western Hemisphere, replacing them with new, more evenly distributed criteria that emphasized occupational skills and "family reunification." Yet, as Mae Ngai has shown, even as the 1952 and 1965 reforms seemed to mirror the civil rights reforms that emphasized equal access and protection, they were both progressive *and* reactionary in intention and effect and were meant to reconcile liberal pluralist and nationalist interests in the postwar context. On the one hand, American liberalism during and after World War II posited cultural pluralism, a discourse with roots in the late Progressive Era, as the converse of fascist ideals of white supremacy. But this sensibility, with its tolerance or embrace of cultural diversity, also subtly comprised a belief in national superiority.[61]

Moreover, by the late 1940s, such pluralist ideals were regarded in terms of strategic Cold War interests. As immigration reformers urged Congress to repeal the quotas that the 1952 law had retained, they portrayed the racism behind the national origins principle as "an anomalous interruption in the national narrative," which impaired the nation in its struggle against Communism.[62] Although conservatives worried that immigration reform opened the door to subversive elements, the integrationist case of liberal reformers held sway in the 1960s. And, in addition to their political objectives, immigration reforms served the nation's economic interests by giving preference to sorely needed professionals and laborers, while retaining numerical restrictions against a much-feared flood of migrants seeking economic mobility.

Despite being prominently framed in the language of democratic pluralism, these changes, as Ngai contends, actually "hardened the distinction between citizen and alien," casting the latter as the "citizen's silent double."[63] Constructed as a figure of lack, bereft of the axiomatic right to have rights that citizenship secures for individuals, the alien signals the limits of a liberal imaginary of integration that approached social and political justice as a matter of abstract and formal equality. Liberal nationalism granted no space for alternate perspectives, originating for example from a human rights or nonaligned politics, and it approached the question of equality as a formal, rather than a substantive one. The new, evenly distributed quotas did not take into account the differing size or need of individual nations, nor redress the way in which particular nations had been historically excluded from immigration prior to 1952.[64] As Ngai concludes, the liberal nationalism that underwrote the immigration reforms of 1965 (which, in turn, continued to structure immigration policy into the twenty-first century) "resists humanitarianism and remains blind to the causal connections between the United States' global projections and the conditions abroad that impel emigration."[65]

And yet, the new policies enabled patterns of immigration, especially from non-European regions of the world, unforeseen by Congress and unprecedented in American history. Asian Americans and Latinos have been the fastest growing populations in the United States since the 1960s, dramatically altering the nation's racial landscape by the twenty-first century.[66] Although the Hart-Celler Act was meant primarily to placate ethnic European American constituencies, and although the rapidly changing racial and ethnic demographics of the nation begot neoconservative backlash in the 1980s, the act has been crucial in securing the ongoing liberal fantasy of the United States as a "nation of immigrants" and therefore a "global nation." While it rendered undocumented aliens into "impossible subjects" of law and politics—and even, in a variety of instances, did so to legal permanent residents (e.g., in 1996, Congress terminated welfare benefits for legal aliens), the liberal imaginary proclaimed these reforms as being of a piece with the nation's progressive achievement of democratic freedom and equality for all.

This American imaginary of integration, in both its domestic and international aspects, brought to "other" peoples a conception of liberal individualism long enjoyed by white male Americans, who were its ideal(ized) subjects.[67] In the liberal imaginary, individual personhood and property ownership exist in a mutually constitutive relationship of political economy. The liberal individual possesses, first and foremost, himself—free to labor, move, and live according to his own will. The political order of liberal democracy, in turn, exists to protect the freedom of the self-possessed individual, his capacities in himself and that which he acquires as an extension of himself through those capacities, namely private property.[68] The self-possessed individual therefore stands as the ideal person who enjoys full citizenship rights. Those historically deemed incapable of self-possession because of deficiencies in their ability to think rationally, labor independently, or otherwise command authority over themselves (such as children, women, and the mentally ill) have been relegated to attenuated forms of citizenship or foreclosed from it altogether (as was the case for free blacks and slaves prior to the Civil War and Asian immigrants before 1952). Nikhil Pal Singh thus argues that a "normalizing claim to whiteness" has always already preceded and predicated the exceptionalist construction of national belonging that supposedly transcends prior differences: "Racial definitions enabled the very process of thinking about U.S. national belonging as both a normative and a universal condition."[69]

Because the American democratic project has been interconnected with a tradition in which white men of property determine who is and is not fit for self-government, both domestic and global integration into a liberal democratic order has always been informed by social and cultural assumptions about what type of subject, in the United States and in other parts of the world, has the capacity to become the individuated person of modern liberalism. The racialized subjects against whom such idealized personhood is constructed have, in turn, been rendered "'exceptional' figures and legal fictions," as they are "never individuated enough" to enjoy individual rights "nor collective enough" to justify their claims to sovereignty apart from the liberal rights-granting nation.[70] The "three-fifths person" of blackness, the "domestic dependent" Indian nation, the "separate but equal" African American, the "foreign in a domestic sense" inhabitants of U.S. Pacific and Caribbean territorial holdings, and the Asian "immigrant ineligible for citizenship" comprise these primary "figures and fictions" of American law and history.[71]

To be sure, by the late twentieth century, the civil rights movement and the postwar reforms it accomplished enacted very real transformations in racial discourse and structures, most significantly in revealing that the logic of "separate but equal" underpinning legalized segregation was, in the language of the 1954 *Brown v. Board of Education* majority opinion, "inherently unequal." The passage of the Civil Rights Act of 1964 and the Voting Rights Act of 1965 accordingly prohibited discrimination and mechanisms for disenfranchisement and exclusion of African Americans and other racial minorities from national life, extending to them the "equal protection" of civil and political citizenship guaranteed by the Fourteenth Amendment. At the same time, the civil rights movement heralded the transfiguration of racial consciousness (decades in the making) as an oppositional political project for people of color, wherein racial difference could be a source of collective identity and agency, rather than (only) the basis for exclusion and denigration.[72]

And yet, the restructuring of American life remained limited, as liberal (and later even neoconservative) proponents of civil rights discourse embraced the merits of individualism and colorblindness, characterizing racism as the misguided belief system of reactionary individuals, rather than a systemic ideology that had long and thoroughly organized political, economic, and legal life in the United States. Since the 1980s, then, mainline liberalism, neoliberalism, and neoconservativism have endorsed a formal conception of racial equality that disparages and penalizes *any* overt investment in racial identity, whether on the part of white Americans or people of color. Meanwhile, stark racial disparities, especially for African Americans (but also Latinos, Native Americans, and in some cases Asian Americans) persist in almost all areas of life, including wealth, life expectancy, unemployment, incarceration, and education.[73] While (neo)liberalism attributes the gulf between minority and white experience to individual choices or "cultural" differences, it masks the structural hierarchies that have made access to material and social resources persistently uneven. As George Lipsitz has deftly demonstrated in *The Possessive Investment in Whiteness,* with respect to key areas such as home ownership, education, and employment, a "coordinated collective politics characterized by resistance, refusal, and renegotiation" protects the social and economic privileges accumulated by white Americans over decades and centuries, forestalling the possibility of substantive equality for racialized minorities in the United States.[74]

Also since the late 1980s, the era that Lisa Duggan has astutely and succinctly described as the "twilight of equality," the refusal to recognize social and economic security *as rights* and the increasingly rapid dismantling of the social and economic securities that the state provided citizens have generated new experiences of vulnerability in the United States. As Duggan and others have shown, *neo*liberal hegemony has never been only a fiscal program, even as it represents itself as pursuing neutral principles of governance and economics.[75] While it overtly dismisses social differences as cultural and private matters, neoliberalism actually "organizes material and political life in terms of race, gender, and sexuality as well as economic class and nationality, or ethnicity and religion."[76] By prizing and naturalizing certain forms of life—namely, whiteness, maleness, heteropatriarchy, the middle class—and by drawing a fixed distinction between the realms of the private/family/domestic and the public/civil society/state, the biopolitics of the neoliberal state works to sever a politics of class from that of identity.[77]

The panacea of market-provided "choices," "personal responsibility," and "tolerance" as ideological solutions by which to diminish, or at least to rationalize, economic and political inequities, as well as to reconcile cultural differences, has had a drastic social impact. Neoliberal policymakers, politicians, and corporate elites advocate a "law and order" approach that has resulted in skyrocketing rates of surveillance and incarceration.[78] Reforms in social programs and safety nets steadily have displaced the cost of child- and healthcare, education, and other needs onto individuals and families. Following sustained mass unemployment in the 1970s, years of inflation, and the consolidation of the "New Right" as a political force, the predominant political and popular discourse in the United States has involved an almost unrelenting condemnation of "welfare dependency" and policy changes that mandate participation in workfare (mostly in low-wage service-sector jobs), education, and training programs.[79] While purporting to enable the social and political agency of the autonomous and self-possessed subject, (neo)liberalism systematically dismantles institutional supports and privatizes the resources and protections afforded that subject, rendering entire populations at home and abroad disposable in the process. With its function reduced to the protection of property rights and the rights of (usually corporate) property holders, the state's policing operations take prominence, and everyday life becomes increasingly militarized. My use of "(neo)liberal" here and in the following chapters marks both the ideological continuities as well as the global permutations of American liberalism during and after the Cold War.

A neoliberal order thus compounds "older" forms of racism, such that the effects of economic and political restructuring continue to fall most severely upon people of color, despite the official and popular discourses of colorblindness, multiculturalism, and postracialism prevalent throughout the country—and does so even as neoliberalism morphs its idealized subject from the white citizen to the multicultural American and eventually the multicultural *global* citizen, so as to permit the ascendance of some people of color into positions of privilege while generating newly stigmatized others who are "the un-American, the overly race conscious, the monocultural, and the illegal."[80] The rise of multicultural literature at the end of the twentieth century participated in the cultural logics of neoliberalism, channeling much antiracist energy into a representational politics of diversity, tolerance, and inclusion, while detaching those politics from the structuralist critiques of racial capital at the heart of prior radical social movements. The new popularity that U.S. writers of color, as well as postcolonial literatures, began to achieve in the 1980s seemed to make good on the promise of inclusion, wherein visibility came to stand as evidence of (neo)liberalism's political transcendence of social difference. Despite being constantly hailed to represent the progressive incorporation of racial others into the American good life, however, these same writers, I argue, often transfigured the American lives they were conscripted to represent into the political subjects of human rights.

Generic Americans, Minor Literatures, and Morphing the Human

Numerous critics have described how specific literary genres employed in the field of human rights actually put the category of literature into crisis by confronting it with the material and political conditions of its own existence. These include, for example, John Beverly on the *testimonio,* Barbara Harlowe on revolutionary writing, and Kay Schaffer and Sidonie Smith on life writing. On the other hand, scholars such as Lynn Hunt, Joseph Slaughter, and Jodi Melamed have documented how rights discourses have been constitutive of the human subject in its prevailing modern form, the individual citizen of political personhood, as well as that subject's legibility in and through modern literature and culture. Distinct generic forms therefore contribute to the making of the human subject, perhaps none more so, as Slaughter contends and I elaborate in more detail in the following chapters, than the *bildungsroman,* the novel of individual development that seems endlessly transposable across the globe.

In proposing human rights literacy as a dialectical method, *Writing Human Rights* builds upon but also diverges from this scholarship by theorizing how the ethico-politics of minor literatures revise, if not altogether disregard, such generic distinctions in order to counter the eventualities of Cold War and post-1945 U.S. history. Thus, while Hayden White has described the historian's work to be the writing of a narrative that is essentially literary or poetic in character, the minor literatures I consider in the following pages self-consciously enact historical recoveries of that which has proven heterogeneous to the time and space of the modern state and ungovernable by it.[81] To be sure, any number of U.S. multiethnic literary works from the 1980s to the present yield a recuperative cultural politics that hews closely to the governing principles of neoliberal multiculturalism. Inasmuch as the subjects of these texts have been excluded from full recognition in terms of social and legal belonging, these texts seek to make them legible as "generic" Americans in order to secure the political and civil protections and entitlements that neoliberal multiculturalism promises to send their way. Nevertheless, I contend that they carry within them at least the traces of "the empirical complexity, the real histories of material violence, fragments of materiality, and empirically real experiences" that a human rights method reads otherwise.[82] Even more to the point, in the texts on which I have chosen to focus, these traces surface as the primary subjects of fiction. The first half of *Writing Human Rights* thus attends to the generic morphs of the human that minor literatures perform in relation to the *bildungsroman*. The second half then moves our attention from the individual *bildung* to the family saga, in order to situate the development of the human person—and the family romances she dreams up—within the social lifeworlds and political communities that she wants.

Both the family saga and family romance precede the *bildungsroman* in Western literature and culture. Originating during the thirteenth century in the Nordic region before traveling throughout Europe and the West and composed primarily of sets of short narratives, family sagas chronicled the fortunes of Icelandic families, especially during moments of widespread social and political change. Family sagas have proven highly portable, hence enjoying tremendous success as a form of world literature, and even the earliest examples were distinguished by "a stratified yet mobile society where identities are unstable and where there is an ongoing struggle between individuals climbing the social ladder."[83] Eventually often taking the form of the family novel, the family saga is never simply about the heroics or fortunes of an individual protagonist, not even the paterfamilias; rather, it concerns the reproduction and status of a family line. The genre intrinsically situates its characters in a social world that is also not the abstracted body politic of the state.

If family sagas provide some of the earliest instances of the novel, by the eighteenth century, the novel form became especially concerned with narratives akin to what Freudian psychoanalysis would term "the family romance," that is, the child's fantasy of alternate parental figures who compensate for actually existing and imperfect biological parents. As a fantasy in individual development, the family romance indexes the child's wish for a more noble lineage (often drawn from literary and other iconic images) and surfaces as the pre-oedipal staging ground for the articulation of selfhood by the child, as he comes to see himself as an individual detached from his given family. In regard to the development of Western literature, Christine van Boheemen has gamely argued that "the generic function of the novel may well be to serve as the family romance of Western culture," the form glorifying "the power of language to evoke presence, which is used as a remedy against awareness of alienation."[84] The "fully rounded life story," which the *bildungsroman* in particular delivers, thus serves as an "*imago* of a distinct, self-present subjectivity," and the realist or mimetic novel seeks to "deny the ineluctable otherness, the presence of absence, the ontological gap that necessitates discourse."[85] Enabling the *bildung* by which the individual person's advancement into autonomy is imagined, the novel's family romance serves as a repository for the contradictions and losses that the modern subject undergoes but must repudiate in order to transcend the contingencies of his existence.

In employing the term "minor literatures," I am concerned with how contemporary writers of color work across these different genres of narrative prose fiction—where the family's seemingly severed relations to the individual protagonist often materialize in unexpected, troubling, and moving ways, and realism regularly gives way to the miraculous, the utopic, or the impossible—in order to memorialize the losses of the past. In minor literatures, the failures of incorporation and integration come to constitute "an alternative site where the palimpsest of lost memories is reinvented, histories are fractured and retraced, and the unlike varieties of silence emerge into articulacy," so that the very subject of humanity comes to us in altered terms.[86] Published in 1987, at the pivotal juncture when neoconservative moral imaginaries of racialized social pathology began to collude with an ascendant (neo)liberal doctrine of possessive individualism, Toni Morrison's milestone novel *Beloved* proves such a rewritten palimpsest. For Morrison, imagining how a family devastated by the legal fictions of individual and incorporated personhood recovers itself entails imagining the human otherwise. As it confronts the violence borne by those foreclosed from legal incorporation and social recognition—those who, in turn, claim freedom on their own terms—*and* those whose very disintegration founds the personhood of other others, *Beloved* provides an exacting ethical account of the racialized terror encrypted at the heart of the American good life made global by the end of the twentieth century.

Your Best Thing

Although the novel begins with a ghostly haunting of the house known as "124," it is the arrival (or return) of Beloved in 1873, when it is set, as a *living* human person that compels a diegetic reckoning between the former slave woman Sethe and the original traumatic event at its core: Sethe's killing of her unnamed daughter, when she is threatened with return to slavery after her escape to Ohio from Kentucky in the years leading up to the U.S. Civil War. At the novel's outset, having committed the unthinkable, Sethe has been exiled from the local community as well as the history that transforms former slaves and free blacks into "African Americans," as Morrison catalogs:

> No more discussions, stormy or quiet, about the true meaning of the Fugitive Bill, the Settlement Fee, God's Ways and Negro pews; antislavery, manumission, skin voting, Republicans, Dred Scott, book learning, Sojourner's high-wheeled buggy, the Colored Ladies of Delaware, Ohio, and the other weighty issues that held them in chairs, scraping the floorboards or pacing them in agony or exhilaration. No anxious wait for the *North Star* or news of a beat-off. No sighing at a new betrayal or handclapping at a small victory.[87]

Near the novel's end, in regard to the widespread racial violence that surrounds him, Stamp Paid (who had years before ferried Sethe and her newborn other daughter, Denver, into free territory) observes: "Eighteen seventy-four and whitefolks were still on the loose" (180). The excruciatingly slow pace of racial transformation in the postbellum era exhausts the promises of progressive freedom granted to African Americans.

Sethe's emancipation, however, has come not as a spoil of war or as a legislative gift, but from her own staggering, world-shattering act, which also removes her, Denver, and, when she returns, the title character, Beloved, from the progressive temporality of that national history altogether. Beloved arrives on the heels of Sethe's reunion with another former slave from Sweet Home, Paul D, who becomes Sethe's lover and who offers to her and Denver the possibility of a new start, a reentrance into history and community, as he appeals to her: "We can make a life, girl. A life" (46). Prior to his arrival, for Sethe, "the future was a matter of keeping the past at bay," such that the "better life" available to them "was simply not that other one," namely of enslavement in Kentucky (42). Paul D expels the ghost of the infant who has for years haunted 124 (and driven away Sethe's two older sons) and has impeded all social ties with others, a constant, furious reminder of Sethe's "unnatural" crime. The exorcism in turn conjures Beloved as a living human presence—a young woman with almost no recollection of her own past, but who seeks to absorb all of Sethe's attention, even if it means diverting Paul D into a sexual relation with herself so that he eventually is "moved" out of Sethe's house.

Ultimately, it is the revelation of Sethe's crime that drives Paul D from 124 altogether. As he censures her, saying "You got two feet, Sethe, not four," he accuses her of the animalistic barbarism that Sethe has associated with that "other life" at Sweet Home, from which she had desperately hoped to save herself and her children (165). As the analeptic recollections of Sweet Home relate, it is the contingency of her (and her fellow slaves') status as human beings that renders Sethe the object of both humane benevolence *and* tremendous violence under slavery. Under the Garners, their original masters, the Sweet Home slaves are treated with a modicum of dignity, as Garner declares his male slaves to be "men." But—as Paul D comes to realize subsequent to Garner's death, the family's financial decline, and the arrival of the Garners' brother-in-law, known as "schoolteacher," to oversee the estate—this has been a tenuous reality at best: "They were only Sweet Home men at Sweet Home. One step off that ground and they were trespassers among the human race. Watchdogs without teeth; steer bulls without horns; gelded workhorses whose neigh and whinny could not be translated into a language *responsible* humans spoke" (125; emphasis added).

In fact, after Garner's death, the rapid conversion of men back into enslaved animals (who observe how *other* animals enjoy more freedom than they in fact do) ultimately leads Paul D to wonder, "Garner called and announced them men—but only on Sweet Home, and by his leave. Was he naming what he saw or creating what he did not?" (221). The biopower of white patriarchal authority likewise confronts Sethe most bluntly when she accidentally overhears schoolteacher instructing his students to tabulate her "human characteristics" and "her animal ones," and she queries Mrs. Garner to learn that a "characteristic" is "a feature" or "a thing that's natural to a thing" (193, 195). Sexually assaulted by schoolteacher's nephews (who "took my milk," as Sethe describes it, since she was lactating at the time) and brutally whipped by schoolteacher (so that she is left with a "chokecherry tree" of scars on her back), Sethe too learns how terribly fungible is the humanity that the Garners have granted her (16–17).

While the lifeworld that Garner has established at Sweet Home is also idiosyncratic—strictly delimited to the boundaries of his property—it is an essential component of *his* personhood, where proto-liberal inclinations enable his power to grant (or, conversely, withhold) recognition to other forms of (human) life. After his death and schoolteacher's revaluation of them, the slaves begin stealing from the estate, understanding their actions as "not only their right but their obligation," an effort to resignify their worth to one another and to themselves (191). But the emphasis on "responsibility" and "obligation" in these passages also signals the difficult ethics of Morrison's work, where, as I elaborate further below (and in chapter 2), responsibility to others *precedes* the emergence of agency and self-possession. That is, unwilling to posit her subjects as pure and total victims of history, Morrison counters a liberal conception of freedom with a phenomenology of responsibility that is the very *condition* of human freedom, rather than its antithesis.

The Sweet Home slaves' plan to steal *themselves* away—a plan that goes awry with only Sethe and her children able to make the escape—culminates their elusive claim of self-possession against the "thingness" that chattel slavery attributes to them. But of course, under the law, and in particular, the Fugitive Slave Act, her escape makes Sethe over into an "outlaw," whose self-claimed freedom is inconceivable and whose personhood is thoroughly violable. As Morrison describes Sethe and Amy Denver, the white woman who delivers Denver during Sethe's trek to Ohio, they are "two throw-away people, two lawless outlaws" (84). Moreover, as Paul D further realizes in his own later escape from Kentucky, the right to rights belongs to "men who had the guns. . . . Men who knew their manhood lay in their guns and were not even embarrassed by the knowledge that without gunshot fox would laugh at them" (162). In these various reflections on the legal and social status of slaves, Morrison meticulously delineates the "characteristics" of the self-determined and self-governed American citizenry from which Sethe and Paul D are repeatedly abjected as the legal personhood, the rationalized and calculating "humanity," and the brute force of heteropatriarchal masculinity that white Americans enjoy.

Thus, in the moment Sethe is threatened with return to Sweet Home, Morrison recalls and rewrites the impossible legal situation in which the historical Margaret Garner (upon whom Sethe is based) found herself caught, between state and federal law that assigned to her divergent statuses, although neither of them emancipatory: the Fugitive Slave Act of 1850, under which her owners could lay claim to her, on the one hand, and murder charges in Ohio, on the other, which ascribed to her legal personhood, if only to hold her culpable for the child's death. While, in the historical case, a federal judge overruled the state of Ohio and returned Margaret Garner to her Kentucky masters, Morrison obviates the legal contradiction by having the schoolteacher determine, after he finds Sethe with her dead child, that "there was nothing there to claim" (149).[88] In the eyes of the law, Margaret Garner's freedom was indistinguishable from her outlaw criminality. But the novel transfigures the moment of violence as a *gathering* or *incorporation* of self, a human *becoming* that is assembled in the face of the inhumane assault she is up against: "She just flew. Collected every bit of life she had made, all the parts of her that were precious and fine and beautiful, and carried, pushed, dragged them through the veil, out, away, over there where no one could hurt them. Over there. Outside this place, where they would be safe" (163).

In casting this moment of world-shattering violence as an incorporation and safeguarding of Sethe's personhood, Morrison throws into severe relief how liberal political philosophy and state governmentality abstract human persons out of heterogeneous bodies, sundering them from the collective lifeworlds that sustain them, in order to integrate them as citizen-subjects of the nation. As I further elaborate in chapter 3, a liberal imaginary of state formation and political subjectivity presumes for the self-possessed individual a "natural" body—a uniform, self-contained organism with discrete borders, which is legible to and before the law. A metonym for the legal person under the modern state, it is this body "animated" by reason, the self-possessed human, whose natural rights are protected by the U.S. Constitution's representation clause and who simultaneously constitutes the self-governing body politic of a democratic society.[89] Conversely, "if there was not a full body, it was not entitled to full personhood."[90] Such "self possession" of human persons reconstituted more archaic relations of property, kinship, and social difference in the liberal political philosophies of the modern state (in particular in the writings of Thomas Hobbes and John Locke).

But, the modern legal state also always already depended upon social conventions that distinguished between those bodies that were "naturally" autonomous and self-possessed by the reasoning person and those that were dependent or somehow incomplete, in need of development, and thus under the dominion of (reasonable) others. In the case of U.S. law, as Karla Holloway observes, "The association of black bodies to enslavement and to 'blackness' as vulnerable to this particular biologic constructionism" enfolds racial difference into constitutive categories regarding who "could be disentangled from the visibly distinct bodies that populated the newly composed Americas": "When identity matters . . . the legal origin never wanders too far from the substance of the claim."[91] The "three-fifth's compromise" in Article I of the Constitution, which counted slaves as "three fifths of all other Persons" for the purposes of determining congressional representation, never mentions black racial difference. But it nevertheless codifies the social conventions differentiating between heterogeneous bodies, absorbing some into the "natural" and whole personhood of American national life and according them the "natural rights" that such standing makes available, while dispersing others into their fractional parts.

At the same time, such social distinctions prove more pliant, unpredictable, and unruly than the law that strives to discipline them according to its own reason might wish. Thus, as Holloway further argues, while the law "effectively erases the standing of any penumbral questions," black writers "play with this complexity that makes for the compelling tangles of fiction": "Legal determinations may be arbitrary but they are nonetheless concretizing. Literary imaginations liberate and allow, indeed encourage, the leak of one to the other."[92] The fictional characterization of Margaret Garner as Sethe incorporates such fugitive unruliness, a willful human being other than the "thing" over which property owners enjoy their right to "use and abuse," as property owners are wont to do. But neither is she the humanitarian object of benevolent ministrations by liberal allies, who seek to save her and make her over into a sign of their own self-possessed self-righteousness, the type of person Morrison embodies in the somewhat comic character of Edward Bodwin, the former abolitionist, who laments the passing of the "old days" fighting for the abolishment of slavery, "good years . . . full of spit and conviction" and for whom Sethe's act of infanticide affords simply another upright cause to champion (260).

Instead, rearticulating her response to victimhood as an emergent and terrifying agency constituted through inconceivable violence, Sethe proves frightening to all around her: "This here Sethe didn't know where the world stopped and she began. . . . More important than what Sethe had done was what she claimed" (164). In seizing "all the parts of her," she at once lays claim to herself *and* unmakes all the terms by which she is recognizable; for both schoolteacher and those around her, there is indeed "nothing" familiar left of her character. She has hence been left, for years after, to her own devices, as it were, living with Denver and the baby ghost in the hard-won but utterly isolated space of 124 until Paul D arrives. Nonetheless, her emancipation also generates a relation of responsibility with which Sethe must belatedly reckon, initiated by the return of Beloved as a real person. As seemingly impossible as Sethe's choice has been, and as attenuated as Sethe's personhood is, Beloved demands a confrontation with the loss that has made Sethe's own being possible. The relationship between Sethe and the returned Beloved hence attests to how radically new forms of political subjectivity arrive only through a network of recognition by and obligation to others.

Beloved's appearance is at first one of deep, if mysterious, consolation and fulfillment for Sethe and Denver, and the prospect of losing her again feels for them "ungovernable" (123). However, Beloved's presence eventually evokes only compulsive fixation and horror. Beloved herself remains, as Avery Gordon has argued, haunted by what those around her cannot discern.[93] If her familiars want Beloved to complete them and remove the losses of the past—as indicated in the incantation of "I am Beloved and she is mine" that threads through the novel—Beloved's own desires exceed this recovery and remain illegible. As Sethe is all consumed with a need to at once justify and make amends to Beloved, she is led into a vertiginous relation of self-sacrifice. The relations of possession, identity, and responsibility become indistinguishable from one another, and, unable to work or to care for her family, Sethe is debilitated by a vortex of guilt. She begins wasting away, as a now pregnant Beloved grows increasingly insistent in her accusations and demands on her (141).

It then takes the reprise of a community of older black women, who, out of the very human flaws of jealousy and negligence, had failed to warn Sethe of the arrival of schoolteacher in the first instance, to save Sethe from the terror of her past. As they approach 124, they first encounter younger versions of themselves, so that the scene of Sethe's recovery is also a reenactment of their own part in the past trauma, their redemption obtained when they prevent a frenzied Sethe from attacking Bodwin, whom she mistakes for the returning schoolmaster. The congregational speech act of these women provides a scene of *communitas,* assembling a nascent political community—one that prefigures the civil rights movement to come—that saves Sethe from the ruinous consequences of killing a white man, even one who "never turned us down" and who is "steady as a rock" in his alliance to the former slaves (265).

But recovering Sethe also entails the necessary disappearance and forgetting of Beloved, as the novel's conclusion affirms: "Everybody knew what she was called, but nobody anywhere knew her name. Disremembered and unaccounted for, she cannot be lost because no one is looking for her, and even if they were, how can they call her if they don't know her name? Although she has claim, she is not claimed. . . . They forgot her like a bad dream" (275). *Beloved* has been defined as, in the term that Morrison has Sethe herself employ, a work of cultural "rememory," in that it recalls and rewrites the situation of Margaret Garner through its construction of Sethe. But Sethe can be incorporated as a fictional person only through the cyclical recovery and loss that Beloved undergoes. In this way, I suggest, the novel instructs in a human rights method that reads for disappearances, where the very memory of the disappearance is made to disappear. Disappearance, as Gordon has also observed, involves a temporal apprehension distinct from torture, suffering, and murder, even as it often entails these other forms of terror. Disappearance is never exactly past, but a contemporaneous absent presence. To apprehend the disappeared, to find ways to "talk to them," entangles us in an ongoing relationship of responsibility with those who have been lost.[94]

In "having claim" but remaining unclaimed, the story of Beloved, which we are also told at the novel's end is not one "to pass on," poses disappearance as the mode of devastation and terror that exceeds our conventional histories of slavery and its aftermath. Beloved's scattered and disjointed utterances seem to recall, not so much Sethe's murder of her, but death in the slave ship. Her "rememory" hence casts the conditions of responsibility and reckoning beyond a single act and agent of infanticide to the scene of the black Atlantic, a time and space that exceeds both individual biography and precedes national history and that can be recovered only by way of a transnational imaginary bound to the possibility of what, in chapter 1, I will discuss as other humanities. In other words, as an institution, slavery has certainly not been forgotten or made to disappear from national time. But what always escapes and exceeds the received histories and positivist methods by which slavery has been made known in the present are the other ways of being and the other futures to which the institution of chattel slavery in the United States laid waste—lives and futures unmade and rendered impossible at the nation's very founding. Insofar as Beloved not only offers up fragmented memories of the slave ship, but is also modeled on the Yoruban orisha Oshun, Morrison posits intimations of those other lifeworlds that might have offered black subjects entirely other forms of recognition and of good life.[95]

The human rights method that *Beloved* articulates, then, actually disorganizes progressive temporal markers.[96] By the novel's end, Sethe is brought back into the fold of her contemporary African American community by the recognition that the other black women and Paul D grant her. Thus, as Paul D pulls her out of her mourning, insisting to her that "you your best thing, Sethe," he urges her to reorient her desire toward a collective future: "Me and you, we got more yesterday than anybody. We need some kind of tomorrow" (273). But as a political subject in the immediate postbellum years, this recognition granted Sethe is also a far cry from the robust forms of U.S. citizenship reserved for the ideal personhood of the American good life—namely, white men. Instead, whatever bodily integrity, self-possession, and social security Sethe has achieved is bestowed by those whose own standing is also in turn quite tenuous and truncated, and becomes only more so with the failures of Reconstruction and the consolidation of the Jim Crow social order. Literary critic James Berger describes the revelation made possible in *Beloved*'s "apocalyptic scene" as catalyzed by an "alliance of political forces" that made it impossible for any African American "to genuinely own property or live as a subject in a society that gives overriding value to property rights."[97]

But Berger further describes how *Beloved* responds to the liberal discourses regarding racial difference and equality ubiquitous at the moment of the novel's composition in the 1980s. Encapsulated in the infamous "Moynihan Report" (the 1965 report titled "The Negro Family: The Case for National Action," authored by then–Assistant Secretary of Labor Daniel Patrick Moynihan), the liberal imaginary that emerged from the 1960s onward shared with more conservative perspectives an assessment of black life, and in particular black family life, as pathological and damaging to both African Americans and the health of the nation. Such liberal constructions attributed these deficiencies to the *cultural* havoc wreaked by slavery (rather than the inborn biological inferiority that white supremacy assumed), especially the breakdown of heteropatriarchal authority in African American families. However, they retained the assumption that black life constitutes a degraded form of humanity. Liberal concerns with black "welfare" thus eventually converged with a conservative political agenda to strengthen the rhetoric of "traditional" family values *and* to remove the state supports (such as they were) that created "welfare dependency" in order to foster "personal responsibility" within African American communities. As Berger discerns, Morrison displaces the ideological discourses of race from the 1980s to the 1870s, in order to propose that not only has the nation not yet successfully "worked through" the trauma of slavery for black life, but it has nested that loss within the extremely limited options it came to offer for black personhood at the end of the twentieth century.[98]

Thus, the ongoing and unfulfilled obligation to Beloved that the novel constructs can hardly be Sethe's alone.[99] It instead remains for the nation to do justice to the lost daughter, returned to the zone of the unimagined, unclaimed, and forgotten "like a bad dream." What do we mean, then, by the claims of justice here? We can certainly stipulate reparations for the national and original trauma that is slavery, which by the end of the twentieth century seemed to have become a social and political dead end.[100] But an ethical reckoning also means grappling with how the *universal* norms disseminated as measures of good life *across the globe* under the auspices of American internationalism have always already been founded on a Constitutional calculus that accorded black life "3/5th" personhood. The American good life entails the constant counting up of "feet" (as Paul D is compelled to do) before admitting "equal footing" to others in the American global nation. The black racial form materializes as a corporeal trace that haunts all attempts to get over or get past this violent dismemberment without actually and fully addressing its responsibility to the Other.

Beloved insists that the American good life, which neoliberalism posits as universally available at the "end of history," is in fact a globalized "white life," whose transcendence of violent and mass death *depends upon* the collective disasters that beset (and that it visits upon) other forms of life for its own reproduction and universalization.[101] As Dylan Rodriguez argues, such idealized "white life" is "generally alienated from and systemically *unfamiliar with* forms of collective, unexpected bodily violence and premature death," while anti-black racism naturalizes the latter.[102] The neoliberal logic of multiculturalism has rendered the American good life flexible enough, by the twenty-first century, to incorporate some others into the white life it secures, but it does so only against the immense production of physical and social death that is an integral component of modern "development" across the globe. The American good life produces and requires unlimited warfare (against drugs, against crime, against terror, against infidels), the militarization of everyday life, environmental catastrophe, and ever-increasing economic and social inequality on a planetary scale.

If, therefore, as Kenneth Warren has argued, *Beloved* amounts to an attempt (a wrongheaded one, in Warren's assessment) "to politicize a melancholy truth about the human condition, namely that, for most of us, our lives and what they meant to us are destined to be forgotten by the living," a human rights literacy nevertheless confronts the profound unevenness in that loss to reveal how some of "our lives" are hastened to their end, or relentlessly emptied of meaning, *in order to secure the good (white, American) life of others.*[103] To the extent that the exceptional American nation has adjudicated the terms of personhood, good life, and freedom across the planet for the duration of the long twentieth century, the return of Beloved in Morrison's novel disturbs not only 124, nor only the "house that race built" (to employ the title of an important early collection of critical race theory, to which Morrison contributed the opening essay titled "Home"), but the stranglehold that the American good life exerts across the globe. In describing *Beloved* as an instance of "minor literatures," I am hardly suggesting it is overlooked or unknown in either academic or commercial venues.

Rather, because it reckons with the legal logics and social fictions of personhood that naturalized and perpetuated the "peculiar institution" of slavery in the United States, the profound challenge that it issues in regard to the *global* configurations and implications of American exceptionalism remains less appreciated. In *Death of a Discipline,* Gayatri Chakravorty Spivak does briefly turn to Morrison's novel as an example of "planetary" literature, observing how all that remains after Beloved's disappearance is "weather." As Morrison writes: "By and by all trace is gone, and what is forgotten is not only the footprints but the water too and what it is down there. The rest is weather. Not the breath of the disremembered and unaccounted for, but wind in the leaves, or spring ice thawing too quickly. Just weather" (275). As Spivak explains, planetarity moves according to a "geologic time" that is equally inaccessible to all of humanity, however conceived, even as the space and time of the planet is the condition of existence for such human life. In this sense, "just weather" resonates with Warren's "melancholy truth about the human condition," whereby all organic, sentient life eventually disintegrates and returns to the rock-hard limit condition that is planetary existence.

But Spivak's account *also* simultaneously grants priority to the world-making projects by which human life does endure. Consequently, she concedes, "One might be obliged to claim history from the violent perpetrator of it, in order to turn violation into the enablement of the individual," even as she insists that "one must not make history in a deliberate way. One must respect the earth's tone."[104] In the slow time and "justness" of the planet, every such necessary production of human being is also compelled to reckon with the planetarity that precedes and enables it. Thus, if Warren reads *Beloved* as participating in the production of a past that did not "really" happen to "us," the "just weather" of *Beloved*'s conclusion nevertheless brings us into a relation of *responsibility,* rather than one of straightforward identity, with that past, now translated as a form of planetary reckoning. The irruption of "Beloved," as the novel's final word, against a tableau of forgetting and erasure of all that is human then interjects the name as a placeholder for those other humanities being expunged with the installation of the American good life across the globe.

The Human Rights Record

As I hope to have begun showing above and continue to illustrate in chapter 1, the political aspirations of anticolonial movements often diverged substantially from the paramount liberal objective of establishing states in the service of free trade and global capital. It is useful to bear in mind that, as Westad points out, in the 1960s, "the idea of the Third World" pertained to a conception of *the future,* which "linked the European and American 'New Left' to the politics of Africa, Asia, and—increasingly—Latin America."[105] Liberation movements in the global South offered a transnational vision of alternative modernities, divergent from the geopolitical stranglehold perpetuated in the standoff between the United States and the Soviet Union during the Cold War. As I will continue to elaborate in this book, these movements contributed substantially to the postwar human rights "record," as Micheline Ishay calls it. Drafted between 1948 and 2007, this record offers a dialectical, progressive, although neither linear nor emancipatory, history, in which human rights designate, not "natural" properties, but outcomes of international social struggle and political contest since 1945.[106] As a record, human rights remember the historical struggles and debates that informed the construction of an international human rights regime and continue to signal what the performative force of these concepts might yet be. Furthermore, as I explain throughout *Writing Human Rights,* the human rights record grants recognition to those political subjects—thought to be improbable, unlikely, or impossible by imperial racial and (neo)liberal logics—who nevertheless "become" or arrive to lay claims to rights that they do not have.[107]

These alternate imaginaries have frequently referred to socialist conceptions of equality, freedom, and justice. The Universal Declaration of Human Rights, the International Covenant on Civil and Political Rights, and the International Covenant on Economic, Social and Cultural Rights (i.e., the tripartite "International Bill of Rights") accordingly forward much fuller notions of good life and human well-being than does a more constrained set of negative freedoms that Americans often conceive of as natural rights.[108] But the human rights record has also come to include other, often transnational social movements (some of which I also consider throughout this book) such as feminism and environmentalism, as well as religious movements such as liberation theology or transnational Islam, all organized around divergent modes of social being.[109] Rather than romanticizing or idealizing any of these various social and political projects, which have often enough been in conflict with one another, the human rights record archives varying conceptions of good life from the 1940s onward, which in turn calls for a human rights "literacy" to inform our methods of social and cultural analysis.[110]

In contrast to the "end of history" that the devotees of (neo)liberalism championed (prematurely, even by their own later admissions), the human rights approach I propose in this book avers that "what remains, of socialism and post-socialism, colonialism and post-colonialism, is history—a history which has set itself on a different path than that of Enlightenment teleology in its capitalist or socialist forms."[111] It requires "thinking between the Posts" (that is, between postsocialism and postcolonialism) to grapple with racisms that "rely not necessarily on biological conceptions of race but on institutional mechanisms" (such as incarceration, medicine and health services, [un]employment, and border control), in order to "differentiate populations into subgroups having varied access to means of life and death."[112] Countering the naturalized predominance of (neo) liberalism that secures the American way of life *as* good life, a human rights methodology poses both a more constrained *and* an expanded set of aspirations for thinking about ethical regimes, political projects, and moral norms. Against the perspective of an American global nation that naturalizes and universalizes human rights across the globe, human rights *as a historical record* suggests that human rights are *one of many* possible ethical regimes by which "the good" can be imagined and lived across time and space. As Jack Donnelly explains, human rights provide only one of an array of conceptions of justice, political legitimacy, and flourishing of human dignity that have been available since the mid-twentieth century.[113] To thus cast human rights principles as an "ethical regime of living" renders them much more provisional, contingent, and dynamic than a universalizing discourse admits.

As I note above and throughout this book, and like other political and social theorists of human rights, I describe *embodied vulnerability* as a "universal" condition of human life; human beings, in other words, are characterized not by the particular capacities or properties they possess, but instead by a shared bodily exposure to the world. Yet, my focus on minor literatures and writers of color avers that such vulnerability has never been distributed evenly. Rather, some lives have been rendered more contingent or even expendable than others, and the biopolitics of neoliberalism produces ever new categories of superfluity. Contemporary racial formations hence constitute, as Lisa Lowe contends, a material trace of the historical exclusions to which particular(ized) populations have been subject in the United States. As Lowe explains, the persistence of racial difference—that is, its ready intelligibility in and on the body—provides "material evidence" of ongoing economic stratification and social exclusion that systematically persists in an era of formal political and legal equality for persons of color: "Race remains, after [incorporation by] citizenship, the material trace of history and thus the site of struggle through which contradictions are heightened and brought into relief."[114] Because equality for people of color in the United States after liberal integration remained circumscribed to formal political rights and national belonging, it failed to encompass the economic and social rights that many civil rights leaders had long understood as central to thoroughgoing racial transformation.[115] But the more immediate postwar context, to which I return in the next chapter, intimates a very different—if still deferred—imaginary for thinking about this broader panoply of rights and protection.

Thus, when we posit people of color in the United States as the *political subjects* of human rights and attend to their material and imagined linkages to others elsewhere, a human rights method makes visible the limits of a domestic regime of liberal rights. A human rights literacy reanimates vital aspects of the social justice movements in which civil rights politics took place, ones too easily obscured by (neo)liberal individualism, to remarkably expand the forms and ways of life that the American global nation has failed to recognize or refused to protect. In this sense, ethical regimes of living, while achieving "a certain systematicity or regularity . . . that give them a provisional consistency or coherence" do not "necessarily have the stability or concrete institutionalization of a political regime."[116] Human rights have not, in fact, enjoyed political and legal institutionalization *in* the United States. Rather, as a *counter-* or *ethico-*politics to a liberal formulation of rights, the human rights regime poses a *"minor"* genealogy made possible by the transnational movements of peoples and the global networks of cultural and social exchange.[117] What the human rights record therefore reveals, and what I would like to elucidate further, is the substantial contestation undertaken by the "darker races" against the ideological limits of the united nations world and a (neo)liberal vision of the American good life.

Beginning in the 1970s, it was not only humanitarian organizations that adopted human rights discourses; opposition groups in varied locations (especially, for example, in Latin America) did so as well, in efforts to protect themselves from state persecution and impunity.[118] No doubt, as I will further explain in chapter 1, "the minimalist cry not to be tortured" eventually displaced "more robust panoramas of social change" in the global South, and "the construction of human rights in the 1970s served to elevate the neoliberal world of the future as a model of global citizenship while subjugating alternative visions that emphasized social or economic rights or the right to self-determination."[119] Nevertheless, despite the fact that human rights present themselves in a "putatively antipolitical language"—or precisely because they do—they have proven valuable for political activists, especially those such as exiles fashioning transnational solidarities, to effect social change in their home countries.[120] In such cases, local actors do not simply "translate" a set of foreign norms imposed from outside, but articulate human rights with local values, "exploiting zones of overlap and tweaking what they [find] in the directions they want to [pursue]."[121]

If, moreover, during and after the late Cold War, political activists living under, or exiled by, authoritarian regimes adopted the language of human rights precisely because it offered the patina of depoliticized and enduring moral claims, then *Writing Human Rights* focuses on the corresponding thesis that such political claims become embedded within the supposedly neutral space of literary production.[122] Human rights document how racialized peoples have wanted otherwise and comprise a critical paradigm by which to read the "belated" assertions of self-determination and "deferred" dreams of social and economic justice that minor literatures hold out for a future yet to come. As the Cold War gave way to a "new world order" in the late 1970s and 1980s, the "culture wars" raged in the U.S. academy, revealing the inability of an American literary canon to reconcile the contradictions of race, class, and gender into a unified national culture. Concerned with the value and place of minor literatures—which were being recovered by scholars as well as newly produced by writers of color—the debates worried the terms (such as aesthetic criteria, "political correctness") by which such work would be included as reflections and expressions of the nation.

If the rise of multiculturalism did not exactly resolve the issue, it has nevertheless provided the logic by which liberalism elicited consent from marginalized groups without addressing the material inequities they faced.[123] However, as my analysis in the following chapters suggests, an array of writers (including Morrison) were satisfied with neither a glib pluralism nor the national limits by which they were hailed to imagine belonging, rights, protections, and responsibility. Rather, because, as Jodi Melamed observes, "literature has been a form in which it is theoretically possible to say anything," it can "reveal the conditions of violence that official antiracisms sustain and disguise."[124] By adjoining subjects from seemingly disparate times and places, the "minor transnationalism" of these "minor literatures" imparts visions of human being and good life otherwise abandoned by the American global nation and its formulation of (neo)liberal citizenship. The human rights record and minor literatures thus do not offer a merely pluralist recognition of moral values, cultural identities, and social practices. Rather, because the ethical regime for living that they embody has a dynamic and flexible character, one not bound to a single polity, human rights impinge upon and deform the civil order of (neo)liberalism and its privileged subjects, the U.S. citizen and the American way of life. The human rights record grants viability to forms of good life that the American global nation cannot be made to represent, despite its claims to universality.[125]

Finally, because I have posed Morrison's *Beloved* in this introduction as a kind of ground zero for querying and writing personhood, self-determination, and rights anew, I want to call attention to how the novel locates one of those other humanities in the nation's settler colonial history. In Paul D's subplot of escape from the Georgia chain gang and his period of respite in an encampment of Cherokees, Morrison catalogs the latter's history in an encapsulated manner akin to that of abolition and emancipation described above:

> Decimated but stubborn, they were among those who chose a fugitive life rather than Oklahoma. The illness that swept them now was reminiscent of the one that had killed half their number two hundred years earlier. In between that calamity and this, they had visited George III in London, published a newspaper, made baskets, led Oglethorpe through forests, helped Andrew Jackson fight Creek, cooked maize, drawn up a constitution, petitioned the King of Spain, been experimented on by Dartmouth, established asylums, wrote their language, resisted settlers, shot bear and

> translated scripture. All to no avail. The forced move to the Arkansas River, insisted upon by the same president they fought for against the Creek, destroyed another quarter of their already shattered number. (111)

The outline of Cherokee history for which Morrison creates space in *Beloved* lays the disappearance of Native sovereignties alongside the violent fracturing of black humanity, where the recovery and endurance of the latter depends upon the event of the former.

As Chickasaw cultural critic Jodi A. Byrd suggests, there is no easy reconciliation to be made between indigenous claims to home and self-determination that have been demeaned, dispossessed, and displaced by the entrenched structures of settler colonialism and the racialized ways of life that minor subjects—to whom Byrd refers as "arrivants"—have been made to inhabit. As Byrd explains, in contrast to the postwar decolonization of European empires, settler colonialism persists to the present day: "The emphasis in international law on nation-state formations predicates that indigenous peoples remain still colonized liminally within and beside the established geopolitical and biopolitical borders and institutions of (post)colonial governance as stateless entities."[126] Moreover, precisely because the United Nations precludes from its definition of colonialism those indigenous peoples enclosed within breakaway settler colonies (according to what is referred to as the "blue water" or "salt water" thesis, in which colonies are defined as geographically distant from the colonial power), the right to self-determination of Native American peoples has gone largely unrecognized in international human rights discourse. Because the postwar consolidation of a united nations world installed the nation-state as both conceptual and political horizon, the provincializing of indigenous political and critical thought and the spectacular failure to grant indigenous peoples self-determination provide the fundamental but occluded condition of possibility for multicultural neoliberalism and the American good life to develop.[127]

To the extent that Native American nations are continually reduced in national culture and multicultural political discourse to racial minorities "with no prior claim to nation or territory that exceeds the U.S.'s will," the right to self-determination becomes nothing more than a mirror version of "the fictions of U.S. multicultural settler democracy," with very little possibility for addressing the contradictions and incommensurabilities of the past, in particular "the [Native] nation's ability to define for itself the self and other, the inside and out," and to receive as guests and as members whomever indigenous peoples desire on their own terms.[128] In response to this impossible situation, *Beloved* places the black man's freedom in relation to the travails of indigenous sovereignty, where his being granted provisional recognition by the other, across disparate forms of historical subjection, proves the *only* possibility for his refuge and recovery. Morrison's inscription of the Cherokee as essential in a story that is as much about the U.S. state's biopolitical and disciplinary practices in the twentieth century as it is about the nineteenth-century fugitive slave intimates that emancipation for minor subjects then and now must bypass the received constructions of (neo)liberal humanity handed down to the present moment. The rights and freedoms of minor subjects instead entail a necessary reckoning with the submerged history of settler colonial displacements. My contention and hope in the following pages is that the dialectical animation of human rights that minor literatures enact offers a first step toward thinking of self-determination apart from modern state sovereignty and instead through the kind of ethical hospitality with which Paul D is received.

UN International Convention on the Elimination of All Forms of Racial Discrimination
Ernest Gaines, *A Gathering of Old Men*
Maxine Hong Kingston, *The Woman Warrior*

1

Other Humanities

The Bandung Spirit and the Right to Self-Determination

> *The Conference is agreed: (a) in declaring that colonialism in all its manifestations is an evil which should speedily be brought to an end; (b) in affirming that the subjection of peoples to alien subjugations, domination and exploitation constitutes a denial of fundamental human rights, is contrary to the Charter of the United Nations and is an impediment to the promotion of world peace and co-operation; (c) in declaring its support of the cause of freedom and independence for all such peoples, and (d) in calling upon the powers concerned to grant freedom and independence to such peoples.*
>
> —Final Communiqué of the Asian-African Conference of Bandung (24 April 1955)

> *Solidarity is a desire, a promise, an aspiration. It speaks to our wish for a kind of unity, one that does not exist now but we want to produce.*
>
> —Vijay Prashad, *The Karma of Brown Folk*

One of the "old men" of Ernest Gaines's *A Gathering of Old Men* (1983), Johnny Paul, looks out over a Louisiana sugarcane field, recalling where his parents' house, "gone like all the others had gone," once stood.[1] He observes to the white sheriff of the small town, "What you see is the weeds, but you don't see what we don't see," as a way of explaining the murder of a white Cajun farmer, Beau Boutan, whose death provides the central catalyst for the plot (89). The assertion, backed up by other black members of the community, confounds Sheriff Mapes, especially as the men offer this uncanny absent presence as the motive behind the murder for which each of them claims responsibility. Told as a series of fragmented, first-person accounts from the perspective of the individual men, as well as a few white characters and black children, the novel unfolds as a mystery about who has shot Beau, as well as a tale of growing resistance by an African American community long subjected to de facto racial violence and de jure segregation.

A Gathering of Old Men has been rightly received as a treatment of newly forged black masculine agency in the face of ongoing racial stratification in the American South during the late twentieth century.[2] However, its insistence that one "had to be here to don't see it now" offers the suggestive possibility that the absences that haunt the novel go well beyond the conventional measures of personhood that civil integration into American life affords (89). Instead, it asks us to consider the limits of an American imaginary of integration in order to see, and not see, what and how its subjects might "want otherwise." The minor perspective of a minor character like Johnny Paul makes evident how a white supremacist culture and even a more liberal official discourse, both of which Mapes comes to represent over the course of the novel, has "only little knowledge" in "how to deal with black folks," which amounts more or less to "knocking them around" (93).

In this chapter, I consider how the institution of the "united nations world"—that is, the international order of formally equal, sovereign states meant to serve as containers of political energies and guardians of world peace described in the introduction—foreclosed those dimensions of antiracist struggle in the United States that, in solidarity with anticolonial struggles in the global South, laid claim to social and economic rights and the right to self-determination as crucial to the freedom of subjugated peoples. Considering the political principles elaborated in the International Convention on the Elimination of All Forms of Racial Discrimination (ICERD) alongside *A Gathering of Old Men,* as well as *The Woman Warrior* (1975) by Maxine Hong Kingston, I demonstrate how a human rights approach traverses the disciplinary border between critical American studies and postcolonial studies to ascertain how minoritarian struggles in the United States have been, and might once again be, attached to decolonization and socialist movements in the global South. Rendering visible the limits of an American formulation of rights, justice, and good life as it has been represented on a planetary terrain since the Cold War, minor literatures record, in Johnny Paul's words, "what we don't see" any longer.

In illuminating forms of solidarity and political community rendered illegible within the united nations world and the great power politics of the Cold War, minor literatures might be said to reanimate a "Bandung Spirit," or in Cynthia Young's terms, the "soul power," associated with the Non-Aligned Movement (NAM) of 1961. The Asian-African Conference, held in Bandung, Indonesia, in April 1955, with representatives from twenty-nine countries in attendance, was hailed by its host, Indonesian president Sukarno, as "the first intercontinental Conference of colored peoples in the history of mankind" and served as the forerunner of the NAM, which sought autonomy, neutrality, and solidarity in the face of an increasingly bipolar international order during the Cold War.[3] Fred Ho and Bill V. Mullen identify the "Bandung era" of 1955 to 1973 as momentous for Afro-Asian solidarity movements around the world, observing that it was "both the watershed and high-water mark of black-Asian affiliation and the unfinished and imperfect dream of a road still being pursued and paved."[4] Scholars have debated the diplomatic, strategic, and historical implications of the Bandung Conference and NAM for international relations.[5] My point in retaining the conference's moniker, however, is to keep alive "the *feeling* of political possibility presented through this first occasion of 'Third World' solidarity" and to consider the normative principles at which delegates to the conference arrived by consensus: economic cooperation and development, cultural cooperation, human rights, self-determination, and world peace.[6] Furthermore, I aim to retain Bandung and NAM's ambitions, ones also registered in the ICERD, for a postcolonial order (including Latin American nations) that generated alternative forms of political community beyond national states, even if those forms have remained deferred for a future yet to come.[7] Hence, the Bandung Spirit and the ICERD provide analytics by which to read U.S. writers of color at the end of the Cold War, as they animate the seemingly impossible political demands of this earlier era. In the United States, as Young observes, U.S. Third World leftists in the 1960s and 1970s sought to build "transnational forms of solidarity" that "attacked imperial practices abroad as a way of overturning the domestic forms of oppression facing them."[8]

Despite the inevitable ideological limits and pitfalls, this cultural politics continues to offer an important lesson for the "disturbing historical juncture" of our current century.[9] This chapter therefore considers how, beginning in the late 1970s, just as a burgeoning market for writers of color materialized in the United States, authors like Kingston and Gaines took stock of the radically altered domestic and international landscapes of the late Cold War. Although such literary production has been examined largely in terms of the domestic "culture wars" and the intra-racial divisions between feminist and nationalist politics, I argue that these works grappled with the breach, which, obtained between domestic civil rights politics and Third World decolonization movements, was an artifact of a united nations world, wherein the nation-state form served as *the* horizon for *all* politics. I am thus concerned with how this literature depicts integration in the United States, delineating the compromises demanded of Americans of color and the foreclosure of radical politics and transnational solidarity in exchange for the promises of national belonging. The Cold War enterprise of liberal democracy in the United States induced the reformation of domestic civil rights and racial integration. But minor literatures preserve and re-member planetary horizons of Afro-Asian solidarity organized around the right to political self-determination and cultural cooperation, as well as rights to social security and economic development, that human rights instruments record.

Freedom from Want

Concepts of social and economic rights developed and transformed rapidly in the postwar era, as they reflected the shifting interests and priorities of great power and anticolonial politics. During World War II, Anglo-American leaders understood national security as being integrally tied to economic stability for postwar internationalism.[10] This became expressly apparent when they apprised the way in which *in*security in these areas, especially in the Weimar Republic, had contributed to the rise of Fascism.[11] The Atlantic Charter thus adopted the language of Roosevelt's famous "Four Freedoms" from his 1941 State of the Union address, which explicitly included "freedom from want" alongside the more familiar freedoms of speech, religion, and from fear. While the other freedoms enumerated what have come to be known as "negative liberties," requiring the state to abstain from interference or action (such as imposition of censorship or of a state religion), the freedom from want calls upon the state to actively secure the welfare of its citizens. The "positive liberties" of social and economic security include access to food, shelter, clothing, fair wages, employment security, health and safety, education, old age protection, and recreational activities.

Insofar as the Four Freedoms relayed to an American public the nation's ideological interest in entering the war, it proposed what Elizabeth Borgwardt has called "a New Deal for the world," effectively internationalizing a vision of the incipient U.S. welfare state crafted through New Deal policies.[12] Just as important was the way that "freedom from want" furnished the basis for the Roosevelt administration to draft a domestic "economic bill of rights," which it considered to be fundamental for a domestic program of democratic justice in the United States.[13] Yet, by the close of the Cold War, a range of (neo)liberal and conservative officials cast such a notion of rights as an affront to the tradition of American individualism, and since the 1980s, they have steadily attacked all such government programs. Moreover, even in its initial implementation, Roosevelt's economic agenda sustained the southern labor market and its deep-rootedness in the color line by excluding agricultural, domestic, and other casual laborers, sectors that have included disproportionate numbers of people of color, from Social Security benefits.[14] Likewise, federal housing policies refused to insure mortgages in integrated neighborhoods, thus readily reproducing patterns of residential segregation. And meanwhile, Southern Democrats successfully filibustered federal antilynching legislation. In this failure to abolish such entrenched social and economic inequity, "racial hierarchy continued to serve as an explicit limit within the expanded field of government practice."[15]

A parallel incompletion marked the history of postcolonial national development. As Frantz Fanon prophesied in *The Wretched of the Earth,* the failure of international economic redistribution for newly established nations has meant that, despite the formal equality and political independence propagated after World War II, decolonized peoples have remained subject to relations of economic inequity with and dependence on the former imperial powers.[16] As they assumed the mantle of international "leadership" after World War II, U.S. policymakers, political leaders, and scholars initially excluded the Third World from Bretton Woods, adopted modernization theory, and approached such inequity as a problem of "development." This was as much an ideological project as an economic one; while American capitalists invested only hesitatingly, if at all, in the Third World during the Cold War, U.S. foreign aid was insistently tied to an agenda of structural reforms meant to produce "free men and free enterprise."[17]

Assuming modern development to be an expression of scientific, "rational action" by which these peoples would be "liberated" from stultifying "traditional" cultures and ideologies, American foreign policy maintained striking continuity with the "civilizing mission" that propelled late nineteenth-century colonial governance.[18] Expected to overcome "underdevelopment" according to a Western model—regardless of the fact that the West accomplished its own modernization by exploiting natural and human resources in the colonies—postcolonial development was to proceed by progressive, evolutionary stages that would be culturally, politically, and socially transformative as well.[19] At the same time, American officials worried that postcolonial nations might be swayed by an "incorrect" form of Communist modernity.[20] A host of policymakers, social scientists, and other prominent Americans led the charge to infuse new nations with Western capital and technical knowledge toward modernizing ends, in hopes of countering the Soviet "economic offensive" that began with Nikita Khrushchev's 1961 pledge to support "wars of liberation" in the decolonizing world.[21]

In the end, of course, "development proved an uphill battle," as Third World countries were compelled to participate in an international economic system organized by former colonial powers. Prices for raw materials, which the existing international division of labor mandated the global South produce for First World nations, were kept low. Ultimately, the development project in most postcolonial states could sustain little more than state officials and a small capitalist class, and the demand for intensified production wreaked extensive environmental damage.[22] Meanwhile, even by the late 1940s, Truman had revised Roosevelt's "freedom from want" to connote free enterprise and had dropped "freedom from fear" altogether from his Cold War version of the Four Freedoms.[23] Likewise, American officials discounted economic, social, and cultural rights "as anathema to free enterprise and limited government" and as representative of Soviet ideology, and they turned as readily to authoritarian governments as democratic states to carry out modernizing schemes.[24]

Nevertheless, the international version of "freedom from want," inaugurated in particular in the Marshall Plan and the Bretton Woods charters and institutions, remained "surprisingly expansive," in part because, in Europe, they did not involve the United States in the thorny questions of racial hierarchy and segregation that domestic policies did. As such, postwar international planning offered "a high-water mark for economic rights as human rights in mainstream American politics."[25] As the New Deal at home sought to incorporate the working class through a blurring of leftist and liberal ideologies, it also provided a transnational model of democratic sovereignty in the postwar era.[26] While Articles 55 and 56 of the UN Charter obligated member nations to promote "higher standards of living, full employment, and conditions of economic and social progress and development," "solutions of international economic, social, health, and related problems[,] and international cultural and educational cooperation," the World Bank and the International Monetary Fund (IMF) provided foreign aid toward payment imbalances, stabilized exchange rates, and convened members on international monetary matters in what Borgwardt describes as a "multilateralist moment" that "reconfigured the very idea of sovereignty."[27] In the early 1970s, moreover, Third World leaders put forward a call for a "New International Economic Order"—elaborated for instance in the 1975 UN Charter of Economic Rights and Duties of States—which articulated an international obligation for states to aid in "the economic development of other states along the path chosen by its government" as a remedial measure for the structural advantages Western nations had enjoyed over newly developing ones.[28]

And yet, although the World Bank and the IMF were the most innovative of the global New Deal institutions, they inherently favored market-oriented states, anticommunist regimes, and countries that already retained Western investments.[29] By the 1980s, as modernization theory evolved into neoliberal doctrine, these financial institutions became central to the promotion of anti-Soviet ideology, especially by intervening in the developing world and pushing market-driven policies that created or intensified social problems in postcolonial nations.[30] Such "structural readjustment" programs, anchored in notions of the minimalist state and fiscal "discipline," facilitated capital flight, fiscal decentralization, deregulation of industry and markets, tax subsidies and grants to multinational corporations, the privatization of space, services, and goods, and an array of other capital-friendly mechanisms that resulted, beginning in the 1970s, in a deeply polarized landscape of globalization. Well over a billion people across the globe have actually experienced economic decline since 1970, with wealth being increasingly concentrated in centers of affluence.[31] Structural adjustment programs instituted in the 1980s by the IMF and the World Bank (and the trade policies later set by the World Trade Organization [WTO]) in the wake of debt crises and recessions in Latin America and Africa, required developing nations to implement immense cutbacks in social programs in order to attract capital investment.[32] By 1990, the gap between the wealthiest and poorest nations had increased by 60 percent. At the end of the twentieth century, over 10 percent of the world's people were afflicted by hunger, and more than a billion lived in extreme poverty, all while disease and environmental damage wracked the globe.[33]

The bifurcation of the international bill of rights into two separate covenants, the International Covenant on Civil and Political Rights (ICCPR) and the International Covenant on Economic, Social, and Cultural Rights (ICESCR), readily reflects the Cold War context in which the composition of contemporary human rights took place. "First generation rights" (civil and political rights) were delinked from "second" and "third generation" ones (social and economic rights, and cultural or solidarity rights, respectively), despite human rights scholars' and advocates' insistence that the panoply of rights is actually indivisible. Moreover, not only did it take until 1978 for the United States to sign on to both covenants, but the Carter administration did so with a number of "reservations, understandings, and declarations" (RUDS) that included a provision declaring human rights treaties to be "non-self-executing," that is, in effect only when implemented as legislation by Congress. With respect to the ICESCR, the Carter administration further specified that the goals described in Article 2 (the general obligations provision) were "to be achieved progressively rather than through immediate implementation."[34] At the same time, many newly independent states argued that, given the problems of unemployment, trade imbalances, social conflict, and disease that plagued their societies, social and economic rights could not be immediately implemented in their countries either.[35]

Because most postwar accounts of human rights assume the sovereignty of modern states, they tend to equate the vulnerability of human life with those living in conditions of statelessness or those living under weak, rogue, failed or failing states, which are unable or actively refuse to extend protection to their citizenries. But, as the account above suggests, scholars of neoliberalism have cataloged the many ways in which global capitalism not only increases the number of people displaced as refugees and migrants, but has also steadily diminished the capacity of citizens everywhere to participate in state processes. Globalized states "introduce new threats and provide declining opportunities to citizens, while increasing numbers of residents who lack citizenship claims."[36] Accordingly, human rights ideationally address not only the rights and protections that international actors are to extend to the stateless, but the responsibilities of states to their own constituencies as well, even if this aspect too often goes overlooked in practice.

Indeed, since the end of the Cold War, social critics and activists have returned to the original kernel of social and economic rights that underwrote the "freedom from want," linking it in various ways to a newly conceptualized "right to development."[37] The shift to structural aid programs in the 1980s gave rise to a formulation of reciprocity in international aid, governance, and decision-making, requiring states to "act in certain ways in order to qualify for development assistance or to be treated fairly (justice as impartiality) in international economic decision-making."[38] While such norms arose and were meant to accord with Western nations' interests during the Cold War, since the 1990s, they have been rearticulated as human rights norms by various organizations seeking justice for vulnerable individuals and groups. Thereby querying the limits of state sovereignty, these political challenges once again open up the subject and meaning of self-determination as a human right.[39] At the same time, numerous nongovernmental organizations (NGOs) have begun focusing on the implementation of socioeconomic rights and on the United States as a site for human rights activism.[40] These projects often "build on the theory that many poor or otherwise disadvantaged Americans already have some sense that they have a 'right' to food, health care, education, and other basic needs" but want "the language and legal status of the international instruments outlining those rights."[41]

To be clear, then, it is not my contention that political subjects and disenfranchised peoples should simply *not* make appeals to the state. In fact, to the extent that it has been effective at all, the international human rights regime has perhaps been most so in establishing standards for states' obligations to their own citizens. Nevertheless, as I explain further in chapters 2 and 3, in its sovereign form, the state (and the legal and juridical practices through which the state grants recognition) can too easily simply "disappear" violence, loss, and deprivation altogether, especially when the state authors those forms of social abandonment. Thus, we urgently need other methods for reading such abandonment and for imagining political subjects and communities from within, but also in difference from, the state. The point is not to fault political struggles that address and attempt to remake the state so much as it is to remind us that the sovereign state is, despite its own projections otherwise, a historical formation that, in its dialectical contradictions, might give rise to other forms of political community that it puts under erasure. A human rights record proves one resource for wanting and imagining such other possibilities, despite the ongoing attempts of states to instrumentalize it otherwise.

Anticolonial Self-Determination and Antiracist Humanity

Despite the outsized influence the United States exerted in its activities in the postwar years, by 1960, the United Nations was no longer a straightforward extension of U.S. power. The inclusion of Third World nation-states transformed it into a "more diverse forum, less susceptible to American influence than before"; by 1970 the global political map had been entirely redrawn to include 142 nations, compared with 56 independent nations in 1910.[42] But by the 1968 UN International Conference on Human Rights held in Tehran, where the Afro-Asian nations formed a coalition that wielded much control over the human rights agenda, the majority of Third World countries were ruled by authoritarian systems that openly disparaged political rights and civil liberties.[43] Ultimately, then, for most of the twentieth century, the United Nations failed to prove the "central forum for and singular imaginative custodian of the norms" of human rights, whether political, social, economic, or cultural.[44] Instead, as historian Samuel Moyn has shown, it was primarily NGOs (and Amnesty International in particular) and "delocalized grassroots agents" who led the way with respect to human rights advocacy.[45] Moreover, although contemporary human rights discourse had been penned in the late 1940s, it was not until the 1970s, with the repression of "revisionist" socialism by both the Soviet Union in Prague and the United States in Latin America, that it emerged as something like a "plausible utopia" in an international arena.[46] Accordingly, with the collapse of the Communist bloc in the 1980s and the acceleration of globalization, transnational human rights discourses became increasingly conflated with humanitarian rhetoric, whereby guarantees of self-determination, state sovereignty, and nonintervention, at least for postcolonial nations in the global South, became increasingly subject to globalized moral imaginaries and sentiments.[47]

Nevertheless, a human rights approach enables us to recover a moment during the Bandung era of significant engagement by leaders of a newly emergent Third World and of the U.S. black freedom movement with human rights that is otherwise obscured by the official memories of the united nations world.[48] After all, billions lived in African and Asian lands that had been subjected, "in the name of 'progress' and 'humanity,'" to European colonialism, and by the end of World War II, their leaders began to want "to conquer modernity for themselves."[49] Most of the NAM nations became members of the UN Group of 77 Developing Countries (G-77), established during the 1964 Conference on Trade and Development, and have since dominated the agenda of the UN General Assembly.[50] If we thus take seriously the right to self-determination and the social and economic rights inscribed as part of what I am calling "the human rights record," we recover the real force of possibility that the Bandung Spirit and NAM posed to the emergent postwar assumptions of the American good life. Due in good part to the advocacy of Third World leaders, Article 1 of both the ICCPR and the ICESCR declare first and foremost: "All peoples have the right of self-determination," reflecting the absolutely vital, anticolonial aspiration that, in the United Nations' early days, the great powers jealously guarded for Western nations.[51] Critically, though, while Third World diplomats argued vigorously for the adoption of self-determination as a fundamental human right, the *meaning* of self-determination at this moment was itself highly contested, and anticolonial leaders did not necessarily equate or limit self-determination to unassailable state sovereignty.

Not incidentally, then, the Afro-Asian bloc of nations undertook the next major human rights initiative, the ICERD, adopted in 1965, which, while focused primarily on apartheid and ongoing colonial abuses in Africa, also included an optional right to universal petition meant to apply throughout the world.[52] As the first completed human rights treaty, the ICERD represented, as historian Steven L. B. Jensen observes, "a successful crack at the hard nut of international law-making, namely the problem of sovereignty."[53] In fact, the standoff between the Cold War powers since the adoption of the Universal Declaration of Human Rights had hampered the completion of the two human rights covenants. It was the precedent set by the NAM nations (with notable leadership by representatives of Jamaica and Liberia) who brought the ICERD to the General Assembly, where it was completed in one session, that blazed the path for the subsequent completion of the ICCPR and the ICESCR.[54] Below, I consider how the ICERD queries the relation between formal political equality, material well-being, social security, and legal standing. Here I would underscore how the convention regards colonialism and racism as cut from the same historical cloth; for example, in its preamble, the convention cites *both* the 1963 UN Declaration on the Elimination of All Forms of Racial Discrimination *and* the 1960 Declaration on the Granting of Independence to Colonial Countries and Peoples as indispensable precedents for its own provisions. As such, I suggest, the ICERD regards self-determination as an essential characteristic of racial equality, and vice versa.

Between 1950 and 1966, when the ICCPR and ICESCR were adopted by the UN General Assembly, the interpretation of the right to self-determination did indeed shift from a concern with individual, democratic rights to a strictly anticolonial state prerogative that was indifferent, if not explicitly hostile, to democratic practice.[55] In the early 1950s, Third World diplomats such as Charles Malik and Jawdat Mufti promoted an essential link between human rights and national self-determination, which necessitated both democratic domestic governance and nonintervention by foreign powers. However, by the early 1960s, many representatives endorsed separating the right to self-determination from questions of political freedoms.[56] Hence, rather than a means to individual, democratic rights, the right to self-determination became an end unto itself, such that the attainment of sovereignty "exhausted" the "idea of self-determination" and became aligned with the international state system I describe in the introduction.[57]

For this reason, Moyn dates the true advent of a "human rights revolution" as commencing in the 1970s, arising from the frustration of international jurists with decolonized nations whose claims to self-determination shielded them from international scrutiny and rebuke. By excoriating Third World regimes for their human rights abuses, former imperialist powers continued to horde the prerogative to determine who might control their own political destinies and on what terms. Here, human rights discourse readily appeared to be a flexible and strategic neocolonial *and* neoliberal rhetoric, selectively assessing the moral fitness of postcolonial governments from a Western perspective.[58] Already by the 1968 Conference on Human Rights in Tehran, representatives from most Third World nations, even those not circulating in the Soviet orbit, criticized the UDHR as "an irrelevant artifact from a past age," unable to address a postcolonial Third World, for which economic development and maintaining national liberation were the most pressing priorities.[59] For example, Article 1 of the 1986 UN Declaration on the Right to Development (and its precursor, the 1981 African Charter on Human and Peoples' Rights) gave pride of place to economic development and self-determination, before declaring in Article 2 that "the human person is the central subject of development and should be the active participant and beneficiary of the right to development." Moreover, Article 2 accords to states "the right and the duty to formulate appropriate national development policies that aim at the constant improvement of the well-being of the entire population and of all individuals, on the basis of their active, free and meaningful participation in development and in the fair distribution of the benefits resulting therefrom."[60] While the 1986 Declaration did not wholly repudiate individual rights, its primary aim in both its preamble and main body was to advance guarantees of national and economic security from which the Third World had historically been excluded.[61]

Indeed, most leaders of nationalist *and* Marxist resistance movements in colonized nations preferred the sovereign state form when it came to organizing the postcolonial societies for which they struggled.[62] While such elites fought against foreign rule, they did not typically disavow the conceptions of modernity extended by colonial powers, and they usually believed the state form was best able to mobilize resources and to counteract the colonial "underdevelopment" from which their people suffered.[63] These modernizing projects included the expansion of education, health and sanitation, public works, communication networks, national censuses, and agricultural reforms, as well as the implementation of organized police, judicial, and penal apparatuses. In keeping with these social and political objectives, postcolonial states usually adopted constitutions that, at least in governmental kind, were "isomorphic" with former imperial rule.[64] The establishment of such states, often, in Odd Arne Westad's words, "substituted for the nonexisting 'nation' in territories otherwise arranged by colonial powers" and aggravated social tensions, especially around ethnic and religious differences.[65]

Because self-determination found limited legitimized expression in the sovereign state form, domestic repression and abuse executed by authoritarian or one-party regimes led to the well-publicized scandal and "decisive failure" of postcolonial governance beginning in the 1960s.[66] The principle of state sovereignty, especially as manifested in the domestic jurisdiction clause that I discussed in the introduction, rendered the recognition and protection of all *other* rights subject to the dominion of individual nation-states.[67] Military leaders, dictators, and other authoritarian governments fashioning themselves as modernizers who could meet their nations' economic needs through development while holding Communists at bay eagerly sought support from the United States. In places like the Philippines, South Korea, and the Dominican Republic (all of which I discuss in *Writing Human Rights*), as well as South Vietnam, Guatemala, Iran, and Indonesia, the United States provided aid, training, and advisers, with little concern for how such regimes flouted even the liberal political rights that were supposedly part and parcel of modernization.[68]

In the 1980s, the detachment of economic development and national self-determination from individual political rights was further compounded by the rise of a discourse of radical cultural relativism, which dismissed human rights as altogether foreign and irrelevant constraints imposed in order to control non-Western nations.[69] Rather than simply replicating a Soviet rhetoric about political sovereignty and economic security, postcolonial avowals of cultural relativism emphasized the inconsistency of individual rights with traditional cultures.[70] After the end of the Cold War, in the 1990s, this debate came to be framed as one between, on the one side, (neo)liberal claims to individual political and civil rights—thought to characterize the democracies of the global North—and, on the other side, communitarian or traditional values promoted throughout much of the rest of the globe (although they were often referred to by the shorthand "Asian values"). Those such as Lee Kuan Yew, the former prime minister of Singapore, argued that "traditional" values did not include political freedoms, which were much less important to developing nations than obeisance to national authorities. Even worse, the rhetoric from authoritarian regimes who violently abused their own citizens came to uncomfortably mirror that of those Western advocates of relativism who championed respect for Third World cultures, as they identified democratic human rights to be pernicious neocolonial missives.[71]

Thus, in a postsocialist era, claims to social and economic rights had been folded into *either* demands for liberal, first-generation individual rights *or* third-generation cultural ones, fracturing what human rights activists and scholars had maintained to be an indivisible panoply of the three generations. Official, academic, and popular discourses in the United States and elsewhere conceived of international politics as the contest between first- and third-generation orders of rights, and of those orders as themselves irreconcilable. The social and economic concerns that second-generation rights reflected were rendered *either* as products to be purchased in the free markets of liberal democracies (and their ever-shrinking welfare states) *or* as goods that the communitarian state (often with barely any welfare infrastructure to speak of) allocates according to antidemocratic "cultural" norms. That the rise of cultural relativism and the shift away from individual rights in postcolonial politics took hold at the same time as authoritarian postcolonial governments replaced democratic ones was neither coincidental nor a merely cynical turn of events. Rather, the historical conditions of national liberation, economic restructuring, and Cold War bipolarity that I have traced in the introduction and in this chapter overdetermined the turn to culturally conservative and politically repressive agendas.

And yet, during the early Bandung era, nationalist aspirations were hardly limited to the capture of the state; rather, they were driven by a fervent desire to be free of colonialism. Bandung participants shared an understanding of the structural causes of their nations' underdevelopment by colonial rule.[72] Moreover, this desire for liberation was based not so much on conceptions of a homogeneous racial or cultural nation, as on a shared struggle against empire that made possible the broad continental and intercontinental imagining of Third World solidarity and cooperation. This sort of "internationalist nationalism" reveals the crucial way in which mass-based social movements expressed desires for freedom, justice, and belonging that were distinct from, if not always in contradiction with, the state form.[73] The Final Communiqué from the Asian-African Conference of Bandung in 1955, which I cite in the epigraph to this chapter, fully endorsed the UN Charter principles of human rights and the UDHR. Diplomats such as the Philippines' Carlos Romulo, who had served as his country's ambassador to the United Nations and signed the UDHR, urged delegates at the Bandung Conference to pursue both national self-determination and individual human rights, as he rebuked Western imperialism and Communist repression in equal measure.[74] Bandung, NAM, and the intergovernmental organizations and instances of cooperation that followed thus illustrated the possibility of political communities as alternatives to both nation-states and "outsized political entities" such as the United Nations, the World Bank, the IMF, and the WTO.[75] Moreover, Third World formulations of procedural justice, including equitable representation in international institutions and decision-making, along with principles of international diplomacy that included peaceful dialogue and problem-solving, marked a notable departure from the coercive and domineering modes of both earlier imperialism and the great powers during the Cold War.[76]

To be sure, neither the Bandung Conference, Afro-Asian internationalism, nor, as I discuss below, the American black freedom movement can simply be shoehorned into a human rights container.[77] But this alternative genealogy of human rights can animate the interlocked antiracist and anticolonial demands for self-determination, as well as social equity, political freedom, and economic justice that racialized U.S. subjects articulated alongside anticolonial and socialist movements in this era. During and after World War I, the rise of American influence around the world was contested by what Mullen calls a "deliberately miscegenated internationalist politics," which in turn anticipated the character of anticolonial movements before, during, and after World War II.[78] This internationalism promoted the role of Marxism in twentieth-century world revolutionary struggle, but it also seriously considered pan-African, pan-Asian, and pan-Arab endeavors (as well as dialogues between them) as crucial to its mission.[79]

After World War II, many postcolonial regimes looked to a Soviet model of development (one organized, for example, around a central plan for industrialization, building infrastructure, and collectivizing agriculture), which they found to align with their own "state-centered and justice-oriented ideals."[80] American elites accordingly perceived in Soviet Communism the possibility, and the possible threat, of "an alternative modernity; a way poor and downtrodden peoples could challenge their conditions *without* replicating the American model."[81] But NAM nations also struggled to maintain political and cultural autonomy from both superpowers, giving rise to the original, positive meaning of a "Third World" founded in human rights, self-determination, and world peace.[82] Although Bandung participants were careful to emphasize that they did not form a trading bloc, they nevertheless called for the need to stabilize international commodity prices, for diversification of exports by way of raw material processing, for greater participation in international economic and governance institutions, and for consultation between members in the interest of economic cooperation.[83]

Concurrently, in the United States, the existence of the American Communist Party (founded in 1921), albeit with a relatively small membership, suggested "to some of those whom Americanism had disenfranchised that other methods for organizing society could be envisaged, even in America."[84] Black radicals "voiced visions of communal possibility that consistently surpassed the conceptions available in the prevailing idioms of U.S. political culture" and took up anti-imperialist critiques as a response to newly emergent relations of power and development across the globe.[85] During the Black Power era of the late 1960s and early 1970s, black internationalism flourished, drawing and expanding upon the earlier anti-imperial politics advanced by figures such as W. E. B. Du Bois and Paul Robeson.[86] Movement intellectuals such as Malcolm X, Amiri Baraka, Elaine Brown, Harold Cruse, E. Franklin Frazier, Claudia Jones, Huey Newton, Robert Williams, and Richard Wright oriented their own expressive and political activities toward the alternative modernity envisaged by the NAM alliances, beyond and in tension with domestic integration.[87] At the same time, black nationalism inspired and influenced the radicalization of other communities of color, as Asian Americans, Chicanos, and Puerto Ricans, along with the American Indian Movement, elaborated theories of "internal colonialism" against which they organized in alliance with one another.[88] Members of this "U.S. Third World" Left differed from the larger New Left coalition by insisting that capitalism is a fundamentally racialized system.[89] As a result, their efforts were informed by intertwined experiences of racial and class inequity, which subsequent activist-scholars have theorized as "racial capitalism."[90]

As I have explained in the introduction, the internationalism of such resistance movements was eventually contained, if not eradicated, by way of various ideological and coercive measures, in the United States and elsewhere. Fracturing domestic and international alliances from the 1950s onward, the liberal imaginary of integration redirected antiracist efforts toward achieving the equal rights and political freedoms promised by U.S. citizenship. But in the waning years of the Cold War, a mounting backlash against civil rights gains also accompanied the ascendant rhetoric of multicultural tolerance, and the prevalence of autocratic and dictatorial regimes across much of Asia, Africa, and Latin America provoked a parallel debate in regard to "cultural relativism" and universal human rights norms. Within this context, many mainstream reviewers and academic critics have cast minor literatures as trading in more radical aspirations for the "identity politics" of national visibility and belonging. But, I suggest, these conclusions are perhaps more symptomatic of the reading practices brought to bear on the works of U.S. writers of color than of the imaginative possibilities such literature harbors. As I turn to consider below, minor literatures from this period also recorded the dialectical contradictions that the norms of state sovereignty and liberal individualism could not reconcile, contradictions that can and should (re)animate antiracist and transnational human rights politics.[91]

The "Nothing to See" of Integration

Gaines has been celebrated primarily as a writer of regional fiction, documenting in particular the oral traditions and folkways of rural Louisiana, where he spent much of his life. Written late in his career, *A Gathering of Old Men* certainly conforms to that description, but also, I contend, ponders the implications of national integration in a mode that has transnational reverberations into the twenty-first century. The taut structure of the novel resembles that of a deposition, with the various narrators (introduced by both their formal names and the more familiar nicknames by which they are known to the other characters) serving as witnesses who also participate in the aftermath of Beau's death. For the black characters, the death immediately stokes fearful memories of the Boutan family, Beau's father Fix "and his drove," and the brutality they have doled out toward African Americans in the past (13). It also recalls the more quotidian forms of discrimination and racism that have structured Jim Crow society for the span of the men's lives in the twentieth century (38, 45).[92] Although the overriding assumption throughout the novel, on the part of both white and black characters, is that their friend and neighbor, the stoic Mathu, has killed Beau—Beau's body lies in Mathu's yard until the coroner departs with it—each of the men claims responsibility for the murder (as does Candy Marshall, the white heir of the sugar plantation, who is especially close to Mathu, as he helped raise her after her parents' deaths). Having shot rounds from their shotguns identical to the one that killed Beau and gathered the empty shells before arriving at Mathu's place, the men offer individual motives, all having to do with the indignities, insecurity, and loss they suffer as black men. Thus, Sheriff Mapes is unable to gather conclusive evidence on the identity of the killer.

As the multiple narrators tell of the events following Beau's death, another story emerges, one of the integration of the surrounding region into a national and international political and economic order. From the privatization of land, to the arrival of new technologies, and the mass migration of young adults from the area, the characters emphasize the erosion of local, traditional ways of life in the haunting emptiness, the "nothing to see," that surrounds them (20).[93] To return to the scene with which I opened this chapter, in describing what he recalls and "don't see it now," Johnny Paul recollects his own parents and other black men and women working the fields. He recognizes that the arrival of what Mapes refers to as "progress" threatens to expunge the memory of the slave and of the impoverished black labor that long cultivated the land: "One day that tractor was go'n come in there and plow up them graves, getting rid of all proof that we ever was. Like now they trying to get rid of all proof that black people ever farmed this land with plows and mules—like if they had nothing from the starten but motor machines" (92). The landscape thus offers a poignant trope of the belated but certain integration of the region into a modern nation that, for the novel's characters, portends an erasure of their lifeworld. Cherry describes the empty cane fields, leased and farmed by the Boutan family, as evoking a sense of solitariness: "The rows looked so naked and gray and lonely—like an old house where the people have moved from. Where good friends have moved from, leaving the house empty and bare, with nothing but ghosts now to keep it company" (43). In a metonymic chain that traces this sense of abandonment, the empty cane fields give way to empty homes, which give way in turn to a hollowing out of the elders who stand as "the final living testament to the history and struggle of their people."[94]

Likewise, a discourse of racial integration and accommodation, allegorized in the figure of another of Fix's sons, Gilbert ("Gil" or "G-bert"), supplements the militant stand taken by the old men against Fix's entrenched white supremacy. Gil is one of a powerhouse duo of Louisiana State University football players, a fullback striving for an All-American title alongside African American halfback Calvin Harrison. Dubbed "Salt and Pepper" by the media and LSU's "publicity people," the pair seems to signal the inevitable desegregation of the Deep South (111–12). While the news of his brother's death momentarily threatens to throw Gil's liberal inclinations off the rails, he eventually pleads with his father not to retaliate by lynching Beau's killer. He explains, "All my life I have heard what my family have done to others. . . . It hurts me to hear that, Papa," and "I couldn't make All-American, Papa, if I was involved in something against the law. . . . Even if our name was involved, the Yankee press would destroy me" (137–38). Gil's brother Jean also implores his father, "We have law out there to do what many of these people would like to see us do" (140). Although disgusted with what he sees as his sons' betrayal of family honor, Fix ultimately resigns himself to waiting for the legal system to do its work, even as he disowns Gil.

When Mapes informs the black men that Fix will not be coming to Marshall, he is overjoyed to point out to them that the very absence of the confrontation is of their own making:

> Y'all the one—you cut your own throats. You told God you wanted Salt and Pepper to get together, and God did it for you. At the same time, you wanted God to keep Fix the way Fix was thirty years ago so one day you would get a chance to shoot him. Well, God couldn't do both. Not that He likes Fix, but He thought the other idea was better—Salt and Pepper. Well? Which do you want? Salt and Pepper to play together, or you want God to keep Fix the way he was thirty years ago so you would have a chance to shoot him? Well, make up your mind. I'm sure God's just sitting there waiting. (171)

The novel thus repeatedly emphasizes a sense of *belatedness* in the communal stand that the men have decided to take, with even the men asking one another: "We wait till now? Now, when we're old men, we get to be brave?" (31).

Similarly, Gil describes Fix's days of racist aggression as an anachronism that belongs to the past: "Those days are gone, Papa. . . . Those days when you just take the law in your own hands—those days are gone. These are the '70s, soon to be the '80s. Not the '20s, the '30s, or the '40s. People died—people we knew—died to change those things. Those days are gone forever" (143). One of the policemen encourages an anguished Gil to "play the best game you ever played" with Pepper and to think of Beau's son Tee Beau: "Tee Beau's future. You want to do something for your dead brother?

Do something for his son's future—play in that game tomorrow. . . . You can help this country tomorrow. You can help yourself" (151). The arrival of a liberal civil rights order to the area forecloses the more extreme forms of opposition all the elderly men, black and white, hope to mount, casting it as a remnant of a time that has passed. When the black men move from the yard into Mathu's shack to discuss his impending arrest, they concede to one another their disappointment. Mat explains, "I don't feel like going back home empty-handed. We'll never gather like this ever again," to which Clatoo replies, "We ain't got a enemy to fight" (180).

Ultimately, though, it is Mathu, who, having remained more or less silent throughout Mapes's interrogation, acknowledges a transformation among them and affirms their courage in gathering to support him. Throughout the novel Mathu is described as "one of them blue-black Singaleese niggers" who has "always bragged about not having no white man's blood in his veins" and is "the only one we knowed had ever stood up" against the routine violence doled out by white men. At the same time, for Candy, he represents the living memory and character of her family's land (51, 31, 177).[95] Thus, when he tells the men of the conversion he has experienced in the face of their valor, he grants them a claim to a black manhood he has represented to them while acknowledging the complete change in himself that their bravery has wrought:

> I ain't nothing but a mean bitter old man. Hating them out there on that river, hating y'all here in the quarters. Put myself above all—proud to be African. You know why proud to be African? 'Cause they won't let me be a citizen here in this country. Hate them 'cause they won't let me be a citizen, hated y'all 'cause you never tried. Just a mean-hearted old man. All I ever been, till this hour. . . . I been changed. Not by that white man's God. I don't believe in that white man's God. I been changed by y'all. Rooster, Clabber, Dirty Red, Coot—you changed this hardhearted old man. (183)

Mathu's praise transfigures the belatedness of the men's assembly into the origin of a new, self-directed future for all of them, however short-lived it might be.

Furthermore, the most significant of these transformations comes with the revelation that it is Mathu's godson, Charlie Biggs ("Big Charlie"), who actually shot and killed Beau. Despite being described as physically imposing in size—"six seven, he weighed about two hundred and seventy-five pounds. . . . His arms bulged inside the sleeves of his denim shirt, and his torso was as round as a barrel"—Charlie derides himself as a "nigger boy" who has "all my life . . . run from people. From black, from white; from nigger, from Cajun, both" (188). Charlie explains that, finally fed up with Beau's abuse, he had decided to quit working for the Cajun farmer and shot Beau in self-defense as the latter tried to retaliate against Charlie's impertinence. Nonetheless, Charlie had initially decided to flee Marshall, leaving Mathu to take the blame for the death.

For Charlie, then, it is not the killing itself, but his decision *to return and take responsibility* that designates his newly claimed manhood: "I'm a man, Sheriff. . . . That's why I come back. I'm a man" (187). Charlie, like Mathu, experiences this moment as a conversion that interpellates him as a new man. He explains that, in trying to run away, he found himself unable to leave Marshall:

> If I turnt and went toward Morgan, something there stopped me, too. Something like a wall, a wall I couldn't see, but it stopped me every time. I fell on the ground and screamed and screamed. I bit in the ground. I got a handful of dirt and stuffed in my mouth, trying to kill myself. Then I just laid there, laid there, laid there. Sometime round sundown—no, just 'fore sundown, I heard a voice calling my name. I laid there listening, listening, listening, but I didn't hear it no more. But I knowed that voice was calling me back here. (192–93)[96]

As Candy's boyfriend, the journalist Lou Dimes who narrates this chapter, remarks, "There was something in his face that you see in faces of people who have just found religion" (193). Charlie insists that Mapes refer to him as "Mr. Biggs" as a designation of his new manhood.

As critic William T. Mallon argues, the "congregational" speech act that acknowledges the injuries and losses of the past, rather than the threatened violence, provides the key vehicle by which all the men achieve this communal black manhood; the shotguns that have been previously used only for hunting become symbols of "a hard-won dignity that regenerates and sustains the community."[97] At the same time, this performative speech has the effect of transforming the space of the former slave quarters into the place of responsibility and affiliation.[98] As a portrait of *communitas*—Victor Turner's concept of the social process by which those grounded in a particular geography come to be defined by their social relatedness in a "community of feeling"—the scene marks the men's "transitory, liminal status," experienced as movement and "an interval moment of creative possibility and innovation."[99] In *A Gathering of Old Men,* it is not the shared condition of subjection that produces affiliation and identification, but rather a *shared desire to negate those conditions;* as a result, Gaines characterizes this *communitas* as both sacred and political.[100] In the hearing that the old men provide to one another's stories of injury and loss, Gaines rearticulates the conditions that constitute their commonality and revises conceptions of rights, responsibility, and freedom that define American citizenship. The performative speech acts in *A Gathering of Old Men* accordingly generate a critique of the limits of the liberal citizenship offered to African Americans by articulating a political community of subjects alternative to that of the national state. Gaines thus radically reinscribes responsibility as an obligation to recognize in one another the *desire* for self-determination, social justice, and economic security, which have continually been foreclosed *as* rights despite their import in the black freedom struggle of the postwar era.

The novel does not conclude, however, with this mutual recognition between all the men. Instead, despite Fix's resolve not to interfere with Mapes's investigation at Marshall, a younger group of Beau's friends, headed up by Luke Will—known for terrorizing the black community in order to discourage desegregation—decides to pursue retribution. A shootout promptly succeeds Charlie's confession, culminating with the deaths of Charlie and Luke. Despite this seemingly calamitous outcome, the novel ends on a distinctly comic note. In his account of the court trial that follows the gun battle, Lou assesses the men: "You've never seen a sadder bunch of killers in all your life—on either side. Everybody had something wrong with him—scratches, bruises, cuts, gashes. They had cut themselves on barbed wire, tin cans, broken bottles—you name it. . . . Everybody was either limping, his arm in a sling, or there was a bandage round his head or some other part of his body" (211). The other reporters who descend on the courtroom "took the whole thing as something astonishing but not serious. No one else laughed nearly as much as the news people did" (212). The judge concludes that "since the two men who had killed were both dead, he could not pass judgment over them," and he sentences the rest of the men to probation, in particular barring them from possession and use of any weapons, which, as Lou parenthetically notes, "was like telling a Louisianian never to say Mardi Gras or Huey Long": "He said if he heard once that any of the defendants picked up a gun, or was within ten feet of anyone with such a weapon, he would send that person to prison for the rest of his natural-born life. He asked if there were any questions. There were no questions, and he slammed down the gavel and said the court was adjourned" (213–14). Lou's free and indirect discourse in relating this conclusion characterizes the liberal, integrationist imaginary that displaces both the reactionary white supremacy embodied by Fix, which is ushered to its death in Luke, and the radical black militancy characterized by Mathu, which is ushered to its death in Charlie. From this newly hegemonic perspective, not only have both of the battling sides sustained equivalent casualties, but the penalty doled out seems negligible, amusing even, given the rewards extended in return, namely, the genuine recognition of African Americans as equal citizens before the law and the implementation of their civil rights. Most critics have concurred with this liberal perspective, which accords the characters their manhood and their humanity.[101]

Yet, when we return to the novel's historical setting during the waning years of the Cold War epoch, the emphasis on firearms in this conclusion proves particularly telling. Critics have debated whether the gun battle is central or inconsequential to the construction of black masculinity in the novel, and Suzanne Jones suggests that the dual ending of the gun battle followed by the trial sends a flawed, ambiguous message, about which "one could argue that the old men lose some moral ground," especially given that Charlie refuses Luke's desperate offer to turn himself in so that he might save himself by ending the shootout.[102] In contrast, I propose that this redoubled conclusion essentially structures the novel's dialectical critique of the historical juncture at which Gaines writes. Of course, this conclusion inscribes the ambivalence toward violence at the heart of the black freedom struggle, in particular the sense on the part of black nationalists that nonviolent civil disobedience was at best a limited response to the pervasive police and mob violence facing African Americans in the twentieth century. But beyond staging diverging *modes* of resistance, the gun battle and the courtroom trial ask us to consider the very divergent aim posited by the black radical imaginary, one that, while not always entirely foregoing the aspiration for belonging in the United States, also held fast to pan-Africanist, Third World internationalist, and "Bandung humanist" visions of future political community.[103]

The novel's dual ending consequently queries the very subject and location of self-determination, drawing out the contradiction that a liberal construction of the American global nation cannot surmount. The judge's injunction imposes very specific conditions on black belonging in the nation, forcibly channeling all political and social claims through the state rather than communal action. In the judge's sentence limiting that which both black and white men in Louisiana take to be a "natural right," the passage obliquely evokes the Constitution's Second Amendment right to bear arms: "A well regulated militia being necessary to the security of a free state, the right of the people to keep and bear arms shall not be infringed." Given the mention of "militia" in the prefatory clause, legal debates over the Second Amendment dispute whether it accords an individual right or a collective one of a "subset" group, such as a state militia. My aim here is not to rehearse the various positions taken with respect to this debate. Rather, I wish to point to the contradiction that is inherent in it and upon which a liberal philosophy of natural rights founders: the irreconcilability between, on one hand, the individual as a subject of rights (including the right to bear arms) accorded by the state and, on the other, the natural right to democratic self-determination, which can, at any moment, portend an insurgent (collective) call-to-arms that might contest the nation-state or undo it altogether.[104] Of course, most recent defenses of the constitutional right to bear arms arrive from a rightist position—either a deeply libertarian individualism that warns against the tyranny of the state or a reactionary conservatism that employs the racialized specter of the armed criminal against whom law-abiding citizens need to protect themselves (or some combination of the two).[105] But returning to the Bandung-era aspirations of numerous black American leaders, I contend that Gaines underscores this restriction on firearms to record a very different dimension of the issue: the compromise demanded of African Americans by liberal integration, where a minor subject finds, like the postcolonial nations compelled to integrate into the united nations world, that he or she may aspire only to "his or her national interest," the dream of freedom being defined by the hegemonic nation, rather than other possible axes of identification and desire, while the state retains its monopoly on "legitimate" violence.

Finally, the seemingly offhand reference to Huey Long also returns us to the human rights record. In the leftist challenge that the populist former

Louisiana governor and senator mounted against his former ally, Long was in part responsible for Roosevelt's crafting of the so-called Second New Deal, which included the Wagner Act, the Works Progress Administration, the Social Security Act, the U.S. Housing Authority, the Farm Security Administration, and the Fair Labor Standards Act—that is, the pivotal provisions that have since come to be known as the signature institutions of economic and social security from the era. This of course is not to promote Long as a particular champion of African American civil rights.[106] Rather, in linking Long, Mardi Gras, and firearms in the same breath, the novel leads us back to the inception of the imaginary of domestic and international integration to uncover the profound social and economic unevenness of that liberal project.

By the early 1980s, when Gaines published *A Gathering of Old Men,* the ascendancy of Ronald Reagan's presidency signaled a scuttling of détente with the Soviet Union—itself plagued by the economic crises that would speed it toward glasnost and perestroika at the end of the decade—and renewed support for anti-Communist campaigns in the Americas, Middle East, and Africa (not to mention the military invasion of the tiny Caribbean island nation of Grenada). The Reagan Doctrine quickly dismissed the Carter administration's incipient concerns with human rights principles as a criterion for foreign policy decision-making, insisting instead that the United States needed to "reestablish order in the natural development of 'newly independent states' " by assisting even "authoritarian" (as opposed to Communist "totalitarian") regimes that could hold the line against socialist insurgency.[107] The shifts in foreign policy were accompanied at home by momentous change. The surveillance and demonization of black nationalism and radical social movements and a backlash against New Deal institutions (and particularly those welfare programs that historically served African Americans), as well as the modest civil rights reforms enjoyed by black citizens, the global restructuring of economic relations, and the influx of new immigrant populations to the United States were well underway. But, despite the "declension narrative" often used to describe the waning of radical social movements and cultural politics since the late 1970s, insurgent ideals of self-determination and solidarity persisted through an era otherwise hailed as one of conservative retrenchment.[108] In light of the wide-ranging transformations of American life, Gaines's depiction of the temporal lag of dreams deferred insists upon the partial and incomplete character of freedom, self-determination, and social justice for his subjects.

Gaines's novel also appeared precisely at a moment when much American literary criticism focused on the inherent tensions between black (and other women of color) feminism and cultural nationalist politics.[109] It is thus important to point out the way in which, even as it focuses on the reinscription of black *men*'s collective agency, the narrative apprehends the claims made by such other subjects. For example, after the men have finished recounting their memories, and Mapes asks dismissively, "You mean y'all ran out of stories?" Beulah, one of the women who has been listening in, replies: "'Nobody ain't run out of nothing. . . . You want me to start? . . . You want any woman here to start? I can tell you things done happened to women round here make the hair stand on your head. You want me to start? All you got to do is say yes. All you got to do is nod" (106–7).[110] Mapes, however, replies with a decisive "no," discounting any further contributions by the black women present. Moreover, earlier, as the men are first hearing about Beau's death, Chimley describes how "that oldest boy of Berto, that sissy one they called Fue," brings word to them: "Something to do with Mathu, and something to do with Beau Boutan dead in his yard. That's all I know, all I want to know. . . . Y'all can go and do like she say or y'all can go home, lock y'all doors, and crawl under the bed like y'all used to. Me, I'm leaving" (29). Registering the heterogeneity of Gaines's subjects, without fully pursuing them, the characterizations of Beulah and Fue bring into relief an otherwise receding horizon of feminist and queer subjectivities that I address in more detail in later chapters.

Indeed, as numerous critics have pointed out, the very structure of Gaines's novel, narrated entirely from the perspective of minor characters (Mathu, Charlie, Mapes, Gilbert, and Candy never take up the first-person narrator's role) considerably revises an African American modernism that homes in on a lone, alienated male subject, such as Ralph Ellison's Invisible Man or Richard Wright's Bigger Thomas.[111] Moreover, Gaines's focus on those who seemed marginal to the social movements of the 1960s and 1970s—elderly, rural residents "left behind" in a region considered "stuck" in the past—transmits an alternate temporality for social transformation than do narratives centered on young, urban activists or highly visible, charismatic political leaders.[112] If, as Karla F.C. Holloway maintains, "black literatures are legal fictions inevitably bound by law," both the testamentary form and the plot's resolution in the courtroom exemplify such literature's investiture by the law and the law's narratives of identity, as minor characters are made over into mature citizens in the public eye.[113] But *A Gathering of Old Men* also evokes how, although the law bounds citizenship and personhood to one another, there have always also been other genealogies for constituting persons in terms of their humanity, apart from whatever standing the state awards.[114] Such "humanity" not only emerges in contradistinction to formal citizenship, but also disarticulates itself from American national belonging in order to register the ongoing aspiration for a self-determined political community that might constitute persons otherwise. Hence, to the extent that integration *did* effectively transform the legal and political personhood afforded African Americans in the United States, as a *minor* literature, *A Gathering of Old Men* trenchantly divulges the limits of the American global nation for imagining black personhood.

Its plot (i.e., both the novel's sequence of events and the scheme in which the characters conspire) remains impossible without the supposedly minor characters who articulate for the novel a collective will to constitute black self-determination.[115] This focus on minor subjects in a peripheral time and place registers what I have been calling a critical Bandung Spirit, which seeks to generate forms of good life other than the ones proffered by liberal integration. Despite its appearance as dealing with provincial subjects left behind in integrationist national and international movements, the self-determination articulated by the text might also convey the desires for social security, economic rights, and antiracist justice that moved the Afro-Asian nations in the 1950s and 1960s. Next, I turn to consider how Kingston's well-known subject of feminist politics finds openings for such a worldly Bandung Spirit and newly emergent transnational affiliations in the confusions of identity that her memoir portrays.

"My American Life Has Been Such a Disappointment"

In the forty years since its publication, Maxine Hong Kingston's "memoirs of a girlhood among ghosts," *The Woman Warrior,* has had a formidable impact on American studies, feminist scholarship, and minor literatures, as the extensive criticism on the work makes evident.[116] Here, I focus on an aspect of the text that has received less attention: its treatment of the social and political transformations effected by the liberalization of immigration policies in the 1950s and 1960s, as well as the civil rights and ethnic nationalist movements of the 1960s and 1970s. In her concern with the relationship between established and more recently arrived Chinese Americans and their connections to African Americans, Kingston engages the Bandung Spirit through a dialectic of departure and return that endeavors to keep open the possibility for new forms of affiliation and solidarity. She raises crucial questions about the implications of the heterogeneous "new immigration" that has radically altered the racial and ethnic landscape of the United States and offers recognition to those who want otherwise with respect to racial democracy and social justice. At the same time, *The Woman Warrior* takes seriously how the "actually existing socialism" of authoritarian states shaped the political visions of diasporic subjects from deeply embattled Asian homelands during the Cold War.

While the figure of Kingston's woman warrior has become emblematic of the desires and agencies that women of color wield, it is instructive that the chapter in which this heroine is most memorably depicted, "White Tigers," abruptly shifts from its fable of Fa Mu Lan, who inhabits a mythic sphere of "perfect filiality," to the narrator's observation, "My American life has been such a disappointment."[117] The narrator proceeds with anecdotes about the cavalier anti-black racism of the supervisors under whom she has worked and, even when not discussing incidences of overt prejudice, she describes the sense of "suspension" that characterizes her family's American life, surrounded by white "Ghosts" (99). As an adult, the narrator worries over her elderly parents' well-being, after they lose their laundry to urban renewal and her mother continues to work for years as a farmhand. Her mother complains, "This is a terrible ghost country, where a human being works her life away. . . . I have not stopped working since the day the ship landed"; and "Factories, canneries, restaurants—always somebody somewhere working through the night" (104–5). Thus, although she "could not figure out what was my village," the narrator nevertheless learns "exactly who the enemy are," namely, the "business-suited in their modern American executive guise," "stupid racists," and "the tyrants who for whatever reason can deny my family food and work" (45, 49). Accordingly, in imagining the significance of the woman warrior's agency in a political-historical realm, she fantasizes about taking up arms against American racism (49).

But Kingston also records the torture and deep poverty that her extended family in the People's Republic of China (PRC) undergoes; the news from there, she writes with understatement, "made my parents, who are rocks, cry" (50). Here, then, the text offers as strident a critique of Chinese authoritarianism—in particular, the Cultural Revolution underway as Kingston writes *The Woman Warrior*—as it does of American racism: "To avenge my family, I'd have to storm across China to take back our farm from the Communists; I'd have to rage across the United States to take back the laundry in New York and the one in California" (49).[118] Thus, when she concludes that "nobody in history has conquered and united both North America and Asia," the feminist subject faces the fractured and contradictory discursive terrain that has come to constitute contemporary Asian American life, one that can be unified only through tremendous violence against the multiple histories that comprise it (49). While critics have long held that *The Woman Warrior* was never concerned with a straightforward recovery of cultural "truth," I emphasize how it holds out the possibility of return for the Bandung Spirit, which generates other possibilities for being human and living the good life.[119]

Although often overlooked, the poignant narrative offered in the chapter "At the Western Palace" opens onto those subjects who want otherwise than what an American global nation offers.[120] In its delicate rendering of the relationship between the sisters Brave Orchid (one of the many versions of the narrator's mother that the text offers) and Moon Orchid, Kingston fashions a minor transnationalism, where immigration cannot be characterized and measured simply according to the liberal nation's generational terms of arrival and assimilation. Although Kingston describes Brave Orchid and Moon Orchid, upon their reunion at the airport, as "two old women with faces like mirrors," the chapter also draws sharply contrasting portraits of the two. The tenacious Brave Orchid, who has over the years carved out a life from the inclement environs of the United States, measures her own achievements against the cultural innocence and, in her terms, "uselessness" of the newly arrived Moon Orchid. The chapter culminates with Moon Orchid's confrontation of her husband—who moved to the United States decades earlier and is so assimilated that he "looked like one of the ghosts"—and her realization of his abandonment of her, despite the regular remittances he has sent to support her over the years. Brave Orchid tries to console her sister by telling her, "We're all under the same sky and walk the same earth; we're alive together during the same moment" (154). But the traumatic meeting, into which she is drawn by her sister, drives Moon Orchid into insanity, manifesting as a paranoia about "Mexican ghosts plotting on her life" (155). As Brave Orchid realizes, while her sister's husband enjoys the benefits of integrated American personhood, "Moon Orchid had misplaced herself, her spirit . . . scattered all over the world," once her traditional bonds to others are rent by the passage of her family to the United States (157).[121]

In light of the damage caused by the integrationist imaginary of the American global nation (and, of course, traditional patriarchal arrangements of social relations, on which most commentators focus, as well as modern authoritarianism), *The Woman Warrior* instead assembles an incomplete subject in the narrator, who famously continues "to sort out what's just my childhood, just my imagination, just my family, just the village, just movies, just living" (105). When she tells of the difficulty she faces in finding her voice as a child, especially at school, the narrator remembers that "I liked the Negro students (Black Ghosts) best because they laughed the loudest and talked to me as if I were a daring talker too. One of the Negro girls had her mother coil braids over her ears Shanghai-style like mine; we were Shanghai twins except that she was covered with black like my paintings" (166).[122] The twin imagery at once recalls that of Brave Orchid and Moon Orchid, but, in suggesting likeness between the racially differentiated girls, also contemplates other forms of possible affiliation.[123] Moreover, the paintings to which the narrator refers are those she creates during a period of self-imposed silence; she perceives them to be "so black and full of possibilities" (165).[124] In this description, the text subtly suggests the forms of nascent solidarity it hopes to initiate out of what otherwise seems a silent void.[125]

Returning to the narrator's incarnation as Fa Mu Lan, we might then consider how the Bandung Spirit revises that chapter's conception of bodily vulnerability, injury, and social transformation. The narrator describes how her parents carve onto her back the "list of grievances" committed against her family and village, so that even after her demise, "the people could use my dead body for a weapon" (34–35). She later marries and becomes pregnant, conjuring a remarkable image of herself: "Now when I was naked, I was a strange human being indeed—words carved on my back and the baby large in front" (39–40). *The Woman Warrior* does not present a simple, atavistic return to a supposedly authentic subject of tradition, but produces the "strange human being," who can articulate new transnational relations between the minor subjects of the American global nation. Later, upon learning that all of their family in China has died and their family home there lost, the narrator tries to assure her mother by echoing Brave Orchid's words to Moon Orchid: "We belong to the planet now, Mama. Does it make sense to you that if we're no longer attached to one piece of land, we belong to the planet? Wherever we happen to be standing, why, that spot belongs to us as much as any other spot" (107).

Near the end of the text, the narrator says, "Soon I want to go to China and find out who's lying—the Communists who say they have food and jobs for everybody or the relatives who write that they have not the money to buy salt" (205). Yet, this actual return is never accomplished, and instead the text concludes with a different, imaginative return, a re-telling of the ancient legend of the poetess Ts'ai Yen (Cai Yan), who, when abducted during a raid on her village, sings to the accompaniment of her captors' music played on reed pipes: "Her words seemed to be Chinese, but the barbarians understood their sadness and anger" (209). When she is returned to her own people, Ts'ai Yen's song is taken up by the Han on their own instruments, and Kingston closes her text by commenting about the song: "It translated well" (209). Critics have variously discussed this ending in relation to the novel's thematic focus on the viability of a coherent Chinese American identity, whether it posits the success of a hybrid subject or the melancholic cleaving to past injury.[126]

I suggest, however, that when read in the context of the late Cold War and the narrator's expectation of a return that nonetheless does not take place, the collaboration and exchange that "A Song for a Barbarian Reed Pipe" allegorizes might be located elsewhere than the PRC or Chinese history and culture—located, that is, in the minor moments of affiliation that open in the text. In its evocation of a "planet" shared by its diasporic subjects, *The Woman Warrior* locates its own textual production of the strange human in the terms of a newly deterritorialized "planetarity" that critics such as Gayatri Chakravorty Spivak and Wai Chee Dimock have conceived from older notions of world literature.[127] At once denaturalizing the entrenched national boundaries that stand in as the political and moral boundaries of social agents and countering the abstraction that neoliberal globalization enacts, planetarity reveals "a crisscrossing set of pathways, open-ended and ever multiplying, weaving in and out of other geographies, other languages and cultures. These are input channels, kinship networks, routes of transit, and forms of attachment—connective tissues binding America to the rest of the world."[128]

It is this conception of planetarity that Kingston's narrator claims for herself and her mother in the face of their displacement and that releases minor American literatures from their domestic(ated) place in a multicultural national canon. Yet, planetarity as such is, as I described in the introduction, inaccessible to the human—that is, its time and space vastly exceed and escape human life and cognition. Rather, transnational imaginaries such as the Bandung Spirit mediate between the local and the global, offering modes by which to locate the human other than in the nation-state. Finally, as expansive as this Bandung imaginary might seem, the affiliations to which it gives rise take place, as Dimock also contends, in the minor, the "most minute, most intimate" acts of close reading, "pursued within the compass of a word, a phrase, a sentence [that] generates relational ties that can nonetheless extend for thousands of miles and thousands of years."[129]

By striking a commitment to the planet through its minor acts of transnational and interracial affiliation, *The Woman Warrior*—along with the other works I consider in this book—also inherently strives to "provincialize" the American good life. In what, retrospectively, we might dub the beginning of the late Cold War and at a moment when U.S. international ascendance and hegemony were in no way a foregone conclusion (i.e., in 1975, when, among other events, the United States withdrew from its disastrous campaigns in Southeast Asia), the spatial imaginary of the planet offers up multiple lifeworlds for the production of the "strange human being" who is the woman warrior. Such a planetary scale scrambles the progressive, "stagist" historicism of (neo)liberal development theory and politics, which, as Dipesh Chakrabarty writes in regard to his own effort to "provincialize Europe," consigns colonial others to "an imaginary waiting room" because they "were not yet civilized enough to rule themselves."[130] Whereas modern politics continually posits "the idea of single, homogenous, and secular historical time," in which "a story of human sovereignty [is] acted out" for those subjected to "a plural history of power," historical time is never "integral," but rather "out of joint with itself."[131] Moreover, while the secular, liberal imaginary of modern integration necessarily dismisses "gods and spirits" as "mere social facts," *The Woman Warrior* (like most of the other minor literatures I consider in this book) not only concedes the "coeval" existence of those "gods and other agents inhabiting practices of so-called 'superstition'" that "have never died anywhere."[132] It constantly conjures them as stubborn remainders of multiple pasts—"all the seemingly nonmodern, rural, nonsecular relationships and life practices"—that are never "fully conquered by" the developmentalist history of global capitalism and the modern state system.[133] Other beings, natural and supernatural, animal and divine, prove indispensable ethical counterpoints to the alternative humanities that minor literatures track.

To provincialize America in the history of human rights is to offer recognition to the aspirations for racial justice and self-determination archived in that record, as my return to the ICERD in the next section means to demonstrate. In *The Woman Warrior*, the most potent threat that the narrator, as an angry adolescent, lodges against her mother is one of departure. "I'm going away. I'm going away anyway. I am" (201).[134] As an adult, she tempers this warning by assuring her mother, "I'll be back again soon. . . . You know that I come back. I think of you when I'm not here," to which her mother responds, "Yes, I know you. I know you now. I've always known you. You're the one with the charming words. You have never come back" (101). If *The Woman Warrior* is unable to establish once and for all what constitutes the truth of Chinese, American, and Asian American identities and, conversely, "who's lying," a human rights approach significantly transfigures the memoir's project. Rather than simply reporting grievances in order to enact a wholesale return and exact vengeance, Kingston's text harbors a desire for new social and political worlds to sustain the vulnerable and resilient subjects engendered by transnational migration and exchange, and it constitutes its woman warrior through, but in difference to, the historical record.[135]

The ICERD and Human Rights Futures

A human rights approach animated by the Bandung Spirit recalls that in the postwar moment, the most vocal exponents of a cultural relativist perspective were not Third World nations but, in fact, representatives of imperial power, who insisted that human rights were inappropriate and meaningless for peoples "at the lowest stage of development."[136] In contrast, anticolonial leaders denounced this "colonial cultural relativism" and successfully defeated the insertion of a colonial clause in the draft covenant that succeeded the UDHR, ensuring that basic human rights were codified as universal in the human rights instruments that followed.[137] With its recognition of the racial and national hierarchies that organized an international division of labor and distribution of resources, this human rights approach provides a very different perspective on the post-1989 controversy over universalism and cultural relativism. During the Bandung and NAM eras, anticolonial intellectuals and activists, while certainly cognizant of the many factors that differentiated their peoples from one another, founded their political solidarity on a shared experience of colonialism, racism, and economic oppression.[138] In this way, the Bandung Spirit directs us "to consider the locations, practices, and politics that *created senses of community* across the Afro-Asian divide," radically remaking our notions of community beyond cultural pluralism and tolerance.[139]

Various human rights instruments, including the international bill of rights, do indeed confirm a "right to culture." And yet, international law has been loath to extend a rigid definition of what precisely "culture" *is*.[140] At turns, UN agencies and instruments describe culture as "a coherent self-contained system of values, and symbols as well as a set of practices" reproduced by specific groups, meaning mainly minority, subnational, and indigenous groups whose cultural practices diverge from those of a dominant national culture.[141] But the ICESCR enumerates a right to "cultural life" alongside the rather modern rights to social and economic rights, such as the right to education and the right to employment, and Article 15 of the covenant, which most expressly addresses cultural rights, does so in the same breath as it insists on the "right of everyone" to "enjoy the benefits of scientific progress and its applications" and emphasizes states' obligations to take steps "necessary for the conservation, the development and the diffusion of science and culture," as well as to "respect the freedom indispensable for scientific research and creative activity."

The history of minority rights in international law is likewise notoriously vexed. For various UN agencies and documents, the definition of a minority group, states' obligations to minority groups, whether minority groups enjoy rights *qua* collectives, and to what protective measures states are contractually bound in regard to minority groups all remain contested matters.[142] Both internally and in relation to the international bill of rights, the ICERD reflects this complexity with respect to minority groups. In fact, the ICERD makes no particular reference to minority rights. Instead, it maintains the central objective of establishing legal and social equality between racial and ethnic groups, without establishing separate rights for such groups.[143] The Committee on the Elimination of Racial Discrimination has concomitantly proceeded with a notion of equality that treats racial distinctions in the law (with the exception of expressly affirmative action measures, which I describe below) as discriminatory. UN instruments subsequent to the ICERD have come to replace the language of "racial minorities" with that of "ethnic minorities." Besides being consistent with conventional and scientific wisdom that there is no biological basis for designating racial differences, the language of "ethnic minority" means to signify the more capacious shared history and culture that distinguishes minority populations. Nevertheless, sometimes interchanged with "national minorities," the term has come to "denote both minority groups whose members are nationals and/or citizens of a particular state as well as groups characterized by a striving for self-governance, including a will for independence."[144]

Several related conceptual and practical problems then hamper the international effort to eliminate racial discrimination. First, the ICERD stipulates both negative duties—that is, it bars states from engaging in racial discrimination—as well as positive ("affirmative") ones with respect to "public life," including addressing the discriminatory actions of nonstate actors, encouraging multiracial integration, and taking necessary measures to encourage the development and protection of racial groups that have suffered past discrimination.[145] However, the meaning of "public life" remains indeterminate in the convention, and Article 4 also prohibits racist speech and activities, requiring that not only state institutions and representatives refrain from such discourse but that states declare such activities on the part of nonstate actors to be illegal. Insofar as legal scholars find these provisions to be in conflict with the rights of free expression and free association, the ICERD contradicts not only U.S. First Amendment rights, but also core first-generation human rights norms enumerated in the UDHR and the ICCPR.[146] Likewise, in itself, the ICERD does not oblige states to protect *any* rights; rather, it is meant to ensure that there is no discrimination in the enjoyment of rights that a member state grants its citizens. Yet, the ICERD intends to procure for racial minorities equality before the law and substantive material and social equality. Thus, on the one hand, "the CERD Committee is concerned with discriminatory practices only, and not the absence of economic or social rights in general terms."[147] But states must also put into practice *some* ideal of social security and economic justice, if any type of substantive equality is to be practicable.

In any case, U.S. civil rights law restricts notions of equality to a much narrower domain than does the international bill of rights or the ICERD. In order to compromise with conservative congressional leaders in the passage of the UN Charter, over what the latter saw as the creeping influences of international law on domestic matters (including, especially, as I note in the introduction, race relations in the United States), the Eisenhower administration agreed to refrain from submitting human rights treaties to the Senate for ratification. As a result, the United States had only a small part in the development and adoption of the key treaties—namely the ICCPR, the ICESCR, and the ICERD—which simultaneously guaranteed self-determination and nondiscrimination.[148] When the U.S. Senate did finally ratify the ICERD in 1994, it did so with a number of RUDs. These reservations and restrictions practically "eviscerate" the broader meanings of nondiscrimination that the convention extends.[149] Furthermore, while the initial U.S. report to the CERD Committee (submitted in 2000, much overdue) admitted the vast inequities facing racial minorities in the United States, it also denied that the United States has obligations in regard to economic, social, and cultural rights because they are not recognized *as rights* within the U.S. legal system. In keeping with an ascendant neoliberal creed, the report posited that the state *cannot* and *should not* necessarily seek to repair such inequality, insofar as it is produced by way of a combination of "societal conditions" and "individual characteristics."[150]

American law and jurisprudence accordingly permits only very narrow affirmative action practices in areas such as education, employment, and politics; U.S. jurisprudence has insisted on the need to demonstrate discriminatory intent *and* effect in order for laws and regulations to be deemed actionable, and it recognizes most incendiary and racist speech as permissible under the First Amendment of the Constitution.[151] The ICERD is further deemed "non-self-executing," thus precluding its pertinence in and for U.S. jurisprudence (in other words, any and all of the ICERD provisions must be adopted by way of legislative measures to be legally binding). As most courts have viewed even the most restrained affirmative action measures as compensatory for past discrimination, rather than integrative in character, progress in the efforts of public institutions to address de facto inequality have stalled, even while the nation celebrates the superficial markers of de jure equality, a "colorblind" legal system, and a multicultural nationalist ethos.[152]

Scholars such as Karla Holloway and Lisa Lowe insist that the *ongoing legibility* of race—that it remains visible on the body and signifies intelligibly in public life—even after integration has been pronounced, serves as an index of how social norms and forms retain the *material force* of legal exclusion and the cultural fictions through which such exclusion has been justified. After the civil rights movement and ensuing legal reforms, U.S. law construes race as a "fiction" that should have no bearing on legal reasoning, and it is mostly skeptical that race has bearing in the body politic at all. But racial identities continue to refer back to bodies that evidence collective truths about social and economic life elsewhere, truths that the law itself fortified through precedent that upheld such entrenched racial distinctions and their significance in national life. With race, then, as with the ghosts of those lifeworlds that modern liberalism has never fully conquered, "the past is both present and disruptive."[153]

Racial liberalism and multicultural neoliberalism in the United States certainly disavow the de jure segregation, racial violence, and legalized discrimination of the Jim Crow era. Yet they have also failed to grapple with the thoroughly racialized formulation of personhood that has been the mainstay of cultural belonging, social and economic security, and legal citizenship in the United States. Thus, as Lisa Marie Cacho argues, present-day laws inherit and recode those "identity categories" that "functioned historically as excludable or includable statuses in segregation, naturalization, and immigration law," as the state continues to depend upon "the *permanence* of certain groups' criminalization."[154] Populations that are "subjected to laws but refused the legal means to contest those laws as well as denied both the political legitimacy and moral credibility necessary to question them" (including undocumented immigrants, U.S. residents of color, and the poor residents of the global South) remain "ineligible for personhood," dwelling in a form of "social death" that is integral to the law's own self-justifications.[155] They are "imagined to be the reason why a punitive (in)justice system exists" in the first place: "Although they are excluded from law's protection, they are not excluded from law's discipline, punishment, and regulation."[156]

Legal scholars contend that the ICERD recognizes and addresses this structural reality in its emphasis on de facto discrimination and "equality of effect."[157] But they also note, probably correctly, that measures necessary to address substantive inequality impose obligations that are "far-reaching and burdensome" on states (begging the question why the burdens imposed on states should rank higher consideration than those imposed upon minority populations).[158] The U.S. case epitomizes how states opt out of obligations to social and economic human rights by claiming sovereignty over domestic matters and the priority of constitutional law that domestic jurisdiction accords. It also reveals how equality before the law can itself obviate those practices that sustain substantive inequalities. Here then, we face one of the central paradoxes that continually troubles human rights norms, including the normative principles addressed throughout *Writing Human Rights*. The proliferation of particular(ized) human rights subjects—in this case, ethnic or racial minorities, but also, as I elaborate in subsequent chapters, those such as women, children, and the disabled—who need to be specifically named, addressed, and assured of their human rights, despite the universality attributed to those rights, poses a problem of standing: Who is, or more precisely how do we know, the human person who has, or is to have, the right to rights? Moreover, how can those rights that are considered to be inherently natural and definitive of such human beings *per se* at once constitute those rights that have to be cultivated and protected—or are just as likely to be abandoned or disavowed—by the positive power of law?

That Article 27 of the ICCPR already *does* make express mention of such particular(ized) groups further illustrates this conundrum. As the covenant stipulates: "In those States in which ethnic, religious or linguistic minorities exist, persons belonging to such minorities shall not be denied the right, in community with the other members of their group, to enjoy their own culture, to profess and practise their own religion, or to use their own language." Moreover, Article 1 of the ICERD defines racial discrimination as "any distinction, exclusion, restriction or preference based on race, colour, descent, or national or ethnic origin which has the purpose or effect of nullifying or impairing the recognition, enjoyment or exercise, *on an equal footing*, of human rights and fundamental freedoms in the political, economic, social, cultural or any other field of public life" (emphasis added). The qualification of "equal footing" has the potential to complement the right to culture and solidarity rights, which the thrust of the ICERD and conventional interpretations of it seem otherwise to hold at bay because it prohibits states to make "any distinction" among its citizens. Returning to the historical context in which NAM nations sought to secure both anticolonial and antiracist principles in international law, the tension between the right to (collective) culture and the elimination of (individual) discrimination dialectically records how anticolonial leaders viewed collective self-determination and individual equality to be mutually and inextricably intertwined ends. According to such a human rights approach, only through the right to determine for oneself what constitutes an individual and collective good life does formal equality before the law come to have substantive meaning and effect.

The ethico-politics of minor literatures in no way resolves the legal contradictions and ambiguities that hound the international human rights regime. Rather, as I argue here and throughout this book, U.S. writers of color actually heighten and intensify them in order to incite alternative iterations of political community and the production of alternative humanities foreclosed by the American global nation. What from a purely legal or juridical viewpoint might seem a regrettable lack of "textual clarity" might, by way of a human rights *literacy,* direct us to ethical imaginaries in which the recognition of "humanity" is not (only) a matter of proscription and discipline, but of an active production that draws on religious, aesthetic, and other cultural resources to imagine individual and collective good life otherwise. Such a human rights method then also means regarding the production of culture and cultural politics in terms other than the static, homogeneous, and usually retrograde practices too often attributed to minority groups and (post)colonial peoples, who are in turn characterized as subjected (or worse, held hostage) to "traditional" culture and who are as a result at best tolerated by the majority (and just as often subject to xenophobia and expulsion).

In bringing a Bandung Spirit back to bear on racial formations in the United States, a human rights literacy materializes impossible subjects, those persons whose claims to recognition and justice cannot be granted in domestic legal, political, and juridical imaginaries. Historian Mae Ngai has used the formulation of "impossible subjects" to describe how immigration law and naturalization policy from 1924 to 1965 effectively constituted entire national populations as inherently, that is racially, alienated—socially and culturally inassimilable and legally unincorporated—vis-à-vis the U.S. nation-state. Relegated to a paradoxical status as "impossible subjects," they were at once physically present in the nation and unrepresentable and thus put under erasure in both liberal and conservative social and political imaginaries. In adopting the rubric of "impossible subjects," I likewise maintain the specific historical work that the law enacts in "making" (or making impossible) particular(ized) humans and the lifeworlds they inhabit. But I am also casting the implications of this phrase more broadly, suggesting that minor literatures undertake the ethical task of imagining such impossible subjects in order to counter the disappearances that the law and the state perform.

For example, despite her supple analysis of the way in which present racial forms embed past histories of legal exclusion, Cacho also concludes that for such racialized constituencies, "*there is no way out of this dilemma*"; efforts to "recuperate social value" on the part of aggrieved groups "*requires* rejecting the other Other" and succumbing to the "lure of legibility."[159] Whereas Cacho seems to assign the manufacturing of *all* social value to the law and its adjuncts (e.g., corporate media) as functionaries within the bounded territory of the nation-state, she elides the possibilities for reading, writing, and wanting "otherwise" that the ethico-politics of minor literatures can generate and that organize my approach throughout this book. *Writing Human Rights* takes seriously how diasporic and transnational imaginaries of religion, art, and culture can perform unstintingly to, in Elizabeth S. Anker's terms, "flesh" out the complex personhood that the law refuses to recognize or actively unmakes.[160] Admittedly, these are not the predominant forms and norms by which life and being are ascribed meaning—hence, my use of "minor" to describe the literatures, subjects, and transnationalisms to which I attend. And I certainly do not want to overstate the transformative capacities of cultural politics in the face of immense forces of state power and social violence. But I also contend that we cannot afford *not* to recognize the complex and multifaceted modes by which people *do* make meaningful lives for themselves, world-making projects in which literature participates and which it records. A critical anxiety about how the production of social value always involves the dismembering of other others, as Cacho puts it, cannot (and ought not) to forestall political subjects from arriving as legible persons, making intelligible claims upon others.

There is nothing given, pure, or static about the process of imagining good life otherwise. It is constituted and contested through cultural and religious imaginaries that are themselves contested, hybrid, polyvalent, and dialogic. Consequently, the minor literatures from the era of the late Cold War never amount to a wholesale return to a "prior" or "originary" past that precedes the social, political, and legal orders of racial capitalism.

Instead, reading the works of Gaines and Kingston in tandem with the ICERD evokes the Bandung Spirit's fugitive aspirations for self-determination, solidarity, and personhood that arise as internal, but in difference, to the modern state form and neoliberal arrangements of life across the globe. As I turn in the next chapter to focus more singularly on the question of standing, that is, the right to have rights, that minor subjects claim, it is with these other, self-determined lifeworlds and political communities, ones that remain in/different to the disciplinary and governmental compulsions of the modern state, in mind. The literary *ethics* of human rights cleaves to those others rendered impossible by the subject's taking (a) place, involving the latter in ongoing relations of responsibility as the very condition of their being (made human). Nevertheless, an ethico-politics of human rights makes possible markedly different formulations of collective belonging, social security, and economic equality than are posited in and by the American good life. As a *literary* ethics, this human rights method also harbors the dissident spirits and beings that refuse the progressive temporality upon which modern political consciousness insists.

UN Universal Declaration of Human Rights
Jessica Hagedorn, *Dogeaters*
Chang-rae Lee, *A Gesture Life*

2

"Come Almost Home"

The Impossible Subject of Human Rights

> *This impossible claim is what politics is like for us, we who are not alike and are only barely human; what we call justice is the undergoing of this impossibility.*
>
> —Thomas Keenan, *Fables of Responsibility*

> *To be human is to be intended toward the other.*
>
> —Gayatri Chakravorty Spivak, *Death of a Discipline*

From at least the 1990s onward, since the end of the Cold War, (neo)liberal political discourse has channeled objects of violence and suffering through a paternalistic humanitarianism that posits them as unfortunate victims made stateless and rightless by imperialism, fascism, war, and other modern evils and in need of charitable protection. Oriented primarily by such a moral framework, humanitarians do not necessarily act in the name of a legal right, but instead to alleviate experiences of suffering.[1] Human rights, by contrast, "confer a modern inventory of entitlements, where the obligation to victims arises not from the heart, but from the head—from legal-bureaucratic duties."[2] And yet, while human rights originate in a natural law tradition that accords rights as an inherent property of individual human dignity, such rights have very little substantive meaning without "an assertive political agency" that represents the subjects of rights and pursues claims on their behalf—a theoretical and practical problem I have already begun discussing in the previous pages.[3] As Richard Ashby Wilson and Richard D. Brown maintain, "Humanitarianism more reliably delivers emotional rewards," but a "lack of a thick transnational morality and corresponding local attitudes of compassion and sympathy" render humanitarian efforts uneven and "spasmodic," such that the success of any campaign depends upon arousing both sympathy and outrage among observers.[4]

In this chapter, by turning to two well-known Asian American novels, *Dogeaters* (1990) by Jessica Hagedorn and Chang-rae Lee's *A Gesture Life* (1999), I consider how minor literatures trouble the distinctions between the moral responsibilities of humanitarianism and the juridical claims of human rights. I argue that a more intricate understanding of ethical responsibility—what, as I will discuss in more detail below, Emmanuel Levinas describes as a "being for the Other"—can enliven a human rights politics that prepares us, socially and theoretically, as witnesses to the arrival of the *subject* of human rights (in contrast to the administered object of victimhood) and the articulation of her demand, for the right to rights upon the here and now of the nation and its citizens. Distinguishing notions of charitable humanitarianism from the ethical responsibility that a human rights politics might entail, I continue to elaborate the difficult relations and necessary risks involved in granting personhood to desiring, complex human others, a problematic that my discussion of *Beloved* in the introduction evoked.

As I have also already indicated, the problem of recognition within a modern state system is the central theoretical and practical problem for human rights as a legal and juridical regime. For this reason, as any even cursory review of the twentieth century makes evident, human rights principles and instruments have been severely limited in terms of legal implementation and enforceability. And yet, I argue, human rights remain deeply meaningful methods of political and moral imagining, especially for subjects whose recognition by the state is tenuous, if not altogether foreclosed. How might the "impossible" subject of history and politics yet arrive as the "minor" subject of rights and responsibility? As I explain in the following sections with respect to minor literatures, the literary imagination participates not only in a "redistribution of the perceptible"—where "those who don't count make themselves count"—but instructs us in a form of ethical witness to prepare for the standing of such impossible subjects.[5]

Minor Literatures and a Life of Their Own

A human rights literacy enables us to read for what I have been calling the impossible subject of human rights, the subject for whom political justice and legal redress remain unavailable, but whose claims impel the ethical project of human rights politics nevertheless. As Joseph Slaughter observes, one of the virtues attributed to literature is "its capacity to represent contradiction and paradox without a professional disciplinary obligation to offer a logical resolution."[6] This tolerance for ambiguity and ambivalence can certainly normalize the law's own inexorable contradictions, but it is also crucial for "challenging and rearticulating human rights assumptions and practices." Toward this end, minor literatures can offer a crucial staging of the form and meaning of responsibility and protection within a transnational frame of vulnerability, violence, and justice. Conventional approaches to literature, humanitarianism, and human rights have long been yoked to the type of "sentimental education" advocated by Richard Rorty, wherein shared emotions provide the basis for progressive change, and humanitarian intervention depends upon eliciting the assent of "powerful people" and a "leisure class" who consume human rights narratives.[7] In contrast, the ethical critique I propose here emphasizes the alienating or disarming effects that the literary can induce, such that our responsibility to the other resides neither "in the head" nor "the heart," but with a certain discomfort in our own skin, the difficulty of "living (at home) with ourselves" when brushed by the Other who is the impossible subject of rights.

In the context of American literary and cultural studies, certain figures have dominated the question of humanitarianism—for example, refugees from the Communist bloc or victims of sexual violence, including comfort women (as I elaborate below). In such cases, conceptions of charitable humanitarianism collaborate in consolidating a nationalist narrative of American exceptionalism, wherein citizens' rights are equitably distributed and protected "at home" and Americans intervene—whether by way of the military, nongovernmental organizations, or other agencies—to protect vulnerable populations abroad. I argue instead that minor literatures can, despite having been written in the "major language," deterritorialize such established figures, genres, and discourses (e.g., the *bildungsroman*, as my analysis below demonstrates).[8] Minoritarian cultural production offers a countersite to national memory, writing into the established tradition the "impossibility of not writing," despite myriad obstacles, from the position of the minor subject.[9] As I began explaining in my discussion of *Beloved* in the introduction, the cultural politics of such works prepare us for the arrival of the subject of human rights and the articulation of her demands upon the nation and its citizens, shifting our concern from charitable humanitarianism to the irrecusable ethical claims that call forth a response from us.

As Lisa Lowe has described, within our contemporary context, "so replete with assumptions that freedom is made universal through liberal political enfranchisement and the globalization of capitalism," it becomes acutely difficult to "write or imagine alternative knowledges, to act on behalf of alternative projects or communities" and to undertake the task of "visualizing, mourning, and thinking 'other humanities' within the received genealogy of 'the human.' "[10] Minor literatures, I contend, enable us to think in the "past conditional temporality of the 'what could have been,' " thus examining "the positive objects and methods of history and social science" and, at the same time, considering that which remains "absent, entangled, and unavailable" to such methods.[11] In order to understand the ethical production of the human rights subject by minor literatures, we must consider how human rights exhibit a performative character, underwritten by popular desires for justice, such that they have developed "a life of their own." In this chapter, I consider the *formal* dimensions of political belonging that human rights politics makes available, that is, forms of recognition or *standing* that in turn allow the subject to make claims to more specific rights. Article 6 of the Universal Declaration of Human Rights (UDHR) grants universal standing to human subjects: "Everyone has the right to recognition everywhere as a person before the law." In conjunction with Article 3, which grants "everyone" the right to "life, liberty and the security of person," Article 6 extends the crucial "right to rights" on which other rights are founded.

However, such universal recognition is never simply emancipatory. When "everyone everywhere" is guaranteed recognition and equal protection by the law (as is stipulated in Article 7), "the law becomes the dominant force of social regulation across the entire globe to which all bodies are subjects by virtue of their existence. . . . One is not a body at all without this regulation."[12] Furthermore, the standing afforded by the UDHR is rather ambiguous. Not only does the UDHR not specify "*whose* law" provides the necessary recognition, it also evades the entire problem of structural dispossession that characterizes statelessness and made human rights necessary in the first place: "If all individuals are always already, by virtue of being born, granted certain universal rights, then why must some be granted the same rights again?"[13] As I have noted in the introduction, for Hannah Arendt and many subsequent political theorists, without the physical, material, and governmental forms of security the state affords to those it counts as its citizens, human rights proffer only a chimerical form of recognition. Rather than the enlightened and autonomous individual whom natural rights posit the human being to be in an original state of nature, for Arendt the "good life" of humanity becomes animated by the sovereign power of positive law, which affords vulnerable human beings protection on its own terms. Those lacking membership in such a body politic find themselves objects of benevolence and resources that others might accord them, out of charitable but arbitrary inclinations and not as an inherent right; they are, moreover, as likely to find themselves the objects of physical abandonment and violence as well as social and political exclusion.

Yet contemporary social theorists have also considered the vulnerability of pure "human being," which so worries Arendt, as essential for imagining alternative forms of political community. In this case, contemporary human rights politics recognizes the categorical vulnerability, social dependency, and reciprocity that human life entails and the precariousness of the social institutions necessary to it. Foregoing the dream of transcending the bodily and historical "givenness" of phenomenological existence, an ethico-politics of human rights instead imagines a world "in which an inevitable interdependency becomes acknowledged as the basis for global political community."[14] As Judith Butler surmises, such a project affords recognition to the shared terrain of bodily vulnerability and accordingly constructs the human as a historical-political subject: "If vulnerability is one precondition for humanization, and humanization takes place differently through variable norms of recognition, then it follows that vulnerability is fundamentally dependent on existing norms of recognition if it is to be attributed to any human subject."[15] Instead of a pre-social given, "human nature" is a social project, and human rights politics *create* individuals as free and equal rights-bearing subjects *through* discursive (social, legal, political) practices, or, in Butler's words above, the variable norms of recognition that human rights principles can elaborate.[16]

There is nothing self-evident about *who* is recognized as the subject of rights in these projects. Instead, the subject of human rights is a subject *coming to* rights, by becoming the subject who is recognized as human. Jacques Rancière hence has famously formulated the subject of human rights as one undergoing the "process of subjectivization," enacted by "those who have not the rights that they have and have the rights they have not."[17] The right to recognition, the right to have rights that concerns this chapter, is at once the paramount right of the Other, who cannot be unified with the nation-state or "the people" but who nonetheless takes (a) place in society.[18] As I explain further below, *our* responsibility for this "right of the Other" comprises the ethico-politics of human rights, exhibiting a performative character that produces what I am calling "lives of their own." This production of their own lives is one that reverberates throughout political and intellectual histories of human rights.[19] In other words, although the process of drafting the UDHR and the international bill of rights, for example, was riddled with postwar realpolitik on the part of the Cold War superpowers (a point I have elaborated in chapter 1), the very expression of these principles had a force that exceeded the sometimes more cynical—and always ideologically partial—intentions of state officials.[20]

Throughout this book, then, I correlate *and counterpose* international human rights specifically to *American* life, a good life that, as I have previously indicated, has been historically rendered as white life across the globe. Moreover, I contend that human rights make visible what Françoise Lionnet and Shu-Mei Shih term "minor transnationalism," or the "complex and multiple forms of cultural expressions" and the "micro-practices of transnationality" that minority and diasporic peoples develop in relation to dominant forms of transnationalism, including the charitable humanitarianism I describe above.[21] By focusing on the United States—and on the material and imagined linkages of Americans of color to others elsewhere—I suggest that human rights provide a potent and welcome alternative ethical regime to the domestic hegemony of civil liberties, liberal rights, and the (neo)liberal order by remarkably expanding the forms and ways of life that the nation has failed to recognize or refused to protect. Insofar as human rights politics can create spaces for the production of emergent political subjects who make claims in their own name, it is important to underscore that we cannot pre-script the demands that those subjects make upon their arrival. Any case we consider, such as victims of sexual and political violence, whom I discuss below, can stand only as a singular example of the process of becoming a human person. Thus, my examples in this chapter put the subjects of Japanese imperialism and Philippine authoritarianism, American nationalism and Asian American transnationalism into a historically contingent relation of obligation, one that cannot be replicated in other instances where different particularities of historical encounter and material conditions shape the types of subjects who are made and unmade. It is for this reason that I emphasize the *conceptual* and *formal* staging of human rights politics that a literary imagination makes available, rather than a programmatic or thematic one. Conflating a literary project with a realist politics can lead us to judge authorial decisions and the actions of characters as literally "responsible," or not, as if the literary can actually produce the material results *we* want. Instead, as I explain in this chapter, these novels seek to show how the "peaceful" present is saturated with the losses of the past and how apprehending the disappeared *as such* is vital for the Other to arrive as a "real personhood," what I describe as the "(be)coming" of the minor subject of human rights politics.

While the "problem" of stateless vulnerability makes it difficult to institute human rights actually and effectively "on the ground," this paradox also extends a conceptual flexibility by which to locate those minor subjects who "want" rights and (be)come to claim them. If "human rights discourse cannot protect citizens that it cannot 'see,'" minor literatures play a crucial role in transfiguring the human be-ing of human rights, insofar as these works alienate and rewrite the human form in relation to the performative subject of rights.[22] For a comparative American studies, the nascent human rights subject poses a powerful instantiation of a "wanting otherwise," in my adaptation of Kandice Chuh's now well-known directive to "imagine otherwise."[23] As Chuh argues in regard to Asian American studies, literary works are "epistemological projects engaged in a politics of knowledge," which pursue "an as yet unrealized state of justice by tracing, arguing, critiquing, and by alternatively imagining the conditions that inscribe its (im)possibility. Justice is understood here . . . as an endless project of searching out the knowledge and material apparatus that extinguish some (Other) life ways and that hoard economic and social opportunities only for some."[24] Likewise, my own analysis of Asian American literary works in the following sections suggests that the standing granted by the UDHR incites an ethical witnessing, by which we might seek to do justice to the impossibly violent conditions that constitute the (non)existence of the human rights subject, who has been made otherwise illegible to us.

Certain genres of realism have been considered germane to exposing the conditions of political violence and social suffering, for example, the first person *testimonio* or documentary films. Like the other authors I consider, Lee and Hagedorn enfold a good deal of accurate and realist historical texture into their narratives toward just such an end. Nevertheless, I approach the question of witnessing with a somewhat different purpose, given that the witnesses these authors provide us are patently fictional and thus definitively not testimonial in character. Thus, and as I explain below, I am probing the formal models of responsibility that the novels make available in their characterization of the witness, rather than an account—authentic, realistic, or otherwise—of the event itself. Specifically, minor literatures demonstrate that in order to grant others freedom to arrive as such, without violently making those others over into versions of the self (in this case, versions of the American good life), we must risk the very standing we have been granted, in order to reckon with the losses of the past. Before we can *imagine* otherwise, that is, we must give ourselves over to the other's desire.

Incorporating Persons, Witnessing Others

In both *Dogeaters* and *A Gesture Life,* instances of extraordinary violence bring each novel's plot to a climax. These scenes coincide with a narrative reordering that almost entirely reconfigures the social positions and political subjectivities of those who had, up to that point, served as first-person narrators—that is, as witnesses—of the historical events unfolding before them. In their redistribution of narratorial perspective and reliability, the novels query the line between vulnerability and responsibility, witness and victim, the real and imagined, the reader and text. This production of uncertainty, as I hope to demonstrate, illuminates the ways in which their subjects "want otherwise" and how such desire might materialize as a human rights politics. In *Dogeaters,* one of the central narrators, Joey Sands, witnesses the assassination of the popular and progressive Filipino Senator Domingo Avila by a paramilitary unit of the fictionalized regime of Ferdinand Marcos:

> It only takes a second for the noise, quick spurts of explosion I recognize immediately. I dive for the concrete sidewalk, hoping to be swallowed up by benevolent, unseen forces, hoping to come out of this alive. Something tells me I should've known better, I should've known all along, everything was too quiet and empty

> back there and now, I'm going to die. I'm going to die for something stupid, because I am a witness and I am a thief, I took the German's fucking drugs and money and I don't care about his loving me, I know the Senator's dead like I know my own name.[25]

Until this point, Joey's first-person narration has underscored his cunning urbanity, as he, the orphaned son of a Filipina prostitute and a black American GI, portrays his life as a DJ in a Manila nightclub, as a junkie, and as an occasional sex-worker ("the German" in this passage referring to his most recent client). He depicts his own shrewdness, positioning himself as the omniscient viewer, who watches as others watch others, or as they watch him, whether while he spins records or arranges for tourists to visit sex shows. When comparing himself to his friend Boy-Boy, a shower dancer whom Joey considers to be the most abject of the marginalized people working in the 1960s Manila tourist, drug, and sex industries, he declares, "I'm nobody's slave" (45). Observing that "Maybe I'm lying," Joey also casts doubt on his reliability as a narrator, thus rounding out his construction of himself as someone who knowingly and smoothly manipulates those around him toward his own ends (45).

Nevertheless, when Joey witnesses Senator Avila's assassination, he finds himself almost entirely undone, his fate now inextricably linked to the death he has witnessed. Knowing himself to be endangered because of what he has seen, Joey seeks refuge with Boy-Boy, who, it turns out, is part of an underground resistance movement. Through Boy-Boy's comrades, Joey meets the murdered Senator's daughter Daisy Avila, a former beauty queen who, in a separate plotline, becomes politically radicalized over the course of the novel. Daisy joins the guerilla insurgency after having been tortured and raped by military police, which results in a miscarriage of her pregnancy with one of the rebels (who is himself murdered by the army) (233). By the novel's end, both Daisy and Joey become altogether different "persons," signaled not least by the shift from the first-person to third-person perspective in Joey's story and Daisy's renaming of herself Aurora. As the two hide and train in the mountain jungles with the other insurgents, the narrative transforms the political victim and the witness into political subjects in their own right, even as the outcome of that narrative remains ambiguous and unsure.

A Gesture Life tracks the character of Franklin Hata, a Korean adoptee assimilated first into Japanese society (as Jiro Kurohata) and later as an American citizen. The narrative splits between Hata's tenure serving as a medic in the Japanese Imperial Army stationed in Burma during World War II and as the owner of a medical supply shop in a wealthy New York suburb at the end of the century. His uncertain reunion with his long-estranged, adoptive Korean daughter, Sunny, stirs Hata's troubled memories of his relationship with a Korean comfort woman—known simply as K—in the Japanese camps. The novel intertwines the narrative present with the story of his love for K and her death at the hands of Japanese soldiers in retribution for her murder of Captain Ono, who has taken a special interest in her and has claimed her for himself as well as for the new pan-Asian society that Japanese imperialism seeks to build.

At the crux of Hata's unspoken anguish remains his own raping of K—although notably neither he nor the novel is quite willing to name it rape—as well as K's "concession" to the captain that she exchange her life for Hata's (since Hata has infringed upon the captain's prerogative over K). In particular, his inability to grant K's appeal that he shoot and kill her in order to spare her the "something worse" than death, which she is certain awaits her, culminates (we presume, as the novel only elliptically suggests it) with her brutal gang rape and dismemberment by the other soldiers.[26] Just prior to the narration of the circumstances of K's death, Hata reveals that K has "finally come back for me," in the diegetic present of the 1990s, to his house in Bedley Run. Moreover, he maintains that she is not "a spectral body or ghost": "As deeply as I wished she were some wondrous, ethereal presence, that I was being duly haunted, I knew that she was absolute, unquestionably real, a once-*personhood* come wholly into being" (286; emphasis added). K then proceeds to ask Hata if they might leave the "impressive house and property" in which he resides so that she might finally "die" in a place like Shanghai, Kyoto, or "perhaps even Seoul," to which Hata responds, "I don't want you to die. . . . I want you to live with me forever" (287).

What should we make of the two novels' narrative reconstructions of their subjects: Joey's "I" becoming the vulnerable third person buffeted by historical and political forces, Daisy's new existence as Aurora, and K's return to Hata? Slaughter has demonstrated how the UDHR quickly dispenses with references to "human being" in order to center on the "person," a technical legal term that refers to the abstract "right-and-duty bearing unit" and that "has no necessary relation to the human being," but instead provides "the rhetorical vehicle through which the law personifies (or incorporates) the human as a creature capable of bearing its rights."[27] As Slaughter explains, the cultural form of the *bildungsroman* has been a key, extra-juridical instrument in the construction of human personhood; the plot of development and incorporation secures the individual's personhood, "trans-plotting" rebellious life into "socially acceptable modes of narrative protest" and "claims on the state."[28]

Indeed, in *A Gesture Life,* the sole other place besides K's return where Lee raises the question of "personhood" appears in an early recounting of Hata's own coming of age, a sort of abbreviated *bildung* that describes his departure from his birth family (it is here that he first reveals, rather casually, that he is of Korean ethnicity, living under Japanese imperial rule) at the age of twelve to attend a prestigious school and his adoption by a Japanese family, the Kurohatas:

> For me, it was the heady time of adolescence that unmasked and clarified my sense of obligations, so much so that I now view that period as the true beginning of "my life." This was when I first appreciated the comforts of real *personhood*, and its attendant secrets, among which is the harmonious relation between a self and his society. There is a mutualism that at its ideal is both powerful and liberating. (72; emphasis added)

In two paragraphs, *A Gesture Life* thus dispenses with Hata's coming-of-age narrative.[29] Notably, this section begins with Hata's admission that he, like Sunny, "had been a difficult child" and ends with his impression that he had been "reared" neither by his birth parents nor the Kurohatas, but by Japan's "purposeful society" and "really nothing and no one else" (72–73). Lee quite explicitly, if very quickly, distinguishes the way in which "society" serves as, again in Slaughter's terms (102), the "transitive surrogate" that naturalizes the subject as a recognizable "person," whose existence might then be remade into a "well-ordered life story."

The "attendant secrets" to which Hata alludes hence remark upon the "simultaneously tautological and teleological" process of incorporation, "where one becomes (positively) what one always already was (naturally)," the right-and-duty bearing citizen-person.[30] Hata's passage from the Korean "ghetto of hide tanners and renderers" to Japanese citizenry seems to take place almost instantaneously and magically; Hata remembers the Kurohatas accompanying him to his first day of school and "how the other boys had let us pass without even a murmur" (72). Given that the imperial government selects him for this privilege, the recognition that other Japanese afford him comes as the evident force of positive law, which wavers only later, when Captain Ono begins to question his "ethos" and criticizes "the germ of infirmity" in Hata, shaking Hata's confidence in the national and social status he has otherwise striven to seamlessly occupy (233, 266).

In the United States, by contrast, the process of incorporation proves murkier, and the novel's exposition is especially concerned with demonstrating Hata's opening claim that "People know me here" (1). In a liberal democracy, where *all* subjects are supposed to enjoy natural rights, recognition comes not from a straightforward and exclusive selection on the part of the sovereign, but by an affective mode of identification that Lynn Hunt has called "imagined empathy."[31] As Hunt explains, beginning in the eighteenth century, the seeming "self-evidence" of natural rights, which the American Declaration of Independence and the French Declaration of the Rights of Man and Citizen attributed to individuals, corresponded to a developing sense of individual autonomy that perceived bodies and selves as separate from one another.[32] New modes of empathetic identification "with individuals who are now imagined to be in some fundamental way like you" provided the evidence of this autonomy and, as such, the "psychological foundation of democracy and human rights."[33] The expansion of literacy and the corresponding rise of print culture, especially the novelistic focus trained on individual subjects, was fundamental not only to the liberal political revolutions and new democratic imaginings in the West during the eighteenth century, but ultimately to the "sentimental education" that Rorty promotes as underwriting humanitarianism in the postwar united nations world.[34] As with the tautology/teleology that Slaughter describes, empathetic identification designates the paradoxical creation of the subject of rights; one becomes by way of empathetic recognition what one always (supposedly) already was by nature.

With his own story straddling that postwar division, Hata tells us of his arrival in the United States in 1963, just prior to the momentous shifts in racial formations that the civil rights movement effected. He can describe with only a little disingenuousness that "from what I'd seen during my brief travels in this country, everyone for the most part lived together" except, he notes, for African Americans and the Chinese who "for one reason or another seemed to live apart" (3). Hata himself becomes, over the decades, a "quantity known, somebody long ago counted," and he understands himself as a reflection for "others' certitude" and the "expression of a natural law" (21–22). In becoming a known quantity in Bedley Run, where "the question of my status mostly faded away, to the point it is today, which is almost nothing," Hata obliquely references the new forms of empathetic identification that racial liberalism and neoliberal multiculturalism ushered in during the late twentieth century (3). He proves both a beneficiary and "evidence" of the "natural law" of equal rights, now extended to include Asian immigrants like himself.[35]

I pair these rather distinct moments in Hata's self-narration, his "arrival" in Japan and in the United States, in order to emphasize the central role that recognition plays in Hata's taking his place as the "primary citizen" of two different national societies (275). Hata admits that he has harbored a lifelong fear, "from the day I was adopted by the family Kurohata to my induction into the Imperial Army to even the grand opening of Sunny Medical Supply," that he might suffer a failure that leaves him a burden to "the entire society of his peers": "It must be the question of *genuine sponsorship* that has worried me most, and the associations following, whose bonds have always held value for me, if not so much human comfort and warmth" (229; emphasis added). His anxiety over the authenticity and durability of others' "sponsorship" reveals the insecurity that plagues even a subject like Hata, whose assimilation and affluence would seem to assure his place. The term "sponsorship" further evokes the economic, legal, and psychological dimensions involved in such recognition, where the affective pleasures ("human comfort and warmth") of such relations prove secondary to the formal recognition that state and society supply.[36]

In *Dogeaters*, the United States also provides a *telos* for both Joey and the other first-person narrator, Rio Gonzaga. Joey, who has adopted the last name Sands after the Las Vegas casino, plans to "hit the jackpot with one of these guys" or perhaps "some foreign woman" who will offer him a "green card" marriage (40). Meanwhile, Rio, who grows up the daughter of a wealthy Manila family in the 1950s, learns extensively about American culture through the Hollywood films she watches with her cousin Pucha. She describes her parents' multiple national connections, her father's "dual citizenships, dual passports, as many allegiances to as many countries as possible at any one given time" and her mother's "American papers" that ultimately facilitate their emigration to the United States, where her mother sends her to school and where Rio remains in her adulthood, pursuing her dream to "make movies" (7–8). With an emphasis on the types of legal sponsorship that would make their immigration possible, both Joey and Rio provisionally expect the United States to provide the possibility of incorporation into a "good life" and social freedoms that remain more tenuous in the Philippines because of sexual, gender, class, and partisan constraints. And yet, *A Gesture Life* and *Dogeaters* are avowedly *not* novels about the assimilation of Asian immigrants (in fact, Rio describes almost nothing of her life in the United States, and Joey never arrives there at all).[37] Instead, these moments of incorporation stand as mere preambles to their central concerns, the diasporic subjects' relationship to others who have been subject to violence and foreclosed from recognition, to whom I turn next.

Making Impossible Subjects

In order to understand the novels' construction of personhood for their impossible subjects, we must first consider the way in which each author carefully conveys the historical terms and limits by which recognition can be extended to, or withheld from, such subjects. In *A Gesture Life,* the flashback narration portrays how Hata and the other men in the camp conceive of the women who serve them. Upon hearing K's story that she and her sister (who is killed soon after they arrive in the camp) had been enlisted by their family, in exchange for the protection of their brother, for what they thought would be factory work, Hata admits that he had quite readily believed them to be "volunteers," and for "the men in the queue, they were nothing, or less than nothing . . . soft slips of flesh, a brief warm pleasure to be taken before it was gone" (251). In his portrait of the women's status—or entire lack thereof—in the camps, Lee carefully maps the historical discourses that gave rise to the particular violence and terror of the "comfort woman" system.[38] Certainly, sexual violence, prostitution, and other coercive sexual practices are not an uncommon dimension of warfare, which is itself a highly gendered activity. But, scholars have deemed the "comfort woman" system to have been especially brutal and systematic, and they offer extensive analyses of its practical and ideological underpinnings, which I summarize here.

As came to light in the latter part of the twentieth century, an estimated 200,000 women (mostly Korean, but also women of Philippine, Chinese,

Dutch, and Southeast Asian descent) were forced into sexual slavery by the Japanese government. Following upon the widespread rape of Chinese women during the Japanese advance into China in the 1930s, military officials implemented the comfort system (which was preceded by a legal system of prostitution in Japan), first in China and then in Southeast Asia and Japan itself, to institute order and control over the sexual activities of soldiers.[39] A pervasive belief—what Chunghee Sarah Soh terms "patriarchal fascism"—in the emperor's divinity and soldiers' conscription as a form of veneration for the emperor and empire naturalized the comfort women's role as "gifts" from the emperor, with the women performing as "volunteers" in service of the emperor.[40] Linking the male/paternal privilege to nationalism, the virginity of Korean women delivered an especially prized gift to soldiers. However, the national and racial hierarchies by which Koreans (and other Asians) were thought less than human overdetermined the more traditional discourse of patriarchal fascism. In what Soh refers to as "masculinist sexism," Korean women were considered racially and biologically inferior to the Japanese men.[41] Thus the principle of "patriotic service" also involved representations of Korean women as less than human, or to recall Hata's words, as "mere slips of flesh," which, in turn, coarsened the treatment toward them.

As a result of K's effect upon him, however, Hata realizes that "I was beginning to think otherwise, of how to preserve her, how I might keep her apart from all uses in any way I could" (251). Yet, despite wanting otherwise for K, his abiding desire for her preservation also effects the devastation at the heart of the novel, as Hata remains unable to recognize, much less execute, K's own demand upon him (266). After K has slit the captain's throat and asks again that Hata kill her, she tells him that he does not actually love her, that what he really wants of her is "my sex": "The thing of my sex. If you could cut it from me and keep it with you like a pelt or a favorite stone, that would be all" (300). Captain Ono himself has come to recognize in K a special bloodline, "a commonality between someone like her and me, a distinct correspondence, if one very distant" (268). Ono accordingly explains that he has kept K from her "volunteer" duties to preserve her as a "rare vessel" who needs "to be observed and stewarded" in the service of pan-Asian prosperity (268). Hata's desire for K does not, however, easily translate into such clear-cut imperatives. In the moment of decision, he finds himself, reflected in K's perception, to be "the picture of someone heroic enough to act only upon his own trembling desire," confirming the captain's judgment about Hata's feelings toward K: "What is solid in you but your sentimental feeling and hope?" (295, 266).

Therefore, while both Hata and Ono might have wanted otherwise for K than the conscription of her sexual services, neither recognizes that K wants otherwise than they do. Certainly, Ono's denial of K's desire is much more forthright than Hata's. As K deduces about the captain's demand that she exchange her life—which he already "has," given his position of authority over her in the camp—for Hata's, the "small concession" that he actually wants from her is "what was left of my will" (293). And while Hata might be, as K more than once describes him, "a decent man," he proves "not any different from the rest," and Hata admits that the "fraudulence" he ultimately contributed to the "misery and horror" of K's existence was to put a "gentle boy-face" on the situation with his "yearning and wishing and . . . wanton hope" (295, 300).

Dogeaters similarly probes the gendered, racial, and class formations that supply recognition and engender agency within the Philippines, especially as they have been shaped by U.S.–Philippine relations since the late nineteenth century. Cultural and social historians have written perceptively about how the ongoing cultivation of a so-called special relationship between the two nations engenders a politics of forgetting, whereby a rhetoric of friendship and "benevolent assimilation" obscures the bitterly violent pacification of the Philippine revolutionary army in 1902, as well as radical guerilla forces that staunchly fought against the new colonial state.[42] Even as "the special relationship" between the United States and the Philippines has become a matter of political economy rather than military enterprise (which I discuss in more detail below), it remains one of "entanglement" and dependence.[43] Within this postwar history of shifting U.S.–Philippine relations, Hagedorn portrays the multiple and often contradictory hegemonies that shape domestic life across the stories of numerous, especially female, characters, including not only Daisy, but Baby Alacran, the daughter of the owner of a commercial and media conglomerate, who marries the son of an army general; a lightly veiled characterization of Imelda Marcos referred to as "the First Lady"; Leonor Ledesma, the wife of a military general, Nicasio Ledesma; and the general's mistress, the film star Lolita Luna.

Dogeaters's production of such "uneven femininities" points up the specific conditions of colonial, neocolonial, and global capital relations that the novel critiques.[44] For example (and in a way that is comparable to K's awareness in *A Gesture Life* that what men like Hata and Ono want from her is "her sex"), Lolita chafes against the patronage of the general, who pays the lease on her apartment, as well as reluctantly supports her drug habit and the care of her son: "Disgusting old shit. . . . They were all the same, the old men. . . . Carrying around her used panties as if they were a fetish, like a piece of her they had carved off, like her skin" (176). In response, she considers taking up the offer of "an unusual movie deal," "art films" that would involve "lengthy close-ups of Lolita Luna's vagina, shot by professional cameramen in living color and in a variety of simulated violent settings" (177). For Lolita, the project affords the opportunity for "more shoes, more drugs, her own ticket out of the country. Her debts paid off, once and for all. Her four-year-old son's future finally insured" (177). Thus, Lolita's position closely mirrors that of Joey's early in the novel in that her "choices" are limited to commodified forms of racial and sexual performance, in the service of an elite national and international tourist class of spectators and consumers.

In contrast to Lolita's ambivalent and spectacular negotiation of national and global commercial markets, a different, recurring motif of self-abnegating women in *Dogeaters* shifts attention to forms of more "proper" femininity promulgated by mass media and national culture. While Leonor Ledesma engages in ascetic rituals to redeem her family from the adulterous sins of her husband, Baby Alacran's body becomes the site of various tics, a fungal disease, and other symptoms that starkly differentiate her from the ideal beauty that her mother Isabel (as well as the First Lady and Rio's mother) represents. As Juliana Chang explains, in their excessive or "hysteric" femininity, both Leonor and Baby "embody certain characteristics . . . that are acceptable to patriarchal norms, namely self-denial and self-infantilization," even as they register an ambivalence toward patriarchal structure as a whole.[45]

As Hagedorn further writes, "Our country belongs to women who easily shed tears and men who are ashamed to weep," a succinct formulation of the gendered nationalism that reconciles temporal and affective ambivalence by naturalizing sexual division (105).[46] Accordingly, Baby, whose wedding coincides with Senator Avila's assassination and whose husband (unbeknownst to her) has likely been involved in the death, suffers another "mysterious illness" and bout of sadness in the chapter "The Weeping Bride," which describes her "furtive innocent life," spent lying in bed, watching television, regretting her pregnancy, and inventing "a cleansing ritual for herself," bathing in the "black blood of a pig . . . [to mourn] the death of a man she never knew" (157–58). Indeed, Daisy herself is early on beset with tears, after winning a national beauty pageant, finding herself sobbing continuously, but unable to "pinpoint the source of her mysterious and sudden unhappiness" (105).

Cautioning against too easy sentimentality, however, the novel couples Daisy's emergence from this period with her political awakening in a chapter titled "Sleeping Beauty." Thus, although Baby and Daisy's "tropical melancholy" incorporates the losses that the nation otherwise collectively disavows, and hence comprises a necessary step in the formation of critical consciousness, these weeping women also register the way in which the privatization of shared injury into femininized emotion defuses the political and economic contradictions of the postcolonial nation.[47] In contrast, Daisy's more muddled feelings eventually come to exceed the limited forms of recognition granted to women and their desires; she first denounces the beauty pageant she has won "as a farce, a giant step backward for all women," then quickly marries and separates from a British banker, as the tabloids volubly chide her "ANO BA, CAN'T SHE MAKE UP HER MIND?" (109–11). When Daisy undertakes her affair with Santos, her cousin Clarita warns her "Run away with him. Just don't be shocked by how much you're going to suffer. After all, you're still a married woman in everyone's eyes" (116). By the novel's end, then, Daisy and Joey are affiliated with one another in an insurgent solidarity, not only as victims of political violence, but also by way of their illicit and illegible desires, a point to which I return below.

Apprehensive Witnesses and the Ethics of Recognition

Given the illegibility of desire that both novels accentuate in K's, Joey's, and Daisy's wanting otherwise, I submit that the form of recognition that *A Gesture Life* and *Dogeaters* ultimately extend to their impossible subjects is *not* that of the empathetic identification to which the sentimental education of multiculturalism aspires. Rather, minor literatures such as these induce the ethical obligation to witness and provide standing for those others who have been made impossible. As such, *Dogeaters* cannot literally construct a form of mutual and reciprocal identification between its political victims and insurgents, the Philippine nation, and the diasporic Asian subject (embodied by Rio). Nor can *A Gesture Life* do so for the former comfort woman, the imperial Japanese subject, and the liberal American one. Instead, both novels offer what Butler describes as an "apprehension" of life by way of an ethical witnessing, which comes to reframe the question of which lives, and forms of life, can be grieved and accordingly ought to be sustained and protected. Contrasting recognition with apprehension, Butler describes the latter as "bound up with sensing and perceiving," detecting shadow lives that haunt and disturb more clear-cut norms of recognition: "We can apprehend, for instance, that something is not recognized by recognition," even as we cannot precisely say what that "something" is.[48] Indeed, throughout his narration of his encounter with K and the other comfort women, Hata describes vaguely his "feelings," to which he cannot give expression in precisely intelligible terms, because they occur in contexts where he has "no protocol" for understanding them (233).

Dogeaters further instructs us in this method of apprehension in the "The Weeping Bride" chapter, in a brief anecdote about the dentist who bakes Baby's wedding cake, a woman whose son is "a poet of the underground" and who is detained, placed under house arrest, tortured, and ultimately "disappeared": "The dentist is dead. The dentist never existed. The unforgettable wedding cake has actually been designed and baked from scratch by the bride's glamorous mother, Isabel Alacran" (154). The disappearance, and the encryption of that disappearance—so that the very memory of the disappearance is made to disappear—provides a short but incisive parable, by which to apprehend that something is not recognized by recognition. The temporal suspension of disappearance—which is not exactly past, but, rather, a contemporaneous absent presence—phenomenologically distinguishes it from torture and murder, even as it often entails these other forms of terror. As I began explaining in the introduction, the disappeared implicate us in relations of responsibility; our apprehension of their absence calls for us to transform *the conditions* that make their lives impossible.[49] This method of reading becomes urgent when later, another character, Romeo Rosales, an aspiring actor from a small village, diegetically disappears from the novel altogether, with only one final, oblique reference to him embedded in a piece of gossip ("The man confessed") after he is detained by the military police and framed for Senator Avila's death (182). In its disappearance of Romeo, the novel *formally* apprehends yet another impossible subject of human rights who has been foreclosed from the prospect of justice that the literary work wants for him.

These are subjects to whom Jenny Edkins refers as the "missing missing" or "the doubly missing," those whose disappearances remain unremarked upon, because no one misses them (and, if they do count, it is only as "objects . . . of humanitarian aid or intervention—not as persons with political views of their own").[50] But if they are "unmissed," it is not because they lack relations of care, but because the law not only does not recognize them as "the missing," but, in these cases, enacts their very disappearances. Thus, as Edkins warns, international efforts (such as by the International Committee of the Red Cross in 2002) to grant recognition to those who have gone missing by defining them as "anyone unaccounted for as a result of an armed conflict or a situation of internal violence" and hence "locates responsibility for preventing disappearances and tracing the missing on the shoulders of government authorities and armed groups," risks buttressing the very forms of police and administrative power that refuse to acknowledge the "person as such."[51]

Both novels thus demand a different kind of ethical accountability from those witnesses who apprehend disappeared subjects.[52] In *A Gesture Life,* in his new "feelings" for K, Hata apprehends K's life as one worth grieving and protecting, even as it takes his entire life—both in terms of time and in terms of the stakes involved (i.e., he must give over his life)—to reckon with the new rights and responsibilities that such an apprehension initiates. As Anne Anlin Cheng observes about the novel, Hata's survival of K "represents not a release from but an entry into a ceaseless engagement with the Other-left-behind."[53] Hata's ultimate admission of K's death issues as a strange form of confession, and he never directly admits responsibility for it. Indeed, in a conventional sense, he cannot be found "guilty" of the "most terrible of things" he has witnessed (345). And yet, because the narrative begins with Hata's sense that he should seek a "reckoning of what stands in the here and now," the novel *formally* holds Hata accountable for the impossible subject (5).

In *Dogeaters,* Joey similarly confesses to a priest in a church his own sense of responsibility for witnessing Avila's death: "Father, my name is Joey Sands. I'm a whore and the son of a whore. I just saw Senator Avila murdered. How come I feel guilty?" (191). Hagedorn returns to a language of responsibility in the ambiguous ending of Daisy and Joey's narrative. First, as Boy-Boy's comrades drive Joey to the guerilla camp, he comes to the realization that "these curious strangers are somehow responsible for him" (230) and, finally, in his growing closeness to Daisy:

> "I claim responsibility for everything I do," [Daisy] says to Joey.
> They will get drunk together on cane liquor one night. She cries while Joey describes his mother, what he remembers of her. She reproaches herself, and apologizes for being sentimental. She will not cry when she describes how her lover was captured while she was in detention, or how her unnamed baby girl was born premature and dead. They are together all the time. She teaches him how to use a gun. (233)

As Joey departs his former life for a new existence with Daisy and the other insurgents, the latter rearticulate his sense of guilty spectatorship to one of responsibility toward "the Other-left-behind," which mobilizes them as political agents.[54]

This formulation of responsibility poses a phenomenological ethics that enables us to distinguish forms of charitable humanitarianism from the human rights politics that orients my reading of both novels. As Levinas, who most thoroughly expounds this ethical theory, describes the relation of responsibility, the subject's very existence is beholden to some "Other," that is, other possibilities of existence, which a being displaces in its own being-in-the-world. Ethical responsibility to the Other is thus for Levinas a pre-ontological obligation; responsibility founds our very being. As he writes in "Ethics as First Philosophy," "My being-in-the-world or my 'place in the sun,' my being at home, have these not also been the usurpation of spaces belonging to the other man whom I have already oppressed or starved, or driven out into a third world? Are they not acts of repulsing, excluding, exiling, stripping, killing?"[55] The obligation to the Other, Levinas explains, is irrecusable and ongoing because it makes possible my own taking place. Subjectivity is fragile and continually exposed, because the Other will not remain cordoned off from the self. The Other demands a response from us, an accountability for our own "being at home," our own "place in the sun."

This ethical model of obligation thus counters a conventional humanitarian form of recognition and service to the Other. That is, it fundamentally links those who enjoy the good life of the citizen-person to the arrival of what I call the minor subject of politics and rights, those whom the law and state at best hold in waiting and at worst disappear altogether, but who nevertheless demand to make claims in their own name. Our obligation is neither about moral self-righteousness nor about charitable recognition of those who are less fortunate. Rather, the ethics that Levinas describes concerns the incontrovertible dependence of the self's existence upon the Other and the displacement of the Other that my being in the world enacts. As Edith Wyschogrod explains, Levinasian ethics does not observe an abstract categorical principle, but rather speaks to an embodied condition of existence that nonetheless is shared by every "other as other."[56] Levinas's phenomenological ethics thus allows us to perceive human rights as corresponding to the very fragile and continually exposed position that even the privileged person of citizenship occupies.

In the ethical response to vulnerable corporeality and alterity, a "radical generosity of altruistic existence" empties out a "structure of the self as an egology"; one's own corporeality becomes available to or "at the service of" the Other.[57] Even when one refuses to reckon self-consciously with one's responsibility to the Other (as seems to be true of Hata, Joey, and Rio for much of their lives), one does not escape responsibility, but makes a particular kind of response to it, which in turn sustains a particular kind of (irresponsible) existence for the subject at the cost of many other possible ones. That Other *will* arrive regardless to confront the subject—as K does to Hata and Daisy does to Joey. Precisely because the relationship of dependence is the very pre-ontological condition of the subject's existence, an ethico-politics of human rights that reflects upon vulnerability has neither an epiphenomenal nor a voluntaristic character. But how that encounter takes place remains contingent on the response the subject has afforded her, as evident in the very different experiences that Hata and Joey undergo.

Dogeaters and *A Gesture Life* accordingly recast the project of ethical reckoning by attending to the *conditions* that have made certain lives ineligible for personhood, rather than by "making" them live.[58] Returning in the diegetic present of *A Gesture Life,* as a "real, once-personhood," K demands exactingly that Hata relinquish his own bodily and social security (symbolized throughout the novel in his "immensely beautiful house," which is generally recognized as a "special property") in order to enact her justice, in that Hata's old age and American good life have been made possible by K's loss. In calling for him to leave his house, K indicates that one's responsibility to the Other involves risking one's own being, or one's way of being in the world, in the face of that which has made that being possible. The novel hence ends with Hata preparing to depart Bedley Run, but firm in the understanding that he is not on "any kind of pilgrimage," not "seeking out my destiny or fate," nor attempting "to find comfort in the visage of a creator or the forgiving dead": "Let me simply bear my flesh, and blood, and bones. . . . Tomorrow, when this house is alive and full, I will be outside looking in. I will be already on a walk someplace, in this town or the next or one five thousand miles away. I will circle round and arrive again. Come almost home" (356).

Dogeaters ends with a similar displacement, with Rio depicting herself as "anxious and restless, at home only in airports" (247). The conclusion of her story, which follows immediately that of Joey and Daisy, describes a dream that haunts Rio's adulthood, lived in the United States but with frequent trips back to Manila:

> In my recurring dream, my brother and I inhabit the translucent bodies of nocturnal moths with curved, fragile wings. We are pale green, with luminous celadon eyes, fantastic and beautiful. In dream after dream, we are drawn to the same silent tableau: a mysterious light glowing from the window of a deserted, ramshackle house. The house is sometimes perched on a rocky abyss, or on a dangerous cliff overlooking a turbulent sea. The meaning is simple and clear, I think. Raul and I embrace our destiny: we fly around in circles, we swoop and dive in effortless arcs against a barren sky, we flap and beat our wings in our futile attempts to reach what surely must be heaven. (247)

Immediately after this conclusion, Pucha—whom Rio mostly describes as a frivolous girl with superficial interests and desires—gently ribs Rio for the mistakes in her account of their family's history and concludes: "Nothing is impossible, I suppose, with that crazy imagination of yours. I'm not surprised by anything you do or say, but if I were you, *prima,* I'd leave well enough alone" (249).[59]

This sense that nothing is impossible for the literary imagination (and nothing *is* well enough to be left alone) signals the ethico-politics of human rights that configures the relations between the novel's many dispersed characters, fragmented plots, and manifold symbols. Rio claims that the dream's "meaning is clear and simple" without actually delineating the content of that meaning. Rather, she posits, as Hata does, that one's destiny is "to fly in circles," constantly striving to reach "what surely must be heaven" without actually arriving home. Positioned just after she recounts her disappointment in visiting the ruins of her family home in Manila, the dream house recalls the past family romances and political intrigues that comprise the stories of her adolescence in the Philippines. But it is also bookended by Hagedorn's famous "Kundiman" closing of the novel, a mash-up of Catholic and popular religious forms in which she accuses: *"Dammit, mother dear. There are serpents in your garden"* (250). Thus the dream posits a heaven in which brutalized victims of those same sexual violence and political crises might achieve some alternative form of justice and peace. These closing sections of the novel turn to emblems of faith in order to figure an otherwise seemingly impossible solution to the political corruption and violence that the novel has bluntly represented. As Victor Mendoza explains, Pucha's exposure of Rio's unreliability implies that "Rio's narratives might be feminist, utopian revisions of her family's dissatisfying present" in which "lack constitutes desire."[60] In short, if most of *Dogeaters* insists upon a stark political realism, Rio's dream of the luna moths poses an equally compelling demand to employ our "crazy imaginations" where "nothing is impossible."

Moreover, if, as Mendoza convincingly argues, "Rio's deterritorialized self affords her a political agency predicated not upon the practice of an identity but upon tactical associations" and, in particular, "a metonymic association . . . with queer male Joey Sands," I would insist that, in its divergent endings—with Daisy's claim to responsibility and Joey's learning to use a gun—the novel retains a certain obligation on Rio's part to the subject of human rights.[61] Daisy-cum-Aurora's final words, "I claim responsibility for everything I do," requires that someone like Rio, who is in a conventional sense innocent, offer recognition to the impossible conditions of threat and violence under which Romeo, Joey, Daisy, and countless others (cease to) exist. It is not any particular characterization of Rio that grounds such an ethical obligation. In fact, Rio's narrative primarily relays her observations of other characters, even while her narration never intersects with those characters who suffer state violence and are disappeared.

Instead, it is the *formal* relationality that the novel produces between her capacity as witness, a capacity enjoyed by any speaking subject who lives to tell a tale, and the others, that teaches us how to read for the disappeared.

But the novel also wants for this attention to the other to amount to more than a scorecard of the psychic costs borne by the citizen-person who survives (such as remains the focus of Cheng's astute Lacanian reading of Hata's "ethics of survival" that I cite above), by giving voice *to the desire of the Other* in and through the speaking subject. Constantly pointing up the limits of formal procedures of justice, the unsettled and unreliable positions that Hata and Rio occupy by the novels' ends remark upon the way that a transnational human rights imaginary not only apprehends the disappeared but can materialize the claims of the human rights subject upon and through us.

Recognizing the Limits of Justice

The personhoods recognized in the novels are ones that have remained consistently unavailable to living human beings in a domestic, civil court of claims, whether in Japan, the Philippines, or the United States. The very conditions and the subjects of redress have become impossibly lost at the novels' historical junctures. This point becomes especially instructive when considering, for example, the comfort women redress movement, which began in the 1990s. War trials after 1945 concluded with the executions of many Japanese government officials. However, because these trials took place during a period of shifting alliances, with the early onset of the Cold War and with American interests—especially in Korea soon thereafter—at stake, the full extent and nature of Japanese war crimes, including the violence endured by comfort women, went undisclosed. Even where the women's experiences were known, officials did not construe them as war crimes or human rights violations.

Securing an official admission by the Japanese government since then has been a challenge because of the legal implications such an apology portends, and a 2007 decision by Japan's Supreme Court seems to have decisively excluded individual claims on the Japanese government.[62] The political and ideological aftermath of the war has also contributed to the difficulty. On the one hand, its loss to the United States resulted in Japan's incorporation into the United Nations and an international system of law and diplomacy. This might seem to occasion the demands and context for the Japanese nation to make an account of its wartime history (and, in fact, a 1998 UN report found the Japanese government liable for war crimes and crimes against humanity in its investigation). But the formative role of Japan's earlier victories in China and other Asian nations for geopolitical relationships in the region and its rise as a global economic power in the second half of the twentieth century, despite its military loss, have made redress for comfort women elusive, and this denial has been shored up by the state officials of other governments, even the People's Republic of China and the Republic of Korea.[63] Moreover, the resurgence of contemporary right-wing discourse that remembers the war not as a "morally bankrupt disaster," but as a "noble, although failed, enterprise" fuels resistance to any admission of official wrongdoing.[64]

Thus, although the redress movement organized by Korean and Japanese feminists did not necessarily espouse an account of Japanese war crimes as especially exceptional, the search for reparative justice has nevertheless been enmeshed in the politics of globalization that lends itself to such a characterization. As Lisa Yoneyama argues, an "Americanization" of the pursuit of "world justice" for "Japanese war crimes" made redress an increasingly American concern, as part of a larger cultural project to remember the U.S. war against Japan as a "good war" that delivered "liberation and rehabilitation" to Asia.[65] The rhetoric of liberation and rehabilitation configures an uneven and asymmetrical relationship between Koreans (and Korean Americans) and the United States, where the liberated are always seen as indebted to their liberators (a point crucial to my discussion in chapter 3 as well).[66] As I have been suggesting, a human rights framework can offer a rather distinct vision, one that accords a "real" and complex personhood to subjects who want otherwise. In regard to comfort women, an ethical reckoning thus entails attention to the generic constraints that a legal framework places upon the stories that survivors seek to impart, to the consumer market that commodifies such testimonials in the search for a rarefied notion of the victim's "truth," and to the limits of existing institutions for securing reparations (all questions that have indeed been taken up by transnational feminists since the 1990s).[67]

In the case of the Philippines, the possibility of justice proves equally vexed, given the nation's history with successive Spanish and American imperialist occupations and the conditions of economic interdependence with the United States, as well as the maintenance of U.S. military bases there (even after the nation's formal independence), the legacy of police and security apparatus instituted under U.S. colonial rule in the Republic's postcolonial era—including American collaboration with Ferdinand

Marcos's autocratic rule during fourteen years of martial law—and the nation's ongoing cooperation with the United States as a member of the "Coalition of the Willing" in the "war against terror" in the twenty-first century. Critics have written extensively about the way in which *Dogeaters* represents the complex histories of colonialism, neocolonialism, and (trans)nationalism that inform, for example, the novel's pastiche structure (where the plots I have been examining intertwine with excerpts from historical, anthropological, and journalistic documents) and postmodern aesthetics, as well as its recurrent interest in the phantasmatic spectacles of consumer culture and mass media.[68] Nevertheless, very little of this work examines closely Hagedorn's representation of authoritarian state violence and terror, nor considers its significance in the post-Marcos moment in which the novel was published.

Moreover, most critical commentary does not treat the key chapter, "The Famine of Dreams," which recounts Daisy's interrogation and rape by members of the special forces, including General Ledesma.[69] Here, Hagedorn alternates between the script of a melodramatic radio serial and the officers' questioning of Daisy, which begins with veiled politeness and gradually escalates with more pointed accusations about Daisy and her father, followed by the general showing Daisy the photographs of the brutality inflicted upon the murdered Santos and other rebels, and culminating with the men taking turns sexually assaulting her as she "prays silently to pass out" (216). The chapter closes with the general describing to her "the special equipment set up in another room" where "he promises to make her dance" (216). "The Famine of Dreams" reveals the devastating state violence that accompanies postcolonial modernity and its commodification of national culture. While I consider the specifically gendered implications of such state violence against women in chapter 4, I am especially concerned here with the way in which the novel worries the possibility of justice for the political victim, even after the fall of the Marcos regime.

In its depiction of state violence, then, *Dogeaters* succinctly mines the history of police power and political corruption in the Philippines, which stands as the legacy of U.S. rule in the early twentieth century. As Alfred McCoy argues, "At this edge of empire, freed of the constraints of constitution, courts, and civil society, the U.S. regime deployed its information technologies to form what was arguably the world's first surveillance state."[70] Not only was this police power key to American political control of the Philippines, but it remained crucial in the shoring up (and excesses) of presidential power after 1946, when the United States granted formal independence to the nation.[71] The colonial policing that the United States developed in the Philippines also provided the launching pad for security technologies that were used both domestically and in other parts of the world and central to American statecraft, beginning in World War I.[72] Furthermore, such exchanges between the two nations continued throughout the twentieth century (and into the twenty-first), with American military aid as well as covert operations that stemmed political dissidence and insurgency in the Philippines, as part of a larger U.S. Cold War containment policy. As a result, "These two states have forged powerful instruments to fortify themselves against the processes of political change, slowing progress toward civil rights in America and social justice in the Philippines."[73]

This political repression manifested itself most intensely during the twenty years of Ferdinand Marcos's presidential power, from 1966 to 1986. Marcos declared martial rule during his second term in office, in 1972, and received millions of dollars in assistance from the United States toward counterinsurgency campaigns, used also to quash protests and demonstrations.[74] U.S. aid and advisers helped establish the infrastructure for martial rule, and it is not unlikely that the CIA recruited and trained Filipino officers in torture techniques.[75] Marcos's regime saw thousands of extrajudicial killings and tens of thousands more arrested and tortured, all with tacit U.S. support; "salvagings," in which the scarred remains of torture victims were dumped for public display to induce terror, were also not uncommon.[76] The case of the Philippines thus exemplifies the troubled historical situation of decolonizing nations in the twentieth century, where a U.S.-mandated international order required, above all else, a stable state system. As I have explained in the introduction and chapter 1, for colonized peoples striving for self-determination, especially after World War II, the recognition of formal independence and political sovereignty was made contingent upon the maintenance of internal "order," especially against Socialist and Communist agents.[77] A persistent paternalistic racism (continuous with nineteenth-century imperialist ideology) ascribed the need for these societies to "develop," "mature," and "stabilize," which dictatorial regimes like Marcos's were assumed able to accomplish.[78]

Only in the late years of his regime did American military observers come to believe that Marcos's continuing power would *accelerate* the growth of the communist New People's Army, which had arrived in the Philippines in the 1960s and became a formidable presence by the 1980s.[79] Galvanized by the 1983 assassination of opposition leader Benigno Aquino (upon whom *Dogeaters*'s Senator Avila is based), a coalition of liberal and religious parties, headed by Aquino's widow, Corazon, and Cardinal Jaime Sin, ousted Marcos in 1986 by way of mass demonstrations, termed "People Power" and the "EDSA Revolution" (for the highway on which demonstrators assembled after the February election, which was marred by widespread fraud and won by Marcos).[80] However, political, social, and economic reforms have been halting ever since. Broad inequities persist, and even Marcos's democratically elected successors, Corazon Aquino, Fidel Ramos, Joseph Estrada, and Gloria Arroyo, have employed the police and security apparatus in varying ways to maintain their presidential powers.[81] Indeed, Estrada's reliance on police repression led to a second "people power" movement in 2001, which culminated with his removal from office. With the infrastructure of state violence still in place, an oligarchic ruling class long sustained by U.S. aid and the interests of global capital, and ongoing "low intensity" warfare (albeit with Islamicist "terrorists" replacing peasant and student rebellions), the possibility of recognition and redress for human rights victims remains practically impossible.[82]

Hence, the human rights literacy that I bring to both *Dogeaters* and *A Gesture Life* employs the vocabulary of "freedom" and "choice" as empty signifiers in a literary recognition of the historico-material constraints that shuttle the human rights subject into a zone of speechless nonbeing. Freedom and choice are not simply meaningless or irrelevant to these subjects. Rather, by signifying what it is they "want," such ideals mark the Other as a paradoxical figure of what has been rendered historically and politically impossible and make visible the limits of those juridico-political regimes that cannot grant her standing. In ethical terms, to subject those who have been incorporated into the American good life to the desire of others is to put them into contact with the infinitude of existence that continually exceeds the finitude of their own being. The loss of the Other lives on, then, in the subject as a longing or yearning, which the self might experience as an absence or void within him- or herself. But, for Levinas, this desire is in fact the expression of "a superabundant presence—of a positive force and drive within the heart of the subject," which steers the subject away from the self, toward the Other.[83]

In the end, neither *Dogeaters* nor *A Gesture Life* aspires to a documentary realism that recovers and restores the lost subjects of human rights to their rightful (or rights-full) place in history and politics. Rather, the novels enact a form of justice other than that which any procedural state recognition and redress might provide, but which performative human rights principles want for their subjects anyway. The displacement of Hata and Rio from their American lives, which they initially achieved under the aegis of a tolerant liberal pluralism, remarks upon the ethical stakes of a human rights imaginary, where the very being of the (Asian) American subject must be risked to make right and accord rights to the Other. It is only through such a transnational human rights imaginary that the novels can materialize the Other's claims.[84]

Future Obligations

In the conclusion of *A Gesture Life*, K's personhood unravels Hata, making him a ghost of himself and removing him from the prosperity and security he has enjoyed as he seeks instead to arrive "almost home," in some other, undetermined time and place.[85] In coming to this conclusion, Hata must return to his own obdurate desire to have K and to have K "live forever," which had induced his earlier refusal to kill her quickly and spare her the suffering she experienced. The dissolution of Hata, with which the novel ends, thus also concedes to K's wish to die. Certainly, choosing "a death of one's own" seems to offer the most intense perversion of agency by which to register K's emergent subjectivity, and retaining a language of rights to describe her situation at the novel's end risks a seeming endorsement of state sovereignty. In other words, with its power to order life and death according to its own overriding priorities, only the state seems able to guarantee one's right to life; the subject of human rights is instead left with seemingly only the right to die. But conceiving of human rights as an ethical regime requires that we grapple seriously with the forms of existence that normative social and political communities make possible for minor subjects, and the responsibilities to which they obligate those nascent subjects in turn.

The subject of human rights arrives as a political agent, not ex nihilo, but through a network of obligations to others. As scholars of law and politics explain, rights are never simply a matter of entitlement and intrinsic possession. Instead, they involve the rectitude, the "correctness" of others who carry out their obligations toward the subject of rights.[86] Creating subjects as they define the obligations between them, rights are essentially social. Obtained from rules that govern such human relations, rights authorize the moral worth of the rights-holder and demarcate a field of agency in which the subject "exercises" his or her rights.[87] Every right thus requires a corresponding duty from someone else. In the modern theory of natural rights, implemented in the American and French Revolutions, where "all men" are to enjoy rights, the corresponding duty-bearers would, as Michael Zuckert explains, "seem to be 'all comers'—all other human beings and collectivities (e.g., government) when such [institutions] are in place."[88] In the political philosophy of human rights, the "corresponding duty" that accompanies every rights claim defines the obligation incurred by the subject of rights; the (Asian) American subject who enjoys the right to rights must seek to recognize the right of the Other who makes claims in her own name. Rights are both derived from and create relations between those subjects who "enjoy" them and those who are obligated to recognize and respect them, the political collectivities of other human beings, such that "government" secures the rights of its subjects.[89]

Here, however, it is conceptually useful to distinguish between the ordered "state" of political consensus, and alternative, more supple forms of political community and "government" that our recognition of the Other as a subject of rights might assemble. As Slaughter suggests, these latter forms might very well remain aspirational in the present (they are not yet, in Zuckert's words, "in place"), and our recognition of the Other remains "proleptic" in its desire for such alternative political possibilities.[90] In *Dogeaters,* Daisy's claim to responsibility as she trains with other insurgents in the jungle encampment signals a commitment to such possible future political communities. As I note above, the affiliation of Daisy with Joey, the character that critics have aligned most closely with queer desire, in the mountain camp conjoins the desiring subject with the vulnerable one, marking the fundamental ambivalence at the heart of human existence. If at the beginning of the novel, Daisy embodies one of the most privileged of women in the Philippines, *Dogeaters* demonstrates the way in which desire nonetheless propels her back into a state of exposed vulnerability. Sensitive to the openness that intersubjective sociality entails, the novel constantly yokes its vulnerable subjects to the heterogeneous forms that desire takes over space and time.

"Being human" and "wanting otherwise" hence refer not simply to shared lack; rather, they register the complex interplay of bodily vulnerability with the many types of volition that move us into relation with others. The enduring bonds that create and are created by the subject's many negotiations of desire and need come to haunt and contest the biopolitical orders of life and death that statecraft continually seeks to secure and manage through its administration of vulnerable bodies (a point upon which I enlarge in chapter 3). Using trauma as, in Ann Cvetkovich's words, "the provocation to create alternative life worlds," the ethico-politics of human rights demands exactly that, in our obligation to the Other, we attend to the conditions by which such alternative lifeworlds have been made impossible and might be made possible again.[91] Official and media discourses as well as nationalist culture regularly generate a common sense as to which lives are worth protecting and whose rights should be duly recognized and respected, by relegating other lives to a "domain of unreality."[92] They also construct consensus about the state sovereignty and (neo)liberal order that secures such respect and recognition. In contrast, I have been suggesting that minor literatures might trouble the self-evident subject to whom they are addressed, by attending to the "animated and de-ratifying traces" that "haunt the ratified version of reality."[93] From this "animated debris," we might marshal the ethical claim of the Other that pierces the mutually enabling conceptions of personhood and statehood.

Finally, as *Dogeaters* and *A Gesture Life* (and *Beloved*, discussed in the introduction) demonstrate, a human rights politics never brings its subject into being as a fully autonomous and permanently "free" being, and those who *do* gain recognition might be returned to a zone of unimaginability from which they arrived and which remains the constitutive exterior to political consensus. We should also then consider how, in Lee's novel, K herself gives voice to an unending structure of obligation as she contemplates her course of action (i.e., her wish to die), despite the possibility that she might be pregnant: "There's nothing in me. There can't be. If there is, then God forgive me for what I'll do" (294). Caught in the impossible situation where her agency rests only in choosing between a more or less violent death, K nonetheless recognizes her own responsibility, as she faces the possibility of an "other other" that a pregnancy tropes.

In asking forgiveness in the face—and for the fate—of that other other, K rearticulates her response to victimhood as at once an emergent agency, no matter how fragile and fleeting. When Hata arrives to collect

K's remains, he too must then acknowledge not only that which he knows has been lost—his own lost Other that is K—but also the loss of K's Other, whom he actually cannot fathom:

> I walked the rest of the way to the clearing. The air was cooler there, the treetops shading the falling sun. Mostly it was like any other place I had ever been. Yet I could not smell or hear or see as I did my medic's work. I could not feel my hands as they gathered, nor could I feel the weight of such remains. And I could not sense that other, tiny, elfin form I eventually discovered, miraculously whole, I could not see the figured legs and feet, the utter, blessed digitation of the hands. Nor could I see the face, the perfected cheek and brow. Its pristine sleep still unbroken, undisturbed. And I could not know what I was doing, or remember any part. (305)

The "medic's work" that Hata undertakes in this harrowing scene gathers the destroyed body without being able to recover and integrate her as a living personhood or to make sense of the suffering she has undergone. It remains for K to arrive, as a minor subject in another time and place, for such reparation to materialize. Even further, though, in Hata's inability to "sense that other, tiny, elfin form" whom he nevertheless discovers "miraculously whole," the novel preserves the singularity of the emergent subjectivity that it has accorded to K, retaining the other other as distinctly K's impossible obligation. In remembering that singular relation of responsibility without restoring it, the narrative preserves the desire for K to undergo the ethical relation, where she comes to figure not simply as the victim and bearer of truth about the American good life, but as a responsible subject in her own right.

In a similar vein, Daisy's claim to responsibility in *Dogeaters* follows immediately her reflection upon "her unnamed baby girl [who] was born premature and dead," suggesting that this loss impels Daisy's agency-as-responsibility (233).[94] To be certain, *Dogeaters* never quite articulates this singular responsibility as an internal diegetic element in the way *A Gesture Life* does. Yet, as a roman-à-clef—the genre that risks naming names but does so through the veil of fiction that can always also potentially neutralize its pointed political critique—Hagedorn's novel can drive the responsible, responsive reader across disciplinary and political borders that seek to contain the impossible subject of human rights. As a fitting coda to my formulation of rights and responsibility in this chapter, then, it is worth noting here that Nelia Sancho—the winner of the 1971 Miss Asian-Pacific beauty title, who later repudiated such pageants and joined the anti-Marcos movement and upon whom Hagedorn fashioned the character of Daisy—has been involved since the 1990s in the comfort woman redress movement with the Filipino American organization Lolas Kampanyeras.[95] The human rights politics that configures my reading of both novels profoundly counters and reimagines liberal politics and charitable humanitarianism, because it unfailingly asserts the Other's "right to be human" as simultaneously our own ethical responsibility as witnesses to "want otherwise" for her. Aspiring toward a future in which the losses of the past might be put (to) right(s), this literature creates and recognizes modes of nascent subjectivity not (yet) available, embedded in forms of social existence that have yet to be or that might once have been.

UN Convention against Torture
Susan Choi, *The Foreign Student*

3

"A Globe within Him"

Security at the Borderline of War and Torture

> *It is always war that makes things change.*
>
> —Jacques Derrida, *Of Hospitality*

Early in their acquaintance, the two protagonists whose relationship is at the heart of Susan Choi's 1998 debut novel, *The Foreign Student,* have a brief exchange about the Korean War. Katherine Monroe tells the eponymous foreign student Chang, who has arrived to study at the University of the South in Sewanee, Tennessee: "I've always wondered what a war really looks like. There's no way to tell, reading the papers."[1] While at this point Chang simply shrugs off her question, in the relationship that subsequently develops between them, the plot of the novel itself concerns Chang's coming "to terms" with his own wartime experience. *The Foreign Student* hence offers a "telling" of war that seeks to do justice to the radical unintelligibility of the body in pain from a future location and within a future language that, as I will show, the signifying work of war and torture have made present. If, as I concluded in chapter 2, the subject of human rights is made and unmade by the forms of social and political recognition extended to her by those who already enjoy rights—those whose very enjoyment of rights incurs an ethical responsibility to grant recognition to the Other—this chapter explores the considerable intertwinement of one's standing (i.e., the right to have rights) with one's right to the security of person.

In contrast to the primacy of collective or national security for state power, the right to the security of person refers to the *individual's* physical safety and bodily integrity. As such, the right to the security of person is a crucial aspect of the natural law tradition, codified, for example, in habeas corpus laws or, in the case of the United States, the Fourth and Eighth Amendments of the U.S. Constitution; it prohibits unlawful detention and arrest as well as arbitrary physical abuse or death. However, in its depictions of war and torture, Choi's novel conceives of the human body as a *hybrid* biopolitical subject, at once the created object *and* the political agent of state power. She thus locates the body at the gap between natural and positive law, whereby (as we saw with the "human person" in previous chapters) that which is presumed to exist naturally and prior to any juridico-political regime is simultaneously that which is produced and secured by the positive power of the state. *The Foreign Student* stages the right to the security of person, urging us to ask, with regard to human rights instruments such as the Convention against Torture, about what type of human person might instead exist outside, beyond, or, more precisely, in contradistinction to the national state.

In particular, Choi's novel names (as I describe it below) the Asian/American subject as a casualty of war and torture, unable and unwilling to heel to the divisions of domestic and foreign politics that crucially underpin the liberalization of both the postwar international system and U.S. racial orders. In so doing, it excavates an alternative and expanded human rights political project, assembled by the right to the security of person. In this chapter, I am therefore also especially concerned with how the structures of war and torture—as they exploit the vulnerable subject's body in pain—materialize the border between the domestic and the international, the citizen and alien, in order to secure a nation in whose name the state and its war machine operate. When read by way of a human rights approach, *The Foreign Student* shows how the nation-state (and the international order of nation-states in which it is situated) has never been fully consolidated, but remains permanently in need of its own ontological reproduction. *The Foreign Student* demonstrates how war and torture "work over" the human body, and its capacity to suffer pain, in order to stabilize an ideal of national identity. The sovereign state represents itself as consecrated by, and working to secure, the imagined political community of the nation by (un)making and (re)writing the human body.

In chapter 1, I considered how the human rights to self-determination and social and economic justice articulated the minor subject of American cultural politics with postcolonial subjects of (neo)liberal modernity. This chapter is also concerned with the Cold War context of integration, examining the way in which *The Foreign Student* perceptively tracks a genealogy of "Asian/American" racial formation in relation to, but in marked difference from, the U.S. civil rights reforms of this era. In its portrait of transnational and interracial desire, *The Foreign Student* constructs the human person not as a stable identity rooted in an individuated body, but as a borderline and vulnerable intersection of biological material, somatic intensities, and contested social and political knowledge. In the novel, the vulnerable subject is made further insecure in its errant desire for the other, but the ethical encounters in which such unruly desire takes place also position the subject in new forms of sociality. Specifically, in describing Chang's attachment to Katherine as "Asian/American relationality," I mean to highlight the dynamic, discursive "liaison" in which subject-formation takes place and in which *other* possible identifications are undone. Accordingly, "Asian/American relationality" reformulates the question of incorporation and integration (can Asians in the United States be assimilated) to one of how has "America" itself been constituted in and through its encounters with Asians and Asia. How have the naturalized hallmarks of national identity—namely, the liberal political rights (including the right to personal security) that sustained the culture of the so-called Cold War—been secured, if they have at all, through the nation's violent campaigns in Asia and elsewhere?

By exploring the radical alterity with which the pained subject and subject of desire tarry, *The Foreign Student* pressures the border between "inside" and "outside," in order to stage the ethical encounters that displace "reasons of state" justifying nationalist discourses and security practices. If, as legal scholar Robert S. Chang contends, the border is a social construct, and "the properties of the border change depending on the contingent features of who or what is trying to get in or out," *The Foreign Student* also historicizes this contingency, as it tracks the deformation and reconstruction of a "people and its civilization" in Korea and its fallout in and for American conceptions of national unity.[2] By spelling out the social and political contradictions of monocratic Japanese colonialism, brutal civil war, and the bipolarity of the Cold War that have formed—and divided—the modern Korean nation, the novel queries the construction of "consent," by which war and torture are designated as discrete phenomena in international law and liberal political philosophy. The disciplinary distinction between these forms of political violence pivots on an assumed "willingness" to die for one's country that at some level binds citizens to the national state, while torture elicits submission on the part of decidedly *unwilling* subjects. In contrast, with its Asian/American subject of war and torture crossing and being crossed over by shifting state borders,

The Foreign Student discloses how the sovereign state's capacity to inflict torturous violence on all life—a bodily violence that the nation's minor subjects are all too often made painfully to undergo—founds the essential bond between a consenting citizenry and the nation.

At the same time, the novel adumbrates the state-making project of the Korean War in terms of domestic U.S. racial formations for which the Asian/American body becomes a symptom. Ultimately, in the novel, the war machine works to stabilize the border (and the social, political, and legal orders the border contains) designated by the slash, between domestic and international, North and South, past and present, foreigner and citizen, Asian and American, communist and capitalist, oppressed and free. But it also envisions how the inherent instability of the border opens space for a human rights project that challenges the constrictive character of state sovereignty and national unity.

Times of Integration

In accordance with the stipulations on the financial sponsorship that underwrites his college tuition costs, Chang (who has also adopted the anglicized version of his family name, "Chuck," given to him by an American newspaperman in Seoul) gives talks at member churches of the Episcopal Church Council about his homeland and the war fought there. During one such visit in Jackson, Tennessee, Chang begins his presentation: "'I am Chang Ahn. I study at Sewanee, University of the South, but before this I live in Korea.'" As the narrator continues to explain, "he usually began his address by saying that his presence before them was the direct result of MacArthur's Inchon landing. 'I'm not here, if this doesn't happen,' he said, feeling melancholy suddenly" (50). With the novel set in the 1950s, Chang's location at this juncture, between the productivity of war—"his presence before them"—and its predicate of melancholic loss—"I'm not here"—locates for us the geopolitical unevenness, violence, and contingency through which the modern nation and its security state are forged.

In the conventional periodization of American history, the Vietnam War and the 1960s have come to signify a watershed moment of national reckoning for a range of subjects. By opening in 1950, *The Foreign Student* locates Asian/American relationality *prior* to that war, as well as before the momentous passage of the Civil Rights Act of 1964, the Voting Rights Act of 1965, and the 1965 liberalization of policies monitoring and restricting immigration from Asia. In returning to the Korean War, the novel re-periodizes postwar liberalism and Cold War realist politics in the United States by situating both in relation to the anticolonial struggle and civil conflict in Korea.[3] Chang's existence as what I am calling a borderline subject in the U.S. South elaborates how it is always war (and torture) that, in Jacques Derrida's words, "makes things change" by providing a rather different angle of vision on domestic social order and its transformation in the second half of the twentieth century.[4]

Often described as the "forgotten war" (although, in truth, it is one of a number of such forgotten wars), the U.S intervention in Korea is one that barely registers in American national culture. Yet the war was thoroughly definitive of the shape and limits of Korean national independence—divided as it has been, since the 1953 Armistice of Panmunjon to the present day, across the 38th parallel into two mutually hostile states—and the ongoing "special relationship" (again, one of many such "special relationships" claimed by postcolonial nations) that enmeshed South Korea with the United States into the twenty-first century. Since the war—during which at least three million people died on either side of the border—tens of thousands of U.S. military personnel have been stationed in South Korea, as the United States signed a mutual defense treaty and committed itself to ongoing economic aid to the nation. Ji-Yeon Yuh further demonstrates that the partition and the war's long aftermath has been the source of nearly *all* Korean migration to the United States since 1950.[5]

As William Stueck observes, "What is largely forgotten in the United States . . . is very much a living memory in Korea."[6] Indeed, the ongoing involvement of the United States in South Korea suggests that the forgetting of the Korean conflict requires a sustained cultural and political *effort* that belies the significance of this history. As Daniel Kim argues with respect to Choi's depiction of the "repressive, incompetent, and stupendously unpopular" Syngman Rhee government (as Choi bluntly synopsizes it) during this period and its violent counterinsurgency campaigns, which included forcible conscription, torture, and mass executions of South Korean nationals: "Since the illegitimate and repressive regime that committed such atrocities had been created and supported by the US, the history of the Korean War is not a foreign history . . . but one that is deeply American" (65).[7]

This forgotten Asian/American history provides the context and setting for Chang's existence across the two narratives that constitute his character, as a Korean national and as a "foreign student" in the United States. Given the novel's historical setting in the 1950s, Chang's "indifference" with respect to both Jim Crow social order and civil rights politics in the U.S. South is striking. For most of the plot, he remains unintelligible within the black/white binary that historically organizes racial formation, polarized between propertied whiteness and dispossessed blackness, in the United States. His illegibility conveys the way in which Asian-ness at midcentury was represented primarily as an object of prohibition, because various immigration laws and policies precluded Asian migration and barred Asian immigrants from naturalizing as citizens until after World War II. As scholars of Asian American history and culture have well documented, the discursive construction of the "oriental" as a "forever foreign" threat to national purity and unity has thoroughly determined the historical racialization of Asian-ness in the United States.[8] With respect to the novel, then, my use of "Asian/American" does not replace the more familiar designation of "Asian American," which I retain below for reading an integrationist (if multicultural) trajectory contained within the domestic frame of the United States. Rather, Asian/American relationality *supplements* this politicized identity category, offering a "borderline" perspective from which to discern the past histories and forgotten aspirations that impinge upon the liberal rights and freedoms promised by integration and civil rights reform.[9] Hence, as David Palumbo-Liu explains, the slash in "Asian/American" "at once instantiates a choice between two terms, their simultaneous and equal status, and an element of indecidability."[10]

The Foreign Student depicts historical Asian exclusion in its portrait of Chang's reception in the South as a foreigner. Early in the novel, feeling himself silently scrutinized by the employees at a filling station near Sewanee, Chang imparts to Katherine, with a telling solecism, "They don't know what to make me" (37). Later, Choi describes "a subtle, unremitting scrutiny, disguised as politeness . . . [that] followed him everywhere in America, varying in tone or intensity but always bringing with it the same slight electrification, as if he weren't just caught in a narrow beam of light but somehow animated by it" (54–55).[11] The scrutiny under which Chang finds himself countenances the specific historical juncture of the early 1950s; heretofore absent and foreign, he now has to be "made" over into "someone" recognizable.[12] During the lapse between the novel's 1950 prologue, set in Korea, and the beginning of its first chapter when Chang arrives in Sewanee in 1955, the 1952 McCarran-Walter Act initiated a significant reconfiguration of the U.S. color line by reopening immigration from Asia and repealing the bars on naturalization for Asian immigrants.[13]

Yet, while this immigration bill is usually construed as a liberalization of prior and patently undemocratic exclusions (as I have discussed in the introduction), it simultaneously established a new set of criteria for exclusion. In addition to excluding from entry an expansive list of undesirables—those deemed to be feeble-minded, insane, or mentally defective, drug addicts or alcoholics, those afflicted with contagious disease, paupers, or those likely to become public charges, criminals, polygamists, prostitutes, those considered sexually immoral, or unskilled labor whose presence might adversely affect American workers—the legislation permitted the exclusion and deportation of those engaged in activities thought to be subversive to national security.[14] As they simultaneously named those to be regarded as threats and those considered (newly) assimilable, the midcentury immigration reforms worked in conjunction with U.S. Cold War policy and legislative efforts (including national loyalty programs administered by the Truman and Eisenhower administrations in order to vet government employees) to stabilize the boundaries between a domestic national identity and its foreign others. In so doing, David Campbell contends, U.S. officials extended and intensified the domain of the state's interest, as they "multiplied the dimensions of being along which threats to security could be observed."[15]

The novel's historical setting, then, is one of heightened ideological and political volatility, as the specific historical pressures of Cold War containment gave rise, on the one hand, to a security state vexed by differences that might undermine the national unity in whose interest it operated, and, on the other, the integration of those to whom inassimilable difference had been previously attributed. By situating Chang's arrival at this juncture, *The Foreign Student* takes as its task an imaginative inscription of a context in which those who had previously been "impossible subjects" and "alien citizens" become legible within a national frame.[16] But, at the same time, it recognizes that in the national legal and social order, the abjection of Asian-ness has been necessary and constitutive of *generic* national subject formation in the first place. Thus, as Karen Shimakawa surmises, abjection is characterized by its "constantly shifting relation to Americanness," which, in turn, "marks the boundaries of

Asian American cultural (and sometimes legal) citizenship."[17] If, as Shimakawa further contends, there is "a way to conceive of that process from the perspective of the one . . . inhabiting the body and space of abjection," *The Foreign Student* situates its critique of liberal integration and the security state in the borderline subject's "*movement between*" the Asian and the American during the Cold War, as Chang's perspective coalesces within this Asian/American relationality.[18]

The two opening moments of the narrative evoke continuities, which have since been seemingly severed, between Cold War foreign policy and military strategy, including the nation's involvement in the very live war in Korea, on the one hand and the domestic conditions of racial violence and segregation on the other. The prologue (introduced without a chapter heading) recounts Chang's hurried escape from Seoul. It is only near the novel's end that Choi explicates this abrupt, in media res opening as the beginning of an ill-fated trek to Cheju, whereupon he will be captured by the Republic of Korea Army (ROKA) and tortured by the National Police, despite his being a citizen of South Korea. Between the opening scene of escape and the later revelation of torture, the bulk of the novel alternates between the story of the growing friendship and romance between Chang and Katherine from 1955 to 1956 and the extended flashback accounts of Chang's and Katherine's individual pasts. Although Katherine is privy, like Chang, to the comforts of upper-middle-class life, her story centers on a girlhood in Sewanee and, in particular, a scandalous relationship she has when she was fourteen with Charles Addison, a local professor of Shakespeare and her father's college friend. Chang's close friendship with a poor schoolmate, Kim, also moors Chang's story, in which the personal changes he undergoes are otherwise swept up in the social upheaval through which he lives, so that "he often sensed that he was only moving with the earth beneath his feet, as it gathered speed" (71).

Choi situates the novel's opening scene in 1950 as part of the unsuccessful attempt by the United States to counter and push back the second invasion of the Korean People's Army (KPA) from the North. The U.S. "police action" in Korea required substantial increases and reinforcements of military personnel, with assignments filled, for the first time, without regard to the racial makeup of the troops employed. American historiography remembers this as the moment of the U.S. military's effective desegregation and a precedent for later reform at home.[19] In striking contrast to the foreign stage of U.S. racial integration, the novel's first chapter opens with Chang's arrival in Sewanee in 1955, the year of the brutal and highly publicized murder of fourteen-year-old Emmett Till. Although in the previous year, the monumental *Brown v. Board of Education* decision heralded the end of official practices of segregation, Emmett Till's violent death served as a powerful reminder of the bodily and social *insecurities* that continued to plague African American existence, especially given the Court's failure to call for immediate and substantive forms of desegregation in its decision. As a vanishing point against which we might read Chang's recuperated body in the segregated South as well as fourteen-year-old Katherine's sexual coming of age, the memory of the young boy's tortured and broken body, displayed by his mother to the nation in an open-casket funeral, directs us to ask how security is imagined and procured at "home" and elsewhere, a question to which I return below.

The Foreign Student does not make reference to U.S. military practices of desegregation (indeed, Chang's interaction with Americans in Korea is largely limited to the white staff members of the U.S. Information Services, by whom he is employed) or the Till murder. Nevertheless, I contend that the liberal imperative of integration, and the conditions of violence from which it emerges, comprise the central object of critique from the borderline perspective of the Asian/American subject of war and torture. The presence of the borderline subject in turn threatens to scramble the carefully regulated domestic color line and international borders around which regional, national, and international order coheres.[20] Choi's precise location of Chang at the times and places of the novel's two openings yokes together the Cold War and civil rights projects in order to recognize aspirations for futures that have otherwise been foreclosed by the "integration" of South Korea into the postwar united nations world order and the domestic integration of the American South during the Cold War.

The novel's portraits of Sewanee and Seoul denote the way integrative spatial relations manage the temporal contradictions and ruptures that modernization continually engenders.[21] Revisiting and rewriting the South, Choi's novel makes a double excursus into this imagined past. Published nearly a decade after mass media and political leaders alike declared the Cold War over, *The Foreign Student* returns to a moment that has been represented, by turns, as the halcyon days of a dawning modernity when the nation retained its wholesome optimism, and the beginning of cataclysmic, wholesale rupture generated by the twin pillars of global expansion in capitalist production and markets and the (neo)liberal discourse of democratic rights. Folded into this heterogeneous memory-scape of the 1950s are the remnants of the nineteenth-century ideologies of racial segregation and gendered domesticity (which I describe further below), to which the Monroes (who live in New Orleans and who view Sewanee as a "summer refuge" from urbane life) retire every summer (23). In this layered encapsulation of multiple histories, the novel uncovers the ongoing efforts of the nation stridently trying to anchor its own uncertain ventures in technological and political innovation.

"Integration" thus presents, as we have already seen in the introduction, a spatial analytic for mapping the historical process by which regional and national orders come to cohere culturally and politically, to the extent that they do at all. Liberal reforms in U.S. immigration policy and in the racialized distribution of rights during this period advanced integration as a resolution to both domestic racial divisions and international political/economic ones (as I have also detailed in the introduction).[22] Here and in the next section, then, I would emphasize how such integrationist efforts produce what David Campbell and Michael J. Shapiro call "moral spaces," that is, "the bounded locations whose inhabitants acquire the privileges deriving from practices of ethical inclusion."[23] In juxtaposing two Souths, *The Foreign Student* suggests that reinserting the constitutive but occluded Asian presence in America has significance well beyond that of "Asian American identity." Instead, it seeks to "intervene in the dominant practices of intelligibility that enable geopolitical imaginaries" in order to trouble an entire conception of modern freedoms and national security attached to such integrative moral spaces and in which the United States and Korea remained embroiled in the present time of the novel's publication.[24]

Encountering the Modern South(s) of Asian/America

Chang settles on a domestic analogy to explain in his lecture the Korean War, which otherwise remains enigmatic to his American audience: "He always felt hopeless, called upon to deliver a clear explanation of the war. It defied explanation. Sometimes he simply skipped over causes. . . . He would groundlessly compare the parallel to the Mason-Dixon line, and see every head nod excitedly" (51).[25] The particular force of this "groundless comparison" between the 38th parallel and the hallowed Mason-Dixon line depends upon the equating of two *domestic* histories of civil war and *intra*-national antagonisms. Certainly the Korean civil conflict, after the nation's liberation from Japan in 1945 until the founding of the Republic of Korea (ROK) in the south in 1948, suggests the familiar outlines of a rapidly modernizing northern society in tension with an unyielding southern culture that struggles, in turn, against incursions against its own traditional modes of production and social forms of life. And recent historiography of the Korean War rightfully insists—and Choi's novel depicts—that the agency and interests of Korean people were themselves crucial factors in the partition, insurgency, and clampdowns that swept the peninsula from 1945 to 1955.

However, in 1950, most Americans became aware of Korea for the first time primarily as a coordinate in an *international* Cold War that had up to that point seemed centered almost entirely in Europe. The Korean civil conflict was thus absorbed into the bipolar contest between the United States and the Soviet Union, in addition to the historical and political designs of Japan and China, both of which underwent rapid political and economic changes during this period as well. Despite general confusion and a good deal of skepticism about U.S. involvement in Korea among the American populace, the architects of intervention in Korea, in particular Secretary of State Dean Acheson, considered Korea to be crucial to securing American occupation in Japan, limiting the influence of the Communist revolution in China and other anticolonial movements in Asia, and countering attempts by liberals at home to demobilize after the conclusion of World War II.[26] The successful detonation of the atomic bomb by the Soviets and the later rise of McCarthyism (fueled by the perception that the United States had "lost" China to Communism) further contributed to the sense of urgency with which state officials imbued the war in Korea. Nonetheless, the Korean War remained a "police action" for which the executive branch, unable to translate these concerns into full-fledged support for intervention, did not consult Congress.[27]

As such, the hasty troping of Korean history as a discrete parallel to the American Civil War effaces the very aspect of colonial occupation and the jockeying by extra-national forces—including U.S. interests in the region—that have made Chang's passage to the United States possible in the first place. The analogy to the Civil War and his very "saved" presence instead serve more readily to affirm *American* national unity for his Southern audience than to describe the war in Korea. In other words, Choi illustrates how, despite the temporal and spatial *heterogeneity* that Sewanee itself figures *for and in the American South,* U.S. Cold War culture forged a sense of regional and national *identity* out of such difference. When he screens a photograph of the Seoul Railway station, Chang notices that "people [in his American audiences] were often surprised by the vaulted dome of the train station, and the European-looking avenues"; conversely, he hears positive murmurings when he shows them an "image of the farmers, in their year-round pajamas and inscrutable Eskimos' faces" (52). His audience requires a straightforward and familiar account of Korean difference that, ironically, the "inscrutable" Korean face evinces.

In contrast, Chang's family has enjoyed a privileged life that straddled the later geopolitical divisions of the war, with his father's university appointment in Seoul, his family's country estate in the North, and Chang's own continually equivocal and shifting, albeit undeclared, alliances to the Americans (and thus, by default, to the ROK) on the one hand and, on the other, to the insurgency (and therefore to the Communist Party). The Americans he meets know nothing of this complex and conflicted personal history, however, and Chang's presence in Tennessee corroborates for this audience that U.S. intervention in the Asian nation was a mission of redemption. Having been "secured" in the United States, Chang provides a symbol of the liberated other against and through whom white Southerners recognize their own distinct Americanness.

While Chang's presentation reinforces the orientalist presumptions harbored by his audience—an orientalism that actually also corresponds to the possibility of racial *threat* (e.g., "yellow peril") that has shaped Asian American presence in, and exclusion from, the United States—the narrative's present-ing of Chang before that audience offers an early iteration of what I have described in previous chapters, following Christina Klein, as the global imaginary of integration. Supplementing the more well-known cultural imaginary (and geopolitics of) "containment" during the Cold War and departing starkly from an isolationist tradition, the imaginary of integration was crucial for garnering popular support at home for U.S. foreign policy in Asia (and elsewhere) during the Cold War.[28] By casting U.S. expansion in this era as "integration" rather than territorial occupation, both state policies and "middlebrow" cultural production (Klein offers examples such as the films *The King and I* and *Flower Drum Song*) gave rise to a discourse of global interdependence and asserted the importance of tolerance, inclusion, and equality between the United States and decolonizing, non-Communist nations. As Klein argues, the winning of hearts and minds was as significant a domestic project as it was a foreign one, requiring changes in (white) American attitudes. Partially displacing an extant language of racial supremacy, the sentimental education provided by middlebrow cultural productions—which Chang's speaking engagements patently exemplify and which the narrative seeks to challenge—strove to create bonds of sympathy, bridging difference and facilitating reciprocity and exchange, across a middle-class audience and an imagined Asia.[29]

Indeed, as Chang stumbles upon the first day of classes at Sewanee, many of his fellow students have already embraced these "higher sentiments," such that he finds himself not only the goodwill ambassador in such a project but the *recipient* of friendly feeling in return:

> Only the very beginning of the semester was placid, and perilous. That first day the flagstone walk had been lined with pale, tailored, spit-shined bodies completely absorbed in themselves until Chuck grew near. He seemed to be pushing a ripple of silence ahead of himself. Everyone swiveled, and smiled, and stuck out a hand, and the hysterical idea occurred to him that he was a general inspecting his troops. This idea carried him along but it wasn't able to prevent the incessant bobbing of his head and the hand he was using to shake, and the ceremony could have absorbed the rest of the day had someone not offered to show him the bicycle rack. Although he could have found that bicycle rack in his sleep, he allowed himself to be led to it, and then into the lecture hall, where he was stood up in front of the throng, and made the occasion of a speech about America's duty. (12–13)

Underlying the otherwise comic scene of his introduction to the student body, the moment of pause evoked by Choi's parallel, parenthetic phrases, "and perilous," "and smiled," "and made the occasion of" indicates a moment of decision. The Sewanee students implicitly choose between treating Chang as an agent of threat and object of containment *or* as one of hospitality and integration. The "speech about America's duty" then serves as a reminder of a determination already made, highlighting how the Sewanee students perform their national duty by incorporating Chang into their presence. That Chang, having arrived a month earlier in the summer, has already acquired an "odd proprietary arrogance" about the campus of course remains unimaginable to his classmates. And even Chang cannot help but offer himself, in the bobbing head and hand, as the grateful and unpresuming guest. Chang's impression of himself as a "general inspecting his troops" remains instead "hysterical," an inverted sign of the terms by which he is being received.

The benevolent reception of Chang in the American South enacts the ongoing separation between the domestic and the foreign necessary to generate a secure self-image of American liberal modernity. If his presence in the modernizing South reproduces the border necessary to make war, politics, and culture intelligible, *The Foreign Student* as a whole nonetheless insists on the *incommensurability* of any analogizing between the two Souths of Chang's narrative existence. When Chang observes, "I'm not here, if this doesn't happen," he reformulates the postcolonial migrants' trenchant mantra (coined a decade later) "we're here because you were there," as a *melancholic* constitution of the racialized subject called to account for himself in the terms of an American imaginary (50). His positive presence in the American South arises from the foreign stage of U.S. military intervention, and the distribution of violence and suffering "there" sustains a unified image of the benevolent nation "here."

Further, the negative formulation of "doesn't happen," which would result in Chang's being "not here," simultaneously frames his American presence as a *loss* of *other* possible existences, alternative futures in Korea (or elsewhere), which have been foreclosed. The novel thus proceeds to recount through analepsis the past leading up to his arrival "here." This history exceeds the hegemonic narratives of integration—of racial integration in the South, of the integration of the U.S. South as a region in the modern nation, and of the integration of South Korea into the (neo)liberal world order, which the United States instituted during the Cold War. Chang endures separation from his cherished Korean schoolmate Kim and the ravages of war and torture, what I discuss in the next section as the "body in pain," in order to be ultimately delivered to Katherine. And yet, as I also explain below, insofar as it maintains the right to the security of the human person, the novel does not merely forsake the Korean past for the positive present of American integration. Rather, it transposes a utopian desire for a unified, self-determined Korea as a "recognition of desire" that orients Chang's Asian/American liaison not only with Katherine, but ultimately with the other minor subjects of the American global nation.

The Body in Pain

In *The Foreign Student,* the story of Chang's experience in the Korean War is essentially the story of the body in pain. In her well-known and widely influential book *The Body in Pain,* Elaine Scarry contends that political authority, when engaged in war and torture, harnesses itself to the intractable situation of the body in pain. According to Scarry, extraordinary bodily pain creates a void of language and meaning; that is, pain has no referential content and the person who suffers such pain is reduced to speechlessness.[30] Political authority exploits this "world-shattering" quality by seizing upon and filling up the silence or meaninglessness that such extreme bodily pain produces. As forms of political violence with the primary objective to induce bodily suffering, war and torture provide political authorities the opportunity to substantiate representational regimes that are somehow otherwise untenable.[31] Scarry describes "civilization" as the enlargement and expansion of the human body, whereby material culture and social institutions shelter and provide comfort for the vulnerable embodied human.[32] In contrast, systematic processes of violence suspend reality, deconstruct benign systems of civilization, and "alter" the body, which is civilization's "ultimate substance," so as to "realize" an order of meaning and authority that does not yet exist.[33] In short, Scarry posits war and torture as forms of social and political "writing." War and torture substantiate ideological "fictions" about the nation (or other social collectivities) through and on the "matter" of the human body and its "extension" in material culture.

Scarry's distinction *between* the structures of war and torture hinges on the question of consent. She contends that war involves a contest between two sides with conflicting and mutually intolerable political "realities," which deploy the bodies of "believers" to serve as both combatants and the sites on which, at the conclusion of a war, a new political "reality" is inscribed and materialized for the defeated. Thus, for Scarry, in war there always exists an element of consent, even on the part of those who are conscripted by law, as the body politic (i.e., the nation) and citizens exist in an isomorphic relationship to one another.[34] With torture, in contrast, the "crisis of substantiation" plays out through the body of the "unbeliever." In the objectification and "translation" of the torture victim's bodily pain and injury, political authority decomposes the ideological world of the national subject and rewrites it according to the regime's own truth. Torture is thus inwardly directed toward the nation's domestic lifeworld, and indeed, Scarry emphasizes how torturers incorporate the material objects and practices of domestic comfort into their torture strategies to "unmake" the prisoner's world.[35] Although she does not address specifically the sovereign state as *the* sanctified form of modern political authority (a point to which I will return in more detail further on in order to trouble her reliance on the notion of consent), *The Body in Pain* has been invaluable for understanding the centrality of bodily pain, injury, and suffering in the management of geopolitical crisis and rupture.

The Foreign Student countenances both modes of political violence. During his time in Korea, Chang undergoes two instances of extraordinary pain and suffering that typify the purposive injuring that structures war and torture. The first occurs during his confinement in a crawl space of his family's house during the occupation of Seoul by the KPA from the North in June 1950. Tended to by a servant-girl, Chang hides for three months, after having shepherded his parents onto a train headed south to Pusan and the KPA has taken possession of the family residence. After the South is "liberated" by U.S. troops (beginning with the famous "Inchon landing," in which General MacArthur commanded a surprise arrival by sea and fought the KPA to retake Seoul), Chang begins a slow recovery from the illness that wracked his body during his seclusion. At this point, he undergoes the "heartbreak" of realizing that his American employers have been unable or unwilling to protect him and that the Communists, with whom he had fledgling sympathies, were indifferent to his personal suffering: "Sometimes his stomach would seem to drop away and there in the void was the realization he had been discarded" (105). Although in this first case, Chang's bodily pain is an indirect consequence of the KPA's invasion, it occasions his own realization of his utter physical vulnerability to violence and suffering.

Thus, as he recuperates, Chang hopes to free himself of naïve notions of political loyalty: "He regrouped, declared himself a small principality, and pledged his undivided allegiance again," convening what Choi wryly describes as "The Committee for the Preservation and Welfare of Himself," and excising all other bonds in the interest of making himself over into a free agent, blatantly selfish and fully autonomous (164). Yet, Chang's declaration of self-preservation ultimately proves mostly ineffective. He realizes that, simply because he lives—and remains—south of the 38th parallel and because he is unable to declare allegiances to either the Americans (who in any case "went to great length to establish that they were not an occupation government at all, but a facilitating presence") or the Communist Party (because of a promise to Kim that he would steer clear of the party politics), his fate essentially resides with the ROK (164).

Furthermore, not only does the limited agency that emerges as an effect of and response to the first instance of pain generate the narrative's second scene of extraordinary suffering, but that agency becomes the object of the violence he is made to undergo. Namely, as I note above, as he tries to escape being drafted by the ROKA and searches for the insurgent Kim (who earlier fled from Seoul), agents of the South Korean National Police capture and torture Chang. In documenting the damage that the body undergoes, Choi delineates the impenetrable structure of torture in which pain evacuates any sense of meaning the subject holds, until he "confesses" to being a spy:

> On the ninth day his jaws were held open, and the officer took a straight razor and made small cuts all over his tongue; then he was given a bowl of salt. He ate it weeping. "Are you a spy?" the officer asked. He said he was. He could have said, so long ago, I am a spy. The officer unfolded a piece of paper in front of his face. There were words coursing across it. He was only watching them, not trying to read them. Words came from a world which did not exist. (309)

The scenes of torture produce an alternative context, one summoned entirely by the state and its functionaries, where familiar words and devices are written over with contradictory meanings. After subsequent beatings, Chang gives the name of the priest who aided him in his search for Kim and who provided him with a safe haven in Cheju. Ultimately, Chang's desperation registers in language starkly akin to Scarry's concept of "decreation": "To betray the world he'd stopped believing in it" (311).

By characterizing Chang, after the KPA occupation, as a discarded form of life, *The Foreign Student* makes visible the wretched effects of political abandonment for the "bare life," that is, in the words of Giorgio Agamben, one that is "exposed and threatened on the threshold in which life and law, outside and inside, become indistinguishable."[36] When Chang is hiding in the house, where no violence *directly* targets him, the novel demonstrates how the body's safety and well-being is nevertheless thoroughly contingent upon the "society of security," which is withdrawn from him. And when Chang subsequently attempts to remake his political existence according to a supposedly natural right to life and security of person that motivates him, the state more spectacularly constrains his capacity to choose his own political loyalties (including to the "Preservation and Welfare of Himself") through the force of torture.[37] Enacting the state's exceptional authority to create the world in which the body is made to live, the police agents rewrite in the regime's own image the very possibility of choice and consent, which is otherwise the hallmark of liberal subjectivity and political freedom. As with Scarry's formulation of how torture works over the body, political violence rewrites Chang's world, one in which he had declared his own independence from and "nonalignment" with either the North or the South.[38] Here, then, we see that for political communities that insist upon the totality of their own ontology, the body must be (made) a *singular* instantiation of the "population" in need of existential defense. Unable to tolerate the other natural, physical, affective, and social worlds in which the human forms attachments unauthorized by sovereign power, the modern state "demand[s] a totally coherent and unified body" and sets about stamping out disorder and ambiguity with a virulence that renders peace possible only by way of intensified violence.[39]

And yet, because the novel situates Chang at the crossroads of rapid and overdetermined change that sweeps through Korea, as the nation's nascent postcoloniality from Japanese rule becomes engulfed in a civil war that is simultaneously ensnared in the bipolarity of the Cold War, Chang's body figures primarily as a *negation* from which the nation will (have to) be reconstructed in the postwar united nations world. Chang's experiences of extraordinary pain denote the inscription and reinscription of the "friend/enemy" distinction on the body at moments of such cataclysmic upheaval. But because the very nation has been cleaved into two states, Chang's recuperated body carries within it the signs of the *inconclusiveness* that remains after the war. Accordingly, throughout Chang's travails and torture, in his memory of his family's country estate in the North, the property stands as an imaginary homeland, the location of a future redemption for himself and, by extension, the nation (190). When, after the second and final KPA retreat and ceasefire in 1953, he finds—on his family's Seoul estate—the pair of expensive shoes he had earlier given Kim, he speculates that Kim might after all not have been captured in

Cheju (which, as I discuss further below, he fears is the outcome of his "confession" during torture), and that he may have instead retreated north of the 38th parallel to "what was now the other country" (317). In affiliating Kim with the North, Chang harbors within himself a utopian hope for a future when Kim might be returned to him.

As we learn, however, Chang never returns to the North or the estate that "could not possibly exist anymore" (317). Nevertheless, "that memory, of that place, was sealed like a globe within him. . . . The feel of his body when he walked there was within him. . . . It expanded him" (317). In contrast, the "other memory" of torture exists only as a negation that "obliterated itself and took part of him with it": "Although he had witnessed every detail, the pain was as distant from him as the distance between two bodies. . . . It could be another universe, it could not exist at all. He could not imagine what the other body felt, and so he became another to himself; and after this happened, how could he be close to someone, when he was two people?" (318). In figuring Chang's personhood as doubled between these two bodies, one of which has become irretrievably lost because of the damage inflicted upon it, the novel delineates the way in which the disciplined body is always haunted by the possibility of repressive violence.[40]

Locating Subjects of War and Torture

For much of the twentieth century, the "other body," unmade and worked over in the scene of torture, disappears into the conceptual void between the state's domestic jurisdiction over its subjects and the international law of war, a void that the United Nations Convention against Torture (CAT) eventually, if belatedly and incompletely, struggled to address. The Geneva Conventions of 1949—the core documents that regulate conduct in armed conflicts, between states as well as in civil wars, internal conflicts, and the interventions of third states or multinational forces (as established in the Common Article 3 of the four conventions)—stipulate the protections accorded to those who do not participate in combat during wartime, for example, religious personnel or health and aid workers, as well as those who are no longer taking part actively, such as the wounded or prisoners of war. They thus implicitly appreciate that war is inherently an exercise in which two sides seek to, in Scarry's terms, "out-injure" one another and thus cannot proscribe the inevitable suffering that war's "consenting" combatants must face. Instead, the 1949 Geneva Conventions generally address the status and treatment of the various protected categories of persons (such as prisoners of war), who find themselves outside of their own states, subject to the political authority of another. The Geneva Conventions develop from a longer tradition of humanitarian law, with the first convention replacing earlier Geneva Conventions, the second convention replacing the Hague Convention of 1907, and the third convention replacing the Prisoners of War Convention of 1929. Even the fourth convention, which addresses the treatment of civilians and populations of occupied territories, was not meant to govern relations between a state and its own citizens.[41] Mention of human rights was accordingly almost entirely absent from these instruments.[42]

Concomitantly, despite working in the immediate postwar context, the drafters of the Universal Declaration of Human Rights (UDHR) decided explicitly to exclude the law of war from the document's purview.[43] Within the United Nations, there existed a tacit understanding that the UDHR addressed times of peace, of which (as I have described in detail in the introduction) the United Nations was to serve as the guarantor.[44] Here, then, we see reproduced once again the division I examine in chapter 2, where even temporarily stateless people are rendered objects of humanitarian intervention and administration, and the protection of human rights is effectively relegated to nation-states. Even as Article 5 of the UDHR and Article 7 of the International Covenant on Civil and Political Rights prohibit torture and cruel, inhuman, or degrading treatment or punishment, and this prohibition is recognized as *jus cogens* from which no derogation is permitted, the UN Charter's domestic jurisdiction clause effectively makes the security of person—like the many other rights elaborated in the UDHR—a matter of constitutional law and domestic jurisprudence.

As a result, the CAT proves a relatively belated instrument, adopted by the General Assembly only in 1984 and ratified by the United States in 1994 (although not without an extensive package of "reservations, understandings, and declarations," or RUDs, that drastically limit the impact of the CAT for U.S. law), as the need for it arose precisely from the "scandalous" treatment by governments of their own citizens during the second half of the twentieth century. The CAT was to address the gap between the UDHR and the Geneva Conventions, establishing the Committee against Torture to monitor state compliance and to investigate reports of its violation. And yet, even besides the question of enforceability (which, as I have already noted plagues *all* human rights law), the CAT itself maintains to some extent the troubling contradiction between positive and natural law that it was to resolve. Namely, the convention defines torture as

> any act by which severe pain or suffering, whether physical or mental, is intentionally inflicted on a person for such purposes as obtaining from him or a third person information or a confession, punishing him for an act he or a third person has committed or is suspected of having committed, or intimidating or coercing him or a third person, or for any reason based on discrimination of any kind, when such pain or suffering is inflicted by or at the instigation of or with the consent or acquiescence of a public official or other person acting in an official capacity. *It does not include pain or suffering arising only from, inherent in or incidental to lawful sanctions.* (emphasis added)

The convention certainly forbids government officials from inflicting such acts of "severe pain or suffering" (although, as has been apparent in the "war on terror," the definition of what constitutes "severe pain or suffering" continues to be debated).[45] Moreover, whereas most human rights instruments only imply state responsibility to enact and enforce human rights norms in criminal law, the CAT expressly obligates states to prosecute individuals who violate such norms.

Yet, by excepting from its purview "pain or suffering arising only from, inherent in or incidental to lawful sanctions," the CAT upholds the mystical "force of law," as Derrida describes it, by which political authority sanctions itself. That is, against the possibility of justice, the convention contributes to the law's authority, which is founded only through its own performative force and is, as Derrida contends, "neither just nor unjust": "Since the origin of authority, the foundation or ground, the position of the law can't by definition rest on anything but themselves, they are themselves a violence without ground."[46] This is of course not to say that lawful sanctions will necessarily entail pain and suffering that in other circumstances would be deemed torturous. Rather, we must reckon with the CAT's inability to confront how the political authority that doles out "lawful sanctions" *is itself grounded in the (threat of) violence against the human person,* violence that the convention seeks to prevent and make justiciable.[47]

By ceding to "the Law" monopoly over the definition and means of legitimate violence, the convention skirts the constitutive violence by which the state designates and sanctions lawful and "outlaw" subjects, organizations, and actions.

To deconstruct the central role that violence plays in the enactment of juridico-political authority hence requires a methodological shift to an *ethico*-political human rights approach. What might be gained instead by reading "*human* security," as it has come to be called in the burgeoning field of critical security studies (CSS), as a supplement to the "security of *person*" that the Geneva Conventions, the UDHR, and the CAT attempt to address? CSS has productively initiated a shift in the conceptualization of the subject of security studies (a subfield within International Relations) from the security of the nation-state to the "emancipation" of the human person.[48] Toward this end, prioritizing human security can offer a meaningful critique of state failures to provide "freedom from fear" and to guarantee bodily safety and integrity for all human subjects.[49] And yet, with a few notable exceptions, CSS has ambiguously defined such emancipation as the "freeing of people (as individuals and groups) from those physical and human constraints that stop them carrying out what they would freely choose to do," without addressing how human agency itself materializes within historical conditions of power, vulnerability, and recognition.[50]

I suggest that minor literatures demand that we more precisely understand the human as a subject moved by desire between vulnerability (to the Other) and bodily and personal security. *The Foreign Student* insists that human beings can never be said to properly "have" their embodied persons. Rather, as we have already seen, in its staging of torture the novel depicts the *counter*-production of the subject, remade in the image of the state's truth.[51] But, of equal importance, I consider how such a rewriting produces the excesses and incommensurabilities, the "globe within him," by which the subject of war and torture arrives and provides a critical perspective and alternative ethico-political project against the state's truth. As it maps the Asian/American relationality of its protagonists, the novel conceives of "self-possession" for its subjects out of forms of ethical recognition, in contradistinction to and excess of the nation-state. As such, it offers the nation-state as "only one locus of allegiance, identity and rights among many others, whose shapes we do not yet know."[52] Breaking with the defensive enclosures that the sovereign state imposes upon its subject bodies, the novel stages an ethics toward the Other as an aspiration for communal lifeworlds in which one learns to coexist with others.

Lost Persons

For the body that "endures" and survives torture, the "unmaking" of the subject's world can only be temporary. Accordingly, whereas Scarry seems to suggest that the "decreation" of the world through the infliction of pain absolves the prisoner from responsibility, Chang's suspension of belief actually enacts—and makes him contingently responsible for—the betrayal that has both undone and saved him. Upon his release from police detention, after having "confessed" and provided intelligence, Chang immediately spots a face among the other prisoners that he imagines, but never confirms, to be Kim's. In this way, his confession institutes a new order of meaning for Chang. It sediments his image of himself as a traitor of that which he has held most dear (despite his own declaration of loyalty only to himself): his singular loyalty to and love for Kim. At the same time, the assignation of responsibility is neither straightforward nor conventional. That his confession amounts to a betrayal wavers with the uncertainties that the violence of war and torture create: Was it Kim he saw? Did his "confession" in fact save him, or was his release as inexplicable and random as the torture itself?

No one else blames Chang for, or for that matter even knows of, his confession, and hence the model of responsibility that the narrative devises hews closely to the phenomenological ethics, which I have described in chapter 2. Nevertheless, it is as a traitorous subject through which his recovery, including his migration to the United States, proceeds. The subject that survives torture is, the narrative suggests, actually one that has been created anew upon the violent unmaking of reality that torture unleashes. *This* subject's survival depends upon *a losing of the loss* of (a prior) self that has occurred. Chang's distressed assessment of himself as Kim's traitor both makes his return to "reality" possible and carries with it the traces of the violence that removed him from it in the first place. In the novel's closing pages, soon after Choi recounts the experience of torture, which has previously only been alluded to by his recurring nightmares throughout his time in Sewanee, Chang recalls his reunion with his family, whom he locates in Pusan in early 1951. There his mother, mistaking him for a beggar—his body having been so badly damaged by torture, he has become an entirely other person—initially tries to chase him off. Chang's narrative destiny thus imparts the brutal efficacy of war in forcing the body to manifest its ideological fictions.

And yet, the moment of nonrecognition between Chang and his mother unexpectedly brings him tremendous relief, for "in his mother's failure to recognize him, his duty to his family was done; and the suspicion that this could not be his life, that this war would never define him—finally proved to be right. . . . He was already gone, at that moment. He was already free" (325). Ironically, the severance of the familial bond that is a form of final abandonment is experienced as a complete freedom that the war provides him. If the "war would never define him," it is because the war has destroyed the social world(s) that had anchored Chang's being in the first place, generating a kind of social death. And while the state might attempt to substitute the certitude of "national security" for this lost sociality, the novel discloses this as a baldly empty, if performatively potent, claim, not least because "the other country" is (or might be) inhabited by the beloved Other—other Koreans, generally, but in Chang's case Kim. To be absolutely clear, then, the point is not that war and torture prove liberating in a conventional sense, but that the failure of the state to return Chang *as a familiar* to the national family in whose name it performs its violence gives the lie to the ideological fiction that the state promotes.

While the security state, such as the one the United States installed in South Korea, maintains that external threat is forever present—and that security practices can identify with certainty what constitutes such a threat—it in fact depends upon a radical uncertainty for its own condition of possibility. As David Campbell observes, "The inability of the state project of security to succeed is the guarantor of the state's continued success as an impelling identity."[53] Because the state has "no ontological status apart from the various acts which constitute its reality," the appearance of a "primary and stable identity" is effected only by way of "a regulated process of repetition."[54] As a translator for the United States Information Service, even before his encounters with world-shattering pain, Chang thinks of himself as a "third thing" that is "translation's unnatural byproduct" and has "no real place in South Korea," thereby illuminating the state's inability to suture totally the boundaries between material reality and the fictional/ideological working over of the body (84). Even the new orders that war and torture fashion remain inadequate and fragmentary, never establishing absolute security. Thus, when Choi describes Chang as "already gone," well before he actually departs for the United States, it is because in the swiftly changing geopolitical situation of the Korean nation, a more regulated process of performative repetition gives way to the rapid execution of political violence that destroys the unity between himself, his family, and the nation.[55] And yet, while this violence offers almost nothing in place of the lifeworlds it shatters, it also concomitantly writes Chang into radically new and incomplete relations with those others (in the United States) who will come to define him in the future.

The return of the newly recovered, but always vulnerable, body thus simultaneously conjures the loss of family and national unity and their fictions of domestic security as the abject freedom of the borderline subject. In *The Foreign Student,* such a borderline subjectivity contests the fictions of state sovereignty in two historically significant ways. Besides, as I note above, keeping alive utopian aspirations for a Korean national unity that obviates the political border between the North and South, Chang's abjection in Korea and his subsequent *projection into* the United States also forge an Asian/American relationality that brings this "foreign" vision to bear on scenes of *American* domestic security. Chang's presence then remains to haunt the "translation" of the Korean civil war into U.S. Cold War interests, just as nightmares of being tortured by his own government plague his "recovered" presence in Sewanee. It is here, then, that we also find the interpretive switch-point by which to read Choi's fictional portrait of Chang against the historical case of the Emmett Till murder. After all, it is precisely because Till was made unrecognizable to his mother as her son and as a citizen that Mamie Till Bradley chose to display his brutalized body to the nation.

Although my point here is not to provide a full exposition of the events or significance of this case in American history, it is useful to recall that Till—visiting relatives in Mississippi from Chicago when he was killed, presumably in retaliation for flirtatious overtures toward a white woman—was himself a stranger to the social codes and protocols of Jim Crow society, and his transgression of them led to the torturous violence of lynching by which white supremacist ideology was incarnated in the American South. We might say then that Chang's recovered presence in the American South is haunted not only by the body lost in the torture he underwent in Korea, but by Till's destroyed historical body as well.[56] Chang's white housemate Crane certainly drives this point home when, as he invites Chang to visit his family for Thanksgiving in Atlanta, he muses about the racial reception the foreign student will receive there: "They don't hang Orientals. . . . There aren't any down there to hang. I don't think they'd know one if they saw him. I wonder if they would hang him. They might mistake him for a nigger and hang him, or have the sense to see he's not a nigger and *not* hang him just because of that" (50–51).

We ought not, of course, conflate Chang's character with Till; rather, we should see in the evocation of that history a parable for reading the right to security of person against and across national borders. To return to Scarry's analysis of war and torture one final time, we should consider carefully her use of "civilization" to describe the social and material edifices of domestic safety that war and torture interrupt. In rendering war and torture exceptional to the "civilized" life of the nation, Scarry misses the way in which the state *fundamentally* depends upon the threat of an enemy—one always conceptualized as foreign, even if it exists internally to the nation—for its own political ontology. Sovereign power hordes for itself, at every turn, the ability to designate "states of exception," as it identifies the exceptional others who pose extraordinary threats to the life of the nation. Moreover, the lexicon of civilization also participates in the erasure of the inherently gendered, sexual, and racial character of the state's disciplinary power, which distinguishes war from peace, and torture from war. Construing normal life as peaceful and civilized implicitly endorses an imperial moral geography that prizes such life against the images of barbaric others, those "savages" who inhabit the chaotic "state of nature" and always threaten the health and safety of the nation. Liberal political philosophy incorporates such images of savage violence and otherness, figured as "the criminal, the subversive, the Indian and the minority," directly into "the very basis of modern political life."[57] But in Till's case (as with thousands of other lynchings in the United States), such "savage" violence was turned against the black body precisely to *maintain* the civilities of domestic social order. The specter of Emmett Till consequently stands as a counterpoint to the hospitable reception that Chang receives within an American imaginary of integration—a reading that the right to personal security incites. As such, the novel underscores, as I discuss next, the specifically racial and sexual limits of such hospitality, limits that Chang will proceed to violate.

Compromising Liaisons

The rhetorical question Chang asks himself about his body in pain, "How could he be close to someone, when he was two people?" actually comes to merge his and Katherine's seemingly disparate *bildungs* and constitute the Asian/American liaisons of the novel. As I have noted above, Chang's postwar recuperation does not involve a return and laying claim to the grounds that he once roamed in the North. Rather, it transports him to Sewanee and into a relation with Katherine's character. The latter's own story of a tumultuous relationship with Addison, culminating with her return as a young woman to Sewanee, where she resumes an affair with him, intertwines with that of Chang's time in Korea before and during the war. The novel recounts Katherine's sense of ambivalence as she escapes the confines of gendered domesticity and offers an important counterpoint in the novel for understanding what a discourse of domestic security and freedom entails and what it costs those who are subject to it. Katherine lives a modern version of a distinctly Hester Prynne–like existence, freed of the constraints of marriage and social propriety because she has been marginalized by the town for her sexual transgressions. But as the flashback narration recalls, Katherine's autonomy—what looks to Chang to be a "particularly American" freedom, in which "Obligation or dependence would never have entered her realm"—results from a moment when "consent" has been rendered thoroughly indeterminate (17). Given that she is only fourteen when the relationship with Addison begins, Katherine's sexual freedom proves not an effect of an already constituted liberal feminist will but as a disconcerting encounter with an unruly desire that forms her very being.

For example, as a girl, Katherine experiences her desire for Addison as an alienating dissonance from her own body, as she stares into the bathroom mirror: "Glaring into her own eyes, she felt a terrible pang of self-consciousness suddenly, of being 'Katherine,' and the more acute the awareness grew, the more distant and estranged she felt from it. She couldn't feel like herself" (113). And later, at the dinner table, "The unmoored feeling that had struck her in the washroom emerged again, unbidden. She desperately willed it away. Beginning to wonder what it meant that she was behind her eyes, within her skin, feeling the fall of her hair on her cheek, seemed like an irreversible disaster" (115). Undone by the desire that Addison's presence instigates, Katherine experiences her own being as a haunted existence, thwarting her many attempts to present herself as a "sober, self-possessed woman" (118). Disputing a liberal account of the subject's identity and (sexual) freedom, desire, in this depiction of Katherine, moves between and inscribes bodies as subjects and objects in relation to one another; Katherine's will is formed and "deformed" in her subjection to the radical alterity of desire.

At the end of the summer, the sexual relationship necessarily finishes as Katherine's family returns to New Orleans and Addison's interest in her wanes. When her mother, Glee, discovers Katherine's secret, she effectively disowns her daughter (although without disclosing it to Katherine's father). Katherine "live[s] out the rest of that year in her parents' home like a barely tolerated guest," before being shipped off to summer camp the following year, and she passes the rest of her adolescence in a state of isolated loneliness, dropping out of college, eventually moving back to Sewanee to live permanently in her family's boarded-up summer home and restarting the relationship with the older man (128). Having prevailed upon Addison to propose to her, she nevertheless equivocates as to whether she will marry him and what to do with the house if she does. Katherine views the family house, which provides her financial security, with mixed feelings and as a "trashy legacy," with the detritus that has accumulated in it being "evidence of nothing consistent apart from her own inattention" (209). She wants to dispose of it and, simultaneously, to shelter it as the "private hoard she felt she couldn't do without" (208). From this indeterminate social location, Katherine is called upon to serve her community by chauffeuring students and running errands, but is also continually under implicit rebuke for being available to do so.[58] Katherine accordingly wonders whether she should take as models the town's housekeepers and housemothers, women at the margins of other people's lives with "providential and caretaking habits . . . women suited most of all to be needed, who had been somehow left alone" (159). But her own restlessness prevents her from assuming the domestic ethos of the housekeeper who serves as a proxy mother and wife to other women's husbands and sons.

Katherine's autonomy thus arises from a scene of compromised desire, and she lives in it with the ambivalence that distinguishes this abject freedom. Even Addison admits to himself that although he does love her "in his way," he had "begun their affair a finished person, fully formed," so he is doubtful that "she could ever become crucial to him, or decisive, as he had been to her" (136): "Once she really was a grown woman she would feel him in her own arrogant gait and in the dismissiveness of her speech and wonder . . . that everyone else didn't see it as well, blazing on her like a rash. She always felt indebted to him, although she knew he'd exacted a price. He had worn her down, and what remained had grown hard" (136). Disorderly desire impresses itself and actually molds Katherine's *body,* which is described as "minimal," "as if any flesh beyond the requisite betrayed indulgence. She was still thin and small breasted. Her bones seemed too evident, as if to provoke the thought of breaking them, so that the thought would be admitted impossible. She was uninjurable" (136–37). Katherine has been made into a self-possessed individual, paradoxically, by the man who "had carved her out," so that, whereas with other women he observes "a slight, maddening space between his body and theirs," he feels himself to be in "a precise unalterable fit" with Katherine (207).

Crane bluntly derides Katherine: "She's Addison's whore. Everybody knows that," revealing how everyone in Sewanee *does* see the compromising signs of her liaison "blazing on her like a rash," even as they refuse to acknowledge the contradictory terms by which she is held responsible for her transgressions (221). Katherine's *bildung* indicates that the fiction of her "particularly American freedom" requires forgetting the compromised and dispossessing context in which it is brought into being. In the end, as one of the town's housekeepers, Mrs. Reston (with whom both protagonists are friendly), tells Chang: "It's a long time ago now. . . . It's easy to pretend things went differently. [Addison is] an important man here and she's a grown woman. It's nobody's business. She loves him. . . . But she was just a child when he started with her. And he ruined her" (162). As with Chang, Katherine's freedom is functionally identical to her abjection, as her autonomy arises from a scene of devastation.

If both Katherine and, eventually, Chang are characterized by their freedom, the novel marks such freedom as the ruin of those relations of family and community by which the subject recognizes him- or herself. To be sure, the novel does not propose these two *bildungs* as commensurable. After all, in contrast to Chang, Katherine comes through her experience retaining her bodily integrity, as well as the formal privileges that her whiteness and native-born citizenship aver.[59] Nevertheless, the construction of the two protagonists' abject freedom puts them into a relation critical of the liberal freedoms that U.S. citizenship prizes. Freed from social obligation, neither character stands as a deracinated, abstract subject of liberal modernity. Rather, because they are borderline subjects unable to peacefully inhabit their homes, their autonomy makes visible the deeply gendered and racialized modes by which national belonging, domestic safety, and political freedoms are secured.

And yet Katherine's restless uncertainty leaves her open to the changes that Chang ushers into her world. What no one suspects is how "there could be yawning spaces opened in her by the very completeness of [the] fit [between herself and Addison], that the completeness in itself created space, like a miracle, created something by force of its power of exhaustion, and that it was in that space that she was marking out her distance from [Addison]" (207). While everyone in Sewanee (including Addison himself) views her as an object fully formed by Addison's designs on her, Katherine here is the subject of a much more wayward and turbulent desire. This desire moves her as a subject in her own right. In referring to the "yawning spaces" that such desire opens, Choi further characterizes how, at the heart of that which one considers most private and most singular—Katherine as a self—we find the presence of the Other's desire, who undoes the border between public and private, exterior and interior. The opening portrayed here signals the impossibility of sealing the subject off, whether by way of domestic ideologies of racial and gender hierarchy or of liberal autonomy, from the presence of that otherness. Because such desire is unknowable and unpredictable, the novel can mark its taking place only as a "miraculous" occurrence, arriving as if from nowhere. And yet, as a subject of such desire, Katherine can offer recognition to the otherwise impossible, borderline subject of Asian/American history that emerges from Chang's narrative.

Borderline Subjects

The moment of Chang's abandonment/freedom that closes the novel inaugurates radically new affiliations with those others who will define him. Originating in the destructive political violence he has undergone, this radical freedom stands in critical difference to any redemptive story of U.S. intervention in Korea and Chang's integration in the American South. Instead, the narrative of assimilation can be only an epilogue to world-shattering violence that concludes Chang's *bildung* in Korea. Yet, in the complex temporal emplotment of the novel as a romance between

Katherine and Chang, the revelation of Chang's torture appears only near its conclusion, when he has joined Katherine as she cares for her dying mother in New Orleans.[60] Hence, the disclosure of the earlier events serves as a denouement to his winning Katherine over from her engagement to Addison and is inscribed as a transposition of his ravaged body and utopian aspirations:

> He had thought he would always have two things, the great space within him where his [memories of his family's home in the North] had to live, and that diminishment, when his body had imploded. Between the two, the excess of memory and its absence, was left a story he couldn't describe. But the story had begun to circumvent these difficulties. It grew shorter, and simpler. It would close around that event as his memory had closed around the torture and his body around the wound, and constricting, leave no absence behind. (323)

"The story" that sutures the "two things" of Chang's existence—which also resolves *how* he might become intimate with another—refers not to the thematic *content* of political history or personal or familial memory. Rather, it indicates the *form* of relationality by which the fissures within "himself" provide passage to the "yawning spaces opened" in Katherine in the wake of her relationship with Addison (203). With its emphasis on the story as the conduit for this passage, the novel underscores the performativity of an emergent narrative (or minor literature) to morph its subject in its very telling. Because Katherine recognizes in Chang her own "inability to know what she wanted and say what she meant," this recognition places her into a transformative relation with him (216). The novel yokes Asian/American relationality to what Julia Kristeva describes as the "forfeited existence" that abjection purges from the subject.[61]

The narrative's insistence on the body's unexpected endurance and recovery positions Chang's presence in the United States as a remainder of the violence of war and torture in which the nation took part and which it strives to forget. If body, memory, and story close around the wounds of violence, leaving no absence behind in the constitution of a new subject who has survived the loss of self under torture, the novel also constructs Chang's appearance in Sewanee as an index of the absence he leaves behind in Korea and as an artifact of U.S. involvement in its "forgotten" war. His recovery and renewal in the United States signals the extreme violence that has severed him from Korea. But, as crucially, it locates a critical position from which to query the "good life" secured by the exercise of state power.[62]

Initially, Sewanee and the nation receive Chang as an undemanding, undesiring foreign guest whose isolation makes manifest his initial submission to the social and political arrangements he has entered. In this way, sovereign power becomes evident not only in acts of prohibition, but in enactment of conditional *inclusion.* Chang's Thanksgiving visit to Crane's Atlanta home pointedly distills the terms of hospitality and propriety that attend his presence in the South. Despite Crane's ruminations that his fellow Georgians "might . . . hang him" and his father's position as a Grand Dragon of the Ku Klux Klan, Chang actually receives a warm welcome from the senior Crane, who dubs him "an emissary from a distant land" whom he hopes to make "feel welcome" (59). In this characterization, the Cranes readily embody the genteel heritage that racial segregation and white supremacy has always purported to protect.

Chang faces this conditional hospitality most directly at night, in the Cranes' guest room:

> After Crane left him [Chang] sank down on the bed, gazing blankly at the room, and then he got up and began moving through it, with silent caution but voracious, like a thief. He wanted to find something that made an intimate disclosure: a personal object or the trace of a private decision, but the room was for guests, like a room in a hotel. The drawers were empty. There was nothing stored under the bed. He pulled the curtains aside and stared across the lawn at the great dark mass of a neighboring house, its windows gleaming gold through the trees. Everything here was an obstacle, showing him what he wanted by keeping him from it. (62)

Situated early in the novel, this passage articulates desire in the language of property. "Everything here" proves both an obstacle and a spectacle of what Chang "wants," illuminating the distance between Chang's being "here" and the ongoing removal from the objects that constitute that place. In fact, this distance precipitates his knowledge of what those objects are, expressly affiliating the "gleaming gold" of real estate with the properties of whiteness that law and custom have protected. Decorously observing the rules of propriety, Chang makes no claim on either the house or on whiteness. Instead, he allows himself to receive refuge and comfort on the conditions that they are extended.

Likewise, when Chang learns during the university's winter break and after a particularly intimate dinner he shares with Katherine of her relationship with Addison, he finds himself plagued with "a sense of horror so acute that he might have committed a crime," although he is unsure of "precisely what boundary he had overstepped, only that there had been one, and that he'd forgotten himself" (155–56). His growing attraction to Katherine violates the unspoken law of hospitality that Chang has sought to heed in Sewanee, and he begins to try to excise her from his life. He moves to Chicago the following summer in order to avoid Katherine and Addison (now engaged), begins working in a book bindery, and settles into a fledgling, panethnic Asian community, where he "didn't think he wanted anything more" (247). And, despite the harassment of his supervisor, Fran, who accuses him of being a "slanty-eyed son of a bitch," he feels in Chicago as if "the wind had changed direction and sailed him forward" (237, 247). Fran's epithet also marks the first moment in the novel when Chang is explicitly racialized. This *hostility* is actually a counterpart to the "Southern hospitality" that the Sewanee community and the Crane family extend to him, as both forms of social attention originate in the sovereign authority of the nation *to decide between* the inclusion or the exclusion of the foreign student.

In contrast, the relief that the residents of Chicago's Japan-town provide him not only proves more flexible in the recognition it affords him, but also more tenuous in the objects it can offer. Calling upon his "grammatically arcane" childhood Japanese in order to communicate, he moves into a boardinghouse and is adopted there as "Sensei Einstein" and treated "like a shabby aristocrat" (243–44). In Chicago, then, alongside the denigrating racialization that Fran initiates, Chang encounters a nascent panethnic Asian community whose camaraderie is founded as much in the pragmatic machinations of daily life as they are in immigrant idealism:

> If these people knew he was Korean, they didn't seem to care. Arriving Filipinos were eagerly courted by Japanese massage-house proprietors, and Japanese teenagers rode the El to Chinatown to

> work in the restaurants. Old prejudices were irrelevant and unprofitable. Many of the families in the neighborhood who weren't new immigrants had lived in California before being interned during World War II, and their only loyalty now was to the generous Midwest, where it seemed that anyone could do anything. (244–45)

For the first time Chang realizes that "he didn't have to be a student. There were endless other ways to live, endless other lives he could take" (245). Choi sketches, albeit as a transient episode for Chang, the "other history" of Asian American presence, one lived as manual immigrant labor and the slow accumulation of material and cultural capital punctuated by significant, even disastrous, ruptures of racism like the internment, which derail the dream of mobility and assimilation (245). This history accords with the "realities" of collective immigrant existence and is a subject to which the panethnic Asian American movement and Asian American studies have been carefully and necessarily attentive. In Chicago, Chang "discovered the power to make himself, to throw away what he hated and say what he was," an agency founded in the civil rights tradition that mainline Asian Americanist politics and cultural production have heralded (247).[63] *The Foreign Student* thus tracks the particular political promise of "popular sovereignty," the potent appeal of democratic inclusion into a good life that American exceptionalism holds out as uniquely distinctive of the "global nation."

But ultimately, the novel diverges from this promise of gradual and progressive integration to question the limits of any good life founded on the premise of domestic security. Instead, it ponders how the unexpected and unruly desire of the Other, literally incarnated as the desire between Chang and Katherine, generates forms of sociality that are inherently contingent, even perilous, and never fully secure. Thus, when Chang receives a letter from Addison—which, despite its "supremely self-confident tone" seems "to betray" the tenuousness of their engagement—telling Chang that Katherine has returned to New Orleans to tend to her ailing mother, he takes a one-hundred-dollar bill (that Fran planted in a book in order to test him) and departs for Louisiana. In stealing the money from the bindery to finance his trip to New Orleans, Chang jettisons his place in an *Asian American* history for an alternative existence (yet an "other way to live") whose novelty is equal parts imagination and exigency. His departure from Chicago amounts to one of "many solutions" that he pursues "without caring to know how things might have been different" (250). In this moment of willful decision, Chang foregoes his scrupulous adherence to the letter and the spirit of the conventional hospitality he has been afforded. As they observe about themselves to one another after they have sex for the first time, Katherine is a "bad, faithless woman" and Chang "a thief." But these are "names" attributed to them by a social order that cannot afford them recognition as borderline subjects. The novel instead remaps this order according to an emergent transnational cartography of Asian/American relationality brought into existence by the errant desires to which it has granted recognition.

While Chang detects in the self-confident tone of Addison's letter a performative desire to lay what is actually an uncertain claim on Katherine, Katherine similarly finds that a letter from Chang, forwarded to her in New Orleans by Addison, "betrays something": "She recognized that tone. A whole letter had been composed, assembled, and mailed to transmit to her that arctic, careless tone. She sat down in the arbor and smiled. Well, she thought. Well" (272). In this series of letters, then, desire appears as a *tonal* supplement that undermines the carefully composed content of the letters, registering the unruly desire that has moved the novel's subjects across the nation and around the world—Seoul, Cheju, New Orleans, Sewanee, and Chicago. Similarly, submerged in Katherine's and Chang's romance, then, is the homoerotic palimpsest that the consonance and assonance of the various names—Katherine, Kim, Charles, Chuck, Chang—signal. The fluid echoes between the names move along and switch between the axes of racial, class, and national division, as much as gender/sexual difference. The uncertain articulation of who and what each character "wants" propels these subjects across a transnational field of identification, in a movement that unsettles the seemingly fixed properties of gender, race, class, and nation that normatively designate appropriate subjects and objects. Traversing the planet, the novel draws out spaces of ethical encounter that "need to be continually negotiated rather than physically or symbolically secured."[64]

Here then, the human right to security of person not only poses a dialectical critique of state power, but also grapples with the radically undetermined and unknowable future, which always undoes liberal conceptions of emancipation, by challenging the construction of a subject who knows what she wants and says what she means. In *The Foreign Student,* radical uncertainty "is part of a condition that is immanent to being" and cannot be approached "through an externalized moral calculus."[65] The novel instead orients the human subject toward a future where intimate relations and social existence with others take forms not yet imagined in the present, but which are nonetheless built upon past possibilities that remain very much alive. It inscribes this shared recognition most meticulously between Katherine and Chang, but also opens it out onto the historical terrain of racial formation in the United States. The novel ends with Katherine and Chang once again separated, while Katherine patiently nurses her mother as the latter nears death. Chang in turn waits for Katherine in Sewanee, after school officials expel him but offer him a job in the dining hall, among an otherwise entirely African American kitchen staff, to pay off his theft from the bindery.

The novel highlights this chain of waiting and expectation, in which Chang feels his conversations with the "bachelor crew" from the kitchen to be "rare instances of certainty and self-possession," in which "well-worn comments on the beauty of the day" provide "the kind of talk that carried nothing but their feeling for each other, which was reflexive, and affirming. Yes, I'm here, it said. I see it too" (234). The "self-possession" of this scene is instructive. Chang's transgressions evacuate his every claim to conventional hospitality, leaving him bereft of material possessions, and ensconces him in debt, first to the bindery and then, if he reapplies and is readmitted, to the university (since otherwise he has lost his scholarship). The recognition portrayed here, then, takes place not between propertied subjects who have been successfully integrated into the nation. Rather, the "reflexive" and "affirming" feeling links the recognition of desire that Katherine and Chang share—Katherine's recognition of Chang's unutterable desires—to the recognition that the kitchen staff extends to an indebted, extenuated Chang. Choi juxtaposes this scene of recognition with the closing tableau of Chang's return to his family in Pusan and his mother's failure to recognize his broken body. Set against the moment of abjection that "frees" Chang from his duties "at home" in Korea, the scene transfigures human security and emancipation, with freedom no longer a straightforward release from obligation, but rather entry into a responsible sociality toward the other.

African American hospitality concurrently unfolds here as an alternative conception of rights and belonging across a breach that the Cold War will come to install. It is therefore worth recalling one additional significant event in the history of anticolonial and antiracist movements that took place in 1955, the year when Chang is to have arrived in the United States: the Asian-African Conference in Bandung, Indonesia (as discussed in chapter 1). There, representatives from twenty-nine postcolonial nations (and luminaries from the U.S. civil rights movement such as W. E. B. Du Bois) denounced colonialism and racial discrimination and promoted self-determination and development in the global South. Subsequently, the Non-Aligned Movement emphasized the need for the postcolonial and decolonizing societies to remain neutral with respect to the bipolarity of the Cold War. But, notably, both North and South Korea were excluded from the conference's proceedings. Instead, the war in Korea manifested how U.S. foreign policy during the Cold War, beginning with the Truman Doctrine in 1947, gave very little credence to such professions of neutrality, effectively designating decolonizing societies as "with" or "against" the cause of freedom as U.S. officials sought to contain Communism and integrate "free peoples."

As I have already indicated throughout the previous pages and chapters, the Cold War remained a "cold" war, permitting for security and peace on the "home front," only by way of the proxy wars in Asia—first Korea and later Vietnam—and the disciplining of African American social movements and political protest in the United States. The "certainty" of association between the Asian migrant and African Americans therefore rests not upon a shared history or identity. Rather, Chang and his coworkers recognize in one another the subject of desire, of a "want" that exceeds what the nation—organized around the interests of liberal, propertied whiteness—means to or will provide them. It thus moves beyond a realizable utopia and the bounds of literary realism to the fictions of desire as it avows a critical project that "must think and conceive the unthought," and whose "limiting test ought not to be realism but responsibility."[66] The articulation of relationality between the (African) American subjects of rights and the Asian(/American) subject of war and torture in *The Foreign Student,* however, grants a human right to the security of person that neither transcends the historical conditions of Asian American subjectivity nor derides the efficacy of the civil rights movement.

Rather, its suspended conclusion, with all of its characters engaged in acts of peaceful waiting, designates the *many* past openings by which other forms of (human) being might—but do not yet—arrive. The portrait of recognition is one that turns the subject away from the promises of the modern sovereign state and toward the Other, from whose existence one's own being can never and ought not to be secured.

UN Convention on the Elimination of All Forms of Discrimination against Women
Julia Alvarez, *How the García Girls Lost Their Accents* and *In the Time of the Butterflies*

4

Regular Revolutions

The Feminist Travels of Human Rights

> *On my frequent trips back to the Dominican Republic, I sought out whatever information about these brave and beautiful sisters who had done what few men—and only a handful of women—had been willing to do. During that terrifying thirty-one-year regime, any hint of disagreement ultimately resulted in death for the dissenter and often for members of his or her family. Yet the Mirabals had risked their lives. I kept asking myself, what gave them that special courage?*
>
> *It was to understand that question that I began this story. But as happens with any story, the characters took over, beyond polemics and facts. They became real to my imagination. I began to invent them.*
>
> —Julia Alvarez, "Postscript," *In the Time of the Butterflies*

Perhaps no recent human rights instrument has received more media and academic attention, as both an object of celebration and reproach, than the Convention on the Elimination of All Forms of Discrimination against Women (CEDAW). Adopted by the UN General Assembly in 1979 and often considered an international bill of rights for women, the convention defines discrimination against women to be "any distinction, exclusion or restriction made on the basis of sex," which impedes "the recognition, enjoyment or exercise by women" of their human rights and fundamental freedoms. From the establishment of the Commission on the Status of Women (CSW) in 1946, through various UN conferences on women beginning in Mexico City in 1975, CEDAW culminated decades of advocacy and struggle from within and outside the United Nations. CEDAW went into effect in 1981 and has since been ratified by more than

180 nations.[1] In 1995, the Fourth World Conference on Women in Beijing affirmed the principles of CEDAW with the Platform for Action that garnered worldwide attention and called for a broad range of rights for women, including political, education, labor, and property rights.

And yet, notably, the UN Charter and the International Bill of Human Rights had already observed a commitment to the equal rights of men and women. The history of the adoption of CEDAW hence reveals the extent to which the recognition of "women's rights as human rights" was a norm *to be cultivated* rather than one being reflexively affirmed.[2] In other words, since the postwar era, and especially after the Cold War, women have proven an exemplary subset of human rights subjects who, as Jacques Rancière describes it, "have not the rights that they have and have the rights they have not," such that their political recognition actually entails a "process of subjectivization."[3] In asking about what it means for women to be made over into human rights subjects, this chapter takes up several related and intertwined questions at once. How do representations of women's social subjection and political activism travel between First World and Third, and between liberal democracies and postcolonial authoritarian nations, to shape our notions of what it means to "be" both a woman and a human? How do such representations organize diverse feminist imaginaries? And how do the traveling discourses of women's lives consolidate our sense of those very political distinctions in the first place?

The human rights method for reading minor literatures that I elaborate in this chapter is one that thoroughly incorporates a transnational feminist practice of reading and writing "women's rights as human rights," so that we might significantly revise our assumptions regarding both North American liberal or humanitarian feminism and various strands of nationalist politics—such as liberal idealism, realpolitik, socialist utopianism, and cultural nationalism—deployed during the Cold War and its aftermath. In chapter 3, I described the white woman's *liberal* feminist will as situated in (and enabled by) the context of war and torture that "works over" and "integrates" the Asian subject into the American global nation. In contrast, in what follows below, I consider how a feminist ethics can reinscribe our conceptions of women's revolutionary politics and their significance for transnational imaginaries of political community.[4] By granting recognition to Third World and postcolonial women's social and political agency, this transnational feminist imaginary poses a critique of the more limited discourses and politics that often animated advocacy around and aligned with CEDAW, ones that identified (even if only implicitly) such women's primary need to be that of an American "good life," of which they have been left wanting.

Specifically, by considering the feminist figures of reform and revolution in two novels by the Dominican American author Julia Alvarez, *How the García Girls Lost Their Accents* (1991) and *In the Time of the Butterflies* (1994), this chapter asks how we might differently understand the historical conditions that enable, and limit, the (feminist) agency of the minor subject "at home" in the United States, given U.S. hemispheric involvement in what Maria Josefina Saldaña-Portillo describes as "the age of development." Insofar as development discourse proved a unifying regime of truth and subjection in twentieth-century hemispheric politics, I propose that transnational feminist literary practice uncovers the productive fissures, contradictions, and ambiguities of this history. In particular, I examine how the novels critique the political constructions of the Latin American Third World as deprived and depraved. Illuminating the way in which these representations have deeply informed North American cultural discourses of female need and subjection, Alvarez's work also recognizes how significant the collaboration between First World liberal democracies and authoritarian Third World regimes has been for conceiving women's agency in the Americas.

Furthermore, in order to situate women's agency in relation to the geopolitical production of borders, I consider how Alvarez's novels represent what it is that women "want otherwise" about their lives and their struggles with respect to such needs and desires. In these narratives, feminist agency at once remembers and responds to the violence of the past and inhabits a world remade by that violence, thus rendering the "everyday" a significant site for analysis. Evincing from Alvarez's novels a human rights method that conceives of feminist agency as always rooted in the material conditions of history and an original violence in the face of the Other, I argue that this ethics, in turn, demands our recognition of the other ways of being that take form in the lives of "other women," whether they be the white Dominican woman displaced by the assimilating U.S. woman of color, or the white Dominican woman's others displaced by her racial and class privilege, or "other others" whose existence we have yet to fathom.

What becomes clear in the articulation of a human rights method that takes seriously the material and social specificities of women's lives is the extent to which the minor subjects of transnational feminism are embedded within lifeworlds of care, responsibility, and desire, from which they can be severed—in the name of (neo)liberal possessive individualism—only by way of tremendous rupture and violence. This chapter, along with chapter 5 and the conclusion, is thus attentive to the alternative conceptions of good life that emerge from these other lifeworlds, where women's needs, desires, and freedoms are deeply imbricated with the rights of the disabled, the rights of the child, and the rights to family and health, rather than imagined as the isomorphic rights of discretely autonomous subjects. At the same time, each of these chapters suggest that such alternative social and political communities cannot be thought of as existing in a binary opposition to or apart from the structuring processes of global capital. Rather, all arrangements of care, kinship, intimacy, and sociality exist in a supplemental relation to capitalism, dialectically produced or "given up" by the latter but also existing in relations that potentially and performatively contest it.

CEDAW

In the decades-long debates and advocacy that preceded the adoption of CEDAW, feminist legal scholars and activists argued that international law and human rights instruments had, inadvertently or not, adopted a masculine gendered subject as the purportedly universal human rights subject.[5] For example, human rights law addresses itself to the activities of state actors and public officials and effectively excludes domestic violence and other more "private" violations of personal security from its purview. As with hegemonic human rights discourses in general, which garnered particular international currency only after the collapse of the Soviet bloc, international or global feminism was a distinctly post–Cold War phenomenon.[6] Along with the rise of authoritarian postcolonial governments, the treatment of women has, since the 1980s, become an especially spectacular site on which the meaning of "self-determination" has been contested, with political elites and cultural leaders in postcolonial nations justifying the unequal treatment of women through recourse to traditional cultural and religious norms. Mainstream coverage of CEDAW has accordingly represented it as bringing equality and protection to women suffering under the benighted conditions of their "cultures"—women who are living, that is, in a type of cultural captivity. Subsequently, for example, international feminists have called, to great effect in terms of media attention, for humanitarian relief from sexual violence, beginning with the "ethnic" conflicts in Bosnia and Kosovo in the early 1990s. At the 1993 World Conference on Human Rights in Vienna, feminist advocates were able to impress upon political, policy, and other leaders the need for protection of women in war and international conflict, including the recognition of rape as a genocidal war crime.

As such, the international women's rights movement has regularly represented the human rights that Third World women "want" as precisely those political, personal, and civil rights that men (should) enjoy as citizens of liberal democracies. In the past several decades, there has developed a pattern in which local women's organizations produce representations of women's victimization, shaped to elicit concern and sympathy from a "global" audience, which in turn authorizes intervention from elsewhere.[7] In this way, human rights practice becomes rendered (as I have described in previous chapters) as the right to intervention on the part of various state, nongovernmental, and other humanitarian actors to liberate needy women from their oppression. Thus, even while conservative groups in the United States worry about the threat that CEDAW and liberal feminism generally pose for traditional American "family values" and the sovereignty of U.S. constitutional law—and the United States has yet to ratify the convention—a global human rights discourse about women readily reproduces a moral geography that designates entire national societies as "democratic" or as "barbaric."[8]

This is the critique that transnational and postcolonial feminism has repeatedly and extensively lodged against liberal feminism (even while this critique remains invisible in corporate media and commercial culture's cyclically repetitive representations of "shocking" Third World depravity with respect to women's rights). Transnational feminist commentary in the humanities and cultural studies rebukes a purportedly "global" feminism that in fact *globalizes a particular feminist politics,* putting under erasure both local women's activism and considerable historical and structural inequities, as it promotes a Western-centric model of women's rights based on an individualist formulation of liberal subjectivity. Especially where gender inequities and sexual liberties are concerned, transnational feminists make clear how the movement to grant "women's rights as human rights" is largely unable to account for the political struggles and social heterogeneities *within* and across such spaces.[9] In such dehistoricized and abstracted constructions, the "Third World woman" is entrapped within the depravity and deprivation of her national "culture." She therefore stands not as the emergent *subject* of human rights *politics* but as the *object* of *humanitarian rescue,* with First World women (and men) authorized as the true agents of feminist politics and transformation.[10] As Inderpal Grewal surmises, it has been "unfortunate but unavoidable that the 'moral superiority' of American geopolitical discourse should have become part of the new global feminism in the United States . . . constructing 'American' feminists as saviors and rescuers of 'oppressed women' elsewhere within a 'global' economy run by a few powerful states."[11]

In this chapter, however, I am concerned with recalling that it is *not only* such moralizing discourses that travel across borders. Nor does such travel take place only from the First World to the Third (or from the global North to the global South). Rather, I am interested in how the movement of women of color, *into and within* the United States, poses a minor transnationalism that might reorient a human rights approach attendant to "actually existing" women's needs and desires. My approach in this chapter will thus obviously remain critical of hegemonic (neo)liberal perspectives on women's rights as human rights, and I use "transnational feminism" to indicate a perspective that writes back against such global(izing), humanitarian, and/or neo-imperial feminisms. Nonetheless, I also wish to continue elaborating a human rights approach that poses a dialectical critique of such liberal or humanitarian discourses, in order to grant recognition to the political agency that *is* wielded by U.S. women of color and Third World women. Specifically, the human rights literacy called forth by Alvarez's texts recognizes how such women's agency actually makes possible a liberal feminism that nevertheless constantly puts under erasure those very subjects in the construction of the benighted and besieged Third World woman.

A transnational perspective that emerges from the internal or domestic differences of women within the United States—and their contradictory and contested claims as subjects of rights, freedom, and development in relation to "other" women—renders visible, in turn, the history of imperial expansion, military intervention, and geopolitical collaboration between First and Third World states.[12] Much transnational feminist scholarship has been focused on the differential gender impacts of globalization and how the globalization of labor, commodification, marketing, capital and finance circulation, and consumption are gendered practices. Such work informs my analysis here (especially, for example, in my discussion of "free zones" and political and economic liberalization in the Dominican Republic below), but I am especially interested in bridging such concerns in political economy, on the one hand, and, on the other, the questions of political history and political theory that inform our conceptions of political rebellion and social transformation. It certainly remains critically imperative not to overlook the material conditions that circumscribe and obscure the feminist practices of "other women," but it is also as a testament to women's ongoing struggles in the face of such obstacles that I understand Alvarez's work. After all, it is a notable irony that, although CEDAW expressly requires states to change cultural practices that subordinate women, the movement to recognize "women's rights as human rights" also made visible the historical ways in which the *culture of human rights,* even in the global North, had limited ability to address gendered forms of violence as a political question.

By thus inverting the terms of a humanitarian feminism (i.e., one that declares "women's rights as human rights"), I consider how Alvarez's novels pose an ethico-politics of human rights that is at once productive of and grants recognition to women as political subjects. This is not exactly to say that "human rights are women's rights," so much as to grapple with how women, especially Third World women and women of color, as "differentially constructed within formations that are state and nation, geopolitics, economic, sexuality, etc." never stand simply as the victims of benighted or depraved authority, which leaves them deprived of the human rights that others from elsewhere will need to deliver to them.[13] Instead, the various, shifting, multifaceted, and diverse struggles in which women have taken part have shaped the very terms by which we come to understand what being human and human rights might mean.

A Regular Revolution

García Girls is a fictional account (albeit loosely based on Alvarez's own family) of the García family's move from the Dominican Republic to the United States, following Carlos García's involvement with a failed coup attempt against the long-term Dominican dictator, Rafael Leonidas Trujillo. Assisted by the U.S. Central Intelligence Agency (CIA), Carlos escapes Trujillo's national police, the notorious Military Intelligence

Service (SIM), in 1960 and resettles in New York with his wife Laura and four daughters, Carla, Sandra, Yolanda, and Sofía/Fifi. *Butterflies,* by contrast, offers a fictional recounting of the historical Mirabal family, four Dominican sisters, Dedé, Patria, Minerva, and Maria Theresa/Mate, the latter three of whom participated in a revolutionary movement against Trujillo. *Butterflies* describes the politicization of the three sisters, their rise to leadership in the revolutionary June 14th Movement, and their murder by Trujillo's forces on November 25, 1960.

Very little of the criticism available on Alvarez's fiction considers these two novels, which have both been well-received critically and widely taught, in relation to one another. Instead, most critics of *García Girls* approach the novel as a story of immigration and cultural conflict, but bracket the history of authoritarianism against which Carlos and his compatriots rebel.[14] Analyses of *Butterflies,* on the other hand, focus on the novel's central theme of political rebellion, gendered nationalisms, and processes of collective memory, while largely ignoring the broader context of Cold War bipolarism and U.S.–Dominican relations.[15] Here, however, I suggest that, when put into dialogue with one another, Alvarez's novels traverse the disciplinary border between U.S. ethnic literature and postcolonial/ Latin American/Caribbean literature in order to make visible the relationality between women's subjection and feminist agency across the divisions of U.S. First and Third Worlds.

The construction of the United States as a site for refuge from Trujillo's authoritarian regime and the migrant subject's "development" of a liberal feminist perspective entail actively forgetting the history of U.S. (non)intervention in the Americas. In narrating the collective consciousness of two sets of Dominican sisters, Alvarez's novels pose a doppelgänger or spectral relationship between the "deprived" woman under "depraved" Latin American/Third World postcolonial leadership and the freedoms and protections that North American (neo)liberalism purports to make available. This ghostly doubling opens a window onto the twentieth-century *collaboration* between the United States and authoritarian state regimes in the Americas. Whereas a liberal internationalist discourse of rights that circulates in the "united nations world" scrupulously distinguishes between authoritarian repression, socialist revolution, and (neo)liberal reform (as we saw in chapter 1), Alvarez's portraits of women's needs, desires, and everyday life reveal the more muddled history of collaboration that remains behind the image of the United States as a place of refuge from the illiberalism of the Third World.[16]

The title of this section (and this chapter) comes from the curious chapter located structurally midway through *García Girls,* "A Regular Revolution." Narrated in a notable first-person plural ("we"), which approximates the externally focalized perspective of a collective subject, no single sister ever takes up the first person singular ("I"), although each one is nonetheless addressed in the third person singular ("she"). The chapter moves quickly through a summation of the sisters' assimilation, primarily by their attending an elite boarding school, into American social mores and cultural practices. The girls explain the contrast between themselves, and the perceptions of their family's wealth, and those of their white classmates, the heirs of U.S. corporate elites, such as the "Hoover girl and the Hanes twins and the Scott girls and the Reese kid": "Those brand-name beauties simply assumed that, like all third world foreign students in boarding schools, we were filthy rich and related to some dictator or other. Our privilege smacked of evil and mystery whereas theirs came in recognizable panty hose packages and candy wrappers and vacuum cleaner bags and Kleenex boxes."[17] In this portrait, Alvarez pointedly employs what Saldaña-Portillo terms the "idiom of development"—that is, the tropes of "civilization" and civilization's necessary, underdeveloped others—which sustained the structural adjustment policies of the 1950s and 1960s.[18]

As Saldaña-Portillo argues, discourses of "development" prevailed internationally after 1945, seizing the attention of decolonizing elites in Africa and Asia, liberal economists in the United States and revolutionary leaders in the Americas alike.[19] As she further contends, development discourse was remarkably effective in unifying this heterogeneous range of actors around the tenet that the Third World did, in fact, exist in a condition of "underdevelopment."[20] Moreover, as Saldaña-Portillo explains, the object of development became first and foremost, not national economies, but individual subjectivity; that is, development discourse concerned itself with locating the "desired/desiring subject of (under)development" who was ideologically disposed toward "freedom from want."[21] In particular, development discourse assumes that "progress" unfolds according to the history and standards of Western nations, including the desirability of technological mediation, commodity production, and consumer practices for nations in the global South.[22]

In Alvarez's novel, the sisters' adoption of a politics of liberal feminism, portrayed as sexual freedoms, free movement, and public outspokenness, corresponds to their assimilation to consumer culture, which provides the gendered signs of the changes they undergo. Such an idiom of development marks the growing ideological differences between the García girls, on the one hand, and their parents and Dominican relatives, on the other. As the narrators explain, the García girls quickly cultivate "a taste for the American teenage good life, and soon, Island was old hat, man": "We had *more* than adjusted" (108). In this portrayal of "adjusting" and assimilating to American consumer culture—and its self-image of progressive development—the *deprivation* of the island is affiliated with an ideological *depravity* (e.g., the "filthy" "evil and mystery" of "some dictator or other," which, as Americans, the girls seek to transcend).

Their American schoolmates certainly cannot place the name of Rafael Leonidas Trujillo, and, in the United States, the García girls' memory of him only reaffirms the political differences *between* their present home and the Dominican Republic. Indeed, during the era of Trujillo's dictatorial regime, the United States approached the Dominican Republic according to the strictures of the Good Neighbor policy. Building upon the pan-Americanism of the late nineteenth century and implemented by Franklin Roosevelt to secure hemispheric stability, the Good Neighbor policy proclaimed principles of noninterference and mediation between states to solve regional conflicts (an approach very much in alignment with the postwar international order I have described in the introduction). Yet, as Eric Paul Roorda explains, the Good Neighbor policy was steeped in the contradiction "between fraternity with neighboring republics and domination over them": "Its goals . . . [had] always been geared to gain [U.S.] national security and prosperity, by whatever means seem likeliest to work, from persuasion to invasion."[23] The strength of Latin American militaries, combined with nonintervention by the United States, led to the rise of authoritarian regimes in the region, beginning in the 1930s.[24] Although the brutality of governments such as Trujillo's posed public-relations problems that required constant diplomatic attention by the U.S. State Department, the Good Neighbor policy and the desire to protect American interests (private debt held by U.S. investors and national security, to name the two most salient) ensured that the United States did not interfere with the internal governance of the Dominican Republic.[25] The State Department hoped to demonstrate "that the U.S.

government was completely impartial, abstaining from both interference and judgment, neither disapproving nor advocating."[26]

Yet the history of U.S.–Dominican relations is only partly one of non-intervention. That era is bookended by episodes of "gunboat diplomacy" in the early twentieth century—including the military occupation of the Dominican Republic by the U.S. Marine Corps from 1916 to 1924—and the likely role that the CIA played in organizing Trujillo's assassination in 1961.[27] The eight-year military occupation of the Dominican Republic had an enduring effect upon the nation, resulting in an unprecedented national integration of the political system and its military. However, it also resulted in bitter anti-U.S. sentiment and left the Dominican Republic largely bereft of any political infrastructure to sustain a democratic government.[28] The U.S. Marines also founded and ran the Haina Military Academy for the professional training of officers, its most famous alumnus being of course Rafael Trujillo. Most significantly, the United States found it could not overtly act against Trujillo's increasingly authoritarian government after his election in 1930 because of the tremendous hostility that Dominicans felt toward the earlier Marine occupation.[29] Thus, if the Good Neighbor policy implies that the United States begrudgingly extended international respect to the Dominican Republic—begrudging because of the vicious character of the Trujillo government, but respectful of the Dominican people's "self-determination" and sovereignty—this scene took place against the backdrop of earlier U.S. expansionism, where U.S. interests underwrote the Monroe Doctrine's claims to hemispheric solidarity. The effects of those early interventions lasted well into the latter half of the century.

Moreover, Trujillo expertly exploited U.S. anxieties about the Soviet Union's growing international influence during the Cold War, so that by 1948, despite its previous disapproval of the regime, the State Department conferred on Trujillo the status of an ally.[30] The postwar rise of anticommunism in the United States only further consolidated the State Department's alliance with Trujillo's regime, as the bipolarity of the Cold War subsumed and rearticulated all other geopolitical and diplomatic concerns.[31] Poised as "the hemisphere's chief mainstay (self-appointed) against communist aggression," Trujillo was able to purchase from the United States weapons and equipment, used mostly to intimidate and constrain the Dominican populace.[32] Ultimately, U.S. support for Trujillo (and other Latin American dictators like him) was, as Roorda observes, "rooted in the enduring notion that order among nonwhite people can be maintained only by strong discipline."[33] Not until the late 1950s, when Trujillo's grip on power began to plummet and the domestic opposition to his regime grew stronger and more vocal (partly in response to the Mirabal murders, which I address below), did the United States shift its relation to his government.[34] In a hope to avoid a "second Cuba," by taking a role in the transition to a new government (and to distance itself from a dictatorship with which it had allied itself for years, so as to secure its role in the transition), the State Department imposed an arms embargo on the Dominican Republic.[35] It also made clear to Trujillo's opponents that the United States would grant recognition to a new government after a coup d'état, if it consisted of "moderates" rather than radicals or socialists.[36]

Although the geopolitics of this history might seem worlds apart from the daily lives of the Latina women who concern Alvarez, I contend that it is precisely through her attention to women's everyday lives that she establishes a dialectical critique of the collaboration between U.S. (neo)liberalism and Dominican authoritarianism. The "regular revolution" of the *García Girls* chapter title refers to the "constant skirmishes" and then the "open" battle by which the sisters challenge their parents' gendered restrictions on their social behavior throughout their adolescence and young adulthood, culminating in their being shipped off for summers to the Dominican Republic (after Trujillo is overthrown). In the Dominican Republic, the García sisters deride their aunts and cousins for maintaining traditional expectations of women. When their youngest sister, Fifi, becomes involved with a Dominican man whom the other sisters find overbearing, they plot a campaign for "our Fifi's heart and mind," again making use of liberal Cold War rhetoric to ideologically figure the feminist rebellion they undertake (122). Worried that Fifi will engage in sex without contraception, and further, that she might choose to remain on the island rather than return to the United States, they set out to end the relationship. Their cousin Mundín points out to them, with reference to their boasting of their own substantial sexual experience, the irony of this effort: "[Fifi's] got her rights too," he tells them (126). Carla, Yolanda, and Sandi nevertheless assume that because Fifi submits herself to Manuel's sexism, "she's brainwashed" and, as such, is not a capable subject of rights and choice (122).

They employ a metaphor of revolution to describe their plan to save Fifi. However, this trope depends upon a *literal* politics of confrontation, obliquely involving their father, in the urban setting of the island: "We're staging a coup on the same Avenida where a decade ago the dictator was cornered and wounded on his way to a tryst with his mistress. It was a plot our father helped devise but did not carry through, since by then we had fled to the States" (127). Their own plan is a relatively simple one, tactically speaking: when returning from an evening out to the family's compound without Fifi and her *novio,* the sisters reveal that the lovers have been spending time unsupervised, thus putting Fifi's reputation at risk. Their mother, Laura, decides that the four girls must return to the United States: "I'm not going to send them anymore to cause trouble," she tells her sister, which is exactly the result they had hoped for (130). Yet, when their Tía Carmen worries over how much she will miss them, the three sisters feel ambivalent about the success of their plan: "We are free at last, but here, just at the moment the gate swings open, and we can fly the coop, Tía Carmen's love revives our old homesickness" (131). Fifi's anger at them—she bitterly calls them "Traitors," before moving out of their shared room—further heightens this ambivalence (132). The others console themselves: "'She'll get over it.' Meaning Manuel, meaning her fury at us, meaning her fear of her own life. Like ours, it lies ahead of her like a wilderness just before the first explorer sets foot on the virgin sand" (132). The sisters' adoption of this trope of *terra nullius,* "our" lives as "virgin" land yet to be explored and conquered, takes up a colonial construct in service of a liberal imagination that uses and discards the maternal affections and protections extended to them by their aunts and mother. Yet, it is their own selves who are simultaneously rendered as the unsullied object of revolution *and* the knowing agent who will usher in change.

Given the dizzying array of metaphors used in this story—those of discovery and conquest, liberal adjustment, and revolution—and the ambivalent affections and desires these tropes represent, it is extremely difficult to draw out unambiguous lines of agency and subjection. Clearly this is a story about effecting one's will vis-à-vis others, but *who* it is that the chapter privileges as its heroic or enlightened subject remains uncertain. Indeed, who constitutes the *individual* subject of the chapter remains uncertain, since no single "I" ever speaks in her own name. Our attempt to locate a pure agency uncompromised by the sexual and gender hierarchies of "tradition" or, for that matter, class privilege, proves impossible. Instead, the sisters' "revolutionary" plot loops back into and is enabled precisely by the "traditional" social differences that they attempt to transcend. They exploit the same patriarchal attitudes of their Dominican family to "save" Fifi from herself—that is, to produce her as the subject of liberal feminist "choice," despite Fifi's own desires otherwise. But even further, their explication of their plot reveals that members of a parental generation, who are assumed to be held captive to such traditional culture, have themselves been agents in a revolutionary plot that exploited the heteropatriarchal privileges Trujillo abused for his own sexual gains. And, as the later chapter "The Blood of the Conquistadores" portrays, with the girls' mother, Laura, expertly handling the secret police who visit the family's home in search of Carlos, this insurgency directly involves Dominican women as well as men (a point that *Butterflies* in its entirety thematizes).

The girls thus do not destroy this past, nor do they transcend or simply repeat it. Rather, Alvarez portrays a dialectic forged *through* traditional social relations. That their "revolution" depends upon these relations alters the meaning of their freedom—rendering it a betrayal of Fifi and an abandonment of their aunt's love—and they come to doubt their own orientation toward it. In the conventional *bildungsroman*, such moments of emancipation signal the character's coming into "her own" as an American woman. However, in *García Girls,* the stories that precede this one structurally (but succeed it chronologically, due to the novel's regressive chronology) about the adult sisters in the United States revolve around failed marriages, nervous breakdowns, and pervasive self-doubt. The contradiction that inheres in this story's plot—that is, the contradiction that is the plot of a "regular revolution"—thus comes to organize the entire novel, including the story that follows "A Regular Revolution," titled "Daughter of Invention," in which Yolanda's ("Yoyo's") nascent talent as a writer both depends upon but displaces her parents' experience of Dominican postcolonial violence and rebellion to enact her own liberal freedom of expression. Throughout *García Girls,* then, Alvarez insists upon recalling the originary violence that founds American liberal freedoms and refuses any straightforward celebration of the subject of that freedom. This central focus on contradiction and loss hence proves instructive for reading, as I do in the following section, the much-commented upon reverse chronology by which the narrative unfolds, moving from the sisters as adult individuals, embroiled in familial and romantic complications, back to their "origins" in the Dominican Republic.[37]

Breaking Down, Broken Progress

In its drive toward a chronological beginning and a narrative origin, the novel suggests that the loss of the Dominican homeland is not (as the "immigrant narrative reading" would have it) the *cause* of the adult sisters' individual feelings of alienation and estrangement from their parents and from others (with which *García Girls* discursively opens), but rather a *symptom* of a pervasive loss that temporally *precedes* and determines the entire family's displacement to the United States (the chronological beginnings that Alvarez depicts in the last chapters of the book).[38] An early chapter, "The Four Girls," which intertwines memories of "the mother" (as Laura is referred to here) with the daughters' recollections of her, not only directly addresses the developmental narrative as modernity's privileged form of recognition for the human subject, but proposes the dialectical ethics necessary by which to read *García Girls* otherwise.

"The Four Girls" chapter includes a brief anecdote (which has received little notice in the critical commentary on the text) about Sandi's institutionalization in a psychiatric hospital, as she grapples with an eating disorder and exhaustion. Laura explains to a doctor that, while in graduate school, her daughter has rapidly begun losing weight on a "crazy diet" trying to "look like those twiggy models" (54). Sandi also reads voraciously:

> She had lists and lists of books to read. . . . She told why she couldn't stop reading. She didn't have much time left. She had to read all the great works of man because soon—the mother got up her courage to say it—"soon she wouldn't be human." . . . She told us that she was being turned out of the human race. She was becoming a monkey. . . . Already the other organs inside her body were a monkey's. Only her brain was left, and she could feel it going. (54)

In reading "all the great books" (namely, Freud, Darwin, Nietzsche, Erikson, Dante, Homer, Cervantes, and Calderón de la Barca, as the doctor and Carlos list them), Sandi hopes to "remember something important from having been human" and observes to her mother: "Evolution had reached its peak and was going backwards" (54–55).

Although her father describes his daughter as having "a small breakdown" and her mother dismisses these notions as "crazy talk," Sandi's sense of "going backwards" imparts a method for interpreting the entire text's seemingly regressive movement. As Sandi delves into an archive of "great books," she seeks a genealogy of the human in which she might find a reflection of herself, one that will redeem and return her to humanity. This fragmented account of her illness does not provide such a "recovery," but instead ends abruptly with a portrait of her at the hospital, confused and disturbed by the surrounding world. Shifting to a diegetic present, however, in which an older and seemingly healthy Sandi tells her sisters, "I just want to forget the past, you know?" the chapter offers an alternative mode of recognition, one that develops not in a linear and progressive fashion, but by way of the shared memories and affective cues that the women's intimacy with one another constructs (60). Furthermore, in its third section ("1960–1956"), set in the Dominican Republic, *García Girls* locates that intimacy as preceding the family's departure from their home there and involving their extended family, with whom "they lived side by side" (225).

"Reading backwards" in *García Girls* eventually leads us, then, not to an original subject of humanity, but to the embodied conditions of vulnerability and the social contradictions from which agency materializes. In the third section and the final haunting chapter, a young Yolanda steals a newborn kitten from its mother, despite a hunter's warning that to do so would be "a violation of its natural right to live" (285). Riddled with guilt, Yolanda throws the kitten out a window and watches it "make a broken progress across the lawn" back to the coal shed in which she had first come upon it (288). Yolanda finds herself haunted by the mother cat, which (she imagines) sits wailing by her bedside for years afterward. With its wrenching portrait of a "broken progress," this closing chapter decisively refuses a liberal schema that reifies subjects as *either* deprived feminine victims of depraved repression *or* feminist agents of choice and change, the binary that organizes the sisters' lives as adult women in "A Regular Revolution." The final paragraph instead returns to the contradiction of violation that enables the subject:

> Then we moved to the United States. The cat disappeared altogether. I saw snow. I solved the riddle of an outdoors made mostly of concrete in New York. . . . I went away to school. I read books. You understand I am collapsing all time now so that it fits in what's left in the hollow of my story? I began to write. . . . I never

> saw Schwarz [the kitten] again. The man with the goatee [the hunter] and [his dog] Kashtanka vanished from the face of creation. I grew up, a curious woman, a woman of story ghosts and story devils, a woman prone to bad dreams and bad insomnia. There are still times I wake up at three o'clock in the morning and peer into the darkness. At that hour and in that loneliness, I hear her, a black furred thing lurking in the corners of my life, her magenta mouth opening, wailing over some violation that lies at the center of my art. (289–91)

Taken as an allegory for Yolanda's own subsequent displacement from the "motherland," the story of the kitten poses the García girls' migration to the United States as a violation of a "natural right." Yet, in the *literal* story, Yolanda is the agent of violence and, to the extent that it enables her "art," its beneficiary. As in the regular revolution, the literal dimension reinscribes the positions that the allegory seems to assign. Thus, the "stories" that Yolanda constructs as an adult, to fit the "hollow" of the novel, do not offer an ordered account of cause and effect, progress from victimhood to liberation, but rather, return us to the tangle of loss and violation, rebellion and will, that her literary imagination attempts to fill up and to order through narrative.

Moreover, the image of the cat's open mouth that ends the novel recalls for us the opening story of *García Girls,* "Antojos," in which an adult Yolanda returns to the Dominican Republic, hoping that "this turn[s] out to be my home" (11). An American advertisement image on a billboard of a "creamy, blond woman" in a shower, with her "head thrown back in seeming ecstasy, her mouth opened in a wordless cry" closes out this story: "Her head is still thrown back, her mouth still opened as if she is calling someone over a great distance" (23). The woman's open mouth anticipates and calls to the image of the cat, twinning its melancholic "wailing over some violation" and converting the woman's ecstasy into a sign of enduring loss. In her search for fresh guavas, Yolanda seeks to quench her own "antojo," which, as Yolanda's aunt tells her, "is like a craving" and her aunt's maid describes as like being "taken over by *un santo* who wants something" (8). Yolanda cannot, however, find her way to a prelapsarian island home, one that exists before the violence she enacts upon the kitten and before the violence that the state enacts upon her family. As Lucía M. Suárez eloquently argues, the losses that the novel encrypts are not only "the loss of language and the losses necessitated by assimilation" in the United States, but also, "the wound caused by the inherited legacy of the indecipherable horrors of the thirty-one-year Trujillo dictatorship that imposed loss of both memory and geography on many Dominican families."[39]

Instead of a straightforward return home, the story illustrates Yolanda's coming to an uneasy recognition of her contradictory class, national, and gendered status as she travels in the Dominican countryside. Unwilling and unable to identify with her aunts and female cousins and their embrace of "traditional" roles, she "plans to bob up again after the many *don'ts* to do what she wants" (9). Nevertheless, when her borrowed car breaks down as she drives alone searching for guavas and she meets two *campesinos* she perceives to be threatening, Yolanda calls upon her family name and her position as an American to "save" her:

> She has been too frightened to carry out any strategy, but now a road is opening before her. . . . She begins to speak, English, a few words, of apology at first, then a great flood of explanation. . . . The two men stare at her, uncomprehending, rendered docile by her gibberish. Only when she mentions the name Miranda do their eyes light up with respect. She is saved! (21)

From beginning to end, *García Girls* thus figures as ambiguous and contradictory the lines of subordination and agency that define its subjects. This central contradiction brings to bear an ethical truth whereby *any* (liberal, feminist, revolutionary) subject's agency takes place against a scene of original violence and functions to naturalize subaltern others. These others often appear intelligible through grids of racial, national, or class formation. For this reason, the brief narration offered from the point of view of the Haitian Chucha, the Garcías' long-term and loyal servant in the Dominican Republic, after the family has departed for the United States, provides a significant perspective on those "left behind" in the ascendance of (or into) American liberalism. Moving through the house filled with memories of the Garcías, praying to *loas* and *santos,* and ritualistically preparing for her own death, Chucha feels her own heart and blood to be like "something that I have forgotten to turn off in the deserted house" (224).

Emergent only in the margins of the García girls' narrative, Chucha's voice nevertheless spectralizes those others, naturalized and "deserted," whose presence actually and necessarily makes possible the subject's "development." But, just as often, Alvarez represents *other* others by way of an *intra*-subjective violence (such as splitting Yo between the mother cat and her kitten) and demands from us a critical care toward those who have yet to be named, but whose "natural right to live" nonetheless haunts the minor subject of the American good life. This structuring contradiction that interrelates the United States to the Dominican Republic and the First World feminist to Third World women registers, for the transnational feminist reader, the intertwined political histories of the postcolonial Dominican state and American imperialism that so crucially ground liberal metaphors of social change.

The Ghosts of Other Women's Rebellions

The "development" of the four García sisters, who as adults avail themselves as (troubled) subjects of First World liberalism, can serve as a foil for grasping the other four sisters, "the Butterflies," of Alvarez's second novel. The contradictions that structure, and break down, plot and personal development in *García Girls* also afford an opportunity for interpreting Dominican patriarchal "traditions" as discursive *artifacts* that liberalism creates, instead of assuming them to be the preconditions of underdevelopment that the liberal subject transcends. Shadowy doubles to the García girls, the subjects of *Butterflies* offer a type of ghost story to haunt the former, like the "story ghosts and story devils" that trouble Yolanda. As Avery Gordon, citing Walter Benjamin, writes about the "animating" force of materialist historiography, "the oppressed past or the ghostly" provokes "a different kind of encounter and recognition" of that past.[40] *Butterflies*, I contend, reanimates the tropes of revolution and rebellion that otherwise have become sedimented as practically dead metaphors in the liberal common sense of immigrant narratives and feminist individualism. Indeed, in *Butterflies*, Minerva's adult daughter Minou claims to speak to the spirits of the three murdered sisters through the medium of a family servant. And, although the one surviving sister, Dedé, mostly dismisses Minou's contention as superstition, in the novel's closing paragraphs she too admits to hearing the sisters' "soft spirit footsteps" at night as she falls asleep.[41] When Dedé insists, "I'm not stuck in the past, I've just brought it with me into the present," she illumines the dialectical critique that Alvarez's novels impart (313).

As a witness and survivor, Dedé adopts the role of official memory-keeper, maintaining in the family home a museum-shrine to her sisters and serving as a living repository for other Dominicans who wish to share their own memories of the Butterflies. But beyond such official acts of memorialization, which translate individual lives into collective symbols of patriotism and resistance for the nation, Alvarez seeks through Dedé to offer a "different kind of recognition." Crossing the border between the personal/familial and the nation, and between the national domestic space and an international or hemispheric one, Alvarez frames the novel with the character of the *gringa dominicana* journalist to whom Dedé recounts her sisters' stories. Shifting from the third-person narration of the novel's opening to the first-person perspective of the subsequent chapters, in which each of the sisters tells of her own involvement in the June 14th Movement, the novel indicates the need for "a way to enable Dominican history to write itself out of its repressed position in the U.S. historical imaginary without becoming exotically or voyeuristically 'othered.' "[42]

Alvarez imagines each of the Mirabal sisters' involvement in the revolution against Trujillo as materializing from the daily social relations of romance, family, and religion, in which each is embedded. The paths that they follow are quite disparate. Dedé realizes that, despite her own longing for neutrality and security, she ultimately has no "choice" because her fate is entwined with that of her sisters (193). Patria meanwhile understands her involvement as an extension of her religious convictions. Mate follows her girlhood crush (and later husband), Leandro, into the movement. And Minerva approximates most closely a "modern revolutionary consciousness," which Saldaña-Portillo characterizes as having been favored by Latin American socialist movements, embodied in the "risk-taking, resolute, frugal, nonornamental, productive, fully masculine, fully national fellow."[43] Outspoken and unwavering in her commitment to the June 14th Movement that plotted to unseat Trujillo, Minerva occupies the often-idealized role of a female revolutionary. Yet, precisely because Alvarez situates Minerva within the familial relations of sisterhood, never transcending them for a purely masculinist version, I suggest that *Butterflies* posits the subjectivity that she embodies as one among an array of possible positions from which social transformation originates. Thus, even Minerva finds herself at moments exhausted by the demands that her Mariposa image requires, although she tries to bracket those uncertainties as the "woman in her" (267).

In its model of a feminist politics that does not transcend the relations in which women are situated, *Butterflies* simultaneously depicts how such transformation occurs through subjects' difficult but sustained inhabiting of spaces of vulnerability, upheaval, and damage. Feminist anthropologist Veena Das describes such social transformations as women's "descent into the ordinary," which works to repair the past not with "any momentary heroic gesture but [with] the patient work of living with . . . new knowledge."[44] As Das writes, paradigms that dichotomize resistance and submission—and that privilege tropes of "imprisonment" and liberation—are simply too "crude" to discern how "originary moments of violence are lived through" everyday life.[45] Normative cultural paradigms of "female need" can certainly constrain and deflect women from a range of possible social and political subject positions. Yet, she argues: "If the social context alters suddenly, the woman herself or others in her social world might evoke a different definition of female 'need.' Thus, individual lives are defined by context, but they are also generative of new contexts. . . . It is not that older subject positions [are] simply left behind or abandoned—rather, there [are] new ways in which even signs of injury [can] be occupied."[46]

The process of incorporating what Das calls the "poisonous knowledge" of violence and loss into everyday life is supple and long-term. For this reason, it can, from the perspective of a model that dichotomizes power and resistance, merely disappear from sight altogether, appearing as a "return" to previous and repressive conditions. But recognizing the descent into the ordinary as a form of agency allows us to attend differently to the Mirabal sisters' involvement in the insurgency, their return to their families after their arrest and imprisonment, and their subsequent murders. For example, Mate's diary records the experience of her own and Minerva's imprisonment by the SIM in La 40, a detention center. In this secret journal, Mate records her experience of bodily trauma at the hands of the military police. When Mate suspects that she might be pregnant and considers an abortion, so as to prevent a baby being taken from her and given "to some childless general's wife," the novel evokes the question of reproductive rights, so central to a North American liberal feminism, but with the crucial difference that the context of state terror makes for the female revolutionary (240).[47] This entry is followed by one that reads: "Still very weak, but the bleeding has stopped. / I can't bear to tell the story yet. Just this—I've either bled a baby or had a period. And no one had to do a thing about it after the SIM got to me" (240). In chapter 2, I described the "unborn" as figuring the Other to whom the human rights subject becomes obligated upon her arrival as a real personhood "come wholly into being." In *Butterflies*, however, Mate cannot determine whether she has undergone a true loss, as she remains uncertain about whether the infliction of torture (described below) has led to a miscarriage or whether she is "naturally" menstruating, and in any case, she is "no one" who had a choice in the matter. This ambiguity therefore redoubles the woman's uncertain standing as a subject of rights, "caught" as she is between traditional ("natural") family and the security regime of the authoritarian state, as I continue on to explain here.

In the subsequent pages of the diary, the introduction, "Here is my story of what happened in La 40 on Monday, April 11th," is immediately followed by a note: "pages torn out" (242). As I also discuss below, the novel does however return (to) these pages, at the end of the chapter, which have been secretly submitted to a representative from the Organization of American States (OAS) who investigates the conditions in which political prisoners are being held (254). When Minerva earlier urges Mate to share with the OAS representative "about what happened at La 40," and Mate equivocates, Minerva, "all fierce," responds: "You have nothing to be ashamed of!" (243).[48] Mate also notes in this entry that Minerva has begun to collect an "arsenal" of contraband (a knife, sewing scissors, scalpels, and so on), and the younger sister observes: "Sometimes I think revolution has become something like a habit for Minerva" (243). Here Alvarez casts Minerva's revolutionary stance from Mate's perspective as a "habit," echoing the "regular revolution" of *García Girls* and again posing a materialist critique of an idealized notion of rebellion. *Butterflies* interrogates the construction of such revolutionary subjectivity by placing it in relation to the various feminine others against whom it is authorized: the "other" Mirabal sisters (i.e., the daughters of their father's mistress), the "non-politicals" held in the same prison cell, *campesinos,* and Haitian servants.

But even further, in what is perhaps the most difficult but most ethically significant account that the novel extends (and which recalls the kitten's "broken progress" in *García Girls*), *Butterflies* suggests that the production of the privileged subject-in-resistance *requires* a scene of violation such as the one that Mate undergoes. Mate's experience of extraordinary pain and suffering therefore consolidates Minerva's fierce defiance. In the restored account of her detention at La 40, Mate describes first how the

SIM officers force her to witness the beating that they give Leandro and then the electric shocks they administer to her in order to "persuade" Leandro, successfully as it turns out, to supply them with information on the resistance movement (255). Notably, the names of all the insurgents, including Leandro's, are blacked out in this account when she passes it to the OAS investigator; as Mate explains, "I am afraid of getting innocent people in trouble" (254). However, if, as Elaine Scarry has argued (and I have elaborated at length in chapter 3), pain evacuates the subject's grasp of a meaningful reality, effectively destroying that existence, this scene also intimates that it is not only the state regime that seizes upon the vacuum that extreme pain generates.[49] Rather, the moral authority of the *revolutionary* subject is also forged through the foundering of the tortured subject, as the blacking out of names might also suggest the absence of the revolutionary subject prior to the scene of torture. Alvarez thus proposes that the subject of resistance cannot occupy the position of the body in pain, but is instead founded on the undoing of the latter.

At the same time, when Leandro cries "I'll do it, I'll do it!" (i.e., provide intelligence about his comrades) and calls to Mate, "Tell them I had to do it," the scene suggests that the intimate ties of the marital relation overdetermine *his* "betrayal" of the revolution; watching his wife being tortured *is like being tortured himself* (256). Indeed, later, *Butterflies'* depiction of (the memory of) the sisters' husbands as they receive the news of their wives' deaths draws out the SIM's further use of such a mode of "persuasion":

> Manolo tells how that Thursday they were taken out of their cell and marched down the hall. For a brief moment they were hopeful that the girls were all right after all. But instead of the visitors' room, they were led downstairs to the officers' lounge. Johnny Abbes and Cándido Torres and other top SIM cronies were waiting, already quite drunk. This was going to be a special treat, by invitation only, a torture session of an unusual nature, giving the men the news. (309)

What might this use and abuse of women's bodies signify about their humanity in regard to political violence? As I have already suggested, for Minerva the revolutionary project provides "a new way for men and women to be together that did not necessarily have to do with romance" (76). Nevertheless, the persistence of more "traditional" relations becomes manifest in the "special treat" and "unusual nature" of this torture (76). The particularly "inventive" forms of torture to which women's bodies are subject therefore reflect a dual structure, signifying the spectacle of women's pain and suffering not only as a physical wounding of the woman herself, but as a means by which to "get at" her kinsmen.

If, as we have seen in chapter 3, the tortured body reveals the way in which the state creates (and "decreates") the "natural body" that is posited as its fundamental unit of life, here we find the woman's tortured body as suspended between the modern nation-state and those "natural" communities—that is, patriarchal families—that the modern state and modern revolutionary movements purport to transcend and replace, even as they depend upon the family as the locus of biological and social reproduction. It is precisely along this distinction that, under the auspices of the Convention against Torture, the Committee against Torture has in some instances acknowledged and condemned violence against women as a means for obtaining information or punishment of male relatives, but does not recognize "everyday" domestic and sexual violence against women as *in itself* cruel and degrading and thus a form of torture.[50]

Torturous political violence makes over the tortured person into a feminized other, even as it depends upon gendered difference to render the torture of women an especially potent technique for substantiating the regime's own truth—the "truth" of the total and ideal authority of the agent who has effected the body in pain—against men considered enemies of the state. In the context of modern state terror, then, kinship is disarticulated and reassembled as affiliative forms by which men can be newly devastated. Certainly, insofar as the women "belong" to their families as much as they do to the revolution, the state wields the news of their death as especially potent weapons against its (male) subjects, but that familial relationship itself has been remade in the political context of revolution. In their "attachment" to their wives, the men become themselves the vulnerable humans that state officials work over in order to substantiate the state's own truth. But the sisters are never only dupes or shills in their husbands' revolutionary activities; their participation in the insurgency as wives and sisters emerges from and transforms their complex personhood.[51]

Alvarez's novels thus stage the substantiation of power through such original violence and questions the justness of *any* power materialized in this experience. Obviously, this includes an overt critique of Trujillo's regime, but that regime exists in a relation of traumatic rupture from the lifeworlds of Dominican families, even while dictators like Trujillo regularly claim themselves to be "fathers" of the nation. More subtly, the critique also takes aim, as I hope to have shown, at the heroic revolutionary stance that Minerva endorses at the expense of "other women" and the "woman in herself." And, perhaps even more elusively (in that we must return to *García Girls* to recall it), it queries a self-congratulatory American liberalism that deplores the "filth," "evil," and "mystery" of "some dictator or other," as well as a humanitarian liberal feminism that constructs the woman's body subject to violence as both its necessary other and a victim in need of salvation. A global economy of punishment and discipline inextricably intertwines First World disavowals of torture as barbaric with Third World practices of such violence.[52] The spectacles of torture and political repression "comfort American liberals who rest contented in their view . . . that barbarism resides elsewhere, in the other, that other world, unenlightened, steeped in medievalism and bloody cruelty" and that the United States instead offers a space of refuge and healing.[53] In this multilayered and multipolar distribution of violence, truth, and power, a global spectacle of torture can secure, at once, the revolutionary's idealized self-image of resistance, the authoritarian regime's dominion over its citizenry, *and* the First World's sense of political security and moral superiority.

As Alvarez notes in her postscript to *Butterflies* (from which I also cite in the epigraph for this chapter), "November 25th, the day of their murder, is observed in many Latin American countries as the International Day Against Violence Towards Women" (324). We see in this memorializing move women's political agency expressly remade into an occasion of women's victimhood; the sisters' active involvement in the revolution becomes reimagined (only) as their vulnerability to gendered forms of violence (which, in turn, serves as a liberal feminist call to action). Such liberal representations make over women's activism *as* their subjection to patriarchal and authoritarian depravity; their otherness proves an artifact of North American liberalism rather than an "authentic" cultural difference. As such, human rights become something *delivered to,* rather than *forged by,* women in the global South.

Alvarez, in contrast, teases out the way in which feminist agency always emerges from and is folded back into the material, corporeal, and affective conditions that constitute femininity in the first place. Rather than abandoning feminist agency in nationalist politics, I suggest that *Butterflies* casts such agency as radical, but also, as Saldaña-Portillo describes it, as "radically conditioned," emerging from the contradictory conditions of women's lives. Without understanding women's lives as thusly situated in the historical conditions of their subjective possibility, we too easily dismiss Alvarez's novel, as critic Lynn Chun Ink does, as "reinstating gendered national dichotomies" simply because "the Mirabals return to their roles as wives, mothers, and homemakers upon their release from prison."[54] For Ink, the Mirabal sisters "become" subjects of patriarchy rather than "agents of nationalism," presumably because of Alvarez's limited feminist imagination rather than the actual limits of the history they inhabit.[55]

I contend that we might instead understand the Mirabal sisters' "return" to their gendered roles and their subsequent murders otherwise, by recognizing the work that comprises, in Das's terms, the descent into the ordinary as a form of agency. For example, placed under house arrest, Minerva considers herself to be at once both "falling apart" and beginning "a new life" with her sisters, their children, and her mother (258). Unexpectedly undone by her time in prison, Minerva "returns" to a domestic space, but the context and meaning of home has been absolutely altered by her and Mate's knowledge of violence and suffering acquired in prison, not least because their husbands remain incarcerated and the women are placed under house *arrest*. Likewise, the sisters' murders occur as they travel to visit their imprisoned husbands, hoping to keep up the men's spirits but also to relay information surreptitiously about the resistance movement. It is precisely their participation in the everyday roles of wives and mothers that reanimates their active roles in the underground resistance, and vice versa. The descent into the ordinary defines their conditioned agency, as well as the ambivalence with which Dedé remembers their loss.

The novel both opens and closes with Dedé's memory "racing backwards . . . to the moment she has fixed in her memory as zero": "And I see them all there in my memory, as still as statues . . . and I'm thinking something is missing now. And I count them all twice before I realize—it's me, Dedé, it's me, the one who survived to tell the story" (7, 321). Dedé's absence in this recovered past simultaneously indicates her survival into the post-Trujillo era, when she will then be haunted by her other sisters. Their absence impels her to afford them a different type of recognition. As a witness to the violent past and subject to ghosts, Dedé—who otherwise refuses an active role in the revolution—mediates for her audience (notably, the *gringa dominicana*) the knowledge of state violence and women's rebellion in the Dominican Republic. *Butterflies* thus asks us to reconsider the everyday "grounds" of revolution that liberal feminism takes up as metaphor but also screens out in its appropriation.

Free Zones

With its carefully constructed model of political subjectivity, *Butterflies* refutes the representations of Third World deprivation on which North American rhetoric and policies of assimilation, development, and (non) intervention are grounded. At the novel's end, set in 1994, Dedé is reunited, at a reception in honor of the martyred sisters, with an elderly Lío, who had served in the late 1940s as Minerva's conduit into the underground movement. When Lío reassures Dedé that the sisters' deaths contributed to the nation's eventual freedom, she reflects: "He means the free elections, bad presidents now put in power properly, not by army tanks. He means our country beginning to prosper, Free Zones going up everywhere, the coast a clutter of clubs and resorts. We are now the playground of the Caribbean, who were once its killing fields" (318). Moreover, as she scans the room, she notices the other guests: "The boy-businessmen with computerized watches and walkie-talkies in their wives' purses to summon the chauffeur from the car; their glamorous young wives with degrees they do not need; the scent of perfume; the tinkle of keys to the things they own" and later, on the drive home, "the only lights are up in the mountains where the prosperous young are building their getaway houses" (318). Dedé surmises: "Lío is right. The nightmare is over; we are free at last. But the thing that is making me tremble, that I do not want to say out loud—and I'll say it once only and it's done. Was it for this, the sacrifice of the butterflies?" (318).

In "A Regular Revolution," the oblique emphasis on the "goods" of development implies that the García girls' "liberation" is as much about being emancipated into consumer citizenship and neoliberal exchange as it is about sexual freedom and physical mobility. As Grewal has explained, in such an affiliation between consumer culture, market exchange, and rights discourses, political liberalism becomes conjoined with economic neoliberalism such that, internationally, an "American way of life" designates both, "a symbol of 'freedom' and democratic rights" *and* an "imperial power that use[s] disciplinary as well as governmental technologies within transnational consumer culture."[56] With respect to female subjects and femininity specifically, "technologies of feminist empowerment and pleasure that were promoted by late-capitalist consumer culture became yoked to the promise of new discourses of modern female and feminist subjectivity and citizenship and the removal of violence and poverty for female populations in what were called 'developing countries.' "[57] When construed through Dedé's "trembling" reflection on the post-Trujillo Dominican Republic as a chain of "Free Zones," Alvarez explicitly questions the value of such "American goods" for Dominican women. *Butterflies* instead directs us to consider the subject of tyranny and of "development," in the Dominican Republic and in the United States, in the context of a hemispheric history that has been overdetermined by U.S. interests and policy.

Above all, Dedé's reference to "Free Zones going up everywhere" refers to the (neo)liberalization of political and economic institutions in the Dominican nation after Trujillo's assassination, even as it remained, until 1986, under quasi-dictatorial governments. With respect to the Dominican economy, this has been carried out in particular through the operations of Industrial Free Zones (IFZs), where tax and other economic incentives attracted investment by private foreign capital, and through the country's submission to agreements in the 1980s and early 1990s with the International Monetary Fund (IMF), which stipulated austerity measures in exchange for IMF loans.[58] By 1988, there were seventeen IFZs, made up of 220 companies (most of them from the United States) in the Dominican Republic, and by 1990, 10 percent of the Dominican population had migrated to the United States.[59] These transnational linkages and the affiliated discourses of "freedom"—free elections, social freedoms, free markets—have thus come to obscure the former imperial subjection of the Dominican Republic to U.S. interests, a history that bounded the Dominican nation to the United States for decades.

U.S. political and economic interests instituted the cultural marker of "deprivation/depravity" that has characterized a Latin American Third World, and this perception of the region served in turn to justify the nation's political, economic, and military (non)interventions there. In its telling of the Mirabal sisters' political activities, *Butterflies* archives the experience of state terror under Trujillo's regime as one of the effects of

U.S. imperial history. But, further, Alvarez spectralizes the *form* of the four Mirabal sisters in the United States as doppelgängers to the four García sisters. In the migration of Dominican women, "deprivation/depravity" takes on a *racial* form, underwriting the hostility that the García girls (who, like the Mirabals, enjoyed racial privilege in the Dominican Republic over resident Haitians and dark-skinned Dominicans) encounter upon arriving in the United States. Alvarez most notably depicts this racialization in the story "Trespass," where she portrays young Carla's run-in with a sexual predator as embedded in and of a piece with more quotidian instances of racism: "Every day on the playground and in the halls of her new school, a gang of boys chased after her, calling her names, some of which she had heard before from the old lady neighbor . . . 'Go back to where you came from, you dirty spic!'" (153). Coupling the sexual "trespass" of the older man with the racist abuse that the white boys dole out, Carla's story imbues the earlier stories in the novel, of the adult sisters' romantic and sexual predicaments later in life. Carla's account of racialization thus recasts stories such as "Joe" and "The Rudy Elmenhurst Story" (both of which involve Yolanda's vexed relationships with white men); the failure of sexual and emotional intimacy that at first seems rooted in incompatible "cultural" differences—such as differing languages or sexual mores—expands to encompass the asymmetrical national histories of power in which these subjects are situated.

We might therefore read the adult women's espousal of a liberal feminism and of neoliberal consumer citizenship as a disavowal of such racial difference, an attempt—through "adjustment"—to escape the racial signifiers of deprivation/depravity that plague their status as Dominican women. However, as we see in "A Regular Revolution," authorizing oneself as the autonomous subject of North American liberal feminism does not evacuate racial markers, but instead reassigns them as the cultural difference that supposedly debilitates women *in* the Dominican Republic (where, in turn, such difference can be displaced onto racial and class others). A transnational feminist ethics attentive to such ghostly others can reveal how the very notion of "oppressive tradition," against which the García girls' liberal feminist self-image coheres, when refracted through *Butterflies*, proves to be not the source of the feminine subject's Third World underdevelopment, but rather its discursive effect. As I have been arguing, a transnational feminist perspective reencounters women who have been pronounced victims of tradition, regarding them instead in terms of the material circumstances and social worlds that constitute their lives, especially as those conditions are subject to geopolitical cataclysms.

But a human rights approach that recognizes the complex personhood of women as political subjects also compels us to rethink "revolution" itself as a rhetorical claim (one that disparages and displaces its others as premodern, conservative, and/or feminized in character) that is actually only one in an array of options by which social transformations take place. Scholars and political activists alike have contended that international human rights are not essentially revolutionary, but rather are norms that expressly work to defuse revolution and rebellion, in order to promote orderly development and progress and to reconcile individual subjects to social order and political authority. Nevertheless, human rights principles have themselves been products of sweeping historical transformations. This is nowhere more clear than in the organization of rights into a generational model, where "first-generation" rights are affiliated with the American and French Revolutions, "second-generation" rights with socialist movements, and "third-generation" rights with anticolonial and nationalist struggles. As such, human rights and political revolution exist not in diametric opposition to one another, but in a dialectical relationship of order and transformation that, as I have described in chapter 1, human rights instruments record. As Lynn Hunt explains, in the American and French Revolutions of the eighteenth century, the declaration of the "naturalness" of human rights enabled a right of revolution, which induced revolutionaries to "establish or re-establish the natural, equal, and universal right of individuals, and both linked legitimacy [of the revolutionary struggle] to the guarantee of individual, natural rights."[60]

However, the right to rebellion and revolution (even more than the "right to self-determination") proved an especially provoking question in the drafting of the Universal Declaration of Human Rights, as the United States and Britain refused recognition of this provision in the document. The omission of revolution as a right certainly evinces the way in which, since its inception, the United Nations as an institution, along with the hegemonic human rights discourses it promulgates, strives to maintain international stability in keeping with the imperial and neoliberal interests of the great powers. And yet, by considering how women want otherwise, a human rights literacy can discern their (be)coming the political subjects of human rights as in itself revolutionary. Together, *García Girls* and *Butterflies* script the complex, alternative agency of subjects fractured by divisions of gender, race, nation, and class, whose political engagement arises from the daily work that female need and feminine desire call forth. Neither hemispheric geopolitical conditions nor women's lives under them are as static or discretely separate as our conventional histories, maps, and disciplinary divisions would make them out to be. And yet these muddied and shifting grounds also provide the very contexts and contradictions through which social and political transformation takes place.

UN Convention on the Rights of Persons with Disabilities
Jhumpa Lahiri, *Unaccustomed Earth*
Ana Castillo, *So Far from God*

5

Being Well

Minor Subjects and the Right to Health

> *The way we imagine disability through images and narratives determines the shape of the material world, the distribution of resources, our relationships to one another, and our sense of ourselves.*
>
> —Rosemarie Garland-Thomson, "Disability and Representation"

While the *bildungsroman* has proven the privileged narrative genre for the literary construction of personhood and national belonging, we have seen in previous chapters how contemporary U.S. writers of color not only morph the narrative of development in order to imagine the subject of human rights otherwise, but, as discussed in chapter 4, forego the narrative of the individual altogether in order to relate a "sisterhood" of other political possibilities for their protagonists. The minor subject of human rights, I have been arguing, is one whose be(com)ing exists neither as the natural human being, nor the abstract person reconciled to a liberal national or international order, but is a social product whose arrival at once enacts an ethical challenge to those from whom she demands recognition. Thus, as I have hoped to demonstrate, minor literatures grant to human rights a "life of their own," imagining subjects who exist in an aspirational and proleptic relationship to social and political forms of community, in difference to the nation-state and global capital. In this final chapter and in the conclusion of *Writing Human Rights,* I turn from the *bildungsroman* altogether to alternate genres also being rewritten and transformed by U.S. writers of color: the family romance and its predecessor, the family saga. In so doing and as in the previous chapter, my concern also shifts from the more discretely individuated subject of rights to alternative forms of community and collectivity that arise in dialectical tension to global conditions of political and economic modernity.

In these remaining pages, then, I examine how contemporary writers of color adopt the family romance, often by returning to elements of the family saga, in order to respond to the considerable damage and estrangement that the globalized conditions of modern life threaten. Considering minor literatures that script a contemporary version of the family romance, with an emphasis on the missing mother that registers the situation of women, children, and the disabled, spotlights those who have been recognized in the human rights regime as particularly vulnerable populations. But while taking into account the conditions that produce such vulnerability, I am equally concerned with how these literatures conceptualize *affiliation,* beyond "flesh and blood" kin, in order to grant recognition to the *desiring* subjects that modernity produces, subjects who want otherwise than either traditional, patriarchal forms of communal life (which, in any case, are increasingly difficult to sustain except by way of fundamentalist politics) or abstracted neoliberal personhood. Toward this end, I also consider how minor literatures rewrite mother and child into alternate forms of imagined sociality, ones organized around, in this chapter, the right to health, and, in the conclusion, the right to family.

As in chapter 4, then, I continue to underscore the perspective and position of diasporic women of color.[1] This is not to essentialize or reify these subjects as *the* privileged or authentic site of human rights politics, but rather to insist upon the need for rigorous attention to the many and specific social locations from which human rights subjects articulate political claims and critiques. Precisely because the Third World woman and (as I go on to elaborate here) the person with disabilities, as well as children are so often represented by a (neo)liberal imaginary as the humanitarian victim par excellence, characterized as bare life and bereft of all political agency, I am concerned with how minor literatures imagine them instead as distinctly political *subjects* who want otherwise. But in situating them within changing conceptions of the family, I also hope to anchor these subjects in the social worlds that produce them and in which any agency will come to have meaning. In this way, minor literatures not only theorize, in Arne De Boever's words, "the care for the self and the care for others," but appreciate how such narratives of care "can become meaningful . . . as political narratives about biopolitics."[2] In the following sections of this chapter, then, I go on to consider short stories from Jhumpa Lahiri's *Unaccustomed Earth* (2008) and Ana Castillo's novel *So Far from God* (1993) to understand how they each conceive of health and well-being as core human rights principles.

Something Precious

The third book by the Pulitzer Prize–winning Jhumpa Lahiri, *Unaccustomed Earth,* takes as its primary subject U.S.-born South Asian Americans and concludes with the three "Hema and Kaushik" stories, on which I focus here. This short story cycle locates the title characters, Hema (whose last name is never given) and Kaushik Choudhuri, at three different moments. "Once In a Lifetime" begins in 1981 with Kaushik's family's return from India to Massachusetts, where they live with Hema's family for a month, upon learning that his mother, Parul, is dying of cancer. The next story, "Year's End," tells of Kaushik's introduction four years after his mother's death to his new stepfamily, his father having married a widow in India and brought her and her two daughters back to New England. The final story, "Going Ashore," depicts Hema and Kaushik's reunion in Rome nearly twenty years later, as early middle-aged adults. In "Going Ashore," the two begin a three-week-long affair, although Hema is engaged to another man. Upon separating, Hema departs to India for her wedding to Navin, soon after which she learns she is pregnant, and Kaushik, who is on what is meant as a brief holiday in Thailand, dies while swimming during the 2004 tsunami.

Given that these stories, like most of Lahiri's work, address middle- and upper-middle-class Bengali immigrants and their children, it would be simple enough to construe the plots' family romance as an allegory for ethnic immigrant assimilation.[3] In this case, Parul's illness and death would certainly also constitute what scholars David Mitchell and Sharon Snyder call (and as I will elaborate below) the "narrative prosthetic," that is, "the hard kernel or recalcitrant corporeal matter" that shores up the normative symbolic order that cultural texts seek to institute.[4] As Mitchell and Snyder explain, metaphors of disability are an "ambivalent and mutable category of cultural and literary investment," in which, even as disabled characters "provide powerful counterpoints to their respective cultures' normalizing Truths about the construction of deviance," such representations too often ascribe these persons "a programmatic (even deterministic) identity."[5] In this case, Parul's cancer might signify the "handicapping" racial and cultural differences that must be discarded and disavowed in order for the next generation to ascend into an American good life. Certainly, beginning the cycle with adolescent protagonists in a middle-class American suburb seems to set the stage for a *bildung* that resolves the loss of the mother through a heterosexual romance between Hema and Kaushik and their incorporation into the national family.

And yet, in deflecting its characters from this expected trajectory, (dis)placing them instead into alternate possible spaces and modes of affiliation, the narratives want otherwise for these subjects. Indeed, depicted as beautiful, glamorous, and cosmopolitan, even when ill, Parul embodies for both Hema and Kaushik an ideal but lost mother, rather than an object of denigration and disavowal. Hence, in Parul, the biological mother and the fantasy mother are fused as one. Her death takes place in the interstitial space between the first and second story; the narratives never quite repress the loss but neither do they represent it except in Kaushik's memory. Meanwhile, in the interlude between the onset of Parul's cancer in the first story and the expected romance of the third, "Year's End" depicts the way in which Kaushik's new immigrant stepmother, Chitra, can only fail to compensate for Kaushik's loss. While Chitra strives cautiously to care for him and his father in an "old-fashioned" manner, Kaushik measures her against Parul and finds her utterly wanting.[6] Chitra's unworldliness and good health strike him as a jarring affront to what he recalls of his mother, and he is repulsed by his stepmother's presence in his family's house and among their things.

Nevertheless, the story poses a fragile bond that Kaushik begins to construct with his two young stepsisters, Rupa and Piu, while home for a brief visit during his winter break from Swarthmore. He recognizes a loss he shares with these girls—"the knowledge of death seemed present in both sisters . . . marking them in spite of their lightheartedness"—as well as their common "journey from India to Massachusetts, too old not to experience the shock of it, too young to have a say in the matter" (272). It is this shared experience of loss that brings them together, in an affiliation arranged by Dr. Choudhuri, and that they help one another to guard. As Kaushik observes, "My presence was proof that my mother had once existed, just as they represented the physical legacy of their dead father" (283). However, Kaushik abruptly rends that newly emerging affinity between them when he finds the girls scrutinizing photographs of Parul that had been hidden away: "'You have no *right* to be looking at those,' I told them. 'They don't belong to you, do you understand?' . . . Words continued to pour out of me, words that should not have been uttered, should not have been heard" (286; emphasis added). Berating them and their mother further, he harshly declares: "Well, you've seen it for yourselves, how beautiful my mother was. How much prettier and more sophisticated than yours. Your mother is nothing in comparison" (287). In this moment, Kaushik forecloses the shared recognition of vulnerability that the dead mother signifies, instead hoarding the photographs—which he later buries along the coastline, near the Canadian border—as signs of his own private loss. As he recognizes at the end of the story, "The memory of that night was now the only tie between [himself and Rupa and Piu], eclipsing everything else" (293).

It is here, too, as he flees the possibility of this new family, that the story foreshadows Kaushik's death in the final story. Looking out over the ocean, he understands that "the water was the most unforgiving thing, nearly black at times, cold enough, I knew, to kill me, violent enough to break me apart" (289). Despite this threat (and indeed, he will die in warmer, seemingly more hospitable waters on the other side of the world), Kaushik feels that this unforgiving landscape "claimed me as nothing had in a long time," as he at once recalls Hema's family's house, the "last place that had felt like a home" (291). As they are brought into proximity by their parents' familiarity with one another, Hema is neither Kaushik's sister nor girlfriend, and the nascent bond lost with Rupa and Piu anticipates the fragility of the ambiguous tie between the title characters. Thus, as Lahiri describes the first night Hema and Kaushik spend together in "Going Ashore," after finding each other in Rome, "something precious had been stumbled upon, a newborn connection that could not be left unattended, that demanded every particle of their care" (310).

Bound by shared memories of the lost mother ("Hema knew, without having to be told, that she was the first person he'd ever slept with who'd known his mother, who was able to remember her as he did"), their desire appears as an uncanny return of the familiar, made solid in their new discoveries of one another (313). As Susan Koshy writes of Lahiri's fiction more generally, the stories "reveal not only the growing relevance of relationships to those who are less than kin and more than stranger but also, and more important, the dislocation and consequent unreliability of the very categories through which we demarcate the familiar and the unfamiliar."[7] The two embark on a heady romance that Hema—herself recovering from a years-long affair with a married man—finds safe because she knows it will inevitably end with her return to the United States and to Navin (who is practically a stranger to Hema, as the marriage has been more or less arranged, upon Hema's request, by her parents). Thus, when, on their last day, Kaushik insists that she move to Hong Kong with him instead, she bristles against "the fact that he was telling her what to do. Unlike Navin, he was not offering to come to her"; Kaushik dismisses her as a "coward" and remains cold to her when they part because she refuses him (321, 323). And while Kaushik comes to regret his remoteness in these last moments together, Lahiri concludes the story cycle with another insurmountable rift, as she expressly denies that Kaushik fathers Hema's pregnancy. With Navin as the biological father of the child, the story closes by confirming "you had left nothing behind" (333).

How then ought we to read Lahiri's reinscribed family romance, in which Kaushik—the child of an ideal lost mother—figures as a fantasy father impossibly lost to a child not yet born? If "nothing" remains of Kaushik as a subject, the stories nevertheless preserve Hema's secret desire for him, and it is this "wanting otherwise," which is ongoing, impossible either to forsake *or* to fulfill, that opens out onto what I have been describing in this book as a human rights method. "Hema and Kaushik" cautions against a teleological construction of the immigrant narrative and its resolution in and by way of the *bildung,* insisting instead that we remain attentive to the other possibilities imbedded within narratives of development and personhood. Indeed, Hema's own profession as a scholar of Latin commands such sensitivity and thus models this reading practice. Focused on the pre-Roman Etruscan civilization, whose "primary legacy was tombs and the things that were put in them: jewels, pottery, weapons to accompany the dead," Hema searches for Etruscan "fragments" littered in the classical texts she studies (300).

Likewise, Lahiri continually posits material objects in her text as signifiers of *other* lifeworlds—other times and places that are partially remembered but remain irretrievable—around which new affiliations form. For example, "Once In a Lifetime" begins with Hema's earliest recollections of Kaushik; these in turn fade into the story of her mother's and Parul's friendship, which precedes Hema's birth, when, at a park Parul notices "a young Bengali woman in a sari, wearing vermilion in her hair" (224). It is Parul who, as she befriends the other woman, suggests to Hema's mother that she is expecting. While the story delineates the class and educational differences between the two women, it also explains how such "differences were irrelevant in Cambridge, where they were both equally alone" and "they became instant friends, spending their days together while our fathers were at work" (225). This initial friendship lasts until the two families part, when the Choudhuris move back to Bombay. The many household items that the Choudhuris dispense to Hema's family, and which they continue to refer to as "Parul's," include old winter clothes of Kaushik's that Hema finds distasteful and wears begrudgingly. All of these articles, Hema explains, are "gradually replaced . . . until there was no longer any physical trace of you in the house," and by the time the Choudhuris return to Cambridge in 1981, the two families feel like strangers to one another. Parul actually describes their earlier residency in Cambridge as "another life, back then" (249).

The secret of Parul's illness overdetermines the alienation the adults feel toward one another, as Kaushik's mother chooses not to reveal to Hema's parents that she is dying. As Dr. Choudhuri seeks to provide Parul as much comfort and pleasure as possible, with first-class airplane tickets and an enormous new house on the North Shore, these gestures mark out the unbridgeable distance between Hema's more solidly middle-class family, who cannot fathom such indulgences. The adolescent Hema's own reaction to Kaushik's disclosure of his mother's secret at the story's end is one neither of "sorrow [nor] sympathy," but of an "enormous fear of having a dying woman in our home," which leaves her "disturbed that I had been in such close proximity to her disease" and "feeling at once burdened and betrayed" (250–51). A portrait of waxing and waning intimacies, "Once In a Lifetime" depicts the different ways in which shared forms of bodily recognition (as in Parul's recognition of the other woman's pregnancy) nurture—and the failure of such recognition severs—possible affiliations, rendering the objects once associated with those bonds meaningless and empty. As importantly, even the initial bond between the women is represented not as a form of shared Bengali identity, but rather as a shared recognition of displacement and loss.

Read against the extremely brief and fractured *bildungs* that Lahiri provides Hema and Kaushik, these intimations of bonds previously forged and lost are transfigured anew with implications beyond the two families. We learn in "Going Ashore" that after departing his father's house in the previous story, Kaushik has, in the intervening years, remained aloof from his father and stepfamily. Employed as an itinerant photojournalist who documents military and civil violence and human rights violations across the globe, he seeks to separate himself not only from the victims of such violence (even as he remains a professional witness to them), but from all personal and enduring claims that others try to make on him (305). He collects few material objects, and, upon his reunion with Hema, at first denies to her that his work "affect[s]" him, as he is no longer able to "remember all the corpses he'd photographed, their faces bloated, their mouths stuffed with dirt, their vacant eyes reflecting passing clouds over their heads" (316, 305). Kaushik nevertheless realizes "that it was impossible, wherever he landed not to form attachments" and, indeed, that his photography depends upon "the material world, stealing from it, hoarding it, unwilling to let it go" (309). He admits to Hema that photographing atrocities does indeed "affect" him, although not always in ways that make him more humane (309, 317).

In fact, it is a momentary reference to his aging body that most crucially queries this line between himself as the First World, South Asian American citizen and his perception of others as distinct from him, especially in their vulnerable, embodied victimhood. Despite the plot significance of Parul's cancer and Hema's pregnancy, the only in-depth description of embodiment that Lahiri offers in these stories comes in regard to a rather minor ocular impairment that Kaushik develops as an adult, while living in Rome:

> It was in the course of those days . . . that a faint gray speck, smaller than the head of a pin, began floating across his left eye. . . . Kaushik had thought that a gnat was circling his head, and he kept swatting at it, putting out his fingers trying to flick it away. But the speck continued to accompany him wherever he went, quietly tormenting him, and he realized it was within him, that it was not possible to remove it or make it stop. An optometrist explained that it was caused by vitreous gel clumping and pulling away from the wall of his eye, that it was a harmless symptom of getting older. He was told he would grow used to it, and he had, more or less, not bothered these days unless he were in a bright room with white walls, or outside without his sunglasses. It did not affect his driving, or his picture-taking. And yet it felt like an invasion of the part of his body, the physical sense that was most precious: something that betrayed him and also refused to abandon him. (308)

Although Kaushik experiences the speck as "an invasion," the narrative instills it "within him," a cue to the vulnerable humanity he shares with all those others from whom he has physically and affectively distanced himself.

Moreover, Lahiri juxtaposes Kaushik's consciousness of the distracting speck in his field of vision with unexpected recollections of his mother, both of which tellingly reoccur in Thailand as Kaushik swims toward a deserted cove unaware of the imminent surging tsunami wave. These images appear alongside Kaushik's recollection of an object "unlike anything else" that he and Hema have viewed in an Etruscan museum on their last day together: "a bronze sculpture of a severely elongated boy's body, a skeleton more than flesh, standing with his arms at his sides" (331). Just before Kaushik dives off the boat to swim to his death, he likens his own shadow in the water to the sculpture, called "*L'Ombra della Sera:* the Shadow of Evening." This image, together with the appearance of the speck and the memory of his mother as a strong swimmer, constructs a singular constellation of signifiers for Kaushik's embodied being, which is soon to be lost. While his vision impairment remains only mildly troubling, never disabling his "good life," the "floater" once again, and this time with devastating consequences, cues the vulnerable humanity that is "within him" and thus can never be escaped.

Kaushik dies just before he is to begin working in Hong Kong as an editor, where, as Hema observes to herself, "He would not be constantly in harm's way" (315). The irony of his death highlights the extent to which, although Kaushik believes he has chosen (and can also remove himself from) the risks he takes, his own good life has been contingent upon not only the losses suffered by others, but the precarious political, environmental, and economic conditions of globality in which he is situated (315).[8] Thus, when Kaushik likens his own family's displacements to those of refugees—or more subtly, when Hema realizes that the piazza across from the restaurant where she eats lunch served as the point of deportation for Italian Jews during World War II—the references serve not so much to appropriate the figure of humanitarian violence toward sentimental ends. Instead, they acknowledge the embodied vulnerability that constitutes the unrelenting desire for and of "humanity" (263, 309). And, while Kaushik might seem to characterize the autonomous liberal subject having transcended all forms of dependency, the narrative qualifies that accomplishment by posing forms of social recognition, interdependency, and care—first in Rupa and Piu, then in Hema—that might otherwise be available to him.

The stories are told mostly in the first person, although the final story takes up a third-person perspective until its conclusion, whereupon it briefly returns to Hema's first-person narration to relate the loss of Kaushik. This perspective is hence strangely intimate, with the first-person narrators addressing one another through the apostrophic "you," even as one of the two principals goes missing from the plot, as does Hema in "Year's End" and Kaushik, after his death, in "Going Ashore." Interpellating the reader by way of this second-person address, the narratives shift from the expected subjects of flesh-and-blood ties and shared ethnic origins to those of transnational and mobile desires, hailing the reader in an ethical responsibility that demands "every particle" of care to sustain the articulation of a precious "newborn connection."[9] Although Kaushik has misrecognized vulnerability as a state one can and ought to transcend, the stories ask us as readers—standing in and receiving the address meant for him—to consider what material conditions and social supports enable *any*-body to be well—that is to imagine his or her own well-being and to put that vision of self into practice.

When it comes to the right to health, I am obviously pursuing not a *thematic* analysis of the "Hema and Kaushik" stories, but (as I have emphasized throughout *Writing Human Rights*) a *formal* one; these are certainly not sad tales of subjects who cannot *literally* access social resources and various forms of care (including healthcare) and hence evoke sentimentally charitable responses from the reader. Instead, I argue that they provide allegories of the variable and unstable experiences of vulnerability and desire that *formally* unmake and remake the stories' subjects as they lose, re-encounter, and come to new recognitions of one other. Indeed, Min Hyoung Song has described Lahiri's formal strategy as the employment of "allegory against allegory," insofar as, in critical terms, "allegory" can refer to a rhetorical trope, to a genre, *and* to the reader's attribution of hidden meaning in a narrative (as in "allegoresis").[10] As Song argues, Lahiri thwarts readers' expectations of the ethnic *bildungsroman*—that is, their reading of her narratives as allegories of "ethnographic fact" regarding the arrival and incorporation of the South Asian American into the national family—and instead "pulls readers back to the materiality of the text itself," thereby "refusing such interpretation as meaning keeps being displaced onto something other than what has been said, something that operates at the level of the signifier and, just as important, as something other to what the reader may expect."[11]

In pointing to the multiple possibilities by which allegories instantiate themselves, Song suggests how the certainty of meaning that metaphors (such as pregnancy) are intended to secure for the reader give way to the contingencies inherent in the discursive practice of pairing signifiers with material referents. Such figures, that is, might be read otherwise.[12] For Song, the refusal of allegoresis is at once a refusal of reproductive futurism—the social and textual expectations that the present will be seamlessly reproduced into a continuous future, securing familial, ethnic, and national identities.[13] However, rather than an act of willful resistance in the face of such normative expectations, "Hema and Kaushik" records the losses that make such continuities impossible for its minor subjects by highlighting the insecurities of its characters' existences. If the *bildungsroman* is meant to provide a solution to the alienating loss that the family romance memorializes, Lahiri's partitioning of her subjects' lives across three stories refuses the novel of individual development as the answer to addressing such loss. Thus, like the Etruscan artifacts that are Hema's objects of study, "Hema and Kaushik" offer up characters whose distinct, embodied conditions—Parul's cancer, Kaushik's death in the tsunami, and Hema's pregnancy—present *synecdoches* of lifeworlds made unavailable by the temporal and spatial disjunctures of the three stories. Rather than metaphors for the nation into which they are to be incorporated, the characters' embodiments are only fragmentary remains, emblems of the complex and shifting historical conditions and networks of social affiliation that have produced them. And like the Etruscan artist's remaking of the human form, a human rights response to the human being caught in such rapidly changing conditions demands tremendous conceptual flexibility with respect to our notions of who embodies the subject of human rights, as the "matter" of that subject mutates over time and space, re-presented by various actors to themselves and to others.[14]

The cultural politics of "Hema and Kaushik" then are not to construct disability and illness as political identities in and of themselves, but instead to inscribe embodied vulnerability as the subject of a social project that remakes what it means to "be well." In the time of these stories, that subject, the "something precious," remains yet to come, at present unformed and still in need of care. Positing a shared ("universal") embodied vulnerability, while also attentive to the uneven historical and spatial distribution of that vulnerability, a human rights literacy can generate an expansive notion of "being well" made possible by alternative formations of social and political community seeking not to transcend the conditions of vulnerability, but instead to transform them. Hence, as Robert McRuer has contended with respect to the "geopolitics of disability in the new world order," "a re-cognition of bodies beyond boundaries, bodies not (yet) legible according to the terms of our canonical claims—will continue to open up new horizons for thought and action, for solidarity and coalition."[15] In the following sections, then, I explain how a transnational disability perspective that imagines "bodies and desires otherwise" radically animates a human right to health that has remained otherwise foreclosed in a neoliberal American imaginary of good life.[16]

Disabling the American Good Life

In 2006, the United Nations adopted the Convention on the Rights of Persons with Disabilities (CRPD), the purpose of which, as stated in Article 1 of the convention, is "to promote, protect and ensure the full and equal enjoyment of all human rights and fundamental freedoms by all persons with disabilities, and to promote respect for their inherent dignity."[17] The CRPD in fact *reaffirmed* the rights, such as the freedom of expression and the right to bodily security, catalogued in many other instruments, most significantly, the international bill of rights, for people with disabilities.[18] The adoption of the CRPD thus made visible how, although persons with disabilities theoretically were to have enjoyed the same rights as other human beings, these individuals have historically been denied such rights and, indeed, were often considered barely human at all.[19] By contrast, previous attempts at recognizing the rights of persons with disabilities, such as the 1971 Declaration on the Rights of Mentally Retarded Persons and the 1975 Declaration on the Rights of Disabled Persons, tended to adopt a medical and charitable model in addressing the needs of people with disabilities.[20] In response, beginning in the 1980s, disability activists pressed international bodies and human rights nongovernmental organizations (NGOs), most of which made no acknowledgment of disabled people's rights, to draft and implement a legally binding convention based on a social model of disability (in which social organization, in terms of inclusion and exclusion, rather than physical impairment and biomedical treatment, is foregrounded as the locus of intervention).[21] Adopting a range of methods similar to those of other human rights watch groups (including undertaking in-depth investigations of abuses, publishing reports, and establishing alliances with other human rights organizations), disability activists successfully developed a text that endorses a full range of rights for persons with disabilities.[22] As a result, the convention not only calls for the elimination of discrimination, but makes an implicit claim regarding the *standing* of persons with disabilities, that is, that these individuals have a right to rights as human beings.

Like the International Convention on the Elimination of All Forms of Racial Discrimination (ICERD) and the Convention on the Elimination of All Forms of Discrimination against Women (CEDAW) (as well as the Convention on the Rights of the Child, which I will discuss in the conclusion), the CRPD recognizes the specific needs of particular(ized) groups of people, as part of a broader trend that legal scholar Frédéric Mégret calls the "pluralization of human rights."[23] At the time of its development, the UN General Assembly administrative mandate actually stipulated that the CRPD be conceived as an "implementation convention," one that did *not* create any new rights. Yet, as Mégret points out, in adding "extra semantic texture" to its enumeration of rights with respect to how they pertain to people with disabilities, the convention acknowledges the extent to which previous proclamations that regard human beings as "naturally" equal cannot but fail to account for and to remedy the extant social and political inequities that define particular(ized) groups such as the disabled.[24] Even when the rights claims themselves are not entirely new in content, instruments such as the CRPD seem on the *verge* of establishing new rights because of the measures required of states to ensure that these rights are met for persons with disabilities, as for example in the adaptation of infrastructure to ensure freedom of mobility.[25]

In short, while Mégret remains uncertain as to whether the CRPD generates rights particular to persons with disabilities or "simply rights which exist in some form or other for all human beings, but whose existence needs to be highlighted in this context because of the particular vulnerabilities of those with disabilities," he concludes that the convention opens a normative space for bridging "the gap, sometimes uneasily . . . between general formulations of rights and the need to craft categories of rights that better take into account the irreducible experience of those with disabilities."[26] In turn, as Rosemary Kayess and Phillip French assert, the CRPD contains measures that have the potential to affect and benefit *many* persons, such as the right to an accessible environment—as well as the potential to turn rights conventionally assumed to be negative liberties into positive ones of state obligation (such as provisions for augmentative or alternative communication as part of the right to free expression).[27] The recognition in the convention of the specific modes by which disabled persons have been excluded from enjoying rights claims generates what might actually be new rights, such as "the freedom from exploitation, violence and abuse," "the right to participation," and international cooperation in implementation and monitoring, which are not expressly enumerated in other instruments.[28] As a result, Kayess and French argue, the CRPD "modified, transformed *and* added to traditional human rights concepts."[29]

As we have seen, in a liberal genealogy of rights rooted in the natural law tradition, autonomy is understood as the *precondition* for standing, and thus one assumed already possessed by those who are not disabled. The CRPD, however, acknowledges the "extra work"—the prosthetics, infrastructure, and instruments—needed for a particular population to arrive as fully autonomous and equal human persons and seeks to guarantee access to such accoutrements to secure the dignity and personhood of the disabled as political subjects in and of themselves.[30] Ultimately, the convention seeks to supply to disabled persons the *means* for social autonomy, which, in turn, accords them legal and political personhood, that is, standing or the right to rights. Thus, the convention does not actually spell out a right to autonomy; instead, as Mégret observes, "the absence of autonomy is not so much a given, but *a result* of persons with disabilities' treatment by the state and society, so that a 'right to autonomy' would, at any rate, involve less the granting of what cannot be granted than the organization of society in such a way as to maximize each individual's degree of autonomy."[31]

Hence, I contend, the CRPD dialectically records how human rights construct political subjects, legal rights claims, *and* social communities in a mutually constitutive relation to one another, expressly *producing* a kind of "human person" whose political and legal autonomy and equality necessitate specific political, legal, and social transformations. And yet, *as a human rights instrument,* the convention's very existence is made possible by a prior and necessary recognition that disabled people *are* in fact human persons to begin with. We therefore find ourselves, once again, facing the "tautology/teleology" problematic I have described in chapter 2, whereby human rights are meant to produce precisely those (abstractly equal) human beings that they already are (supposed to be) "in nature." The CRPD further underscores how an *ethic* of solidarity must underpin human rights principles that center on the person, whereby *others* provide the means for the autonomy, equality, and participation of persons with disabilities in their social and political communities.[32] Accordingly, Article 19 of the CRPD stipulates both the right to independent living *and* to inclusion in the community.

Who, then, are these humans on the verge of personhood and how do they come into being? Article 1 of the CRPD defines disabilities as "long-term physical, mental, intellectual or sensory impairments which in interaction with various barriers may hinder [a person's] full and effective participation in society on an equal basis with others." The ambiguity of this definition reflects the fact that many state members party to the convention opposed applying the convention to all impairment groups and therefore "open[ing] the floodgates" in terms of domestic implementation of the convention's provisions; these members sought to limit state obligations to only those already recognized by any given state as suffering from unjust discrimination, those who, in other words, are recognized as disabled. As a result, not only does the convention's definition prove to be "open-ended and indicative, rather than closed," but it "ultimately produces an element of circularity."[33] The vague language regarding disability in the convention certainly permits states to limit which forms of impairment, injury, and illness it is obligated to recognize and support, and which forms continue to subject individuals to discrimination and dehumanization.[34]

But at the same time, we should appreciate that at the time that the convention was adopted, disability activists also resisted medically based definitions of disability that "ran the risk of time-locking the CRPD, and of imposing a western view of disability on non-western cultural systems."[35] Consequently, Article 1 also opens conceptual space for political dissent regarding how impaired, injured, or ill subjects come to make claims in their own name. Similarly, Article 8 of the CRPD requires its members to raise awareness about "the skills, merits and abilities of persons with disabilities" and to foster attitudes of respect for these persons and their rights; thus, it speaks not only to material conditions of life for disabled persons, but also to representational regimes by which such life has been imagined. It is precisely here, I suggest, that minor *literary and cultural* forms, rather than hegemonic juridical and legal norms, might undertake the "extra work" necessary to transfigure disability in human rights politics.

Disability theorists such as Tobin Siebers have in fact insisted that we ought not to understand disability as the unique feature of a select population, but as a "property belonging to all human beings," thus urging us to reimagine the subject of human rights otherwise.[36] Whereas in Hannah Arendt's influential formulation (as we saw in the introduction and chapter 2), the subjects of human rights are characterized by nothing *but* their vulnerability, Siebers (like other social theorists I have discussed) directs us to "fragility, vulnerability, and disability as central to the human condition," rather than as a paucity. In so doing, he explains, we radically alter Arendt's "melancholia" for humanity to serve as "a positive foundation for the right to have rights—a goal that requires disability to play a universal role as the guarantor of human rights."[37] A critical disability perspective can re-present human society, "not as a collection of autonomous beings, some of whom will lose their independence, but as a community of dependent frail bodies that rely on others for survival."[38] As in "Hema and Kaushik," above, the "human" hence comes to name a being-in-the-world shuttled in contingent and unpredictable ways between bodily vulnerability and the desire for recognition: "Humanness is defined by the aspiration to be human but in a paradoxical way" that requires as part of that aspiration "that one concede to other beings the status of human being in order to be recognized as human oneself."[39] And, like Jack Donnelly, Siebers encourages us to define the human person as a "work in progress" and thus human rights as *creating* persons through ongoing acts and variable norms of recognition, rather than beginning with such personhood as a biological or ontological given.[40]

A human rights approach conjoined to disability critique allows us to discern where illness, impairment, and injury serve not as metaphors to secure narrative closure and normalcy, but as synecdoches of the social, cultural, and political conditions of "disability environments" that "produce disability in bodies and require interventions at the level of social justice."[41] As in the rest of this book, then, in describing this human right to health, I conceive it not as a self-evident, universal norm imposed upon others, nor as an alibi for a paternalistic humanitarianism that reifies passive victims in need of charity. Rather, human rights supply the political sign under which subjects lay claims to protections and privileges they have not been granted, transforming themselves as political agents in the process. In turn, "health" signifies not simply as freedom from illness and injury but as a granting of dignity to subjects other than the idealized able bodies of liberal fantasy and, as such, yields the possibility of reconfiguring "the very idea of welfare for all."[42]

At the same time (and again, as I have cautioned throughout this book), such a universalist conception of disability can easily obscure how unevenly impairment and injury are distributed as social realities. If *everyone* is (potentially) disabled, then why do any particular subjects need to be singled out for political recognition and redress?[43] Once again, the critical solution is not to forego embodied vulnerability as the central analytic in the human rights method, but to attend to those lives that are continually rendered disabled, if not altogether disposable, while others are tolerated, enabled, and/or celebrated. As McRuer discerns, a turn to "global bodies"—and, I would add, minor subjects—effectively challenges official state and commercial or mainstream incorporations of disability. As this "supplement supplements," it can disrupt entirely those whom the nation recognizes as disabled subjects, incorporable to the body politic, and those human lives deemed disposable, constitutively necessary to, but abjected from the body politic.[44]

Insofar as such recognition has been tethered to (neo)liberal images of an American good life that transcends such bodily limitations, human rights discourses have too often negated how disability figures "the precariousness of the human condition, for the fact that individual human beings are susceptible to change, decline over time, and die."[45] Staging instead what McRuer calls the "disability to come," Ana Castillo's novel *So Far from God,* to which I turn next, shifts our attention to the specters of "disposable domestics" that haunt the borderlands of the domestic and the foreign, the national and the global.[46] Breaking from strict social and political realism with its commitment to the magical and fantastic, *So Far from God* also diverges from a rehabilitative logic in order to tend to the "animated debris" of an American good life that is otherwise given up as lost and dead by the neoliberal imaginary. Thus, like Lahiri's story cycle, Castillo's novel not only considers the intersubjective relations of support and recognition by which bodies come to enjoy well-being. It also counters the insistent incorporation of personhood that the *bildungsroman* achieves by ultimately disintegrating, decomposing, and disappearing its embodied characters, while nevertheless sustaining them as integral parts of the family saga and as essential signs of desiring social and political subjectivity.[47]

Impairment, Injury, and Illness, or the Embodied Relation to the Modern World

In chapter 4, I described how neoliberal discourse, especially as it interfaces with humanitarian or global feminism, takes Third World women as special objects of interest, envisaging the liberation of women—previously held hostage by their cultures—into the political and market freedoms that global capital and liberal democracy make available. Structured thus as a developmental narrative, these women's entry into modernity as autonomous subjects is to be of a piece with postcolonial nations' entry into modern political and economic relations. In the case of diasporic women and women of color in the United States, the transcendence of the oppressive patriarchal past is even further heightened by the spatial distinctions that border-crossing makes available. As she leaves behind the depravity and deprivation of her past, this woman is meant to ascend into the abstract personhood and formal equalities that the American good life avers.

In pointed contrast to such hegemonic narratives of women's development, *So Far from God* offers a catalogue of the various and ongoing threats to well-being under which a family of women live and work. Blending elements of myth and legend, historical romance, magical realism, poetry, folk literature, social and political commentary, allegory, and tragic, absurdist farce, its hybrid narrative strategies correspond to and negotiate the uneven development and hemispheric migrations that comprise the disability context of its U.S. borderland setting of Tome, New Mexico.[48] In particular, Castillo reinscribes the family saga to portray the material contradictions of global capital as a series of bodily injuries and social indignities leveled at vulnerable, but resilient indigenous and migrant populations. Beginning with the "astonishing" death and resurrection of one of its protagonists, La Loca, Castillo immediately establishes a milieu in which "the magical . . . falls within the realm of possibility," and the fantastic and miraculous become integral to the text's political vision (192).[49] The novel's subsequent conclusion with the founding of the "M.O.M.A.S." organization—"Mothers of Martyrs and Saints"—completes its rendition of the "mundane fantastic" (Grace Kyungwon Hong's term for the reworking of magical realism in U.S.-based literatures), where the specters of dead women make regular "ectoplasmic appearances" to communicate with their loved ones (248).[50] In so doing, I will demonstrate, the text lays claim to a right to health for its subjects in the face of the seemingly impossible conditions they inhabit.[51]

The harms wrought by the (post)modernity of global capital are addressed most directly in the plotlines of each of the text's main characters, Sofia (Sofi) and her four daughters—Esperanza, Caridad, Fe, and La Loca (as she comes to be known), each of whom dies over the course of the novel. With their given names readily intimating an allegorical dimension to their stories, the characters' embodiment of traditional Catholic virtues signals the martyrdom of hope, faith, and charity in the modern world, whether through Esperanza's involvement in political and social justice movements, Fe's investment in a bourgeois work ethic, or Caridad's loving benevolence toward others.[52] Moreover, in La Loca's character, Castillo rewrites the hagiography of the twelfth-century Saint Christina the Astonishing to embody, as I elaborate below, a visionary character who breaks with the received knowledge of those around her, standing as an ethical counterpoint to the calcified moral norms of church and state.[53] Ultimately, Sofia's hard-won position not only as mayor of Tome but as the president of M.O.M.A.S. (both of which I discuss further below) esteems the alternate epistemology acquired through the loss of her four daughters, a wisdom (i.e., *sophia*) that breaks with modern rationality, technical knowledge, and liberal values in order to want otherwise.

Told by an immanent third-person narrator with a gossipy and archly ironic, although not unreliable voice, *So Far from God* forwards a vision of social justice bound to a political critique of modern warfare, environmental degradation, and sexual violence. The women of Sofi's family are those whom neoliberalism "gives up," insofar as it produces *and* abandons these subjects, many of whom nevertheless, in the end, remain literally to haunt that (post)modern world.[54] In *So Far from God,* women of color experience global modernity not from the standpoint of a liberated personhood, but from their position of extreme vulnerability to the countless injuries and impairments that the current historical juncture spawns and to the violent tearing away of kin and community that might otherwise sustain their lives when disabled. Yet, in addition to its remarkable expansion of what comprises "violence against women," the novel articulates the "virtues" that these women embody as crucial to their good life, as desiring subjects and political agents, even beyond their deaths.

The narrative opens with the scene of the mysterious and sudden death of Sofia's youngest daughter while sleeping, and it mostly takes place in the house Sofia has inherited from her family, where animals wander "freely in and out" and from which she also runs a *carnecería* to make a living—having been seemingly abandoned by her husband, Domingo (whose return nearly two decades later ends the first chapter) (19). Revived during the funeral procession (and flying up to a rooftop church from where she expounds for the townspeople upon her passage through heaven, hell, and purgatory before being sent back by God "to pray for you all"), La Loca suffers a "phobia of people" for the rest of her life, an aversion that the narrator distinguishes from "an exaggerated fear of germs and contagion" (23). As La Loca explains, "*all* humans bore an odor akin to that which she had smelled in the places she had passed through when she was dead," such that her aversion signals a type of allergy to the human condition itself. She grows up and dies, barely leaving her mother's house, but possessing a supernatural sensitivity, for which she is regarded as a saint by the surrounding community (23; emphasis added). Meanwhile, Sofia's other daughters "had each gone out into the world and had all eventually returned to their mother's home" and, although "the occasions when La Loca let people get close to her, when she permitted human contact at all, were few," she never falters in her duty to "[heal] her sisters from the traumas and injustices they were dealt by society—a society she herself never experienced firsthand" (25, 27).

The opening chapter thus also portrays such occasions of social trauma and injustice as it introduces the other sisters. In the case of Fe, who mostly disdains what she deems her family's backwardness and poverty, injury is depicted as a comic situation, as she responds to her fiancé, Tom, breaking off their engagement by "letting out one loud continuous scream" that lasts for months in its duration (30). On the other hand, Caridad (who responds to the heartbreak over the end of her marriage and several abortions by having drunken, anonymous sex with men she meets at bars) is violently and mysteriously attacked and left for dead, "a nightmare incarnated" (33). The novel portrays the resolution to both sisters' initial suffering as, once again, an enigmatic and miraculous recovery that, this time, La Loca's prayers beget. With Caridad fully returned to her previous body—"not what had been left of [Sofi's] daughter, half repaired by modern medical technology, tubes through her throat, bandages over skin that was gone, surgery piecing together flesh that was once her daughter's breasts"—and the end of Fe's wailing, Castillo poses "reparation" to be a kind of "holy restoration," which is how Sofi refers to Caridad's "phenomenal recovery" (38, 43).

In fact, Caridad realizes that, as part of that restoration, she has become clairvoyant, and she moves out of her family home to become herself a healer by apprenticing with doña Felicia, the *curandera* who has been her landlady. Not only does doña Felicia observe to Caridad that "*you* healed yourself by pure will," but she comes to realize (as does La Loca), by way of her communication with Caridad through dreams, that it was neither a man nor an animal that had attacked Caridad (55). Rather, Caridad was assaulted by a *malogra,* an evil spirit that, according to New Mexican folklore, terrorizes the nighttime wanderer.[55] Portrayed by Castillo as a monstrous and ruinous power, the *malogra* is "both tangible and amorphous"; it "held the weight of a continent and was indelible as ink, centuries old and yet as strong as a young wolf . . . and mostly, as Caridad would never forget, it was pure force" (77). In the face of this impossibly ferocious force, the narrative must posit an alternative form of social agency for the otherwise impossibly injured subject who has borne the brunt of its violence.

Caridad's healing comes to completion when, while on a pilgrimage with doña Felicia, she falls in love with a woman she meets in Chimayo. Caridad thereafter disappears into a hermitage for a year, emerging from this retreat to rediscover Esmeralda, the "Woman on a wall" who had previously "bowled" her over, working at the spa she visits immediately thereafter (89). Meanwhile, although Fe remains more "earthbound," the aftermath of her own extended screaming fit includes damaged vocal cords so that "when she spoke now her voice was scratchy-sounding, similar to a faulty World War II radio transmitter, over which half of what she was saying did not get through," and this damage is rendered in the text by the literal omitting of words from Fe's dialogue (85). Nevertheless, Fe does not see herself as disabled, as she later happily marries her cousin and acquires the many signs of middle-class respectability for which she longs, most of which are paid for "with her own hard-earned money from all the bonuses she earned at her new job" (171). In both of these cases, Castillo portrays the return to integrated personhood as an inexplicable but indisputable arrival of the subject who makes claims in her own name, but who is also at once "sponsored" by the recognition La Loca grants to her sisters in her prayers (this "arrival" of their persons thus resonating with one that I discussed in chapter 2).

And yet, recuperation and health can only prove a temporary state for the sisters, as desire continually moves the novel's subjects into new forms of vulnerability. In Caridad's story, then, one of the group of men who discover her during the year she has gone missing, Francisco el Penitente, a *santero,* who makes religious images, and doña Felicia's godson, nurses an obsession with and begins stalking her. In the process, he discovers that Caridad herself keeps vigilant watch outside of Esmeralda's house, where the latter lives with her own lover, Maria. Having fallen in love with Esmeralda, La Santita Armitaña (as villagers have dubbed Caridad because the men were unable to remove her physically from her hermitage) nevertheless remains silent about her feelings, knowing that "everyone and everything that Caridad had ever given her heart to had gone away" (204). The narrator asks of this chain of desire: "How could [Caridad] not feel [Francisco's] own nearby yearning for the impossible, which was so akin to her own?" As "nobody was talking to nobody about nothing and everybody meanwhile was in a constant state of the willies, feeling like they were being followed all the time, because of course, they all were," this sequence of expectant watchfulness peaks with Francisco abducting Esmeralda (205–6). The narrator reports that the "worst" happens, implying (although never explicitly stating) his rape of Caridad's beloved and quickly qualifying this statement by observing, "well, maybe not the worst," which would have amounted to "a dead body" (207).[56]

This plotline culminates with yet another mysterious turn, as Esmeralda visits the nearby Acoma Pueblo with Caridad and Francisco trailing her and ends with a moment of clairvoyant revelation to Caridad that Francisco is a *coyote* (in the sense of trickster-figure in various Native legends). She and Esmeralda leap together off the mesa, but rather than ending up the "morbid remains of splintered bones tossed to the ground," Caridad and Esmeralda simply vanish (211). The narrator attributes their disappearance to "the spirit deity Tsichtinako," "the Invisible One" who, in the origin myth of the Acoma people, "had nourished the first two humans, who were also both female." It is thus understood to be Tsichtinako who guides "the two women back, not out towards the sun's rays or up to the clouds but down, deep within the soft, moist dark earth where Esmeralda and Caridad would be safe and live forever" (211). Francisco commits suicide soon after, unable to bear the loss of Caridad.

Meanwhile, shut out of promotions at the bank where she initially works because the "handicap" of her irregular speech makes her unintelligible to those unfamiliar with her, Fe decides to take a position as an assembler at the nebulously named Acme International, which subcontracts the cleaning of military weapons parts (177):

> As far as Fe could figure out that's how weapons for the military came to be made, manufactured like anything else in factories by people like herself, plastic and metal, undecipherable shapes, pieces and bits, down assembly lines and one day, somewhere, they were all put together and went off to be used for what they were made to do.
>
> Very important work, when you thought about it. (181)

Not only does Castillo ironically understate the function of the weapons themselves ("used for what they were made to do") and subtly convert the weapons from objects ("they were all put together") to subjects ("went off to be used") in the sentence—but the ambiguity in the reference to "very important work" further blurs the lines between agent and instrument, leaving unclear whether it is the laborers or the weaponry whose "work" is deemed "very important." This indeterminacy ultimately comes to index how the interlinked processes of global capital, state securitization, and modern warfare locate women of color in disability environments as "parahuman" subjects. For these not quite/not humans, recognition of their personhood is withdrawn and their political subjectivity disintegrated, even as the demands of state and capital keep them animated as necessary implements toward other ends.

At Acme International, then, not only does Fe apprehend "something eerie and full of coincidences" about the many ailments from which her coworkers suffer, but, as she takes on new responsibilities that require her to handle industrial solvents, she finds herself increasingly ill; headaches and skin irritations give way to lost fingernails, chronic indigestion, and eventually cancer (180). The medical treatment she receives is equally as distressing, as Fe likens it to a form of torture, and the company makes her the scapegoat for the improper disposal of the illegal chemicals she has been assigned to use and which become the subject of an FBI investigation. Learning eventually that one of the chemicals is "heavier than air," Fe comes to see that it has been her body that absorbed the particulates as they evaporated, and she rages to her supervisor: "WHERE DID _ GO, PENDE_, SON-_-A . . . IF NOT IN_ ME?" (189). Fe's initial and seemingly negligible injury (the speech impediment that remains after her original romantic debacle) derails her from the hegemonic vision of an American good life and drives her, in a compensatory effort, into the extraordinarily devastating conditions that result in her death. Critics have readily identified the environmental racism that structures the injustice of Fe's plot, in which her adherence to the American dream is met with the structural inequities that not only exclude women of color from its achievement, but necessarily abject and decompose them in securing the good life of others.[57]

The subtext of warfare in Fe's story implicitly articulates with the plot of her sister Esperanza's narrative, whose death, in contrast to the others, takes place offstage, during the first Gulf War of 1991, which she covers while working as a journalist for a local news program. This oldest sister's plotline in Tome centers on her relationship with the man who brings her into the Chicano movement, Rubén, but who nevertheless treats her with casual disrespect. Finally ridding herself of Rubén, Esperanza travels to Saudi Arabia at the behest of her employers, where she is abducted and murdered. Eventually the family receives official notice from the Army that "Esperanza had been disappeared for months," and "Army officials claimed to know for a fact that she was dead [although] they also claimed to not be able to locate her body so as to send it home" (159). However, it is La Loca who first reports to her mother that, "la Esperanza is died . . . she got killed over there. Tor . . . tured," after having learned of the loss from La Llorona, the cursed mother of Mexican legend, who visits La Loca regularly and whom I discuss in more detail below (158, 160).

Finally, and closing the circle opened with her passing and resurrection in its opening pages, the novel's last death takes place with La Loca's succumbing to AIDS, as she is inexplicably inflicted with HIV, despite her lifelong aversion to touching or being touched by other human beings. Sofia entrusts the ailing Loca's care to the Filipino Doctor Tolentino, whom she has known her entire life, and the doctor in turn undertakes a hybrid treatment that combines medical and spiritual remedies to temporarily alleviate La Loca's suffering from the "mystifying" disease. But, as the physician realizes, "although sometimes a disease could be stopped, death ultimately could not be" (229). When La Loca does finally pass away, many months later, she does so in the arms of yet another mysterious presence, a nun-like "Lady in Blue"—an allusion to the seventeenth-century Castilian nun María de Agreda, who, according to New Mexico folklore, bilocated in order to apprise the native Jumano Indians of the imminent arrival of Franciscan missionaries. The Lady in Blue visits and keeps Loca company until she "went to sleep in the Lady's arms thinking that for a person who had lived her whole life within a mile radius of her home and had only traveled as far as Albuquerque twice, she certainly knew quite a bit about this world, not to mention beyond, too" (244–45).

In offering a realist account of the disability environments that industrial capital, modern warfare, and heteropatriarchy engender, *So Far from God* never dismisses conventional social affiliations and political mobilization. Yet, as should be clear from the foregoing summary, given the extensive injury that these conditions pose, in order to sustain its minor subjects, the novel must also ascribe a magical and mysterious dimension to supplement more expected forms of contestation and resistance. While many critics tend to read *So Far from God* as a straightforward parody and dismissal of religious and familial institutions for their inherent patriarchal and heteronormative orientations, I suggest that in terms of both form and content, the novel seeks to transfigure extant local traditions and spiritual convictions into alternative social resources for those whom the (neo)liberal imaginary has given up as lost. Without a critical emphasis on this dialectical relationship, such analyses reduce women's suffering *either* to their position within repressive cultural traditions *or* to racial and class inequities that organize borderland life. Unable to grapple with the complex interrelations between the two, such readings have elided how, despite neoliberal claims that modern industrial labor relations and global circuits of exchange have destroyed traditional patriarchy, they often recompose and elaborate masculine, national, and racial privilege in especially potent forms.[58] To offer a political vision that might counter the refunctioning of traditional norms by (post)modern relations of production and social life, the novel does not wholly forego, but instead continually adapts indigenous and Chicano historical forms and norms to apprehend its characters' lives and grant them social meaning, even beyond their physical deaths.

Thus, for example, critics have extensively detailed how the lesbian feminist sensibility of Caridad's story is rendered by way of an indigenous consciousness. The narrative accordingly articulates a response to contemporary reconstructions of traditional sexual mores by patriarchal fundamentalisms that inflict tremendous violence against the women it polices.[59] But the turn to an Acoma origin myth also offers a dissent from secular, (neo)liberal feminist conceptions of women's sexual autonomy. As critics have also further documented, Caridad and Esmeralda's return to Tsichtinako places them in a matrilineal tradition that regards women as creator-figures; this tradition is indigenous to the region about which Castillo writes and exists prior to the religious, social, and economic institutions that otherwise organize women's lives according to the restrictive binary of oppressive tradition and individual liberation.[60] Similarly, given La Loca's rootedness in her mother's home, itself a legacy from Sofia's family who are otherwise only barely invoked, and the relatively peaceful death her character is afforded, critics have described a feminist politics of domesticity in Castillo's novel concentrated in the care and nourishment that Sofia and La Loca provide the other women, who face an external world that brutalizes them, regardless of the political and ideological orientation they adopt toward it.[61] Such a feminist cultural politics in fact rearticulates the public/private divide, shifting political borders in the interest of creating new "home spaces" for the novel's subjects.[62]

The inscription of such feminist domesticity in *So Far from God* further entails a critical transfiguration of La Llorona, the legendary "Weeping Woman [who] astral-traveled all throughout old Mexico, into the United States, and really anywhere her people lived, wailing, in search of her children whom she drowned so as to run off with her lover. For that God punished her forever on earth" (160). When La Loca conveys to her mother that La Llorona regularly visits her, the narrator avows that this "nonsense"—as Fe deems it—must be true, "since Loca did not know how to lie," and, more to the point, "what might be attributed to 'imagination' in others, in Loca's case was nothing short of what had happened, like it or not" (159). (Indeed, the whereabouts of Esperanza's body actually remains more of a diegetic mystery than the identity of the mysterious woman who visits La Loca, since the novel promptly identifies the latter as La Llorona.) However, *So Far from God* also at once repudiates the disciplinary function of La Llorona; not only does Sofia refuse "to repeat this nightmare to her daughters," but the narrator observes that "Sofia had not left her children, much less drowned them to run off with nobody. On the contrary, she had been left to raise them by herself" (161).[63] While for Sofia, "all her life, there had always been at least one woman around like her, left alone, abandoned, divorced, or widowed, to raise her children, and none of them have ever tried to kill her babies," she also concludes, on the rare occasion when she had heard "in the newspaper or maybe it was on the radio" about a woman killing her children, that "the mother was only human and anyone is capable at some point when pushed into a corner like a rat to devour her babies in order to save them, so to speak" (162).

In this sliding chain of signifiers, mothers are "only human" and also at once "like a rat," emphasizing the limits of any woman's ability to maintain her own well-being and the health and safety of her family as social and economic resources to do so disappear. Consequently, by materializing—or more precisely spectralizing—La Llorona as the medium through which Esperanza communicates to her family, the novel maintains the legend to register the constrained and inhospitable material and environmental conditions in which women of color live and labor and the extent to which their humanity must be cultivated through express political will. Eventually, the spirit of Esperanza herself begins appearing, not only to La Loca, but to the rest of her family. Yet, after recounting the trauma of Esperanza's death and the ghostly visitations, the chapter seamlessly returns to yet another decidedly domestic scene, with Fe receiving cooking lessons from La Loca and a section relating "three of La Loca's favorite recipes just to whet your appetite" (165). In addition to her inscription in terms of feminist domesticity, critics have also attributed to La Loca a queer abjection, as she remains indispensable to but also located at the margins of family and communal life, and, of course, she dies of AIDS.[64]

The narrative moves easily, then, between realism and the fantastic, and both aesthetic modes are integral to its rendering of character and plot. But, as Marta Caminero-Santangelo has convincingly argued, if we conflate the moments of magic in the novel with magical realism, *per se,* we risk romanticizing and exoticizing (and contributing to the commodification of) that which in "Latin American (and, by association, Latino/a) culture . . . to a Western audience seem[s] to be magical, mystical, primitive and superstitious."[65] As important is that we risk missing how often the magical actually *displaces* or *replaces* the possibility of collective action in the novel, where "Castillo forcefully highlights the chasm between the magic and the real."[66] However, whereas Caminero-Santangelo infers from such fantastic moments the "threat of passivity" and "escapist romanticism" against which Castillo warns, I contend that the tension between the novel's literal, local politics and its literary speculations mediates its adoption and adaptation of allegorical forms.[67] As in Lahiri's story, this move to allegory is one intimately tied to the narrative's feminist and queer visions. Here, the feminist and queer, however, are both rooted in social realism yet also continually break with it, opening their concerns for nurturing domesticity and wandering desires to the fantastic order that marginalized lifeworlds make available.

In so doing, the novel also extends a remarkable commentary on critical norms that would relegate the narrative to being on the side *either* of praxis *or* of escape and therefore fail to recognize that, as Daniel Y. Kim has written in a different context, the work's value resides not in the politics that it "could never give us anyway" but rather in the "politics that it might make us *want*."[68] In *So Far from God*, then, we might read La Loca as an ethico-political switch-point for relating its thematic treatment of "real" social, environmental, and bodily damage and the seeming extravagance of the novel's allegorical execution. If there is no way to reconcile literally La Loca's illness and death with her nearly complete physical isolation from other humans, the occasion of the second death she undergoes moves us once again to read the mystery of her story as, precisely, formal allegory in which an impossible subject is nevertheless conjured or invented as a political agent.

Specifically, as McRuer has argued, to declare oneself as "HIV positive," regardless of one's actual serostatus, "for the purposes of solidarity" is "to come out as something you are—at least in some ways—not."[69] By traversing the borders between the real and unreal, health and illness, life and death, La Loca's plot fuses feminist, queer, and disability perspectives in order to refuse "the fixation on life as understood in strictly medical terms" and to propose instead "a communicable disability agency" that operates according to the logic of an impossible but enduring political desire.[70] This process of "coming out crip," as McRuer further explains, "involves embracing and at times disidentifying with the most familiar kinds of identity politics."[71] The narrative's indifference to generic, spatial, and temporal boundaries proves imperative if the novel's disabled subjects are to live on and endure, in the face of their many injuries—injuries that the novel recognizes as being too often *mortal* ones.

Animating the Right to Health

For Castillo, the cultural animation of indigenous and Chicano forms is hence vital to the political vision and agencies needed to address the disability environment of the U.S. borderlands. When, for example, Sofia is inspired by Esperanza's example of political engagement to run for mayor of Tome, the narrative casts the decision as a quite radical break with local commonsense.[72] As Sofi surprises a friend with her pronouncement about this political post (in a town that "wasn't even an incorporated village" and "never had no mayor"), the *comadre* exclaims, "You're the one who's . . . always had a lot of imagination," in what is less a compliment than a veiled rebuke, and Sofi counters: "It's not 'imagination' that I've always had, comadre, it's faith" (137–38). In the process of organizing her campaign, she helps launch a "sheep-grazing wool-weaving enterprise, 'Los Ganados y Lana Cooperative,'" which over the course of many years comes, along with Sofia's stewardship, to rejuvenate the local community (146). Posing such realist politics to be in many ways as unlikely and astonishing as the supernatural incidents she portrays, Castillo thematizes the work of both the literary imagination *and* religious faith as crucial to mobilizing political struggle that normative belief poses as impracticable.

Likewise, while the narrative nominally restores the normative nuclear family with Domingo's return in the first chapter, his reappearance coincides with "the spontaneous recoveries" of Fe and Caridad, which are "beyond all rhyme and reason" (39). The narrator recounts the passionate beginning of the couple's relationship, recalling how Sofia first meets the charming and handsome Domingo at her *quinceañera* and elopes with him against her family's wishes three years later. On his return, however, Domingo mostly proves no more useful in alleviating the family's troubles, and Sofia pays no more attention to him than "an old chair in the corner of the room or a table passed on from one generation to the next" (109). In fact, what Sofia finally does remember near the novel's end is that it was actually not Domingo who had abandoned the family in the first place, but she who had ordered him to leave as he accumulated gambling debts that threatened the family's welfare. And after his return and resumption of gambling, when he loses her house in a bet to an Anglo judge, Sofia finally divorces him. The repression and recovery of this memory of Sofia's decision mark it as yet another example of the negotiations that women in the borderland must make, simultaneously astonishing and routine, to keep themselves and their dependents alive.

At the same time, the plot supplements its representation of quotidian family troubles, as Castillo situates it in a much longer history of displacement that is telegraphed by Sofi's friend in a brief conversation, as "the gringos took most of our land away when they took over the territory from Mexico—right after Mexico had taken it from Spain" (217). But La Loca, with her signal gift for discerning the suffering of others, also literally "sniffs out" that during his many years away, her father "was in hell," recognizing the smell from when she herself passed through this abyss during her own death (41). As she explains to Sofi, "Only in hell do we learn to forgive and you got to die first. . . . Mom, hell is where you go to see yourself. This dad . . . he was in hell a long time" (42). La Loca's account of his extraordinary suffering mediates what otherwise might be attributed *either* to Domingo's personal failings, on the one hand, *or* to the ongoing debasement of Chicano manhood in colonial history, on the other. Instead, as someone returned from the hellish abjection that his addiction to gambling engenders, Domingo must learn to inhabit anew the family of "daughters in crisis who had become women during his absence" and the mother who tends to them, a family to whom he remains responsible but over whom heteropatriarchal privilege is no longer guaranteed (110).

Finally, near its conclusion the novel merges traditional religious forms with its realist political critique, when Sofia and La Loca attend a Way of the Cross procession. In this version of the Catholic Good Friday tradition—about which the narrator remarks, "No one had never seen a procession like that one before"—Castillo replaces the conventional stations of the cross with *testimonios* given by the native and Chicano residents of Tome about the many types of damage the local residents have endured (238, 244). Bearing witness to the environmental toxins and contaminants, wracking illness, ongoing international conflict, and economic destitution and homelessness that beget the disabled parahumans of Sofia's family, this chapter makes visible how the entire borderland region is subject to what Rob Nixon calls the "slow violence" of colonialism and globalization, wherein the environmental effects of imperial states and transnational corporations long outlive the presence of those entities themselves.[73] In particular, *So Far from God* is concerned with forms of displacement that a globalizing modernity produces, even for those peoples not forcibly removed from the world they know and to which they belong, since, as Nixon contends, the "loss of land and resources beneath them . . . leaves communities stranded in a place stripped of the very characteristics that made it inhabitable."[74]

As might be apparent from the foregoing discussion, the many stylistic and narrative components of Castillo's text are difficult to distill as discrete formal and structural elements, without involving its other aspects. Not only does the narrative blend a remarkable range of aesthetic and generic forms, but its many different plots are intricately interwoven in order to render what one critic designates its "sisterhood of social ills."[75] Further interlaced with the stories of Sofia and her four daughters are chapters and portions of chapters that recount the lives of other, more minor characters, who nevertheless play pivotal roles in the protagonists' lives. As they provide context for the novel, these sections further elaborate aspects of the indigenous, Catholic, and Chicano lifeworlds in the U.S. borderland of New Mexico. For example, Castillo devotes a chapter to doña Felicia's story—spanning a century, several wars, and multiple husbands and children—and "a brief sampling of doña Felicia's Remedies," a catalogue of traditional therapies, emphasizing organic cures and affective measures of health. Similarly, near the novel's end, while doña Felicia helps tend to a dying Loca, there appears a list of "a handful of . . . tried and proven remedies" that she shares with Doctor Tolentino. Another chapter, "An Interlude: On Francisco el Penitente's First Becoming a Santero and Thereby Sealing His Fate," describes Francisco's vocation as a *santero* (94). The same chapter also includes, as the extended chapter title goes on to report, "what appears to be a deviation of our story but wherein, with some patience, the reader will discover that there is always more than the eye can see to any account"—namely, an anecdote of a disturbing highway encounter between two women driving through rural New Mexico who find themselves mysteriously tailed, sideswiped, and shot at by a man in a pickup truck. Eventually, the chapter "connect[s]-the-dots" to reveal one of the women as Maria, the lover of Caridad's "woman on the wall," Esmeralda (120).

In its meticulous construction of these many subplots and layered representations of the regional setting, the narrative further disregards clearly demarcated borders between past and present, fantasy and reality, the personal and the communal, the queer and the straight, the indigenous, the Chicana/o, and the Anglo-American, the human and the animal, and, most significantly for our purposes, health or well-being and injury, impairment, or illness, as well as life and death.[76] In its hybrid form and content, *So Far from God* inscribes the complex mediations that assemble its minor subjects and the inevitable concessions that those subjects must undertake. Nothing and no one in this borderworld, not even La Loca, is pure, uncontaminated, and immune to the biopolitics and security technologies of the modern state and global capital. But neither are they entirely unmoored and adrift from the specific social, cultural, and political histories that have constituted the borderlands as such. This "contaminated" and yet "faithful" construction of the region as an "antiutopic utopia of impurity and cultural hybridity" in turn configures the specific approach to identity politics that the novel wields, especially in its conclusion.[77]

As a vital supplement to the grim realities represented in the Way of the Cross (and even La Loca's more peaceful death), the institution of the M.O.M.A.S. in the final chapter offers an ultimately hopeful, if more ludic, turn to a speculative future. Described as being similar to conventional NGOs—including an annual conference that comes to overshadow the World Series and the Olympics—the narrator insists nonetheless that "the conference of M.O.M.A.S. was very serious business, hombre!" where spirits of those being revered communicate "news and advice that was, as part of the bylaws, generously passed on to relatives, friends, the petitioning faithful, and community agencies, as well as to relevant local or federal governments" (251). Brian Norman astutely identifies M.O.M.A.S. as an alternate counterpublic, in which the "dead women talking are not ghosts, but citizens" who "facilitate very real political activity," which "harbor[s] the capacity to alter the course of the present, as well as the future."[78]

But, as constituted by Castillo, M.O.M.A.S. also imprints the dilemma inherent to translating race-, gender-, and nation-based movements into the idiom of human rights: in order to avoid flattening out specific legal and political claims in the name of an abstract "humanity," social and political movements risk reifying the "wounded" identity as the source of all rights and agency. For example, the narrator challenges the mother of Fe's former fiancée, Tom Torres, who has protested her exclusion from membership in M.O.M.A.S.—despite the fact that she fails to meet the organization's most fundamental criterion, namely, "that the martyr or saint up for consideration would have to have transcended this life already" (247). Meanwhile, we are told, Tom has "lived well beyond the national average for anybody and kept Mrs. Torres company as her dutiful son until his mother's passing" (247). The "wounded identity" required to become recognized by M.O.M.A.S. is one provisionally open to all mothers—insofar as any of their children might become ill, injured, and impaired, and hence a martyr done in by the damage and terror that global capital and modern states wreak upon vulnerable humans in the borderland. Tom's ongoing (more or less) good life, however, maintains that such "universal" vulnerability does not, in fact, instantiate itself as disability and disposability evenly and uniformly. Moreover, the narrator's dismissal of Mrs. Torres's petition for membership queries why anyone would *want* such damage to be the grounds of belonging.

However, if the novel repudiates a fixed politics of race and nation, neither does it prize a postracial or liberal pluralist vision of humanity. Rather, it tracks the differential distribution of privilege and lack, protection and vulnerability by which disciplinary power assembles "integrated" persons and bodies, where racial forms comprise material traces of historical exclusion (as I have discussed at length in the introduction and chapter 1) and some forms of life are rendered more contingent and dispensable than others. In this case, as disability scholars have begun to argue, racialized and disabled subjectivities are not only analogous to one another but in fact "coterminous" with each other, such that "*all* subjectivity is implicitly prosthetic."[79] The reparation and restoration embodied by Caridad and Fe in the novel's first chapter thus allegorizes the aspirations of many contemporary political struggles and, indeed, are taken to be no trivial matter. Caridad's story, for instance, concatenates the disabled subject's well-being (restored by her own will in conjunction with La Loca's prayerful recognition of her personhood) with a social agency that, in turn, allows her to serve as a healer to others. But such reparation also provides no permanent guarantees of a good life and well-being, which are once again risked in the name of desires that exceed the boundaries of sovereign identity. Well-being and a good life are never secured once and for all, but must instead be constantly cultivated as a project of political justice.

Ultimately, the novel's feminist, queer, and disability perspectives disorder identity categories in order to imagine new types of affiliation between bodies given up in and by the U.S. borderlands, while remaining attentive to the historical conditions that produce those very bodies in the first place. As in many of the narratives I have considered in *Writing Human Rights,* including "Hema and Kaushik" above, Fe and Caridad both figure as persons ultimately lost to a global imaginary of the American good life, even as the losses signify in strikingly divergent ethico-political terms. The loss of Fe remarks upon the limits of a (neo)liberal imaginary that prizes possessive individualism, privatized domesticity, and bourgeois respectability and instrumentalizes, only ultimately to disintegrate, the subjects it creates. In contrast, Caridad's return to Tsichtinako suggests a constitutive exteriority to the postmodernity of global capital. However, because that exterior remains inaccessible to subjective being, it can be figured only as the mysterious alterity of a death that undoes those, such as Francisco, whom it leaves in its wake. Between these extreme ends of human life, the narrative resurrects La Loca and spectralizes Esperanza precisely to make claims for a speculative future justice harnessed to the subjects of these disabilities "to come" for global bodies and minor subjects.[80] A human rights approach to *So Far from God* thus not only preserves the novel's place as a hybrid narrative of borderland modernities, lived at the juncture of colonial history, global capital, the security state, and patriarchal fundamentalisms, but discerns a disability critique that mobilizes an expansive human right to health and health citizenship, which "reimagine[s] disability, to reveal how the storied quality of disability invents and reinvents the world we share."[81]

Moreover, casting M.O.M.A.S. as on the verge of becoming like any other NGO, *So Far from God* further addresses how easily, without an eye toward critical dissensus, such political projects are absorbed and repurposed by global capital and state actors as humanitarian agencies, rendering health a matter of charitable administration.[82] At the novel's close, then, the right to health remains a live and ongoing question. If, as I describe below, the human right to health entails providing "individuals and communities with an authentic voice in decisions defining, determining, and affecting their well-being," *So Far from God* insists upon the achievement of "well-being" through something other than biomedical administration or humanitarian charity.[83] This resolution, I contend, returns us to the international bill of rights to formulate a human rights claim to health citizenship that rearticulates the terms of health and well-being in the United States.[84]

Human rights scholars have described "health citizenship" and the "right to health" as a key component of second-generation human rights. Conceived of as a positive liberty, because it requires active intervention on the part of states, the right to health has not been traditionally recognized within the United States as a "natural right"—that is, as one of the civil and political liberties enumerated in the Constitution's Bill of Rights and referred to, in human rights discourse, as "first-generation" rights. Bryan S. Turner argues that "health citizenship" names an essential human right and that public health entails the physical (including environmental) conditions to maintain good health.[85] Unlike civil liberties, which are conceived as the state's refraining from interference with the activities of individuals, health citizenship is fostered through the active effort by the state and/or other political collectivities. Moreover, as a human right, the right to health extends to all people within a national territory, regardless of citizenship or immigration status.

The definition of the "right to health" is itself deeply contested, with some scholars and practitioners advocating for the "right to healthcare" or the "right to health protection" as more realistic than the rather ambiguous and subjective concept of a "right to health" per se.[86] Disability scholars and activists have shown that empiricist conceptions of health readily undergird moral panics that disciplinary regimes organize, usually against already marginalized subjects. As Jonathan Metzel cautions, health can too easily prove "an unattainable ideal, one that [makes] no room for suffering, aging, dying, or other natural processes."[87] Biomedical and consumerist rhetorics of health accordingly convert the ideal of well-being into normative sets of moral obligations and privatized goods.[88] It is thus imperative to distinguish health citizenship from what might be termed "biological citizenship," where, divorced from social justice claims and concerns over social power, both personal (genetic) inequities and the imperative to correct them become individual responsibilities.[89]

In contrast, a human rights approach frames health and well-being not as matters of charity or special privileges, but in terms of social justice claims, which extend to migrant workers and other noncitizens as well.[90] The human right to health therefore marks the *limits* of biopolitical and neoliberal regimes to address more expansive conceptions and conditions of well-being. For example, Article 12 of the International Covenant on Economic, Social and Cultural Rights (ICESCR) stipulates "the right of everyone to the enjoyment of the highest attainable standard of physical and mental health," as well as stating that

> steps to be taken by the States Parties to the present Covenant to achieve the full realization of this right shall include those necessary for: (a) The provision for the reduction of the stillbirth-rate and of infant mortality and for the healthy development of the child; (b) The improvement of all aspects of environmental and industrial hygiene; (c) The prevention, treatment and control of epidemic, endemic, occupational and other diseases; (d) The creation of conditions which would assure to all medical service and medical attention in the event of sickness.

To the extent that it recognizes the structural, environmental, occupational, and economic conditions that must be in place to secure well-being, the broader concept of the right to health that prevails in international human rights discourse moves well beyond the therapeutic and rehabilitative logics of health services and biomedical institutions in order to recognize those aspects of human life that cannot be attained without political will and collective action.[91] Without such rights-based guarantees, the servicing of health needs is imagined in the more limited terms of marketplace commodities for those (increasingly fewer) individuals who can afford it, or as the dispensation of charity.[92]

Such a framework of justice and equity is consistently omitted from discussions about healthcare in the United States (e.g., in the debates surrounding the passage of the Patient Protection and Affordable Care Act).[93] Indeed, the United States is the only industrialized country that does not recognize the obligation to provide healthcare, which human rights scholars see as a central component of securing the right to health in any nation, since the right to health obligates governments to respect, protect, and fulfill that right.[94] Americans have nevertheless long considered access to bodily and psychological well-being to be more than merely and rightly a privatized luxury, even while they have debated vociferously how such access should be institutionalized.[95] Meanwhile, a number of other countries, such as Cuba, Mexico, Venezuela, and Vietnam, include the right to health in their national constitutions, although the practical translation and implementation of such commitments remain highly uneven within and between states.

As we have seen in chapter 1, as the panoply of human rights principles is elaborated in political theory and international instruments, it is integrated and indivisible, and the concept of the right to health has a number of important social, cultural, and political implications. States and international bodies are expected to ensure equitable distribution of health services; the privatization of such services does not relieve states from having to guarantee adequate access to healthcare. The right to health calls for the achievement of the "underlying preconditions for health," such as environmental and occupational hygiene and health education, as well as particular attentiveness to vulnerable groups and respect for traditional cultural practices.[96] Yet, at the same time, the right to health maintains central political and civil liberties and thus proscribes coercive policies, such as forced testing and treatment. In short, a human rights approach focuses on facilitating individuals' "capabilities to be healthy and on their ability to determine what comprises their own well-being."[97]

Formulated in this way, the human right to health (like all human rights principles) poses an undoubtedly complex and daunting challenge that might very well be impossible to achieve and sustain. Like the other human rights claims I have considered in *Writing Human Rights,* "health" and "well-being" provide yet another set of empty signifiers that index historical and structural constraints, indicating what the subjects of human rights "want" to be otherwise about their existence. But, as a World Health Organization study concludes, provisions for the right to health, in constitutional frameworks for example, are "valuable aspirational statements on which domestic legislation and policy directives are based," and instruments that integrate a human rights approach can serve as crucial propositions to state parties, human rights activists, and health services providers, by which "willing governments can identify and gradually implement targeted and concrete actions through a participatory process where priority medical needs and available resources are considered."[98] As one health advocate observes, a human rights approach to health involves "identifying an entitlement and then patiently insisting that it be fulfilled."[99] As such, "health" and "well-being" are not simply meaningless or abstract ideals, but offer a critical perspective on what has been rendered historically and materially impossible in the present.[100]

The right to health thus provides a potent opening for political critique and moral imagining, and minor literatures present one significant site from which these emerge. As my readings of "Hema and Kaushik" and *So Far from God* in this chapter suggest, minor literatures can also render the possibility of newly flexible and hitherto unthought modes of interdependent community with others, grounded in experiences of vulnerability. Minor literatures shift our conception of the subject of rights from the autonomous individual citizen, who is defined by his capacities (to reason, to labor, and so on) to that of the vulnerable, embodied subject whose well-being must be actively fostered by the political community that engenders and cares for her.[101] Both Lahiri and Castillo's texts cast families, rather than individuals, as the protagonists of contemporary narrative in order to consider how the well-being of minor subjects is to be found in the intimate relations of care that neoliberalism relegates to private matters of the home. Yet both family narratives also reveal starkly the inadequacies of the heteropatriarchal family for responding to the wide-ranging insecurities of the contemporary historical juncture as well as the mobile desires of the minor subjects they portray. Both "Hema and Kaushik" and *So Far from God* therefore appeal to new forms of kinship in the face of such failure. Next, in the conclusion, then, I turn to the "right to family" to consider how minor literatures craft new visions of family to enable the minor subjects that they write into existence.

UN Convention on the Rights of the Child
Aimee Phan, *We Should Never Meet*

Conclusion

An Aesthetics of Kin and the Rights of the Child

In the summer of 2014, U.S. media outlets began reporting of a surge in the numbers of unaccompanied children crossing the nation's southern border. From October 2013 to August 2014, well over 60,000 undocumented minors had been apprehended arriving from Central American nations, especially from El Salvador, Guatemala, and Honduras, as well as Mexico. Fleeing poverty and violence, and often seeking to reunite with family members living in the United States, they lacked lawful immigration status and were usually detained at the border or U.S. ports of entry. Congressional Republicans and conservative commentators blamed their presence on the Obama administration's lax immigration controls and executive overreach in deferring deportations of underage border-crossers. Immigrant advocates and media watch-groups disputed this portrait of the minors—who were often also described as disease-ridden gang members, fronts for narcotics operations, and "anchors" for the rest of their families in the United States—insisting instead that those escaping violence in their home countries could and should be conferred refugee status in accordance with the United Nations 1951 Refugee Convention and that such a move could "dramatically alter the way we view and legally treat [unaccompanied alien children]."[1]

Toward these ends, activists pointed to the skyrocketing levels of violence and corruption arising from the international drug trade and criminal activity in Mexico and Central America, where Latin American governments were at best unable to provide any type of basic security or protection to their populaces and at worst were fully infiltrated by and complicit with such enterprises. This political strategy seemed to gain some traction, with President Obama pronouncing the children's arrival as part of an "urgent humanitarian situation" and even the chairman of the House Committee on Homeland Security, Michael McCaul, describing the situation as an "escalating refugee crisis." But conservatives also steadily continued to refer to the minors as illegal immigrants and ramped up efforts to hasten deportation for those who had already been detained. Deeming them to be vulnerable victims of illegal violence and humanitarian suffering, on the one hand, or avaricious and willful agents of illegal border-crossing, on the other, this polarized representation of the unaccompanied minors corresponds to the conflicted and contested relationship between (neo)liberal humanitarianism and practices of personal, social, and national security.[2] (This divided construction also characterized contemporaneous images of Syrian refugees and helped fuel a backlash against migrants in the 2016 presidential election, the devastating consequences of which are still unfolding as *Writing Human Rights* goes to press.) Despite the fact that cataclysmic economic, geopolitical, and social changes since World War II have "contributed to making separated and unaccompanied child asylum seekers a truly global—and not just regional—phenomenon," only a very small portion of such children are recognized by the United States as holding legitimate asylum claims, and the rest are left to fend for themselves in "a system designed for adults and ill-suited to their needs."[3] Thus, for example, although international law and U.S. criminal law require official guardianship and legal representation to be provided for a child facing legal proceedings, the nation's immigration laws do not stipulate such protections.

Ultimately, these children "have not the rights that they have and have the rights they have not."[4] While legal scholars rightfully propose the introduction of "child-specific" legal provisions in U.S. immigration law and the judicial review of asylum claims, in this short conclusion I have a somewhat different purpose in mind.[5] I suggest that through the literally minor subject who is the unaccompanied child, we might critically reencounter the attenuated personhood of global modernity, where routinized and pervasive warfare, rapidly shifting economic and employment opportunities, environmental disaster, civil unrest, and state violence debilitate the free, full, and harmonious "development of personality" for a range of human beings (to paraphrase language that appears in both the Universal Declaration of Human Rights and the Convention on the Rights of the Child). Minor literatures—here I turn to Aimee Phan's short story collection *We Should Never Meet* (2004)—advance an "aesthetics of kin" in response to the "right to family" claimed by the child, even the adult child, who has been partitioned from her "natural" community and set afloat in the world. As I conclude my discussion of the family romance and family saga, I contend that in minor literatures the families "given up" and assembled by global modernity prove essential crucibles of recognition, provision, and justice for the difficult subjects of human rights who arrive, and have yet to arrive, to make claims in their own names.

The Child in Law

The media spotlight on unaccompanied children in 2014 made widely visible the morass of social, legal, and geopolitical factors involved in a situation with a much more extensive history in the twentieth century. While unaccompanied children in need of resettlement are most highly concentrated in the global South in nations that have experienced natural or political catastrophes, since 1945 most separated and unaccompanied children officially admitted into the United States did so under the terms of authorized resettlement programs.[6] Unsurprisingly, the largest proportion of children evacuated and resettled in the United States has mostly come from Communist (or formerly Communist) states, including about 14,000 Cuban children in the early 1960s and 3,300 Vietnamese children in Operation Babylift in 1975 (to which I return below); those being placed in American adoptive families, especially from Korea, China, and Russia, also make up a significant number. Refugee status and asylum are granted only in cases of direct "danger or persecution," and this has applied as much to children as to adults. For other minors seeking immigration protections in the United States the approach is, as Jacqueline Bhabha and Susan Schmidt observe, "Kafkaesque—surreal in its application of adult procedures to some of society's most vulnerable children."[7]

In this regard the treatment of children confirms the state's unimpeded prerogative to survey and choose from all of humanity those whom it considers to be eligible for an American good life and, conversely, those who are to be categorically excluded from it. In most popular and legal perceptions, the child possesses diminished or no physical and intellectual ability; she is in need of protection with almost no "voice" or capacity to represent or sustain herself.[8] As we have seen throughout *Writing Human Rights,* though, this kind of existence—of pure vulnerability and "bare life"—is exactly what has defined the "human" in contradistinction to the personhood of the citizen under the modern state system. Thus, insofar as "humanity" is conferred upon migrants, refugees, and other national aliens, the child proves not an exceptional figure of the human, but rather an exemplary one. Indeed, the infantilization that so often characterizes the "merely human" objects of humanitarian traffic, abuse, and charity results from the sharp distinction drawn between the person granted recognition and hence enabled before the law and the stateless object of geopolitical crisis and humanitarian care.

Yet, the state's regnant power over the child's life recedes from view as parents come to bear the responsibility for the plight of children, with children standing as little more than appendages of or accessories to individual adults and the social and economic decisions that they make.[9] Citizenship, and legal status more generally, is assumed to be a "one-way descending flow of familial transmission," whereby not only are children always "naturally" attached to their parents' physical presence, but they inherit their parents' legal personhood as well.[10] (As a result, even if procedurally the *unaccompanied* child's status differs almost not at all from that of the adult migrant, the image of this child, bereft of the parental protection and obligation that are supposed to always accompany them, evokes much more vexed social and cultural responses, as in the divided reactions to those who arrived in 2014.[11]) Likewise, the child *citizen* is also one whose personhood is mediated and diminished in relation to other citizens before the law. The child's rights to direct political participation (e.g., at what age the child can vote, sit on a jury, or be drafted) certainly differ substantially from those of adults. But different nations also accord different forms of parental power in relation to the state's own role as *parens patriae* to the child. Children are assumed to be almost entirely apprentice-like in character, "citizens in the making, 'future' rather than actual citizens," and a vast range of adults, first and foremost parents, but also teachers and school administrators, physicians and healthcare workers, social workers, police, judges, and others mediate children's access to rights.[12]

The child is, thus, a difficult and disputed subject of law and rights across the globe, as different legal and governmental regimes approach the child in markedly dissimilar ways, which often also prove internally contradictory.[13] Under a welfare framework, the child is primarily an object of social administration and regulation. Neoliberal legal frameworks, to a further extent, construe the child as an (almost) adult rights- and duty-holder, as, for example, in the United States, where juveniles are regularly charged as adults under state and federal criminal law (and the caricature of the unaccompanied minor as an illegal security or economic threat shares this viewpoint).[14] And from an authoritarian, conservative, or common law perspective, the child amounts mainly to an object of possession and discipline.[15] None of these legal and political vantages on its own does justice to the concatenation of vulnerability, will, and possibility that the child has become in a globalized terrain of late modernity, and as typified in the example with which I began this conclusion, legal and policy officials often find themselves scrambling to reform and update the substantive and procedural norms to accord with the changing social and economic circumstances to which the child is subject. The child's "rights deficit," in which children nominally have claim to any number of rights but those claims are constantly debilitated by the child's deferred right to have rights, constitutes children as paradoxical political subjects, whose vulnerability to exposure and abandonment is at once spectacularly visible in political speech and national culture but nonetheless always being enacted by the very institutions that are meant to extend protection and belonging.[16]

The Universal Declaration of Human Rights (UDHR) was of course meant to include children under its purview, insofar as they are considered to be human beings. Yet almost no specific mention of the child is made in that document, and the Convention on the Rights of the Child (CRC), drafted nearly forty years after the UDHR, responded to the "special needs" of children for which the more abstract notion of the human person will not suffice. Like the other human rights subjects I have addressed in *Writing Human Rights* (such as women or the disabled), the child designates a particular kind of human being that human rights discourses presume already exists across the globe, even while the construction of "childhood" has certainly been historically specific and culturally variable. Indeed, the CRC defines the child very broadly as "every human being below the age of eighteen years unless under the law applicable to the child, majority is attained earlier." What seems to distinguish the child in particular is the need for special protections and safeguards "by reason of his physical and mental immaturity." The convention therefore emphasizes that states must act in the best interests of the child, including providing the child with a legal identity and protecting her from abuse, exploitation, trafficking, and capital punishment. But the CRC also affirms the provisions and participation that the child, as a human being, is already entitled to enjoy and ascribes the full panoply of rights granted in human rights law (e.g., the right to free expression, the right to health, and the right to education). Ratified by all governments except the United States and Somalia (and more recently South Sudan), the CRC intended to secure standing for children, specifically as they are situated within their families, schools, and local communities, but also as legal persons "with evolving capacities," whose own opinions and wishes about decisions affecting them need to be granted due respect and dignity.[17]

The CRC emphasizes that the child's right to family is particularly vital, for example in Article 5, where it calls upon states to respect the rights and responsibilities of parents and other family members, and Article 9, where it prohibits states from separating children from their parents against their will and against the best interests of the child as determined by judicial review. In turn, the "right to family" has been widely recognized in human rights law, beginning with Article 16 of the UDHR, which observes: "The family is the natural and fundamental group unit of society and is entitled to protection by society and the State." This language is repeated in numerous other instruments, including the International Covenant on Civil and Political Rights, the International Covenant on Economic, Social and Political Rights, and many regional conventions and treaties such as the European Convention on Human Rights. The CRC similarly obligates states to respect family unity on the grounds that family is "the fundamental group of society and the natural environment for the growth and well-being of all its members and particularly children."

However, taken together, these documents hardly impart anything like a unified or seamless distribution of rights to the child or to the family. For example, the CRC obligates states to respect family unity, *except* where it threatens the security of the child. Indeed, as legal scholars have noted: "In order to protect the rights of all family members adequately, international law must be both sufficiently flexible to accommodate a wide range of different family structures and values, while simultaneously enshrining universally-agreed upon minimum standards on the rights of those family members."[18] Even as "family life is perceived as being a product of its historical time and its culture," human rights norms recognize the family as an abiding element for the cultivation of human flourishing and good life.[19] Thus, human rights instruments manifest the difficulty of locating an individual subject of rights in an institution that is, at its core, one of social interdependence.[20] To the extent that international human rights law attempts to incorporate the child as a member of a "natural" community, namely the family, the latter is depicted, paradoxically, as organic and self-evident *as well as* that which needs to be fostered and monitored through other institutions.[21]

As I do throughout *Writing Human Rights*, however, I suggest here that rather than viewing such paradoxes as obstacles to political recognition and ethical obligation, we take them as incitement to imagine how minor subjects want otherwise and the kinds of good life—specifically, good family life, to which everybody before the law is said to have a right—that might flourish if we grant the child the recognition she demands. As Kathryn Bond Stockton so astutely observes with regard to her conceptualization of "growing sideways," "growing up"—"toward full stature, marriage, work, reproduction, and the loss of childishness"—is not the only way one might grow.[22] The strange being who the child is before the law, with and without her family, might also tender the opening by which to imagine into existence relations and futures other than straightforward progress from dependence to autonomy, from minority to majority, from vulnerability to sovereign security.

Forming Family

Rather than disavowing the claims of family in favor of the autonomous individual subject of rights, or turning to family as an authentic site of refuge and integrity in an alienating world, then, I suggest that minor literatures instead concern themselves with the varied but incontrovertible forms of precariousness against which the family might offer some measure of care and protection. Any number of social theorists and cultural critics have fairly challenged the romanticized ideal of "*the* family" as an alibi for the institution of heteropatriarchal norms (as in "family values"), for the reproduction of "traditional" forms of life (and the sexual and gender hierarchies they entail), and the procreation of biopower that the state and global capital absorb and instrumentalize for their own ends.[23] I am instead concerned with how minor literatures construe families, especially transnational families, as also highly unstable and promiscuous, their boundaries shifting, "faked," undone, and remade in response to the demands of the security state, international and domestic divisions of labor, immigration law, religious and heteropatriarchal norms, ecological transformations, and technological innovations.[24] The kinship crafted out of these various and often contradictory historical forces also results from migrant practices that exploit the ambiguities between seeming and being a family. Whereas the state often defines practices such as "green card marriages" and "anchor" babies as fraudulent and unlawful, minor literatures treat them as, in Eithne Luibhèid's words, a "competing system of knowledge that is brought against the state" by those subject to its coercive and disciplinary power.[25]

Thus, to cite Kath Weston's groundbreaking study, *Families We Choose,* about lesbians' and gay men's kinship ties and affiliative community-building, for minor literatures, "family is not some static institution, but a cultural category that can represent assimilation *or* challenge."[26] By "treating family as always and everywhere the same entity," we risk evacuating the "context-dependent meanings that have given life to the concept and allowed it to become an object of contention."[27] In minor literatures, the *right* to family calls forth an aesthetics of kin, which pieces families together through the traffic and transformations that globalization entails, materializing the families that the migrant child otherwise wants. The transnational family and the migrant child do not exist prior to such modes of exchange, but come into existence through the global circulation of bodies, goods, money, property, and desires, and minor literatures seek to imagine provisional forms of family flexible and creative enough to respond to the multiple threats and injuries that global modernity triggers. This literature retains the entitlement to family that has been codified as a human right, while also dialectically rethinking what family might yet come to mean and how it might serve as an alternative source for the provision of the right to have rights that eludes the impossible subjects of the American global nation.

Focused in particular on the bare life that modern warfare spawns, Aimee Phan's short story collection, *We Should Never Meet,* tells of severed attachments between mothers, prospective mothers, and their children. The stories pivot around Operation Babylift, the U.S. campaign in the final days of the Vietnam War to evacuate several thousand Vietnamese children, most of whom were considered orphans (although some mistakenly so) and many of whom were fathered by American servicemen, for adoption in the United States. In the opening story "Miss Lien," the adolescent girl who is its title character recalls how as a child in a rural South Vietnam village, she imagined growing tall enough to reach into heaven, where she would announce to her maternal grandparents who died before she had been born: "I am your granddaughter. I am your family. Love me."[28] However, unlike "Miss Lien," where deaths from natural causes are what separate Lien from her grandparents, the other stories in Phan's collection center on family bonds sundered by the Vietnam War and its aftermath, where any claims to kinship become nearly impossible to sustain without mediation and self-conscious efforts to "make" others love and care for the vulnerable child. Those efforts involve an array of motivations and outcomes for adults and children alike.

For example, the final two stories of the collection depict the intention of Bridget, an American pediatrician stationed as part of a humanitarian mission in Saigon, to adopt Huan, an Amerasian toddler. Having left her own two-year-old daughter and veteran husband behind at home in Pittsburgh, Bridget extends her two-month stint to tend to children orphaned or abandoned during the war into three years and eventually evacuates Saigon with Huan during Operation Babylift. Locating in the mixed-race child a justification for her long absence from home and the solution to the rifted ties between herself and her husband and daughter, Bridget's overriding desire to claim him as family seems to make their union an inevitable conclusion. Yet, in the following and final story of the collection, "Motherland," Phan introduces an adult Huan, returning with his adoptive mother, Gwen, and friend Mai to Vietnam. Thus, we infer that not only was Bridget unable to adopt Huan but that Huan has no memory of her. The only trace of Bridget's love in this story persists vaguely when Sophie, the founder of the adoption center where Bridget first encounters Huan, tells him, "So many people loved you, Huan, so many wanted you for their own. I remember" (226).

This final story merges the two temporal and plot trajectories that organize the rest of the collection, one of which tells of the young Vietnamese adults who live through the final years of the war in Vietnam in the early 1970s, and the other about the Vietnamese American children who have come of age in Orange County, California, during the early 1990s. The latter includes Huan's friend Mai, as she reaches the age of "emancipation" from the foster care system, under whose administration she has lived since her arrival as a refugee in the United States; Mai's friend Kim, another Babylift child who struggles to achieve economic independence as she mistakenly convinces herself that a shopkeeper who has shown her some kindness is the mother who abandoned her years ago in Vietnam; and Vinh, Kim's erstwhile boyfriend who pegs his own future on his relationship with Kim and on his leadership of a fledgling gang, Brookhurst 354, made up of foster-care brothers.

"Mother's love" both eludes and enables Vietnamese American life, insofar as the absence of birth mothers makes possible a nominal American good life for these Vietnamese children. In the story "Emancipation," Mai fabricates her own yearning for her missing Vietnamese mother, who died when Mai was very young and whom Mai barely remembers, for her college application essay, which in turn wins her financial aid:

> Remembering all the sympathies people had projected on her all her life, Mai wrote of her longing for her dead mother and native land and her resolution to return to Vietnam one day and help her former countrymen. Though difficult at first to exaggerate her emotions in such a way, Mai was soon swept up in the embellishments. Perhaps she really did think this. (147)

As her friend Tiffany assures her, "It is an advantage that you're an orphan. . . . There's no way [Wellesley, Mai's top choice of colleges] can reject you after what you told them about your childhood" (158). Meanwhile, Mai is unable to announce her current, desperate hope that her foster family, who has raised her for years and always treated her kindly, will formalize her place in their home by adopting her.

In *We Should Never Meet,* familial bonds are hence rendered shifting and contingent, encoding loss, vulnerability, and desire as inextricable from one another, but also unstable and mobile. Phan describes Mai, Kim, and Vinh as (being like) siblings, whose bonds are forged through the shared experience of a foster care system that makes parental presence at best impermanent (as in Mai's relationship with the Reynoldses) and at worst, predatory and exploitative (as Kim becomes the object of sexual advances from various foster fathers). Parental figures—such as the shopkeeper to whom Kim becomes attached and Mai's foster father, Sherman Reynolds—become unfamiliar, "strange again" (44), when the girls make what turn out to be excessive claims upon them, that is, demands for them *to be or become* "real" families. The stories set in Vietnam, such as "The Delta" and "The Gates of Saigon," where nuns and aid-workers provide care for orphans, depict a glut of babies, all faceless and interchangeable. If the Amerasian children are more distinct in this mass of unwanted life, it is because they are marked as especial objects of scorn and shame. Like the ducks that the family of one character, Truc, raises to sell, the infants amount to bare life, "born to die"—a perspective that Kim, herself one of those mixed-race children, affirms when she acknowledges that she depends upon Vinh's affection and protection because "she was so weak, vulnerable, stupid" (51). Vinh has thus long served as a brother and lover (and the father of the pregnancy she aborts), but Kim also resents her reliance on him.

Nor are the relations of interdependence limited to the vulnerability of the very young. In stories such as "We Should Never Meet" and "Visitors," older Vietnamese American immigrants in the United States become the object of home invasion, burglaries, and assaults, arranged by Brookhurst 354, whom Vinh sees as "doing these people a favor. All of them in such a delusion about attaining this material dream of fortune and comfort, but at what expense? . . . They were fools to believe they could actually live among the Americans and become one of them" (108). Exploiting their cultural knowledge of their "own kind"—for example, that Vietnamese Americans are hesitant to call upon law enforcement and that they store their valuables, including cash, in their homes for safekeeping—Vinh and his gang distance themselves from the bare life ascribed to them by claiming a retributive, outlaw agency, aimed in particular at anyone who seems to have bought into the promise of an American good life. In Phan's collection, every possibility of intergenerational affiliation acknowledges the social and political vulnerabilities of the subjects involved, and all too often culminates in a physically violent rending of the fragile affective bonds that the characters create. But the children in these stories are also often unruly, demanding, intentional, resourceful, and knowing as they find their way in the world.

As a set of family romances, *We Should Never Meet* bears witness to the way in which (neo)liberal claims to abstract, universal equality proliferate, rather than deflect, the contradictions of global modernity for migrant children and the families they want. But while traditional family ties remain irretrievable for the characters, a family saga of sorts nevertheless materializes, as Phan charts *for readers* the types of care that have been necessary to keep alive these otherwise abject reminders of the war. Besides Bridget's maternal affections and physician's labor, which I have already mentioned, such efforts figure in all of the stories set in Vietnam, even if only as subplots to their central narratives. Lien transports her newborn infant, the offspring of a rape, to an orphanage. Nuns shuttle orphans from orphanages to the adoption center. One of Sophie's coworkers in the adoption center, Hoa, forges birth certificates and medical charts to secure safe passage for the children through a bureaucratic maze, what she considers to be "a necessary guiltless crime," for "orphans [who] had arrived without names or documentation . . . [in order] to convince the government that they legally existed, were in legitimate danger, and needed to exit the country immediately," even as Hoa's own family's well-being is in profound danger as the Communists close in on Saigon (135).

In the stories set in the United States, however, a parental generation goes mostly missing, such that for the Vietnamese American adolescents, claiming family can be no simple matter of return. Rather, *We Should Never Meet* insists upon asking under what *conditions* families come to be—and to be recognized as such—and, in turn, what good lives might flourish through such recognition. The trip to the "motherland" in the final story proffers no dramatic revelation to Huan (or to readers) about his birth mother or even about Bridget, but does serve as an occasion for a reunion between Huan and Mai after several years, the latter having completed her education and moved to work in Asia, first in Beijing and then Japan. Finding themselves on the receiving end of harassment by those who resent "overseas Vietnamese," both Mai and Huan feel ambivalent about returning there and squabble with one another about their reactions to a country that "orphaned" them. Mai further locates the present whereabouts of Kim, now "married to a man she doesn't respect, with kids she doesn't want" as she buys a beautiful bracelet for her former foster sister (234).

Adapting the form of the family saga, the story comes to supplement the lost parental affiliations with the migrant children's *lateral* recognition of *one another* constituting a provisional family of sorts, and one that moves their plots into a future not hopelessly bound to the losses of the past but also not fully detached from nor transcendent of them. The story hence closes with the two friends spending their final evening in Ho Chi Minh City at a sidewalk café, watching young people on motorbikes cruise the boulevard:

> They look out onto the street again. The cruisers, so proud and happy they are young, born after the war. They only know Ho Chi Minh City, while Saigon is a memory that their parents and grandparents speak of. Their futures are pure.
>
> A young man and woman slowly ride past the café. He is wearing a leather jacket, his hair slick with styling gel. She wears a

> bright yellow dress, her hair in a braid down her back. The woman's arms are wrapped around the man's waist, not because she needs to, but because they are obviously in love. When the couple passes their table, they wave. After a moment, Huan and Mai wave back. (243)

As the antecedent for the collective third-person "they" in the concluding paragraphs slips between Huan and Mai to the "cruisers" and then specifically to a young man and woman who seem to mirror the protagonists back to themselves, the passage suggests a final integration of the united nations world, in which even the last holdout socialist states have been incorporated into the American global nation. As such, memories of the devastating global Cold War fade into an irrecoverable past that holds no significance for the "pure" futures of the Vietnamese and Americans alike.

And yet, a "moment" of delay separates the scene of reflection between the two couples, in which the narrator assumes that the young man and woman are "obviously" in love, as Mai and Huan might themselves appear to be. In fact, elsewhere in the story, Mai and Huan's friendship is explicitly disavowed as a romance even as it enjoys no official status of siblinghood. What then do the two couples mirror one another? Do the Vietnamese couple reflect back an American good life that after the close of the Cold War absorbs all of Asia, as Mai's itinerancy might indicate? Or, insofar as Mai and Huan trail them in returning their greeting, does the couple pose an alternative postsocialist humanity born out of a past from which Mai and Huan were altogether displaced as minor subjects and which bespeaks the limit of what an American good life can integrate into its own image? Ultimately, the point seems not to be that if we could only somehow fill in the stories of the young Vietnamese adults, those like Mai and Huan displaced by the war would have unlocked the secret to evading the disciplinary practices, security strategies, and transnational circuits of the modern state system and global capital that have assembled their lives. Rather, it is precisely as an opaque *ethical figure* that the Vietnamese couple inspires momentary uncertainty in what otherwise seems to pose the most "obvious" portrait of a neoliberal family romance. Seemingly familiar, they might nevertheless reflect something stranger about the conditions of Mai and Huan's own lives, where the state has authorized what type of family they can lay claim to and that has laid claim to them.

Although global modernity puts the diverse forms of family that exist across the planet into contact with one another, has generated a slew of new family forms, and has put family members into motion across national borders, most of these formations enjoy little support in the way of legal recognition or state provision. While, as we have seen in the preceding pages, neoliberal narratives script an account of individual and nationalist development in which people "grow up," from dependent to independent, from vulnerable to secure and sovereign, the heterogeneity of actually existing families encompasses structures of care in which older generations come to depend upon younger ones, disparate life-events mark the transition between different stages of childhood, adolescence, and adulthood, the contingencies of impairment and illness interrupt progress through such stages, and there is much likelihood that adults and guardians charged with protecting children will be in disagreement with the children's nascent sense of their own "best interest."[29]

Meanwhile, in the United States the heteropatriarchal nuclear family associated with the white middle class maintains its hegemonic normativity, compelling all manner of marginalized subjects (racial minorities, transnational migrants, queer people) to assimilate to that ideal.[30] In this respect, as David L. Eng argues, transnational migrants, including transnational adoptees, are conscripted to perform a vital form of affective and symbolic labor, working to sustain the promise of the white, heteropatriarchal nuclear family, a form that otherwise cannot hide the strain and decline it has rapidly undergone in the twentieth century.[31] For example, the exploitation of Third World women—domestic servants and sweatshop labor, to name two of the most widely recognizable forms—has been essential to sustaining the reproductive and consumption practices of the hallowed middle-class family in the United States (and elsewhere in the global North).

Likewise, the phenomenon of transnational adoption, as Eng further explains, "installs racial alterity and otherness in the privatized space of the white American family," verifying the (neo)liberal family's putative commitment to colorblindness and benevolent rescue of those most needy in the global South, even as immigration regulation becomes ever more draconian in the name of national security.[32] The nominal incorporation of these children into "good" American families and American good life disavows the global division of labor and U.S.-instigated wars (whether official armed conflicts, or in the case of the child migrants with which I began this section, the "war on drugs") that generates such "neediness" in the first place. By the end of the twentieth century, as social means such as education and healthcare became scarce in the global South and increasingly denied as public goods to those in the global North, migrant subjects of all sorts found themselves becoming members of transnational families in search of what Rhacel Salazar Parreñas refers to as "care resources."[33]

In response, the aesthetics of kin highlights the multitude of affiliations by which social reproduction and care (potentially) can take place, where minor subjects foster affective, psychological, and bodily well-being in an ethics of intimacy, love, or duty. But these unauthorized families also profoundly challenge kinship itself as a political construct, by which states draw up the terms of their own responsibilities to citizens and others. Insofar as states sanction particular types of sexual and reproductive practices and household arrangements as legitimate and deserving of support, while withdrawing this status from or refusing it for others, they *make* possible seemingly "durable" and natural family forms precisely by repeatedly reinstating that norm.[34] In granting or withholding recognition, a state decrees what resources it will marshal for the "good" family life, what familiars are expected to provide for one another, who will be made to live and who will be "allowed" to die and by whose will, in what spaces, and under what conditions that life and death will take place, and how social, economic, and cultural goods will be transmitted from one generation to the next.[35]

An aesthetics of kin that assembles families according to what, with respect to *We Should Never Meet,* Jodi Kim calls "a new geography of kinship," and with indifference to the law, has the effect of muddling the lines between different types of community that might come to establish themselves as the body and source of dissenting politics.[36] Thus, in Phan's collection, friendships, convents, orphanages, gangs, schools, villages, and relations that might not even have very precise names (yet) all pose protean sites of transnational, in this case Asian/American, "relatedness," where "fundamental forms of human dependency" might be addressed.[37] In animating the right to family, minor literatures do not aim to romanticize traditional and marginalized sorts of family life as authentic alternatives that are somehow external to the estrangement that global modernity wreaks.[38] Rather, these literatures make claims to a "quality" of life for the child and the type of human person whom she might yet become, other than the forms that are available at the present juncture. In exploiting just how "strange" the child is before the law, minor literatures therefore "put the accent on collectively imagined visions of what we want to be or to do" as a matter of ethico-political desire rather than given identities.[39] As minor literatures constitute and enable us to write human rights, the vulnerable, desirous, unpredictable, demanding child arrives in her own right, on a future terrain of community that unfolds in its own time and space.

Acknowledgments

I am deeply grateful to the many individuals and institutions whose support and encouragement were essential in bringing *Writing Human Rights* to fruition. First and foremost, I remain happily indebted to Sangeeta Ray; I was proud to have been one of her first doctoral students and am even prouder now to count her as the closest of friends from whom I have never stopped learning. Jini Kim Watson and Joe Keith read more pages of this book in progress, sometimes more than once, than anyone else, and their advice, enthusiasm, and suggestions were crucial to my thinking and its completion; but it is their friendship that I consider an even more valuable gift. The other members of my terrific writing group also read considerable portions of this work in progress and influenced it deeply, and I am grateful to Cristina Beltrán, Naomi Schiller, and Krupa Shandilya for their unflagging brilliance and critical generosity.

I was the fortunate recipient of a Faculty Fellowship from the New York University Humanities Initiative, and the intellectual community that Jane Tylus built there provided me with the opportunity to begin exploring the ideas that would eventually become this book. Audiences at Indiana University, the University of Connecticut, New York University, the University of California–Berkeley, the University of Maryland, and the University of Miami provided significant feedback while it was in progress. I am extremely grateful to Richard Morrison for his immediate enthusiasm for *Writing Human Rights,* for bringing it to the University of Minnesota Press, and for providing invaluable assistance in determining its central claims and structure at a crucial moment in its development. Thank you to Danielle Kasprzak and Anne Carter for seeing the project through to its conclusion and for their helpful advice along the way.

There have been many others (including extraordinary students) who have cheered me on and helped me keep it together since the beginning of this project. I owe much gratitude to Leslie Bow, andré carrington,

Yoonmee Chang, Tina Chen, Kandice Chuh, Arlene Dávila, Elizabeth Deloughrey, Carolyn Dinshaw, Lisa Duggan, Chris Eng, David Eng, Guadalupe Escobar, Lezlie Frye, Gayatri Gopinath, Sean Goudie, Nina Ha, Phil Harper, Corrinne Harrol, Stephanie Hsu, Doug Ishii, Jane Iwamura, Rana Jaleel, Laura Kang, Ronak Kapadia, Aisha Khan, Daniel Kim, Zenia Kish, Kim Lau, Jim Lee, Justin Leroy, Martin Manalansan, Anita Mannur, Nick Matlin, Maureen McLane, Viet Thanh Nguyen, Emily Orlando, Jan Padios, David Palumbo-Liu, Jo Park, Nels Pearson, Roy Pérez, Matt Potolsky, Mary Louise Pratt, Josie Saldaña, Cathy Schlund-Vials, April Shemak, Anooradha Siddiqi, Lok Siu, Min Hyuong Song, and Emily Thuma.

There have been numerous others I have met along the way who have given me so much food for thought and the many pleasures of their friendship. My warmest thanks to Tamara Bhalla, Nick Boggs, Chris Cannon, Jian Chen, Wendy Cheng, Floyd Cheung, Jigna Desai, Julie Passanante Elman, Ramzi Fawaz, Jonathan Flatley, Donette Francis, Yogita Goyal, Lynn Itagaki, Joe Jeon, Jeehyun Lim, Colleen Lye, Alexandra Schultheis Moore, Greg Mullins, Asha Nadkarni, Rani Neutill, Vanessa Pérez, Sonya Posmentier, Shuang Shen, Elizabeth Swanson, Pamela Thoma, Terri Tomsky, Sara Waisvisz, Belinda Walzer, Janelle Wong, and Cindy Wu.

With every passing year, I learn how crucial are the personal affinities that can span many city blocks, hundreds of miles, and multiple decades. "Friendship" hardly seems to do justice to the kind of sustenance they provide. My deepest gratitude to Fran Bernstein, Eliot Borenstein, Christine Cupaiuolo, Bernie Heidkamp, Anne Lounsbery, Keely McCarthy, Scott Melby, Steve Newman, and Cathy Romagnolo, who have not only let me think out loud with them but have let me be the person I am—hopeful, flawed, incomplete, and all the rest of it—without wavering from my side.

I also have come to recognize with every passing year how rare and extraordinary it is to have a family that never wavers and always provides the care that is needed. Ila, Awanish, Sushrut, Kirin, and Arjun Parikh make me understand in the most powerful ways why family is a right worth fighting for. Drew Hindes and Kealy Ryder provided innumerable hours of often unseen labor, without which I would never have been able to write a single page. And I thank Eric Sobie for the home and life we created together over many years.

My vision of what kinds of worlds are possible when one risks allowing the other into that home and under your skin has been thoroughly and endlessly indebted to the presence of my surprising, resilient, silly, demanding, beautiful son, Nikhil Sobie. He has been his own person from the start, and reckoning with that has made possible a good life I had not thought to imagine before him.

Notes

Introduction

1. Hunt, "The Paradoxical Origins of Human Rights," 3–4.

2. As with a broader move in American studies, I aim to defamiliarize the Cold War as "a congealed historical context," but retain the rubric of the "Cold War" to signal the constellation of historical events, foreign policy perspectives, and geopolitical divisions that the term designates. See Kim, *Ends of Empire,* 11.

3. Chakrabarty, "The Legacies of Bandung," 58.

4. Cvetkovich, *An Archive of Feelings,* 196, 237.

5. Normand and Zaidi, *Human Rights at the UN,* 3–19.

6. Arendt, *The Origins of Totalitarianism,* 351.

7. Ibid., 370.

8. Ibid.

9. Ibid., 372.

10. Ibid., 342, 375.

11. Ibid., 376.

12. Ibid., 380.

13. Rancière, "Who Is the Subject of the Rights of Man?," 298.

14. Butler and Spivak, *Who Sings the Nation-State?,* 45–46.

15. Lewis, "'New' Human Rights," 130.

16. Normand and Zaidi, *Human Rights at the UN,* 102.

17. For an overview of the practicable challenges facing a human rights movement in the United States, see Thomas, "Against American Supremacy," 18–21.

18. This is not an endorsement of American exceptionalism, but rather a question of how, historically and politically, the *imaginary* of American exceptionalism configures U.S. global power, and does so in a way that does not simply reproduce older versions of European imperialism.

19. Bright and Geyer, "Where in the World Is America?," 73.

20. Ibid., 73.

21. Ibid., 66.

22. Ibid., 82–85. See also Chari and Verdery, "Thinking between the Posts," 19–20.

23. Klein, *Cold War Orientalism,* 28. See also Campbell, *Writing Security,* 158–61.

24. Manela, *The Wilsonian Moment,* 35–53; Klein, *Cold War Orientalism,* 28–32.

25. Klein, *Cold War Orientalism,* 13–14.

26. Eckel, "Human Rights and Decolonization," 116.

27. Latham, *The Right Kind of Revolution,* 58.

28. As Ashley Dawson and Malini Johar Schueller (citing Michael Hunt) further detail, such a contradictory worldview and the U.S. foreign policy that ensues from it have been shaped by "a belief in the exceptional greatness of the nation and its promotion of liberty; racial hierarchy; and a distrust of revolution based on the assumption that the American Revolution was unique and unrepeatable" ("Introduction," 4).

29. Ngai, *Impossible Subjects,* 233. See also Singh, *Black Is a Country,* 136–37.

30. Kelly and Kaplan, "'My Ambition,'" 134.

31. Ibid., 136–37. See Samuel Moyn, *The Last Utopia,* for a summary history of how declarations of rights in these earlier centuries occurred within the necessary "context" of a state that reconciled liberties with national unity (11–43).

32. Kelly and Kaplan, "My Ambition," 137.

33. Ibid., 137. See Singh, *Black Is a Country,* 85, for a discussion of how, in a homologous manner, the nation-state becomes the horizon for African American struggle within the United States.

34. As the Cold War proceeded, this was often accomplished by way of covert operations to overthrow democratically elected, left-leaning leaders in the Third World and to provide U.S. support for establishing right-wing authoritarian regimes in their place. Nevertheless, Third World peoples were never simply pawns manipulated by the United States and the Soviet Union, and an accurate account of coups and military interventions during this era also requires analyses of class and ethnic divisions within postcolonial societies. See Prashad, *The Darker Nations,* 143.

35. Kelly and Kaplan, "My Ambition," 141. Also see Moyn, *The Last Utopia,* 30.

36. Kelly and Kaplan, "My Ambition," 142.

37. Westad, *The Global Cold War,* 16.

38. Ibid., 20–21; Latham, *The Right Kind of Revolution,* 6, 32, 53.

39. Louis and Robinson, "Empire Preserv'd," 157. See also Normand and Zaidi, *Human Rights at the UN,* 213–15; Westad, *The Global Cold War,* 112–13, 126. In the immediate aftermath of World War II, however, the United States capitulated to Churchill's more limited agenda for establishing self-determination, one restricted to European peoples and unthreatening to imperialism, and, under the instruction of President Eisenhower, the United States abstained from the UN Declaration on the Granting of Independence to Colonial Countries and Peoples. Of course, when it did come, the transition to independence was not

easily accomplished in most cases, as colonial powers often fought bitterly to retain their colonial possessions, as for example, in the remarkably brutal counterrevolutionary campaigns that France carried out in Algiers and Vietnam. Nevertheless, the political and cultural ravages suffered by European powers during the war eventually resulted in the loss of vast portions of their empires. See Westad, *The Global Cold War,* 86–89.

40. Kelly and Kaplan, "My Ambition," 142.

41. This is of course not to argue that the United States has not engaged in imperial ventures, whether in terms of westward, continental expansion or in terms of its colonial administration of the Philippines, Puerto Rico, and Guam after the Spanish-American War. Moreover, an extensive reproduction of colonial trade patterns and "imperial architecture" also animated the postwar international order, which has been documented extensively by other scholars. See Kim, *Ends of Empire,* 25–26, 28. However, as Amy Kaplan argues in *Anarchy of Empire,* with the closing of "the frontier," by the end of the nineteenth century, national power was measured primarily "by the extension of vaster yet less tangible networks of international markets and political influence" (96). Thus, a necessarily more varied critical vocabulary elaborates the relationship, cooperative and otherwise, between American liberalism and postcolonial governance.

42. Westad, *The Global Cold War,* 21. See also Latham, *The Right Kind of Revolution,* 3–4, 12, 66.

43. Borgwardt, *A New Deal for the World,* 10, 35, 158. See also Dawson and Schueller, "Introduction," 7; Williams, *The Divided World,* 111–15.

44. Bright and Geyer, "Where In the World Is America?," 87; Westad, *The Global Cold War,* 19; Taylor et al., "Geography/Globalization," 16.

45. Normand and Zaidi, *Human Rights at the UN,* 135–36.

46. Anderson, "A 'Hollow Mockery'"; Normand and Zaidi, *Human Rights at the UN,* 135–36. In the 1950s, Southern Democrats also worried enough about the possibility that the UN Genocide Convention could render lynching an international crime that they put forth (and nearly passed) the Bricker Amendment, which would have required that all executive agreements be ratified by a two-thirds majority of the Senate. See Anderson, "A 'Hollow Mockery,'" 91–93, and Lewis, "'New' Human Rights," 118. Also in the early 1950s, a California appellate court ruled to overturn the state's Alien Land Law, which prohibited "aliens ineligible for citizenship" (namely, immigrant Japanese and other Asians) from owning land, basing its decision on the UN Charter's nondiscrimination provisions. Ohio Senator John Bricker and the former president of the American Bar Association, Frank Holman, sounded an alarm about the threat posed to U.S. sovereignty and states' rights by the UN treaties. In 1952, the California Supreme Court overturned the appellate court's reasoning, stating that the charter did not supersede existing domestic legislation. See Soohoo, "Human Rights," 81.

47. Moyn, *The Last Utopia,* 59. The domestic jurisdiction clause also satisfied demands made by the Soviet delegates to the United Nations, who—while maintaining that states were obligated to provide social and economic rights for their citizens—opposed any international mechanisms of implementation or enforcement that would interfere with national sovereignty. See Normand and Zaidi, *Human Rights at the UN,* 135–36, 153, 169. For a discussion of human rights activism as an expansion of dissident politics within the Soviet Union during the 1970s, see Nathans, "The Disenchantment of Socialism," 33–48.

48. Sargent, "Oasis in the Desert?," 140.

49. In *Eyes Off the Prize,* Carol Anderson provides a detailed and absorbing account of the postwar struggle by black leaders, especially in the NAACP, to address the plight of African Americans as a series of human rights violations and the retreat from this tactic forced by the demands of the Cold War, further hastened by internal battles, differences with the Communist Party, USA, and the demands of white liberal allies.

50. Anderson, *Eyes Off the Prize,* 16–17, 58–165.

51. Ibid., 11, 112. See also McDougall, "Toward a Meaningful International Regime," 574.

52. Westad, *The Global Cold War,* 112.

53. Klein, *Cold War Orientalism,* 3–24; Singh, *Black Is a Country,* 161; Westad, *The Global Cold War,* 118, 130.

54. Westad, *The Global Cold War,* 132.

55. Borstelmann, *The Cold War and the Color Line,* 67.

56. Singh, *Black Is a Country,* 165–73; Von Eschen, *Race against Empire,* 107–21; Dudziak, *Cold War Civil Rights,* 13, 56.

57. This, even as European colonial administrations, such as the Belgian Governor-General in Congo, complained about the "bad effect" that the presence of black servicemen in a desegregating U.S. military would have in Africa. See Westad, *The Global Cold War,* 132.

58. Dudziak, *Cold War Civil Rights,* 28–29, 83–88, 91–107; Von Eschen, *Race against Empire,* 116–18.

59. Borstelmann, *The Cold War and the Color Line,* 57.

60. Dudziak, *Cold War Civil Rights,* 46–53.

61. Ngai, *Impossible Subjects,* 233, 238.

62. Ibid., 242.

63. Ibid., 229–30.

64. Ibid., 243–45.

65. Ibid., 264.

66. According to the 2010 U.S. Census Report, over 18 million Americans identified themselves as being of Asian or Pacific Islander descent (5.6 percent of the

total population), and over 50 million as Hispanic or Latino (16.3 percent of the total population).

67. Melamed, *Represent and Destroy*, 10.

68. Here I am summarizing the conception of "possessive individualism" that has been a mainstay of critical American studies. The account of the possessive individual offered by C. B. Macpherson in the 1950s remains the most compelling and influential account of American liberal personhood.

69. Singh, *Black Is a Country*, 20–21.

70. Ibid., 23.

71. Ibid., 37. See also Melamed, *Represent and Destroy*, 58, and Weiner, *Americans without Law*.

72. Omi and Winant, *Racial Formation in the United States*, 96–100. Also see Melamed, *Represent and Destroy*, for an exemplary theorization of what Howard Winant calls "the racial break" and, in particular, the role of literature in the production of, in Melamed's terms, "race-liberal orders" since the 1940s.

73. The reforms in immigration policy that I describe above led not only to an exponential growth in the size of Asian American and Latino populations, but also to their diversification in terms of class status and ideological perspectives. Beginning in the 1960s, Asian Americans in particular have been hailed as a "model minority" that embraces conservative cultural and political values and enjoys socioeconomic mobility as a result. In chapters 1 and 3, I address how a human rights literature rethinks the possibility of Afro-Asian solidarity in the face of such divisiveness. Because an impressively large body of multidisciplinary scholarship already considers the historical origins, social realities, and political impact of difference and conflict between minoritarian racial populations, I do not retread these critical discussions here.

74. Lipsitz, *The Possessive Investment in Whiteness*, 25.

75. Duggan, *The Twilight of Equality*, xiii. See also Melamed, *Represent and Destroy*, 42–44.

76. Duggan, *The Twilight of Equality*, 3.

77. Ibid., 7.

78. Gilmore, *Golden Gulag*.

79. Painter, "The Rise of the Workfare State," 168.

80. Melamed, *Represent and Destroy*, 13, 37–44, 116–17, 152–62.

81. White, *Metahistory*, 5–11.

82. Melamed, *Represent and Destroy*, 227.

83. Tulinius, "Saga as a Myth," 537.

84. Boheemen, *The Novel as Family Romance*, 25–26.

85. Ibid., 17–19. Despite their potential productivity for my analysis, I do not pursue psychoanalytic accounts of fiction hereafter. Instead, I am most concerned

with the cultural politics and moral imaginaries that allegories of subjectivity, and the generic forms they take, make available for minor subjects and minor transnationalisms.

86. Lowe, *Immigrant Acts,* 6.

87. Morrison, *Beloved,* 173. All subsequent citations to the novel appear parenthetically in the body of the chapter.

88. See Smith, *Toni Morrison,* 63–67.

89. Cohen, *A Body Worth Defending,* 50, 81.

90. Holloway, *Legal Fictions,* 16.

91. Ibid., 16–17.

92. Ibid., 21.

93. Gordon, *Ghostly Matters,* 139–40, 181.

94. Ibid., 112–15.

95. See Holland, *Raising the Dead,* 54–55.

96. In "*Beloved*: A Spiritual," Karla F.C. Holloway offers an early consideration of how "the reclamation and revision of history" functions as "both a thematic emphasis and textual methodology" in Morrison's novel.

97. Berger, "Ghosts of Liberalism," 410.

98. Ibid., 415–17.

99. Holland, *Raising the Dead,* 57.

100. Psychic reparations and legal reparations—and the relationship between the two—are themselves complicated conceptual and practical issues. For a discerning theoretical account about the essential role played by reparations in the production of notions of "humanity," see David L. Eng, "Reparations and the Human." For a perceptive discussion of the ethics of reparations that incite the cultural politics of *Beloved,* see Dean Franco, "What We Talk About."

101. Certainly growing economic disparities across the global North have shown the loss of security even for white subjects of the American good life. However, we also need to foreground the material accretion of structural privilege that made white men seem like the *natural* subject of rights in the first place, such that any loss is experienced as incursion, usually by women, persons of color, immigrants, etc.

102. Rodriguez, "The Meaning of 'Disaster,'" 134, 137.

103. Warren, *What Was African American Literature?,* 102.

104. Spivak, *Death of a Discipline,* 88.

105. Westad, *The Global Cold War,* 106.

106. Ishay, *The History of Human Rights,* 4. Ishay seems intent on demonstrating the truly "universal significance" of human rights across tremendously diverse religious, spiritual, and philosophical traditions. In contrast, I restrict my own sense of a global human rights record to the postwar era, without claiming such historical transcendence and only to draw out the efficacy of human rights as political, legal, and imaginative tools in the present. For another discussion of

human rights documents as such a record, see Stanton, "Top-Down, Bottom-Up, Horizontally," 68–74.

107. Ishay deploys the categories of "oppressor" and "the oppressed" so as to suggest that the oppressed exist as self-present subjects of exclusion from rights and privilege, ignoring Foucauldian insights into how disciplinary power creates the very subjects of subjugated knowledge who in turn resist their exclusion. Nonetheless, Ishay helpfully outlines moments of political dissent, by way of radical innovations and ruptures in rights discourses, from the eighteenth century onward.

108. Of these, the United States has failed to ratify the International Covenant on Economic, Social and Cultural Rights.

109. Although the Muslim world is often represented as being averse to human rights, Muslim nations were instrumental in the Non-Aligned Movement (which I discuss in chapter 1), the fight for self-determination, the drafting of the UDHR, and early human rights treaties. Many representatives from these countries also advocated for the indivisibility of political-civil rights and socioeconomic ones. See Chase, "Mutual Renewal," 59, 67. See also Kelly, "Magic Words," 100–105. Jan Eckel describes the "human rights revolution" of the 1970s as a "polycentric and fitful process" with extrinsic sources that included: decolonization in the global South, détente between the Cold War superpowers, the expansion of mass media, the dissemination of images and mobilization of activism around spectacles of mass suffering, transformations in leftist politics, and transformations in churches. See Eckel, "The Rebirth of Politics," 241–52.

110. As powerful as Marxist critique has been at diagnosing the contradictions and abuses of capital, its influence in the United States and elsewhere on progressive and leftist politics has waned, as countless social and cultural critics have detailed, in part because of its own limits in theorizing subjectivity, identity, political aspiration, and historical change not rooted in a class analysis. For only a few, very useful examples of such critical discussions, see Duggan, *The Twilight of Equality?;* Lowe, *Immigrant Acts;* and Slater, "Trajectories of Development Theory."

111. Thompson, "Post-Colonialism, Post Socialism," 8.

112. Chari and Verdery, "Thinking between the Posts," 12, 25.

113. Donnelly, *Universal Human Rights,* 71–84. For Donnelly, however, the alternative visions do not amount to alternative models of human rights per se, because they do not necessarily posit a vision of deontological rights, but instead locate the source of rights elsewhere, in, for example, status or natural law. Donnelly further polemically argues that human rights are the most effective at protecting the individual who is rendered vulnerable by and under modernization. See *Universal Human Rights,* 85, 92. See also Cubilié, *Women Witnessing Terror,* 224–25.

114. Lowe, *Immigrant Acts,* 26.

115. Anderson, "A 'Hollow Mockery,'" 93.

116. Collier and Lakoff, "On Regimes of Living," 31.

117. See Hairong and Vukovich, "Introduction," and Routledge, "Resisting and Reshaping Destructive Development," 316–26, for overviews of political, economic, and intellectual networks that have been emergent in the late twentieth and twenty-first centuries in the global South.

118. Eckel, "The Rebirth of Politics," 229.

119. Kelly, "Magic Words," 106.

120. Moyn, "The Return of the Prodigal," 8.

121. Ibid., 11.

122. Kelly, "Magic Words," 90, 105.

123. Lowe, *Immigrant Acts,* 42–56; Melamed, *Represent and Destroy,* 32–39, 91–99, 114–17.

124. Melamed, *Represent and Destroy,* 49. See Keith, *Unbecoming Americans,* for a survey of a radical cosmopolitan literary tradition that emerged concurrently with the early Cold War and extended a dialectical critique of racial liberalism.

125. Albisa, "Economic and Social Rights in the United States," 35.

126. Byrd, *The Transit of Empire,* xix.

127. Ibid., xxxix.

128. Ibid., 126, 144.

1. Other Humanities

1. Gaines, *A Gathering of Old Men,* 89. All subsequent citations to the novel appear parenthetically in the body of the chapter.

2. See Clark, "Re-(W)righting Black Male Subjectivity"; Harper, "From Sons to Fathers"; Jones, "New Narratives of Southern Manhood"; Mallon, "Voicing Manhood"; and White, "Haunted by the Idea."

3. For a detailed history of anticolonial struggle and Third World solidarity, see Prashad, *The Darker Nations.*

4. Ho and Mullen, *Afro Asia,* 5.

5. Odd Arne Westad marks 1962 as the "beginning of the unraveling of the spirit of Bandung," as the Sino-Indian border war, India's war with Pakistan, and the 1967 Middle East crisis all proved major setbacks for the ideals of mutual support and cooperation. See *The Global Cold War,* 107. Indeed, the conference itself was shadowed by the tense standoff between North and South Vietnam, following the nation's division into two states the year before by the Geneva Accords. For a summary of the multitude of challenges to Afro-Asian solidarity, see Christopher J. Lee, "Between a Moment and an Era," 15–17. *Bandung Revisited*

(edited by See Seng Tan and Amitav Acharya) offers a helpful survey of the practical, political, and historical significance of the Bandung Conference in international relations, especially with respect to Asian states.

6. Lee, "Between a Moment and an Era," 15.

7. Although most Latin American nations had achieved formal independence from colonial rule by 1900, European and U.S. capital interests dominated this region throughout the twentieth century in one form or another. The United States wielded particular influence in the hemisphere, such that, for many in the region, "resistance against the Giant of the North took the form of anticolonialism, in spite of the lack of a formal empire to resist." See Westad, *The Global Cold War,* 78, 84, 143. Consequently, by the inception of the NAM in 1961, Latin American states had been included in this Third World coalition. See also Slater, "Trajectories of Development Theory," 91, and Prashad, *The Darker Nations,* 28–29. Given that, as Greg Grandin argues, Latin America would serve in the twentieth century as a "staging ground" for innovations in both military and "soft" techniques of power, which would eventually prove the hallmarks of "new" American imperialism, its inclusion in the NAM and in the development of human rights politics is especially important to keep in mind. See *Empire's Workshop,* 3. Chapter 4 examines the Dominican Republic as one site of such U.S. intervention.

8. Young, *Soul Power,* 252.

9. Ibid.

10. Borgwardt, *A New Deal for the World,* 7; Anderson, "A 'Hollow Mockery,'" 81.

11. Lewis, "'New' Human Rights," 106–7.

12. Borgwardt, *A New Deal for the World,* 7. See also Latham, *The Right Kind of Revolution,* 31.

13. Borgwardt, *A New Deal for the World,* 136. See also Powell, "Louis Henkin and Human Rights," 57–73.

14. While historians have often described these exclusions as concessions made by the Roosevelt administration to the Southern Congressional bloc, more recently both Larry DeWitt and Mary Poole have argued that in fact these exclusions—at least in Title II, which established only the federally supervised entitlement program that is now commonly known as "Social Security"—originated with the Roosevelt administration itself (in particular, the secretary of the Treasury). Nevertheless, as Poole demonstrates, by instituting a bifurcated system in which African Americans were channeled toward those programs more conventionally described as "welfare" (even while the majority of the recipients of those programs have not been black), the Social Security Act sustained and compounded African American economic insecurity while also dividing notions of social welfare between the entitlement programs serving deserving citizens and those that addressed (and many argue "coddled") the undeserving poor, a

racialized partition that persists into the present moment. See Poole, *The Segregated Origins of Social Security,* 190, 201–3.

15. Singh, *Black Is a Country,* 87.

16. Fanon, *The Wretched of the Earth,* 98–103; Williams, *The Divided World,* xxix. Moreover, global capital has produced a complex reconfiguration of governmentality, resulting in what Aiwha Ong has referred to as zones of "variegated" or "graduated sovereignty." See Ong, *Neoliberalism as Exception,* 99. The uneven incorporation of the postcolonial world into neoliberal life maps extensively upon the earlier unevenness of modernization by imperial powers in the colonies, where urban centers that European powers developed (and from which anticolonial resistance was often launched) often rise as "global cities," while other regions of postcolonial nations experience global capital more sporadically and irregularly.

17. Westad, *The Global Cold War,* 9–10, 31.

18. Ibid., 11–12; Latham, *The Right Kind of Revolution,* 10–25. Westad argues that discourses of humanitarian development have had a long history in the United States, integral even to the ideals of emancipation and reconstruction heralded during and after the American Civil War in the nineteenth century. Emancipation therefore stood as "an indictment of most non-European peasant societies and a stipulation that only the removal of the present form of these societies could prevent the conditions of slavery from reemerging" (*The Global Cold War,* 22). See also Slater, "Trajectories of Development Theory," 90–92.

19. Routledge, "Resisting and Reshaping Destructive Development," 311–13. See also Escobar, *Encountering Development,* 21–54.

20. Westad, *The Global Cold War,* 134; Routledge, "Resisting and Reshaping Destructive Development," 312.

21. Latham, *The Right Kind of Revolution,* 66.

22. Westad, *The Global Cold War,* 91, 154–55; Routledge, "Resisting and Reshaping Destructive Development," 313.

23. Borgwardt, *A New Deal for the World,* 253.

24. Ibid., 51; Lewis, "'New' Human Rights," 110; Latham, *The Right Kind of Revolution,* 4–6, 40.

25. Borgwardt, *A New Deal for the World,* 139.

26. Singh, *Black Is a Country,* 85–86.

27. Borgwardt, *A New Deal for the World,* 122. Borgwardt argues that, because decision-making authority was distributed by way of multilateralist institutions, Roosevelt administration officials and other internationalists in 1945 reconceptualized sovereignty more as a process than an attribute. Beyond economic recovery and stability, the Bretton Woods institutions were meant to help institutionalize human rights ideals. See *A New Deal for the World,* 132–33.

28. Nesadurai, "Bandung and the Political Economy of North–South Relations," 83–84; Normand and Zaidi, *Human Rights at the UN,* 289–95.

29. Westad, *The Global Cold War,* 153.

30. Borgwardt, *A New Deal for the World,* 252–56; Nesadurai, "Bandung and the Political Economy of North–South Relations," 85–92. Slater makes the important point that while there are many continuities between modernization theory and neoliberalism, because the former was deeply influenced by Keynesian economics, it still accorded the state an important role in maintaining a balance between public and private sectors ("Trajectories of Development Theory," 94). See also Painter, "Rise of the Workfare State," 162. Nevertheless, Dawson and Schueller suggest that even by the late 1960s, "the integrated political and economic system created by the United States after World War II began foundering on its own internal contradictions" ("Introduction," 8).

31. Taylor, "Geography/Globalization," 10.

32. Ibid., 11. Nesadurai offers a helpful summary of how developing countries have been subject to global economic governance in ways that intensify inequality and poverty and promote the interests of industrial nations in "Bandung and the Political Economy of North–South Relations," 86–92. See also Normand and Zaidi, *Human Rights at the UN,* 295–98.

33. Latham, *The Right Kind of Revolution,* 8.

34. Lewis, "'New' Human Rights," 123.

35. Ibid., 106, 129.

36. Brysk, "Introduction," 10–14.

37. Borgwardt, *A New Deal for the World,* 257.

38. Nesadurai, "Bandung and the Political Economy of North–South Relations," 92.

39. Ibid.

40. Indeed, given the incursions on civil liberties the nation underwent after the terrorist attacks of September 11, 2001, and the initiation of the "war on terror," lawyers and activists have turned to human rights discourse in trying to reclaim those *political* freedoms that had long been thought to be secure, at least in principle, in the United States, for example, freedom of lawful association, of speech, of religion, and from unlawful detention. See Patten, "The Impact of September 11."

41. Lewis, "'New' Human Rights," 133–34. For a survey of key efforts by organizations and activists working with a human rights approach, see Albisa, "Economic and Social Rights in the United States" and "First-Person Perspectives on the Growth of the Movement."

42. Westad, *The Global Cold War,* 136; Go, "Modeling States and Sovereignty," 107.

43. Burke, *Decolonization and the Evolution of International Human Rights,* 94.

44. Moyn, *The Last Utopia,* 129.

45. Ibid. See also Moyn, "The Return of the Prodigal," 6.

46. Moyn, *The Last Utopia,* 141. Moyn argues that in this context, human rights discourses amounted to a liberal moral stance, one disentangled from imperialism, which responded to a growing sense that anticolonialism had failed as a political project. See also Williams, *The Divided World,* 15; Nathans, "The Disenchantment of Socialism," 43–48.

47. Sargent, "Oasis in the Desert?," 131–33. See also Atanasoski, *Humanitarian Violence,* for an insightful discussion of what she calls the "U.S. postsocialist imperial project," by which the preponderant racial fantasies and nationalist discourses of the Cold War enabled the transition from older European imperialisms to the global ascendance of American power by the turn of the twenty-first century.

48. Anderson, "A 'Hollow Mockery,'" 80.

49. Westad, *The Global Cold War,* 79.

50. Adebajo, "From Bandung to Durban," 113.

51. Burke, *Decolonization and the Evolution of International Human Rights,* 40.

52. Ibid., 70–71. As in the case of the interpretation of "self-determination," the right to petition did, nonetheless, fracture Afro-Asian solidarity, with vigorous support and opposition to the provision from various member nations. See Burke, *Decolonization and the Evolution of International Human Rights,* 69–91. Furthermore, the ICERD *does* seem to permit states to engage in differential treatment of persons on the basis of "alienage," that is, (non)citizenship status, *except* in provisions for determining citizenship and policies on naturalization. Thus, the convention reproduces the identical problem regarding the standing of the stateless, discussed in the introduction, which has been the bane of human rights politics and political philosophy since their inception. See Meron, "The Meaning and Reach of the International Convention on the Elimination of All Forms of Racial Discrimination," 311–12.

53. Jensen, "Universality Should Govern the Small World of Today," 66.

54. Ibid., 64–65.

55. Burke, *Decolonization and the Evolution of International Human Rights,* 37.

56. Ibid., 42, 48.

57. Ibid., 48.

58. Moyn, *The Last Utopia,* 208. See also Sargent, "Oasis in the Desert?," 139–40.

59. Burke, *Decolonization and the Evolution of International Human Rights,* 98–100, 137. By 1968, the draft convention on the elimination of religious intolerance was also abandoned, a "bad omen" for human rights diplomacy and international relations, as wars in the Middle East and Vietnam as well as apartheid in South Africa led to deep divisions at the Tehran Conference. See Jensen, "Universality Should Govern," 68.

60. Moyn, *The Last Utopia,* 224. See also Eckel, "The Rebirth of Politics from the Spirit of Morality," 239.

61. Western states objected principally to such solidarity rights, which they thought shifted the locus of rights-holding from the individual to the collective or state (which, according to their perspective, did not have rights, only obligations), allowing states to justify political repression in the name of social and economic development. Third World leaders saw this argument as a tactic to retain unequal economic relations. The Declaration on the Right to Development therefore proved an extremely compromised instrument that nowhere guaranteed poor countries and former colonies the right to aid, trade, or other benefits enjoyed by industrialized states. It posed a conceptual innovation rather than a practical one. Normand and Zaidi, *Human Rights at the UN,* 303–4, 310–11.

62. Westad, *The Global Cold War,* 81, 86; Prashad, *The Darker Nations,* 127–30, 199–200. Scott has offered a definitive study of how newly independent states undertook the development of national populations by way of large-scale social engineering and "authoritarian high modernist" ideologies. For many postcolonial nations, with diplomatic, military, and economic support from one or the other Cold War superpowers, national development was yoked to authoritarian or dictatorial governments that inflicted extensive violence against their own populaces to crush real and imagined "enemies" of the state and of national development. See *Seeing Like a State,* 3–5.

63. Westad, *The Global Cold War,* 90–91. See also Painter, "The Rise of the Workfare State," 160; Latham, *The Right Kind of Revolution,* 29, 66.

64. Go, "Modeling States and Sovereignty," 109–13. However, Go also demonstrates that a counterlogic to imperial rule tended to prevail with respect to provisions for religion, socialist ideology, and individual rights, evidencing "a nascent set of transimperial, cross-colonial, and thus potentially globalizing influences" (ibid., 109).

65. Westad, *The Global Cold War,* 94–95; Prashad, *The Darker Nations,* 217–18.

66. Lee, "Between a Moment and an Era," 18. Heerten describes how the Biafran campaign for secession in a newly independent Nigeria in the late 1960s marked "one of the last efforts to keep alive anticolonialism as a 'rights of man' movement" and made evident the limits of the "space of political imagination," when revolutionary anticolonialism remained "entirely dependent on the notion of the nation" ("The Dystopia of Postcolonial Catastrophe," 31).

67. Moyn, *The Last Utopia,* 93–98.

68. Latham, *The Right Kind of Revolution,* 123–53.

69. Eckel, "The Rebirth of Politics," 239.

70. Burke, *Decolonization and the Evolution of International Human Rights,* 140.

71. Ibid., 142–43; Prashad, *The Darker Nations,* 163–64.

72. Nesaduri, "Bandung and the Political Economy of North–South Relations," 69.

73. Prashad, *The Darker Nations*, 12–13, 84–86, 170–71, 217. See also Chari and Verdery, "Thinking between the Posts," 19. Cheah provides a useful theoretical account of the earlier and "indistinguishable" origins of nationalism and cosmopolitanism in Europe as ideological and philosophical responses to the absolutist statism of the Treaty of Westphalia. See "Introduction Part II," 22–31.

74. Burke, *Decolonization and the Evolution of International Human Rights*, 959. Accordingly, as Burke explains, a key debate at the conference pertained to the definition of colonialism, in the context of the era of Soviet expansionism. Romulo argued that freedom required more than casting off foreign domination, but a "complete democratic reformation of the repressive colonial state" that prevented an indigenous ruling elite from replacing a foreign one. See also Chase, "Mutual Renewal," 59, 66–67.

75. Lee, "Between a Moment and an Era," 22.

76. Nesadurai, "Bandung and the Political Economy of North–South Relations," 75–76; Jensen, "Universality Should Govern the Small World of Today," 70.

77. Whether the Bandung Conference and NAM ever envisioned (or would endorse) a transnational model of rights and justice remains a point of debate for historians. Moyn contends the concept of human rights had limited, if any, meaningful currency among leaders of the NAM, whose primary concern was that of self-determination and sovereignty. See *The Last Utopia*, 109. See also Williams, *The Divided World*, xxi, 16–17. On the other hand, as Burke argues, delegates to the Bandung Conference were not necessarily hostile to human rights. Instead, human rights formed an "integral part of the political vocabulary at Bandung," where debates over the UDHR significantly resembled those at the United Nations. See "The Compelling Dialogue of Freedom," 950. Moreover, as Jensen has demonstrated, the leadership exhibited by NAM nations at the United Nations such as Jamaica, Liberia, Ghana, the Philippines, and Costa Rica was indispensable to the development of an international human rights regime. See "Universality Should Govern the Small World of Today," 70.

78. Mullen, "Du Bois, *Dark Princess*, and the Afro-Asian International," 219.

79. Ibid. My concern throughout this book is with American political and ideological interests in the postwar period, but it is important to take note of the other side of the Cold War contest, the Soviet's Union's perspective and relations with decolonizing nations. Josef Stalin's approach toward the Third World was somewhat haphazard, as he remained skeptical about the revolutionary potential in these regions to pass through the "stages of development" that he considered essential for Socialist revolution. Stalin's successor Nikita Khrushchev starkly disagreed, believing instead that the Soviet Union needed to support radical and Socialist parties in the Third World. Nevertheless, Khrushchev also maintained a Soviet-centric perspective on the Third World as he sought to develop an internationalist community, an attitude that, for example, plunged

the Sino-Soviet relationship into crisis by 1959. See Westad, *The Global Cold War,* 66–69. Previously, representatives from colonial nations to the Comintern delivered critiques of the Soviet ideological and political agenda, which rejected national liberation for colonized nations in favor of international solidarity. See Westad, *The Global Cold War,* 51–53; Prashad, *The Darker Nations,* 20–22. After 1970, however, many Third World leaders, for example, in Cuba and Vietnam, made more explicit alliances with the Soviet Union, which thoroughly shaped their nations' fates. Where Marxist-Leninist ideals have been instituted in authoritarian, one-party states, totalitarian regimes have often decimated first-generation political rights and freedom, in exchange for social and economic transformations. See Slater, "Trajectories of Development Theory," 96–97.

80. Westad, *The Global Cold War,* 92–93. See also Latham, *The Right Kind of Revolution,* 6, 67–68, 89–90. Nesadurai makes the important point that, while many participant states at Bandung opted for statist approaches to development, the Bandung Communiqué did not actually endorse such approaches, promoting instead "the rights of governments to freely choose their own political and economic systems." See "Bandung and the Political Economy of North–South Relations," 73.

81. Westad, *The Global Cold War,* 17.

82. Lee, "Between a Moment and an Era," 15; Prashad, *The Darker Nations,* xv, 11.

83. Nesadurai, "Bandung and the Political Economy of North–South Relations," 73.

84. Westad, *The Global Cold War,* 18.

85. Singh, *Black Is a Country,* 44, 185.

86. Martin, *No Coward Soldiers,* 18–19.

87. An extensive scholarly literature exists, and is growing rapidly, about the socialist influences and transnational sensibility of the black freedom movement in the United States. For a few examples, see Daulatzai, *Black Star, Crescent Moon;* Keith, *Unbecoming Americans;* Kelley, *Freedom Dreams;* Lubin, *Geographies of Liberation;* Robinson, *Black Marxism;* Von Eschen, *Race against Empire;* and Young, *Soul Power.*

88. See, for example, Alaniz and Cornish, *Viva La Raza;* Behnken, *The Struggle in Black and Brown;* Maeda, *Chains of Babylon* and *Rethinking the Asian American Movement;* and Melamed, *Represent and Destroy,* 29–30.

89. Pulido, *Black, Brown, Yellow, and Left,* 33; Melamed, *Represent and Destroy,* 28–29, 99–108. As Mullen and Smethurst contend, reorienting scholarship on U.S. left politics with analyses of race and ethnicity requires re-periodizing leftist activism in ways that redraw the connections between the Old Left and new liberation movements in the 1960s onward. See Introduction to *Left of the Color Line,* 4–6. In *Hillbilly Nationalists, Urban Race Rebels, and Black Power,* Sonnie and Tracy go even further to demonstrate that black radicalism in fact inspired and collaborated with poor white and working-class activists, those often

written off as too racist, traditional, or ignorant to be organized in multiracial coalitions.

90. Pulido, *Black, Brown, Yellow, and Left,* 59.

91. See Singh, "Culture/Wars," 511–15.

92. For a helpful explanation of the ethnic and class stratification of Louisiana society, in which white Cajuns serve as "racial intermediaries" between Creole landowners and African Americans, see Hebert-Leiter, "A Breed Between."

93. Shelton, "Of Machines and Men," 26.

94. Wardi, "Inscriptions in the Dust," 39.

95. See Griffin, "Creole and Singaleese," for an analysis of constructions of ethnic identity (especially in terms of black Creole and Senegalese or West African identities) and class status *within* black Louisiana society in Gaines's fiction, which prove central to the (trans)formation of "community" that the novel depicts.

96. See Wardi, "Inscriptions in the Dust," for a helpful discussion of how the representation of dirt, graveyards, and swampland in the novel bring together African burial rituals and the Christian Eucharist in order to offer an "ancestral requiem" for the painful histories that the landscape harbors.

97. Mallon, "Voicing Manhood," 50–61. See also Clark, "Re-(W)righting Black Male Subjectivity," 201–3; Heglar and Refoe, "Survival with Dignity," 58.

98. Folks, *From Richard Wright to Toni Morrison,* 64.

99. Lee provides a helpful gloss on Turner's concept, especially as it pertains to political communities, in "Between a Moment and an Era," 25–26.

100. Hartman, *Scenes of Subjection,* 59–60. Hartman explains how "the injurious constitution of blackness" has ensnared black persons in regimes of discipline and subjection by which freedom has been constrained to legal culpability and indebtedness (ibid., 9).

101. See, for example, Hebert-Leiter, "A Breed Between," 114; Folks, *From Richard Wright to Toni Morrison,* 63.

102. Jones, "New Narratives of Southern Manhood," 39–40. For discussions of the shootout, see Clark, "Re-(W)righting Black Male Subjectivity," 200; Jones, "Reconstructing Manhood," 52–54.

103. Kelley, *Freedom Dreams,* 81–84.

104. Indeed, this question plagued the drafting of the ICCPR and the ICESCR, as delegates argued as to what exactly constituted a "people" eligible for the right to self-determination. Although in practice the United Nations doctrine granted the right to "non-self-governing territories," namely, former colonies, the common Article 1 actually seems to leave the meaning ambiguous, providing a powerful, if "empty," signifier orienting various separatist and secessionist movements since the 1950s. See Normand and Zaidi, *Human Rights at the UN,* 222–23.

105. For an illuminating account of how thoroughly anxiety over racial threat has imbued the constitutional right to firearm ownership in the United States, see Cottrol and Diamond, "The Second Amendment."

106. Whether or not Long himself harbored anti-black sentiment is debatable, and, in any case, the Louisiana state constitution disenfranchised the black population entirely by way of restrictive suffrage and election mechanisms, such as poll taxes and literacy requirements. Moreover, Long's demagoguery and strongman hold over Louisiana state politics, even when he was removed to Congress, hardly offers a purely heroic icon of democratic governance.

107. Westad, *The Global Cold War,* 332–33, 358.

108. Berger, "Introduction," 10–12.

109. Estes, *Critical Reflections on the Fiction of Ernest J. Gaines,* 9.

110. Mallon offers a discussion of how the refashioned masculinity of the novel concomitantly extends the promise of new relations between black men and women in "Voicing Manhood," 55–56.

111. Indeed, critics have readily perceived Gaines's Charlie Biggs as a rewriting of Wright's Bigger Thomas and a "countertextual" transformation of the protest tradition that *Native Son* exemplified. See, for example, Clark, "Re-(W)righting Black Male Subjectivity." This should not be, however, to oversimplify Wright's own thoughtful response to the Bandung Conference, which he attended and wrote about in *The Color Curtain.*

112. For a study of how black literary production offers a critique and contests the "fiction" of the ideal of charismatic African American leadership, through which black political modernity has been imagined, see Edwards, *Charisma and the Fictions of Black Leadership.*

113. Holloway, *Legal Fictions,* 62. It is this dependence upon the law to grant African American personhood that leads Warren to argue that the "end" of "African American literature" arrived with the "legal demise of Jim Crow," even if, as in Gaines's novel, entire municipalities lagged decades behind federally mandated desegregation (*What Was African American Literature?,* 2, 15).

114. Holloway, *Legal Fictions,* 29. See Best's *The Fugitive's Properties* for a study of how the figure of the fugitive nonetheless enables the law to consolidate wayward humanity into the commodity form that extends beyond the enslaved black body.

115. See Gaudet, "Gaines' Fifteen Narrators"; Tucker, "(Re)Claiming Legacy in the Post–Civil Rights South."

116. Because there exists an exhaustive body of criticism that addresses the feminist cultural politics of *The Woman Warrior,* including Kingston's debate with Asian American cultural nationalism (especially with the writer Frank Chin), I do not take up these issues here. Likewise, critics have thoroughly addressed the

"transgeneric" character of the text that, while naming itself a memoir, incorporates elements of fiction, myth, and folklore. While this too remains a salient point for my discussion, especially as it morphs the conventional subject of the *bildungsroman* and family romance as they pertain to my discussions in later chapters, I do not undertake the question of genre in this chapter.

117. Kingston, *The Woman Warrior,* 45. All subsequent citations to the novel appear parenthetically in the body of the chapter.

118. For an insightful analysis *of The Woman Warrior* as a record of "history's afterlife," and in particular, the Communist and Cultural Revolutions in China as well as the PRC's involvement in the Cold War, see Kong, "Theorizing the Hyphen's Afterlife."

119. Critics who have discussed the politics of representation that structures both the formal composition and the reception of *The Woman Warrior* include Laura Hyun Yi Kang, *Compositional Subjects,* Chiang, *The Cultural Capital of Asian American Studies,* and Li, *Imagining the Nation.*

120. In a notable exception, Palumbo-Liu describes how the temporal representations in this chapter configure the problematic of a diasporic imaginary and ethnic identity, whereby the formation of the latter entails the sacrifice of the immigrant generation. See *Asian/American,* 348–50.

121. Ibid., 348–49.

122. Sae-Saue describes this scene as codifying "inter-racial proximities in the subjunctive mood," and locates it in relation to the "global landscape of ethnic difference" that Kingston embodies in the multiracial vegetable pickers of which her mother is one laborer ("The Inter-Ethnic Return," 271–74).

123. The much better known image of twinning in this chapter, "A Song for a Barbarian Reed Pipe," comes in the character of an unnamed Chinese girl, whom the narrator torments in an attempt to get the other to speak. As critics have commented, the scene seems to represent the narrator's own vexed negotiation of silence and speech as they shape her perception of the contradictions of a Chinese American woman's identity.

124. Chiang cites the paintings as a trope of "nonrepresentative representation," in which the opaque surface veils the content that it nonetheless maintains does exist. As such, he argues it "illustrates how Asian American racial identity occupies the level of form, as opposed to the Chinese identity that resides at the level of content" (*Cultural Capital,* 157–58).

125. Cheung describes such moments as responses to "provocative silence," in which Kingston "amplifies the glaring omissions [of history]" in order to "invent a braver world," in contradistinction to both patriarchal tradition and American racism (*Articulate Silences,* 75).

126. See, for example, Cheng, *Melancholy of Race,* 65–102; Hunsaker, "Nation, Family and Language."

127. For discussions regarding the rise of the "world novel" and "world literature" in relation to human rights discourse and politics, see Slaughter, *Human Rights, Inc.;* Anker, *Fictions of Dignity.*

128. Dimock, *Through Other Continents,* 3.

129. Ibid., 8.

130. Chakrabarty, *Provincializing Europe,* 8.

131. Ibid., 15–16.

132. Ibid., 16.

133. Ibid., 11, 65–66.

134. Again, with respect to the field of Asian American cultural production, Chiang offers a discerning reading of this conclusion as one that recognizes—even against its own desires—the relation between cultural production and social reproduction, whereby aesthetic value can never be fully disentangled from material interests (*The Cultural Capital of Asian American Studies,* 170). Nevertheless, I aim to supplement this reading with the suggestion that the recognition of desire, in addition to "money" (as Chiang surmises), "translates well."

135. In a telling corollary, Gaines originally titled his novel "The Revenge of the Old Men" before revising it, because "the book is not about revenge. . . . The book is about gathering and standing together for a cause" (qtd. in Mallon, "Voicing Manhood," 62).

136. Burke, *Decolonization and the Evolution of International Human Rights,* 114.

137. Ibid., 120. While the anticolonial endorsement of political rights during this period was more contested when it came to the question of *women's* political and social equality, many postcolonial elites supported women's rights, even if only out of a concern for national modernization and development than for individual personhood. See ibid., 123–26.

138. Lee, "Between a Moment and an Era," 9–10.

139. Ibid., 20; emphasis added. See also Prashad, *The Darker Nations,* 84–88.

140. Xanthaki, "Multiculturalism and International Law," 27.

141. Ibid., 27–28.

142. The 1992 UN Declaration on Minorities does provide more explicit language on the rights of minorities *as* minorities, for example stipulating free association and contact rights that include cross-border contacts. However, the declaration is nonbinding and therefore considerably less effective as a legal instrument than the other texts I consider. See Pejic, "Minority Rights in International Law," 678.

143. Ibid., 676.

144. Ibid., 673.

145. McDougall, "Toward a Meaningful International Regime," 583.

146. While some members of both the Human Rights Committee and the Committee on the Elimination of Racial Discrimination have acknowledged

this conflict, the committees as a whole seemed to have finessed the contradiction with, on the one hand, language of "due regard" that must be granted to political rights and, on the other, by averring that free speech and expression are not unlimited rights but are subject to curtailment in the interest of public order and general social welfare. See Meron, "The Meaning and Reach of the International Convention," 299–301. For a deft theoretical account of the vagaries of regulating "hate speech," see Judith Butler, *Excitable Speech.*

147. Felice, "The UN Committee on the Elimination of All Forms of Racial Discrimination," 211.

148. McDougall, "Toward a Meaningful International Regime," 576.

149. Ibid., 584.

150. Felice, "The UN Committee," 216.

151. McDougall, "Toward a Meaningful International Regime," 585–86.

152. Anderson, "Integration, Affirmative Action, and Strict Scrutiny," 1206–28.

153. Holloway, *Legal Fictions,* 61.

154. Cacho, *Social Death,* 40.

155. Ibid., 6–7.

156. Ibid., 5.

157. Meron, "The Meaning and Reach," 289. As with all such treaties, procedural and practical complications (e.g., the underfunding and understaffing of the CERD Committee) have rendered the monitoring, much less remedying, of such inequality extremely ineffective. See Felice, "UN Committee" for a detailed discussion of these problems.

158. Meron, "The Meaning and Reach," 289.

159. Cacho, *Social Death,* 17, 31; emphasis added.

160. Anker, *Fictions of Dignity,* 22.

2. "Come Almost Home"

1. Wilson and Brown, *Humanitarianism and Suffering,* 8, 11. See also Moyn, *The Last Utopia,* 226.

2. Wilson and Brown, *Humanitarianism and Suffering,* 8.

3. Ibid.

4. Ibid., 19. For an overview of the conceptual and practical complications involved with "neutral humanitarianism," see Forsythe, "On Contested Concepts."

5. Rancière, *The Politics of Literature,* 4, 40.

6. Slaughter, *Human Rights, Inc.,* 43.

7. Rorty, "Human Rights, Rationality, and Sentimentality," 263–67. See Williams, *The Divided World,* 43–55, for a trenchant critique of such humanitarian approaches in cultural texts.

8. Deleuze and Guattari, *Kafka*, 16. See also JanMohamed and Lloyd, *The Nature and Context of Minority Discourse.*

9. Deleuze and Guattari, *Kafka*, 16. In *Immigrant Acts*, Lowe explains how Asian American cultural productions provide such a countersite to national memory and culture in the United States.

10. Lowe, "The Intimacies of Four Continents," 208.

11. Ibid.

12. Cubilié, *Women Witnessing Terror*, 35–36.

13. Ibid., 29.

14. Butler, *Precarious Life*, xii.

15. Ibid., 43. See also Keenan, *Fables of Responsibility*, 172.

16. Donnelly, *Universal Human Rights in Theory and Practice*, 15–16.

17. Rancière, "Who Is the Subject of the Rights of Man?," 302.

18. Lyotard, "The Other's Rights," 183–84.

19. For examples, see Borgwardt, *A New Deal for the World;* Ishay, *The History of Human Rights;* and Normand and Zaidi, *Human Rights at the UN*. All of these scholars use the exact phrase "life of their own" to describe the extra-legal performativity that human rights manifest. Hunt, *Inventing Human Rights*, describes the discursive performativity of human rights as originating in the American Declaration of Independence and the French Declaration of the Rights of Man and Citizen.

20. Normand and Zaidi, *Human Rights at the UN*, 16, 148–57.

21. Lionnet and Shih, *Minor Transnationalism*, 7.

22. Cubilié, *Women Witnessing Terror*, 72.

23. Chuh, *Imagine Otherwise*, 10. Chuh's argument centers in particular on Asian Americanist critique, although I expand this method in *Writing Human Rights* in the interest of a comparative racial and diasporic analysis.

24. Ibid., x, 8.

25. Hagedorn, *Dogeaters*, 151. All subsequent citations to the novel appear parenthetically in the body of the chapter.

26. Lee, *A Gesture Life*, 293, 304. All subsequent citations to the novel appear parenthetically in the body of the chapter.

27. Slaughter, *Human Rights, Inc.*, 58.

28. Ibid., 91.

29. Given the "unmaking" of Hata by the novel's end, which I discuss below, critics have actually referred to *A Gesture Life* as a "*de*bildungsroman" or "deconstructive" *bildungsroman*. See Carroll, "Traumatic Patriarchy," 593; Kong, "Beyond K's Specter," 2.

30. Slaughter, *Human Rights, Inc.*, 99.

31. Hunt, *Inventing Human Rights*, 32.

32. Ibid., 26, 29.

33. Hunt, "The Paradoxical Origins of Human Rights," 13.

34. Slaughter offers an extended discussion of literacy as a crucial element in the "technology transfers" that take place in the postcolonial world, which are construed as essential to the "development of human personality" in Third World nations, as well as the response of postcolonial writers to this injunction to literacy (*Human Rights, Inc.*, 270–316).

35. For select discussions of historical exclusion and contemporary alienation of Asians, for whom the racial image of the "forever foreign" constantly threatens to undermine the claims to formal citizenship and cultural belonging that such recognition authorizes in the United States, see Lowe, *Immigrant Acts;* Palumbo-Liu, *Asian/American;* and Volpp, "Obnoxious to Their Very Nature." In "Traumatic Patriarchy," Carroll describes how the ultimate narrative failure of Hata's incorporation intervenes in and departs from a literature of immigration and assimilation.

36. As Slaughter observes, in modern rights declarations (such as the French and American declarations), even while sovereignty was located in "the people," the people's authority was itself "sponsored" by Nature's God. The contemporary, secularized UDHR (which tries to reconcile heterogeneous religious and political traditions), however, countenances no such superhuman authority and names no guarantor. This vacuum becomes itself a subject of contest. See *Human Rights, Inc.*, 69–71.

37. Gairola hence refers to Joey's narrative in *Dogeaters* as a "counter-bildungsroman," which "counters modes of Western imperialism that manifest through queer sex on the market" ("Deterritorialisations of Desire," 26–30).

38. As many scholars have noted, the euphemism "comfort woman" proves especially ironic, given the brutality of the systematic violence enacted upon the women. I retain the term here to mark both the historical specificity of the practice and the overdetermined ideological conditions by which such sexual violence could be described as "comfort."

39. Oh, "The Japanese Imperial System," 4–9.

40. Soh, "Prostitutes versus Sex Slaves," 73–77. A corresponding if distinct Korean patriarchal nationalism that draws on Confucian principles has further compounded the wounds of former comfort women, where a focus on the "lost chastity" of these women stands as a mark of national shame and stymies recognition of individual women's bodily and psychological suffering. See Fujitani et al., Introduction to *Perilous Memories*, 8.

41. Soh, "Prostitutes versus Sex Slaves," 77–79.

42. See Delmendo, *The Star-Entangled Banner;* Ileto, "The Philippine–American War"; Isaac, *American Tropics;* and Rafael, *White Love*. In "Legacies of the 'Inno-

cent' Frontier," Werrlein addresses this politics of memory specifically through a reading of Rio's nostalgic character in *Dogeaters*.

43. Delmendo, *The Star-Entangled Banner*, 118–19; Isaac, *American Tropics*, 33. See also San Juan, *After Postcolonialism*, for a discussion of the way in which transnational capital consolidates class inequality through what he describes as "comprador or tributary neocolonialism" (9), and Rafael, *Discrepant Histories*, for essays that consider Philippine history and present it as "a site of different and often contentious projects—political, economic, and cultural—whose borders are historically constructed and so remain spatially unstable" (xiv).

44. Chang, "Masquerade, Hysteria, and Neocolonial Femininity," 639.

45. Ibid., 642.

46. McClintock, *Imperial Leather*, 359. See also Lee, *The Americas of Asian American Literature*, 85.

47. Chen, "(Trans)National Imaginary and Tropical Melancholy," 115–19.

48. Butler, *Frames of War*, 5.

49. Gordon, *Ghostly Matters*, 112–15.

50. Edkins, *Missing*, 6.

51. Ibid., 13.

52. An extensive body of scholarship on the phenomenon of witnessing, the concept of "the event" (that is witnessed), and trauma informs my discussion in this chapter. See, for only a few examples, Cubilié, *Women Witnessing Terror;* Sanders, *Ambiguities of Witnessing;* and Douglass and Vogler, *Witness and Memory.*

53. Cheng, "Passing, Natural Selection, and Love's Failure," 563.

54. Cubilié distinguishes between such "guilt-ridden viewing of atrocity-as-spectacle" and "engaged, ethical witnessing" that negotiates the necessary "unknowability" inherent in trauma. But, as she emphasizes, such ethical engagement does not simply isolate the survivors' testimony, but participates in "building ties to the 'human'" and granting recognition through "alternative forms of community" (*Women Witnessing Terror*, 11, 17, 21, 163).

55. Levinas, "Ethics as First Philosophy," 82.

56. Wyschogrod, "Towards a Postmodern Ethics," 63. See Parikh, *An Ethics of Betrayal*, for a fuller discussion of Derrida's contributions to Levinasian ethics with his conception of "every other is every other."

57. Wyschogrod, "Towards a Postmodern Ethics," 63.

58. Butler, *Frames of War*, 23.

59. In particular, Pucha questions Rio's recounting of dates: "*Puwede ba?* 1956, 1956! Rio, you've got it all wrong. Think about it: 1956 makes no sense. It must have started sometime around 1959, at the very least! You like to mix things up on purpose, *di ba?*" (248). This "mix[ing] up on purpose" of dates points to the broader difficulty in constructing a historical chronology for *Dogeaters*, which

condenses historical events and cultural references from several decades (the late 1950s to the 1980s) in a sometimes anachronistic manner. In this way, I would suggest, Hagedorn offers an epochal and structural critique of the Marcos and post-Marcos regimes, rather than a straightforward and chronologically linear roman-à-clef, even as she clearly makes use of this genre. See also Werrlein, "Legacies of the 'Innocent' Frontier," 45–46.

60. Mendoza, "A Queer Nomadology," 820.

61. Ibid., 827.

62. The Asian Women's Peace Foundation, a privately administered fund, has paid reparations to surviving comfort women, but has been denounced for taking a "charitable" approach to these women, in lieu of official recognition. See Choi, "The Politics of War Memories," 396.

63. Ibid., 397.

64. Hein, "Savage Irony," 341–42.

65. Yoneyama, "Traveling Memories, Contagious Justice," 58–59.

66. Ibid., 81.

67. Anthropologists have instead found shamanic ritual to be a particularly rich, extra-juridical resource by which to "speak silence" for former Korean comfort women. See Choi, "The Politics of War Memories," 405. In Asian American literature, Nora Okja Keller depicts the former comfort woman Akiko as just such a shaman in *Comfort Woman* (1997).

68. See Balce-Cortes, "Imagining the Neocolony"; Chen, "(Trans)National Imaginary"; Gonzaga, *Globalization and Becoming-Nation;* Hong, *Ruptures of American Capital;* Lee, *Americas of Asian American Literature;* San Juan, *After Postcolonialism.* Although I argue that "American imperialism" or "neocolonialism" is too reductive a lens to describe the international order established after 1945, in the case of the Philippines, where formal independence came with stipulations about American access to the nation's natural and human resources, "neocolonial" does indeed prove an apt label.

69. Those who do, such as Hong, Lee, or Chen, tend to read it as a critique of broadly commodified, heteropatriarchal femininity rather than considering the structure of torture that the scene enacts, thus eliding the very *different* forms of subjectivity that the novel generates for Daisy, in contrast to, for instance, Lolita Luna.

70. McCoy, *Policing America's Empire,* 16.

71. Ibid., 16–17.

72. Ibid., 17, 37–40. As McCoy writes, "The first U.S. federal agency with a fully developed covert capacity was not the Federal Bureau of Investigation (FBI) or the Office of Naval Intelligence (ONI) but the Philippines Constabulary (PC)" (17).

73. Ibid., 18. See also Westad, *The Global Cold War,* 115–17.

74. McCoy, *Policing America's Empire*, 386.

75. Ibid., 388, 407.

76. Ibid., 403–4.

77. Schmitz, *Thank God They're on Our Side*, 5. See also Westad, *The Global Cold War*, 111.

78. Schmitz, *Thank God They're on Our Side*, 5.

79. Landé, "Manila's Malaise," 8; Adesnik and McFaul, "Engaging Autocratic Allies," 13–15.

80. For a detailed, albeit mainstream, account of the rivalry between Marcos and the Aquinos, Aquino's assassination, and its immediate political fallout, see Burton, *Impossible Dream*.

81. McCoy, *Policing America's Empire*, 14, 36.

82. San Juan, *After Postcolonialism*, 92. See also Anderson, "Cacique Democracy in the Philippines"; Tadiar, "Manila's New Metropolitan Form." There is also a vital history of transnational activism that opposed martial law. In the United States, the Katipunan ng mga Demokratikong Pilipino (KDP), the Anti–Martial Law Coalition, Friends of the Filipino People, the Movement for the Restoration of Civil Liberties in the Philippines, and the Alliance for Philippine Concerns all organized to protest Marcos's dictatorship. See Bello and Reyes, "Filipino Americans and the Marcos Overthrow"; Toribio, "Dare to Struggle"; Choy, "Towards Trans-Pacific Social Justice."

83. Dalton, *Longing for the Other*, 153.

84. See Kurasawa, *The Work of Global Justice*, for social movement theory informed by such a human rights method.

85. Chuh, "Discomforting Knowledge," 16.

86. Donnelly, *Universal Human Rights in Theory and Practice*, 7.

87. Ibid., 8; Freeman, *Human Rights*, 74.

88. Zuckert, "Natural Rights in the American Revolution," 65.

89. As Zuckert further clarifies, "Government becomes the duty bearer corresponding not only to the primary natural rights but also to a derivative right to security in one's rights. This is more than a duty to forbear; it is the duty to supply the protection" (ibid., 65). Moreover, rights entail what Donnelly describes as a "possession paradox," whereby having a right, and having it recognized, are necessary only when it is not automatically enjoyed; indeed, subjects often exercise rights as a "last resort," seeking recourse through other means such as contract or legal claims before acknowledging that recognition and respect has not been automatically tendered. See *Universal Human Rights*, 9, 12.

90. Slaughter, *Human Rights, Inc.*, 26, 33, 81.

91. Cvetkovich, *An Archive of Feelings*, 196, 237.

92. Butler, *Frames of War*, xiii.

93. Ibid., xiii.

94. In raising the specter of the fetus as that responsibility which haunts the subject of political violence, I necessarily raise the thorny question of reproductive rights and politics that concerns much feminist discourse. To be certain, I do not intend to attribute to the fetus a clear-cut "right to life," which has been the mainstay of conservative politics in the United States. As Butler argues, "It is not possible to say in advance that there is *a right to life*, since no right can ward off all processes of degeneration and death" (*Frames of War,* 18). Precisely because, as I have explained in this chapter, personhood—which entails the guarantee of protection from harm and destruction—is a social project and product, not a biological truth, the viability of *any* life (including, for example, animal life or lives lived at a distance) is the result of social and political decision. Nevertheless, in the model of responsibility that I have elaborated here and elsewhere, the ethical implications involved in the singular moments of decision around the fetus cannot be politically pre-scripted nor evaluated in standardized moral terms. If feminist subjectivity is to have any political and historical meaningfulness, it is precisely that reproductive agency involves the subject in a network of social relations that have made her a viable being who, in turn, becomes responsible for other others.

95. Evangelista, "Jessica Hagedorn and Manila Magic," 52; Silverio, "Nelia Sancho."

3. "A Globe within Him"

1. Choi, *The Foreign Student,* 34. All subsequent citations to the novel appear parenthetically in the body of the chapter.

2. Chang, *Disoriented,* 37.

3. Kim, "Bled In, Letter by Letter," 557–61.

4. Derrida and Dufourmantelle, *Of Hospitality,* 143–45. Derrida makes this observation in the context of a discussion regarding the colonial conditions in which Algerian Muslims, initially limited to the status of "French nationals," came to be offered French citizenship in 1919 and again in 1944, a conditional hospitality that parallels that of Asian immigrants in the United States as well as inhabitants of territories such as the Philippines deemed by the U.S. Supreme Court to be "foreign in a domestic sense." In his formulation, Derrida points up not only that war effects social and legal change, but that for sovereign power, any change that arises from other than its own authority is experienced as a kind of warfare.

5. Yuh, "Moved by War," 280–81.

6. Stueck, *Rethinking the Korean War,* 186.

7. Kim, "Bled In, Letter by Letter," 559.

8. For influential accounts of this racial construction in Asian American literary history, see Li, *Imagining the Nation;* Lowe, *Immigrant Acts;* Palumbo-Liu, *Asian/American;* and Shimakawa, *National Abjection.*

9. I develop this concept of the "borderline" Asian/American, a nascent subjectivity whose full articulation is not yet accomplished, from Kristeva's account of the "borderline case." As Kristeva explains, the borderline subject of abjection (i.e., the deject) becomes disoriented as to his or her place and proceeds to "stray" (*Powers of Horror*, 7–8).

10. Palumbo-Liu, *Asian/American*, 1.

11. Ngai offers an incisive account of "animatedness" as a bodily affect with marked implications for raced subjects in *Ugly Feelings*, 89–125.

12. Although Asian immigration to and presence in the U.S. South existed prior to 1950, as Reimers argues in "Asian Immigrants in the South," the social changes wrought by the *Brown v. Board of Education* decision of 1954 and major pieces of civil rights legislation in the 1960s in conjunction with the liberalization of immigration policy in the 1960s were key to the newly substantial increases of Asian immigration to the South in the second half of the twentieth century.

13. A series of immigration laws and policies that effectively restricted most immigration originating in Asia, from the 1870s through the early twentieth century, culminated in the 1924 Johnson-Reed Immigration Act. This law established numerical limits based on a global hierarchy of racial and national identities. At the same time, as I note above, the right to naturalize was restricted to those immigrants deemed white, barring East and South Asian immigrants from naturalizing. As I also discuss in the introduction, the postwar era saw sweeping changes in such policies. The 1952 Immigration and Naturalization Act, or the McCarran-Walter Act, retained the national origins principle by which quotas had been determined, but increased the quotas for previously excluded nations. The Immigration Act of 1965 redrew the criteria for immigration quotas altogether, allocating slots on a hemispheric basis and designing preferences according to occupational requirements and familial considerations. For a thorough discussion of immigration restrictions and reform in the twentieth century, see Ngai, *Impossible Subjects*. For an analysis of the racial restrictions on naturalization, see López, *White by Law*.

14. Indeed, only two years prior, Senator Pat McCarran gave his name to the Internal Security Act, Title II, or the Emergency Detention Act (EDA), which required members of the American Communist Party to register with the attorney general and provided for the building of internment camps (modeled on the Japanese internment camps of World War II) for the detention of those identified as "dangerous individuals" during states of emergency. The legislation was endorsed by political liberals, who believed that, in contrast to the Japanese internment, it would prevent mass incarceration of any particular group. The act nonetheless participated in a logic of the security state by granting legitimacy to declared states of emergency and implicitly permitting the ongoing surveillance of those thought to be subversive, without which speedy detentions would not be

possible. Insofar as the EDA replicated earlier techniques of exclusion, it was not merely an aberration of McCarthyism, but part of the ongoing practices of the security state, in which liberals colluded. See Campbell, *Writing Security,* 178–79.

15. Ibid., 170–71.

16. Ngai, *Impossible Subjects,* 2, 4, 8, 170.

17. Shimakawa, *National Abjection,* 3.

18. Ibid., 19, 3.

19. Dudziak, *Cold War Civil Rights,* 87.

20. Bow refers to Chang's status as that of the "interstitial Asian," who serves "as a vehicle for a commentary on domestic race relations" (*Partly Colored,* 169).

21. See McPherson, *Reconstructing Dixie,* for analysis of how constructions of the South as a region function in American national culture, especially as a figure of recalcitrance in the face of modernity. Eckes provides a detailed discussion of the remarkable increases in standard measures of "modernization" in the American South during the second half of the twentieth century, concluding that, since 1950, national and international markets have well integrated the South. See "The South and Economic Globalization," 50.

22. Klein, *Cold War Orientalism,* 41.

23. Campbell and Shapiro, "Introduction," ix.

24. Ibid.

25. Indeed, historians have long disputed the "origins" and causes of the Korean conflict, as well as the role of Korean political leaders and popular movements in relation to international interests in the nation. See Cumings, *The Origins of the Korean War,* for an encyclopedic account of the complex grounds of this contested political landscape. As new sources, such as memoirs of Soviet officials, Korean-language sources, and Russian archival documents on the war have become available in the past fifty years, historians have debated the extent to which foreign involvement and local power struggles determined the origins and course of the war. Nevertheless, as Stueck details, the Korean conflict *cannot* be characterized as essentially or only a civil conflict. See *Rethinking the Korean War,* 66–83.

26. The Truman administration saw the North Korean attack and the entry of Chinese troops into the war in 1950 as part of a wider Soviet gambit for power, although recently released documents from the Soviet archive reveal that the initiative came from Kim Il-sung. See Latham, *The Right Kind of Revolution,* 38.

27. Gardner, "Korean Borderlands," 129, 142.

28. Klein, *Cold War Orientalism,* 11–43.

29. Ibid., 14.

30. Scarry, *The Body in Pain,* 5.

31. Ibid., 51–57, 116–28.

32. Ibid., 38–40.

33. Ibid., 81.

34. Ibid., 144, 150.

35. Ibid., 40–50.

36. Agamben, *Homo Sacer,* 28.

37. Schmitt contends that the declaration by a "private person" that he has no enemies "can at most say that he would like to place himself outside the political community to which he belongs and continue to live as a private individual only." But this in no way makes vanish the friend-enemy distinction that Schmitt identifies as the essential feature of sovereign political power. See *The Concept of the Political,* 51.

38. Kim, *Ends of Empire,* 158. Scarry takes a largely benign view of the body that exists in "civilization" during peacetime, implicitly endorsing a liberal model of governance that construes torturous violence as exceptional to normal life. More recently, following Foucault's lead, numerous scholars have demonstrated how the state's *biopower* produces the *very life* of the populations it seeks to defend, through the systematic management of biological life and its reproduction (Foucault, *Society Must Be Defended*). Accompanied by physical and cultural violence, as well as forms of knowledge that rationalize and normalize the management of the population, biopower wields the "imperative to live" as justification for even its most aggressive mechanisms of interference and control. Foucauldian inquiry hence renders visible the (threat of) violence by which modern national life is internally secured and normalized. See Cohen, *A Body Worth Defending,* for an impressive study of how liberal political philosophy and the doctrine of natural law come to assume "the body"—understood as an individuated, self-contained organism—to be the "natural" substrate for the body politic through the biopolitical and biomedical concept of "immunity."

39. Shapiro, "Warring Bodies and Bodies Politic," 122.

40. Sáez, "Torture," 133.

41. Kolb, "The Relationship between International Humanitarian Law and Human Rights Law," 417–18. See also Robertson, *Crimes against Humanity,* 168, 182.

42. Kolb, "The Relationship between International Humanitarian Law and Human Rights Law," 411–12.

43. Ibid.

44. Ibid., 413.

45. See Nowak, "What Practices Constitute Torture?," 810–17; Kenny, "The Meaning of Torture."

46. Derrida, "Force of Law," 13–14.

47. Likewise, another troubling aspect of the convention, at least in terms of its enforcement, includes non-*refoulement*—that is, the CAT's explicit prohibition on state parties to "return" an individual to another state "where there are

substantial grounds for believing he would be in danger of being subjected to torture." As former UN Special Rapporteur Manfred Nowak has observed, it should require more than diplomatic assurances from the state in question to certify that a person does *not* face torture, but treaty bodies have proceeded primarily on these grounds, nevertheless. See Rodley, "*The United Nations Convention against Torture* (review)," 1144.

48. For a helpful overview of the field of CSS, see Browning and McDonald, "The Future of Critical Security Studies."

49. Ibid., 9.

50. Ken Booth, qtd. in Burke, *Beyond Security, Ethics and Violence,* 19–20. See also Browning and McDonald, "The Future of Critical Security Studies," 13–15; Edkins, "Humanitarianism, Humanity, Human," 254–56.

51. Sáez, "Torture," 139.

52. Burke, *Beyond Security, Ethics and Violence,* 92.

53. Campbell, *Writing Security,* 12. See also Browning and McDonald, "The Future of Critical Security Studies," 4–6.

54. Campbell, *Writing Security,* 9.

55. Ibid., 9.

56. See Harold and DeLuca, "Behold the Corpse," for a thoughtful discussion of the Till case, in particular, of how the circulation of images of the "human body in peril," reworked the visual tropes of lynching in order to mobilize African American communal politics. Bow persuasively details how *The Foreign Student* repeatedly alludes to African American history and literature in *Partly Colored,* 174.

57. Burke, *Beyond Security, Ethics and Violence,* 14.

58. Katherine's ambivalent existence in Sewanee signals the long residual life of what feminist scholars of the nineteenth century have described as the *continuities* between domesticity and public life. As feminist critics such as Berlant, Brown, Kaplan, and Romero have argued, the "domestic sphere" existed not in isolated autonomy from the market economy and political workings of a (local and national) public world of men, but in a mutually constitutive relation that the *rhetoric* of separate spheres functioned to obscure. Domestic femininity thus articulated a modern subjectivity by which middle-class white women negotiated new forms of material production and political encounter. See Berlant, "Poor Eliza," 636; Brown, *Domestic Individualism,* 3; Kaplan, *The Anarchy of Empire;* Romero, *Home Fronts,* 25.

59. Her abject freedom and the Asian/American relationality to which it opens Katherine do, however, bring those other privileges under scrutiny. The risks are apparent, for example, in the historical terms of the Cable Act of 1922 (repealed in 1936), which guaranteed independent citizenship (i.e., determined apart from their spouse's status) for all women, *except* those who married "aliens ineligible

for citizenship," namely Asian men. Choi dramatizes these measures when Katherine comes under law enforcement scrutiny after vouching for Chang against FBI agents' suspicions that he is a Chinese Communist agitator (275–78). Here, her intimacy with an Asian man renders her national allegiances questionable.

60. Here, I employ the term "emplotment" to further emphasize, as I do in the introduction, the historical imagination that Choi's work of fiction produces as an act of *historical* recovery that cannot be accomplished except in the form of prose fiction. Kim describes this reconstruction of the Korean War in Choi's novel as an act of "postmemory" in "Bled In, Letter by Letter," 571.

61. Kristeva, *Powers of Horror,* 9.

62. As Burke contends with respect to Agamben's description of the camp as the biopolitical paradigm of modern states, it is crucial to understand how the security state generates "'positive,' enabling and seductive forms of power as well as those that are repressive, disciplinary and nihilistic," that in turn "impart to security such a potent, idealistic sheen" (*Beyond Security, Ethics and Violence,* 11).

63. Daniel Kim offers an extended and nuanced discussion of the novel's engagement with this Asian American political formation and the particular literary tradition of ethnic realism representative of it in "Bled In, Letter by Letter," 567–69.

64. Campbell and Shapiro, "Introduction," xviii.

65. Ibid.

66. The more liberal versions of CSS I describe above insist that any critical approach to human security should be grounded in "realizable utopias," that is, political solutions that are deemed possible and realistic in the current historical conjuncture. The minor literatures I consider in *Writing Human Rights* suggest instead the pressing urgency of thinking instead the "impossible," as our ethical responsibility to the Other. Burke, *Beyond Security, Ethics and Violence,* 22.

4. Regular Revolutions

1. See Basu, "Globalization of the Local/Localization of the Global," for a succinct discussion of the history of the UN women's conferences in the late twentieth century.

2. See Charlesworth, "Not Waving but Drowning," for an overview of "gender mainstreaming," and its considerable limits, in the United Nations and other international institutions beginning with the UN Decade for Women in 1975 and especially picking up steam in the 1990s.

3. Rancière, "Who Is the Subject of the Rights of Man?," 302.

4. In reading transnational feminism *against* liberal feminism, I would maintain that feminism itself has no singular definition and has taken multiple historical iterations. Nevertheless, I am here concerned with those social discourses

and political projects that "share the critique of masculinist ideologies and the desire to undo patriarchal power regimes" (Shohat, *Talking Visions,* 2), but also "acknowledge the different forms that feminisms take" (Grewal and Kaplan, *Scattered Hegemonies,* 20).

5. Charlesworth, "Not Waving but Drowning," 6.

6. Basu, "Globalization of the Local/Localization of the Global," 74.

7. Farrell and McDermott, "Claiming Afghan Women," 38–42, 51–52.

8. Dingo, "Securing the Nation." See also Farrell and McDermott, "Claiming Afghan Women," 46–51.

9. Williams, *The Divided World,* 35.

10. Grewal, *Transnational America,* 155–56.

11. Ibid., 152.

12. For example, as Basu explains, in preparation for the 1995 Beijing Conference, U.S. women of color formed coalitions with Third World women which yielded significant critiques of the feminist universalism prevalent in the preceding conferences. See "Globalization of the Local/Localization of the Global," 71.

13. Grewal, "On the New Global Feminism and the Family of Nations," 516.

14. See Chandra, "Re-Producing a Nationalist Literature in the Age of Globalization," for a notable exception in this critical reception.

15. Some recent criticism of *Butterflies* has begun to broach the question of U.S. imperialism in relation to Dominican history. See, for example, McCallum, "Reclaiming Julia Alvarez"; Socolovsky, "Patriotism, Nationalism, and the Fiction of History"; Criniti, "Collecting Butterflies."

16. This image of the United States (and Western Europe) as a land of refuge prevails, even as the nation grants asylum to a proportionally tiny number of refugees, especially in contrast to many Third World nations.

17. Alvarez, *How the García Girls Lost Their Accents,* 108. All subsequent citations to the novel appear parenthetically in the body of the chapter.

18. Saldaña-Portillo, *Revolutionary Imagination,* 27.

19. Ibid., 23.

20. Ibid. This too is an implicit truism of chapter 1 in *Writing Human Rights*—namely, that Afro-Asian solidarity in anticolonial movements gave rise to alternative visions of modernity, which were, nevertheless, premised on the need for national development. As Briggs et al. explain, Latin American "underdevelopment," like the corresponding "development" projects undertaken by states in the region, is the *product* of transnational capitalism, not outside or "prior" to it. See "Transnationalism," 638.

21. Saldaña-Portillo, *Revolutionary Imagination,* 25.

22. Ibid., 23. See also Shiva, *Staying Alive.* Within the United Nations, human rights principles were expressly linked to development goals, as time and again the General Assembly, UNESCO, and other UN agencies affirmed that social and

economic development was essential to the achievement of human rights for all the world's population. See Grewal, *Transnational America,* 132–33.

23. Roorda, *The Dictator Next Door,* 27.

24. Ibid., 32. Of course, numerous factors, not least the tremendous success of his agrarian policies and incorporation of the Dominican peasantry into a national modernity, secured Trujillo's long and repressive regime. Nonetheless, U.S. policy contributed decisively to Trujillo's power (and, more obviously, to his assassination). Indeed, even the distribution of land and the sedimentization of the peasantry began, if fitfully so, with the U.S. military occupation of 1916–1924, during which period, the U.S. military government began institutionalizing a private property regime to benefit U.S. economic, political, and military interests. Against this, the nationalist-populist movement that advanced Trujillo's early agrarian policies formed to espouse "an alternative model of modernity." See Turits, *Foundations of Despotism,* 53, 71–77.

25. Even in the case of the extraordinarily violent 1937 massacre of more than ten thousand Haitians by Dominican soldiers in the northwestern region bordering Haiti, the United States touted the Good Neighbor policy, facilitating a diplomatic resolution between the Dominican Republic and Haiti.

26. Roorda, *The Dictator Next Door,* 62.

27. In his 1904 corollary to the Monroe Doctrine, Theodore Roosevelt accorded to the United States the power to "correct the fiscal irresponsibility of the local states and maintain political order through the exercise of an international police power," which soon led to a receivership arrangement between the Dominican Republic and the United States, whereby the United States served as the collector of customs for the Dominican Republic, and ultimately a treaty giving the United States extensive oversight of Dominican local government (Kryzanek and Wiarda, *The Politics of External Influence,* 31–32). William Howard Taft added to this foreign policy the practice of "dollar diplomacy," actively encouraging U.S. investors to extend loans and private capital in the region. In 1916, following the Dominican refusal to comply with U.S. demands for command over Dominican armed forces and the threat of civil war in the nation, President Wilson ordered the invasion of the Dominican Republic by U.S. Marines on May 5. The ensuing Wilson Plan oversaw the administration of new elections, a reordered financial system, and a newly created national guard in the Dominican Republic. See Atkins and Wilson, *The Dominican Republic and the United States,* 39–41, 46. As Kryzanek and Wiarda explain, there is some evidence, although no direct link, that the CIA later supplied weapons to Trujillo's assassins.

28. Atkins and Wilson, *The Dominican Republic and the United States,* 59.

29. Ibid., 64.

30. Roorda, *The Dictator Next Door,* 231. Such an alliance was only one instance in a decades-long history of U.S. intervention in Latin America and alliances

with dictators. Between 1954 and 1989, the United States also interceded (often covertly) in Guatemala, Cuba, British Guiana, Chile, Nicaragua, Grenada, and Panama. Indeed, in 1965, a few years after Trujillo's assassination, Lyndon B. Johnson dispatched troops to the Dominican Republic to stem a countercoup by the former president Juan Bosch, who had been ousted by Dominican military forces in 1963. On this occasion, Johnson issued his "Johnson Doctrine," whereby the United States would proceed, unilaterally and through military channels, in the Western hemisphere to prevent the institution of any Communist government. See Grow, *U.S. Presidents and Latin American Interventions,* 79–80.

31. Roorda, *The Dictator Next Door,* 233–34.

32. Kryzanek and Wiarda, *The Politics of External Influence,* 39.

33. Roorda, *The Dictator Next Door,* 241.

34. The reasons for the decline of Trujillo's power and popularity were also multiple. These included a major shift in economic policy, whereby Trujillo acquired for himself and his regime a monopoly on the nation's sugar industry (dispossessing large segments of the peasantry in the process) and the increasing use of extremely violent methods by the SIM. Moreover, a major rift between the Catholic Church (which had previously supported the dictator) and Trujillo in 1960 threw many Dominicans' loyalty to the dictator in disarray. See Turits, *Foundations of Despotism,* 232–58.

35. The United States also supported the condemnation of Trujillo by the OAS after Trujillo's involvement in the attempted assassination of Venezuelan President Rómulo Betancourt.

36. Turits, *Foundations of Despotism,* 259.

37. My analysis of the narrative structure and use of terminology regarding different forms of narrative beginnings has been adopted from Romagnolo, "Recessive Origins in Julia Alvarez's *García Girls.*"

38. Many critics have equated a physical return to the Dominican Republic with a "return to the past," as if the Dominican Republic actually does exist "in the past," effectively eliding the specific dimensions of Dominican modernity (the postcolonial state form and its mutual constitution with American imperialism), which impel the departure from the homeland in the first place. See for example, Lovelady, "Walking Backwards," 30.

39. Suárez, "Julia Alvarez and the Anxiety of Latina Representation," 131.

40. Gordon, *Ghostly Matters,* 67. See also Cooppan, "Hauntologies of Form," 82.

41. Alvarez, *In the Time of the Butterflies,* 321. All subsequent citations to the novel appear parenthetically in the body of the chapter.

42. Socolovsky, "Patriotism, Nationalism, and the Fiction of History," 9.

43. Saldaña-Portillo, *The Revolutionary Imagination,* 7, 65.

44. Das, *Life and Words,* 77.

45. Ibid., 78.

46. Ibid., 64.

47. See Sifris, *Reproductive Freedom, Torture and International Human Rights,* for a legal treatment of how the right to personal security can encompass reproductive freedom.

48. Minerva further urges Mate to forego a pardon by Trujillo, because "accepting a pardon meant we thought we had something to be pardoned for" (236).

49. Scarry, *The Body in Pain,* 27–59.

50. Johnstone, "Feminist Influences," 176. See also Charlesworth, "Not Waving but Drowning," 9.

51. See Bergoffen, "February 22, 2001," for a thoroughgoing analysis of the seismic shift that took place in the conception and treatment of sexual difference in international law following the landmark 2001 decision by the International Tribunal for War Crimes in Former Yugoslavia, in which the court found Bosnian Serb soldiers who had raped and tortured Muslim women to be guilty of crimes against humanity.

52. DuBois, *Torture and Truth,* 154.

53. Ibid., 155–56.

54. Ink, "Remaking Identity," 291, 295.

55. Ibid., 291, 295.

56. Grewal, *Transnational America,* 8–9.

57. Ibid., 16.

58. Atkins and Wilson, *The Dominican Republic and the United States,* 151, 206–7; Kryzanek and Wiarda, *The Politics of External Influence,* 128–29.

59. Atkins and Wilson, *The Dominican Republic and the United States*, 203, 161; Kryzanek and Wiarda, *The Politics of External Influence,* 136.

60. Hunt, "The Paradoxical Origins of Human Rights," 7.

5. Being Well

1. Ana Castillo's novel *So Far from God* has been categorized as a work of Chicana literature (a label I use throughout my own discussion as well) because it concerns a family of women with roots in the New Mexico region at a time that precedes the incorporation of the formerly Mexican territories into the United States, following the U.S.–Mexico War of 1848. But I also affiliate it to "diasporic" and "immigrant" women's fiction, in order to keep alive the work of the "decolonial imaginary," as Pérez calls it, which compels scholars to interrogate the very borders by which indigeneity, citizenship, and diaspora are distinguished. See *The Decolonial Imaginary,* xviii.

2. De Boever, *Narrative Care,* 13.

3. See Koshy, "Neoliberal Family Matters," 354, for a discussion of how often Lahiri's work in general is assumed to be "transparent and easily assimilable."

4. Mitchell and Snyder, *Narrative Prosthesis,* 49.

5. Ibid., 48, 50.

6. Lahiri, *Unaccustomed Earth,* 263. All subsequent citations to the stories appear parenthetically in the body of the chapter.

7. Koshy, "Minority Cosmopolitanism," 598.

8. See Ray, "Towards a Planetary Reading," for an ecocritical reading of "Hema and Kaushik" that complements my own understanding of postcolonial planetarity in this book.

9. For discussions of the "scale-jumping" spatial imaginary of Lahiri's fiction, see Koshy, "Minority Cosmopolitanism," and Ridda, "Thinking Global?"

10. Song, *The Children of 1965,* 156.

11. Ibid., 159.

12. Ibid., 163.

13. Ibid., 158–59.

14. I would hasten to distinguish this flexibility proposed by Lahiri from the flexibility prized by neoliberalism. As McRuer explains, although the postmodern sensibilities of global capital seem to entail the ready fragmentation of subjectivity, neoliberalism actually demands the performance of *wholeness* by flexible subjects who can "manage" the economic and social crises that they face, for example, by being increasingly mobile, adaptable, and replaceable. Such flexibility includes tolerance of minority groups, while those minor subjects "flexibly comply" to normative demands, that is, to demands that they approximate normativity. As McRuer further observes, this flexibility is "virtually synonymous with both *heterosexual* and *able-bodied.*" Because queer desire and disability can threaten the performance of such flexibility, they must be "safely contained—embodied—in others." See McRuer, *Crip Theory,* 16–24.

15. McRuer, "Disability Nationalism in Crip Times," 176.

16. McRuer, *Crip Theory,* 32.

17. Because the Bush administration adopted a position of "neutrality" to the CRPD, the United States remained largely at the margins of its development, and it did not sign the treaty until 2009, under the Obama administration. However, Senate Republicans defeated its ratification in April 2013.

18. In 1994, the UN Committee on Economic, Social and Cultural Rights assumed supervision of disability issues, commenting that, although the UDHR and ICESCR made no explicit reference to persons with disabilities, they guaranteed rights to "*all* human beings," and prohibited discrimination based on specific grounds or "other status." See Kayess and French, "Out of Darkness into Light?," 13.

19. Mégret, "The Disabilities Convention," 500.

20. Lord, "Disability Rights and the Human Rights Mainstream," 86. See also Kayess and French, "Out of Darkness," 14–15.

21. Lord, "Disability Rights and the Human Rights Mainstream," 88; Kayess and French, "Out of Darkness," 24–25. See also Sabatello, "A Short History of the International Disability Rights Movement," 15–17. In fact, the government of Mexico led the campaign in the UN General Assembly for a human rights convention addressing persons with disability, as part of the Millennium Development Goals meant to reduce drastically global poverty. Kayess and French, "Out of Darkness," 17.

22. Lord, "Disability Rights and the Human Rights Mainstream," 88–91.

23. Mégret, "The Disabilities Convention," 495. See also Sabatello and Schulze, *Human Rights and Disability Advocacy,* 3.

24. Mégret, "The Disabilities Convention," 505.

25. Ibid., 507.

26. Ibid., 510.

27. Kayess and French, "Out of Darkness," 32.

28. Mégret, "The Disabilities Convention," 507–9; Kayess and French, "Out of Darkness," 6–12. This is especially true if, as Power, Lord, and DeFranco contend, "meaningful participation" is construed beyond a conception of "solely engaging in open competitive employment" (*Active Citizenship and Disability,* 7).

29. Kayess and French, "Out of Darkness," 32; emphasis added.

30. This is perhaps most apparent (and pertinent to the generic question of the family saga) in the convention's purposeful omission of the recognition of family members of disabled persons from its purview. As Kayess and French explain, while the CRPD (like other human rights instruments) recognizes "*both* persons with disability *and* their family members" as having "an active, instrumental role in family life" and clarifies that "the protection and assistance provided to families is for the purpose of enabling them to contribute to the realization of the rights of persons with disability" and not as "compensation for the 'burden' of caring for a person with disability" ("Out of Darkness," 26; emphasis in original).

31. Mégret, "The Disabilities Convention," 512; emphasis added.

32. Flynn, *From Rhetoric to Action,* 13–17.

33. Kayess and French, "Out of Darkness," 23.

34. At its most literal level, as Kayess and French point out, the language of the convention "perpetuates, and perhaps now irrevocably entrenches, the contemporary conceptual confusion between impairment and disability," when it fails to recognize how—according to a social model of disability—impairment is experienced as disability only when discriminatory social practices comprise the "barriers" to "full and effective participation in society on an equal basis with others" ("Out of Darkness," 21).

35. Ibid., 23. See also Sabatello, "A Short History," 17–20.

36. Siebers, *Disability Theory,* 46. Although space does not permit a full discussion of the genealogies of disability politics and disability critique, it is

important to note that Siebers's "universalism," which I find the most productive in articulating a disability perspective for a human rights methodology, is not the only approach to the question of social identity and difference that have informed disability studies. Certainly, many disability activists have adopted a rhetoric and politics that align with the modes of more conventional identity-based movements, even while "actually embodied people with disabilities strain against the content of their imagined political condensation." See Bost, *Encarnación,* 14.

37. Siebers, *Disability Theory,* 92, 178–80.

38. Ibid., 5, 182.

39. Ibid., 93.

40. Ibid., 92.

41. Postcolonial critics also remind us that different cultural contexts generate different conceptions of normalcy and disability, such that individual experiences of illness and impairment do not amount to disability in any universal manner. Even further, the uneven conditions of colonial power and global capital render culturally specific ideals subject to rapidly shifting environmental and material conditions. As such, minor literatures call for innovations in our formal practices of reading, in order to recognize that metaphors and other figures of disability need not always signify as stigmatizing or ableist. See Barker and Murray, "Disabling Postcolonialism," 228–29, 231–34.

42. Power et al., *Active Citizenship and Disability,* 8; Siebers, *Disability Theory,* 25.

43. McRuer, *Crip Theory,* 157.

44. Ibid., 201–8.

45. Siebers, *Disability Theory,* 5.

46. McRuer, *Crip Theory,* 208. I use the phrase "disposable domestics" also to call to mind the important and substantial body of scholarship that women of color and transnational feminism have generated regarding the precarious location of immigrant and racialized women in the global economy, which is also obviously a central concern of Castillo's novel as well. See, for example, Chang, *Disposable Domestics;* Wright, *Disposable Women.*

47. McRuer, *Crip Theory,* 146–70.

48. *So Far from God* appeared at a moment when literary scholars worried over the adoption of a postmodern aesthetic by Chicano and Latino literatures that seemed to break with a nationalist politics of resistance, acquiescing instead to canonical literary standards. See Mills, "Creating a Resistant Chicana Aesthetic" and Rodriguez, "Chicana/o Fiction from Resistance to Contestation" for discussions of Castillo's novel in relation to these debates. Although this is a question largely settled in American literary studies, I find Saldívar's formulation of the *nueva narrativa* (as well as Hong's "mundane fantastic," discussed below) to be

especially helpful for considering the novel's critique of U.S. imperialism and hemispheric struggle. See Saldívar, *Border Matters,* 31–32, and *The Dialectics of Our America,* 16.

49. Castillo, *So Far from God,* 192. All subsequent citations to the stories appear parenthetically in the body of the chapter.

50. Hong, *The Ruptures of American Capital,* 118, 133.

51. For an extended discussion, which complements my own here, of cultural texts that insist on what she calls "accessible citizenships" in "Greater Mexico," see Minich, *Accessible Citizenships.*

52. For discussions of the allegorical allusions in *So Far from God,* see Alcalá, "A Chicana Hagiography for the Twenty-First Century"; Blackford, "The Spirit of a People"; and Porsche, "*So Far from God.*"

53. Alarcón, "Literary Syncretism in Ana Castillo's *So Far from God,*" 148–49.

54. Whereas much similar leftist critique in this vein continues to center the able-bodied as its ideal subject, one *threatened* to be disabled by global capital, Castillo's novel takes as its protagonists women whose lives (and deaths) cannot be separated from those very conditions. See McRuer, *Crip Theory,* 47.

55. Alarcón, "Literary Syncretism in Ana Castillo's *So Far from God,*" 145–46.

56. The narrative further ironizes this violence by making Esmeralda not only a brown belt in judo, but an assistant director of a rape crisis center, who nonetheless finds herself strangely compelled to submit to Francisco's will without any struggle.

57. Specifically, Fe's story fictionally treats the toxic fallout suffered by those living downstream from the Los Alamos National Laboratory, located seventy-five miles north of Tome, New Mexico, as well as the conditions of work for factory workers in high-tech industrial production. See Platt, "Ecocritical Chicana Literature" 147–49.

58. Ong, "The Gender and Labor Politics of Postmodernity," 71; Parreñas, *Children of Global Migration,* 6–7.

59. Morrow, "Queering Chicano/a Narratives," 70.

60. Rodriguez, "Chicana/o Fiction from Resistance to Contestation," 77–78.

61. See, for example, Lanza, "Hearing the Voices." This point is worth underscoring, given how often critics attribute a type of narrative justice in Fe's plot, wherein the tremendous bodily suffering she is made to undergo is deemed her punishment for her adherence to a consumerist and middle-class ethos and her willingness to work in the weapons industry. For example, see Platt, "Ecocritical Chicana Literature," 152. Such readings, I would counter, not only fail to account for the tremendous appeal of the American "good life" as it is marketed to women of color and for the dearth of options available to such women in its stead, but also miss the more nuanced articulation of political responsibility with literary imagination that the novel's formal innovations avow. For a discussion of how

the "consumer durables revolutions of the 1920s" consolidated this normative domestic ethos, where consumerist domesticity came to compensate for the increasingly alienating modern industrial workplace, while pathologizing alternative family and domestic arrangements, see Hong, *Ruptures of American Capital,* 87–90.

62. Johnson, "Violence in the Borderlands," 55–56.

63. For a discussion of Castillo's adaptation of the La Llorona myth, as well as the myth of *la malogra,* see Martínez, "Teaching Chicana/o Literature in Community College," 220–24.

64. Mills, "Creating a Resistant Chicana Aesthetic," 315–17.

65. Caminero-Santangelo, "The Pleas of the Desperate," 83.

66. Ibid., 84.

67. Ibid., 85, 92. See Lawrence La Fountain-Stokes, "Translocas," for an illuminating discussion of the designation of the *loca,* and his elaboration of the *trans-loca* as a figure of critical disidentification (in a Puerto Rican cultural context).

68. Kim, "Do I, Too, Sing America?," 250; emphasis added. I have written elsewhere in more detail about the effort that allegory in emergent literatures undertakes to "invent" its ethical reader. See *An Ethics of Betrayal,* 118–28.

69. McRuer, *Crip Theory,* 57.

70. Ibid., 52.

71. Ibid., 57.

72. See Heide, "The Postmodern 'We,'" 173–75, for a discussion of Castillo's self-conscious epistemological positioning in relation to Chicano Studies.

73. Nixon, *Slow Violence and the Environmentalism of the Poor,* 63.

74. Ibid., 19.

75. Platt, "Ecocritical Chicana Literature," 150.

76. Tellingly, most of the extant criticism on *So Far from God* limits its analysis to particular plots, characters, and themes even when offering theses about the text as a whole.

77. Spurgeon, *Exploding the Western,* 126.

78. Norman, *Dead Women Talking,* 141.

79. James and Wu, "Editors' Introduction: Race, Ethnicity, Disability, and Literature," 8, 12; emphasis added.

80. I would thus caution against too quickly reading the severing of family ties as a liberatory outcome for women of color. While an implicit critique of reproductive futurism certainly pervades the novel, it also worries how the death of each daughter—and the damaging conditions that lead to those deaths—augurs an end to the family's borderland way of life and the alternative futures it could otherwise make available. See Mills, "Creating a Resistant Chicana Aesthetic," 320–21.

81. Garland-Thomson, "Disability and Representation," 524.

82. Castillo's depiction of M.O.M.A.S. invokes Las Madres de Plaza de Mayo (Mothers of the Disappeared) in Argentina—women who, beginning in the late 1970s, famously gathered in the Buenos Aires public space to protest the disappearance of their children by the military government that came to power in 1976. In fact, Las Madres were labeled *locas* by the military junta that executed the nation's dirty war, in order to attempt to counter the demands for political justice that these women performed in their "self-conscious manipulation of the maternal role." See Taylor, *Disappearing Acts,* 187, 194.

83. Yamin, "The Right to Health," 1157. This formulation of the right to health corroborates the type of challenge that, according to Mitchell and Snyder, disability studies poses to the applied sciences and "helping professions," where the "once-silenced object now has the agency to talk back" to those who "would speak its inferiority" ("Compulsory Feral-ization," 629–30).

84. Turner, *Vulnerability and Human Rights,* 112.

85. Ibid., 112.

86. See, for example, Brauman, "Questioning Health and Human Rights," 7–8.

87. Ivan Illich, qtd. in Metzel, "Introduction," 5.

88. Metzel, "Introduction," 5–6.

89. Roberts, "The Social Immorality of Health in the Gene Age," 61–62.

90. Yamin, "The Right to Health," 1159.

91. Toebes, "Towards an Improved Understanding of the International Human Right to Health," 662–63. See also Irwin et al., "Fixing the U.S. Healthcare System," 175–77.

92. Irwin et al., "Fixing the U.S. Healthcare System," 180. In the United States, there does exist a limited recognition that healthcare is a public responsibility vis-à-vis segments of the population who have "earned" it, for example, veterans, who thus receive veterans' benefits.

93. Furthermore, in the United States, public health reform has proceeded largely as a matter of research and lobbying by experts, thus rendering it an especially bewildering and bureaucratic arena of biopolitical governmentality, often with the limited objective of expanding healthcare coverage. See Irwin et al., "Fixing the U.S. Healthcare System," 189.

94. This obligation has meant, in regard to healthcare, that government ensures its availability, accessibility, acceptability, and quality. See Carmalt et al., "Entrenched Inequity," 156–64.

95. For succinct but thorough discussions of the travails of the human right to health in relation to the U.S. healthcare system, see Irwin et al., "Fixing the U.S. Healthcare System"; Carmalt et al., "Entrenched Inequity."

96. Indeed, when applied in conjunction with the ICERD, the right to health casts a spotlight on the tremendous disparities in health suffered by racial

minorities and the poor in the United States and obligates states (and other international actors) to remedy them, "not just as a health issue, but as a democracy issue" (Yamin, "The Right to Health," 1159).

97. Yamin, "Embodying Shadows," 224. The emphasis on the self-determination of well-being registers the often violent or traumatic conditions of disablement, especially for postcolonial and minor subjects. See Barker and Murray, "Disabling Postcolonialism," 230–32.

98. Perehudoff, *Health, Essential Medicines, Human Rights & National Constitutions,* 40.

99. Frasca, "Transforming Practice through Activism," 12.

100. Yamin explains that a human rights framework "simultaneously acknowledges health as inherently political—intimately bound up with social context, ideologies, and power structures—and removes health policy decisions from being matters of pure political discretion by placing them squarely into the domain of law" ("The Right to Health," 1157).

101. As McRuer observes, able-bodiedness has also long carried with it the particular inflections of citizenship conceptualized in the nineteenth century, in relation to industrial capitalism, "being capable of the normal physical exertions required in a particular system of labor" (*Crip Theory,* 8).

Conclusion

1. Longmire, "Should Migrants Fleeing Gang Violence . . . ?"

2. For insightful analysis of how the regulation of immigration, especially with respect to family reunification, constructs and reproduces sexual, gender, and racial hierarchies, see Luibhèid, *Entry Denied.*

3. Bhabha and Schmidt, "Seeking Asylum Alone," 133.

4. Rancière, "Who Is the Subject of the Rights of Man?," 302; Uehling, "The International Smuggling of Children," 837.

5. See for example Bhabha and Schmidt, "Seeking Asylum Alone."

6. Ibid., 131.

7. Ibid., 128–29, 132.

8. Bhabha, "The Citizenship Deficit," 56.

9. Boehm, "For My Children," 790–97; Uehling, "The International Smuggling of Children," 841.

10. Bhabha, "The Citizenship Deficit," 56.

11. Uehling, "The International Smuggling of Children," 847.

12. Bhabha, "The 'Mere Fortuity' of Birth?," 99.

13. Bhabha, "Arendt's Children," 416, 420.

14. See Scheper-Hughes and Sargent, *Small Wars,* 7–12.

15. For an overview of the changing and heterogeneous treatment of children in U.S. civil codes and constructions of the varying need for protection that map quite apparently onto racial, national, and economic hierarchies, see Mason, "The U.S. and the International Children's Rights Crusade," and Uehling, "The International Smuggling of Children," 844, 855–62.

16. Bhabha, "The Child," 1528, 1531.

17. Bhabha, "Arendt's Children," 421; Mason, "The U.S. and the International Children's Rights Crusade," 955. Scheper-Hughes and Sargent explain how the protection from family work and apprenticeship for children ironically often results in a loss of status and respect for the child in *Small Wars,* 10–12.

18. Van Bueren, "The International Protection of Family Members' Rights," 734.

19. Ibid., 736.

20. John, "Children's Rights in a Free-Market Culture," 107–12, 122–32.

21. Stacey, *In the Name of the Family,* 48–49.

22. Stockton, *The Queer Child,* 4.

23. For a succinct and helpful overview of feminist theories of gendered forms of labor since the 1960s, especially as they grapple with the divisions of domestic reproductive care, the Fordist industrial workplace, and post-Fordist production and service economies, see Weeks, "Life within and against Work."

24. To be clear, by referring to an "artifice" or "aesthetics" of kin, I do not mean to suggest that other kinship systems are in fact "true" or more real, only that these representations are ones that self-consciously perform such affiliation. As Joseph explains (citing Gayle Rubin, who in turn draws on Claude Levi-Strauss), *all* forms of kinship are social systems that supplement and organize genetic relationships, drawing boundaries between groups, usually based on the exchange of women. See *Against the Romance of Community,* 169.

25. Luibhèid, *Entry Denied,* 143–44.

26. Weston, *Families We Choose,* 199.

27. Ibid.

28. Phan, *We Should Never Meet,* 5. All subsequent citations from the collection appear parenthetically in the body of the chapter.

29. Bhabha, *Human Rights and Adolescence,* 7, 9, 14.

30. Eng, *The Feeling of Kinship,* 32, 97–98, 135–36; Reddy, *Freedom with Violence,* 161–63.

31. Eng, *The Feeling of Kinship,* 97–98. See also Stacey, *In the Name of the Family,* and Zaretsky, *No Direction Home,* for accounts of the contradictions and anxieties that have plagued the representation of the nuclear family in the United States during the twentieth century.

32. Eng, *The Feeling of Kinship,* 136.

33. Parreñas, *Children of Global Migration,* 14.

34. Butler, "Is Kinship Always Already Heterosexual?," 22–23; Boehm, "For My Children," 791–95.

35. Weston, *Families We Choose,* 5–6; Butler, "Is Kinship Always Already Heterosexual?," 22.

36. Kim, *End of Empire*, 220.

37. Butler, "Is Kinship Always Already Heterosexual?," 15.

38. Weeks, "Life within and against Work," 247–48.

39. Ibid., 248.

Bibliography

Adebajo, Adekeye. "From Bandung to Durban: Wither the Afro-Asian Coalition?" In *Bandung Revisited: The Legacy of the 1955 Asian-African Conference for International Order,* edited by See Seng Tan and Amitav Acharya, 105–31. Singapore: National University of Singapore Press, 2008.

Adesnik, Ariel David, and Michael McFaul. "Engaging Autocratic Allies to Promote Democracy." *Washington Quarterly* 29, no. 2 (2006): 7–26.

Agamben, Giorgio. *Homo Sacer: Sovereign Power and Bare Life* (1995). Translated by Daniel Heller-Roazen. Stanford, Calif.: Stanford University Press, 1998.

Alaniz, Yolanda, and Megan Cornish. *Viva La Raza: A History of Chicano Identity and Resistance.* Seattle: Red Letter Press, 2008.

Alarcón, Daniel Cooper. "Literary Syncretism in Ana Castillo's *So Far from God.*" *Studies in Latin American Popular Culture* 23 (2004): 145–52.

Albisa, Catherine. "Economic and Social Rights in the United States: Six Rights, One Promise." In *Bringing Human Rights Home: A History of Human Rights in the United States,* vol. 2, edited by Cynthia Soohoo, Catherine Albisa, and Martha F. Davis, 25–47. Westport, Conn.: Praeger, 2008.

———. "First-Person Perspectives on the Growth of the Movement: Ajamu Baraka, Larry Cox, Loretta Ross, and Lisa Crooms." In *Bringing Human Rights Home: A History of Human Rights in the United States,* vol. 2, edited by Cynthia Soohoo, Catherine Albisa, and Martha F. Davis, 49–70. Westport, Conn.: Praeger, 2008.

Alcalá, Rita Cano. "A Chicana Hagiography for the Twenty-First Century: Ana Castillo's *Locas Santas.*" In *Velvet Barrios: Popular Culture & Chicana/o Sexualities,* edited by Alicia Gaspar de Alba, 3–15. New York: Palgrave Macmillan, 2003.

Alvarez, Julia. *How the García Girls Lost Their Accents.* New York: Plume, 1991.

———. *In the Time of the Butterflies.* New York: Plume, 1994.

Anderson, Benedict. "Cacique Democracy in the Philippines." In *Discrepant Histories: Translocal Essays on Filipino Cultures,* edited by Vicente L. Rafael, 3–47. Philadelphia: Temple University Press, 1995.

Anderson, Carol. *Eyes Off the Prize: The United Nations and the African American Struggle for Human Rights, 1944–1945.* Cambridge: Cambridge University Press, 2003.

———. "A 'Hollow Mockery': African Americans, White Supremacy, and the Development of Human Rights in the United States." In *Bringing Human Rights Home: A History of Human Rights in the United States,* vol. 1, edited by Cynthia Soohoo, Catherine Albisa, and Martha F. Davis, 75–101. Westport, Conn.: Praeger, 2008.

Anderson, Elizabeth S. "Integration, Affirmative Action, and Strict Scrutiny." *New York University Law Review* 77 (2002): 1195–271.

Anker, Elizabeth S. *Fictions of Dignity: Embodying Human Rights in World Literature.* Ithaca, N.Y.: Cornell University Press, 2012.

Arendt, Hannah. *The Origins of Totalitarianism.* New York: Schocken Books, 1951.

Atanasoski, Neda. *Humanitarian Violence: The U.S. Deployment of Diversity.* Minneapolis: University of Minnesota Press, 2013.

Atkins, G. Pope, and Larmane C. Wilson. *The Dominican Republic and the United States: From Imperialism to Transnationalism.* Athens: University of Georgia Press, 1998.

Balce-Cortes, Nerissa. "Imagining the Neocolony." *Critical Mass: A Journal of Asian American Criticism* 2, no. 2 (1995): 95–120.

Barker, Clare, and Stuart Murray. "Disabling Postcolonialism: Global Disability Cultures and Democratic Criticism." *Journal of Literary & Cultural Disability Studies* 4, no. 3 (2010): 219–36.

Basu, Amrita. "Globalization of the Local/Localization of the Global: Mapping Transnational Women's Movements." *Meridians: feminism, race, transnationalism* 1, no. 1 (2000): 68–84.

Behnken, Brian D., ed. *The Struggle in Black and Brown: African American and Mexican American Relations during the Civil Rights Era.* Lincoln: University of Nebraska Press, 2011.

Bello, Madge, and Vincent Reyes. "Filipino Americans and the Marcos Overthrow: The Transformation of Political Consciousness." *Amerasia* 13, no. 1 (1986–87): 73–83.

Berger, Dan. "Introduction: Exploding Limits in the 1970s." In *The Hidden 1970s,* edited by Dan Berger, 1–17. New Brunswick, N.J.: Rutgers University Press, 2010.

Berger, James. "Ghosts of Liberalism: Morrison's *Beloved* and the Moynihan Report." *PMLA* 111, no. 3 (1996): 408–20.

Bergoffen, Debra. "February 22, 2001: Toward a Politics of the Vulnerable Body." *Hypatia* 18, no. 1 (2003): 116–34.

Berlant, Lauren. "Poor Eliza." *American Literature* 70, no. 3 (1998): 635–68.

Best, Stephen M. *The Fugitive's Properties: Law and the Poetics of Possession.* Chicago: University of Chicago Press, 2004.

Beverly, John. *Testimonio: On the Politics of Truth.* Minneapolis: University of Minnesota Press, 2004.

Bhabha, Jacqueline. "Arendt's Children: Do Today's Migrant Children Have a Right to Have Rights?" *Human Rights Quarterly* 31 (2009): 410–51.

———. "The Child: What Sort of Human?" *PMLA* 121, no. 5 (2006): 1526–35.

———. "The Citizenship Deficit: On Being a Citizen Child." *Development* 46, no. 3 (2003): 53–59.

———, ed. *Human Rights and Adolescence.* Philadelphia: University of Pennsylvania Press, 2014.

———. "The 'Mere Fortuity' of Birth? Are Children Citizens?" *differences* 15, no. 2 (2004): 91–117.

Bhabha, Jacqueline, and Susan Schmidt. "Seeking Asylum Alone: Unaccompanied and Separated Children and Refugee Protection in the U.S." *Journal of the History of Childhood and Youth* 1, no. 1 (2008): 126–38.

Blackford, Holly. "The Spirit of a People: The Politicization of Spirituality in Julia Alvarez's *In the Time of the Butterflies,* Ntozake Shange's *sassafrass, cypress & indigo,* and Ana Castillo's *So Far from God.*" In *Things of the Spirit: Women Writers Constructing Spirituality,* edited by Kristina K. Groover, 224–55. Notre Dame, Ind.: University of Notre Dame Press, 2004.

Boehm, Deborah A. "'For My Children': Constructing Family and Navigating the State in the U.S.–Mexico Transnation." *Anthropological Quarterly* 81, no. 4 (2008): 777–802.

Boheemen, Christine van. *The Novel as Family Romance: Language, Gender, and Authority from Fielding to Joyce.* Ithaca, N.Y.: Cornell University Press, 1987.

Borgwardt, Elizabeth. *A New Deal for the World: America's Vision for Human Rights.* Cambridge, Mass.: Belknap Press of Harvard University Press, 2005.

Borstelmann, Thomas. *The Cold War and the Color Line: American Race Relations in the Global Arena.* Cambridge, Mass.: Harvard University Press, 2001.

Bost, Suzanne. *Encarnación: Illness and Body Politics in Chicana Feminist Literature.* New York: Fordham University Press, 2010.

Bow, Leslie. *Partly Colored: Asian Americans and Racial Anomaly in the Segregated South.* New York: New York University Press, 2010.

Brauman, Rony. "Questioning Health and Human Rights." *Human Rights Dialogue* 6, no. 2 (2001): 7–8.

Briggs, Laura, Gladys McCormick, and J. T. Way. "Transnationalism: A Category of Analysis." *American Quarterly* 60, no. 3 (2008): 625–48.

Bright, Charles, and Michael Geyer. "Where in the World Is America? The History of the United States in the Global Age." In *Rethinking American*

History in a Global Age, edited by Thomas Bender, 63–99. Berkeley: University of California Press, 2002.

Brown, Gillian. *Domestic Individualism: Imagining Self in Nineteenth-Century America*. Berkeley: University of California Press, 1990.

Browning, Christopher S., and Matt McDonald. "The Future of Critical Security Studies: Ethics and the Politics of Security." *European Journal of International Relations*, October 27, 2011, 1–21. http://ejt.sagepub.com/content/early/2011/10/26/1354066111419538.full.pdf.

Brysk, Alison. "Introduction: Transnational Threats and Opportunities." In *Globalization and Human Rights*, edited by Alison Brysk, 1–16. Berkeley: University of California Press, 2002.

Burke, Anthony. *Beyond Security, Ethics and Violence: War against the Other*. London: Routledge, 2007.

Burke, Roland. "'The Compelling Dialogue of Freedom': Human Rights at the Bandung Conference." *Human Rights Quarterly* 28, no. 4 (2006): 947–60.

———. *Decolonization and the Evolution of International Human Rights*. Philadelphia: University of Pennsylvania Press, 2010.

Burton, Sandra. *Impossible Dream: The Marcoses, the Aquinos, and the Unfinished Revolution*. New York: Warner Books, 1989.

Butler, Judith. *Excitable Speech: A Politics of the Performative*. New York: Routledge, 1997.

———. *Frames of War: When Is Life Grievable?* London: Verso, 2009.

———. "Is Kinship Always Already Heterosexual?" *differences* 13, no. 1 (2002): 14–44.

———. *Precarious Life: The Powers of Mourning and Violence*. London: Verso, 2004.

Butler, Judith, and Gayatri Chakravorty Spivak. *Who Sings the Nation-State? Language, Politics, Belonging*. London: Seagull, 2007.

Byrd, Jodi A. *The Transit of Empire: Indigenous Critiques of Colonialism*. Minneapolis: University of Minnesota Press, 2011.

Cacho, Lisa Marie. *Social Death: Racialized Rightlessness and the Criminalization of the Unprotected*. New York: New York University Press, 2012.

Caminero-Santangelo, Marta. "'The Pleas of the Desperate': Collective Agency versus Magical Realism in Ana Castillo's *So Far from God*." *Tulsa Studies in Women's Literature* 24, no. 1 (2005): 81–103.

Campbell, David. *Writing Security: United States Foreign Policy and the Politics of Identity*. Minneapolis: University of Minnesota Press, 1992.

Campbell, David, and Michael J. Shapiro. "Introduction: From Ethical Theory to the Ethical Relationship." In *Moral Spaces: Rethinking Ethics and World Politics*, edited by David Campbell and Michael J. Shapiro, vii–xx. Minneapolis: University of Minnesota Press, 1999.

Carmalt, Jean Connolly, Sarah Zaidi, and Alicia Ely Yamin. "Entrenched Inequity: Health Care in the United States." In *Human Rights in the United States: Beyond Exceptionalism,* edited by Shareen Hertel and Kathryn Libal, 153–74. Cambridge: Cambridge University Press, 2011.

Carroll, Hamilton. "Traumatic Patriarchy: Reading Gendered Nationalisms in Chang-rae Lee's *A Gesture Life.*" *Modern Fiction Studies* 51, no. 3 (2005): 592–616.

Castillo, Ana. *So Far from God.* New York: Plume, 1993.

Chakrabarty, Dipesh. "The Legacies of Bandung: Decolonization and the Politics of Culture." In *Making a World after Empire: The Bandung Moment and Its Political Afterlives,* edited by Christopher J. Lee, 45–68. Athens: Ohio University Press, 2010.

———. *Provincializing Europe: Postcolonial Thought and Historical Difference.* Princeton, N.J.: Princeton University Press, 2007.

Chandra, Sarika. "Re-Producing a Nationalist Literature in the Age of Globalization: Reading (Im)migration in Julia Alvarez's *How the García Girls Lost Their Accents.*" *American Quarterly* 60, no. 3 (2008): 829–50.

Chang, Grace. *Disposable Domestics: Immigrant Women Workers in the Global Economy.* Cambridge, Mass.: South End Press, 2000.

Chang, Juliana. "Masquerade, Hysteria, and Neocolonial Femininity in Jessica Hagedorn's *Dogeaters.*" *Contemporary Literature* 44, no. 4 (2003): 637–63.

Chang, Robert S. *Disoriented: Asian Americans, Law, and the Nation-State.* New York: New York University Press, 2000.

Chari, Sharad, and Katherine Verdery. "Thinking between the Posts: Postcolonialism, Postsocialism, and Ethnography after the Cold War." *Comparative Studies in Society and History* 51, no. 1 (2009): 6–34.

Charlesworth, Hilary. "Not Waving but Drowning: Gender Mainstreaming and Human Rights in the United Nations." *Harvard Human Rights Journal* 18 (2005): 1–18.

Chase, Anthony. "Mutual Renewal: On the Relationship of Human Rights to the Muslim World." In *Religion, Identity and Global Governance: Ideas, Evidence, and Practice,* edited by Patrick James, 57–77. Toronto: University of Toronto Press, 2011.

Cheah, Pheng. "Introduction Part II: The Cosmopolitical Today." In *Cosmopolitics: Thinking and Feeling beyond the Nation,* edited by Pheng Cheah and Bruce Robbins, 20–41. Minneapolis: University of Minnesota Press, 1998.

Chen, Shu-Ching. "(Trans)National Imaginary and Tropical Melancholy in Jessica Hagedorn's *Dogeaters.*" *Concentric: Literary and Cultural Studies* 31, no. 1 (2005): 95–121.

Cheng, Anne Anlin. *The Melancholy of Race: Psychoanalysis, Assimilation, and Hidden Grief.* Oxford: Oxford University Press, 2001.

——. "Passing, Natural Selection, and Love's Failure: Ethics of Survival from Chang-rae Lee to Jacques Lacan." *American Literary History* 17, no. 3 (2005): 553–74.

Cheung, King-Kok. *Articulate Silences: Hisaye Yamamoto, Maxine Hong Kinston, Joy Kogawa*. Ithaca, N.Y.: Cornell University Press, 1993.

Chiang, Mark. *The Cultural Capital of Asian American Studies: Autonomy and Representation in the University*. New York: New York University Press, 2009.

Choi, Chungmoo. "The Politics of War Memories toward Healing." In *Perilous Memories: The Asia-Pacific War(s)*, edited by T. Fujitani, Geoffrey M. White, and Lisa Yoneyama, 395–409. Durham, N.C.: Duke University Press, 2001.

Choi, Susan. *The Foreign Student*. New York: Perennial, 1998.

Choy, Catherine Ceniza. "Towards Trans-Pacific Social Justice: Women and Protest in Filipino American History." *Journal of Asian American Studies* 8, no. 3 (2005): 293–307.

Chuh, Kandice. "Discomforting Knowledge: Or, Korean 'Comfort Women' and Asian American Critical Practice." *Journal of Asian American Studies* 6, no. 1 (2003): 5–23.

——. *Imagine Otherwise: On Asian Americanist Critique*. Durham, N.C.: Duke University Press, 2003.

Clark, Keith. "Re-(W)righting Black Male Subjectivity: The Communal Poetics of Ernest Gaines's *A Gathering of Old Men*." *Callaloo* 22, no. 1 (1999): 195–207.

Cohen, Ed. *A Body Worth Defending: Immunity, Biopolitics, and the Apotheosis of the Modern Body*. Durham, N.C.: Duke University Press, 2009.

Collier, Stephen J., and Andrew Lakoff. "On Regimes of Living." In *Global Assemblages: Technology, Politics, and Ethics as Anthropological Problems*, edited by Aiwha Ong and Stephen J. Collier, 22–39. Oxford: Blackwell, 2008.

Cooppan, Vilashini. "Hauntologies of Form: Race, Genre, and the Literary World System." *Gramma* 13 (2005): 71–86.

Cottrol, Robert J., and Raymond T. Diamond. "The Second Amendment: Toward an Afro-Americanist Reconsideration." *Georgetown Law Journal* 80 (1991): 309–61.

Criniti, Steve. "Collecting Butterflies: Julia Alvarez's Revision of North American Collective Memory." *Modern Language Studies* 36, no. 2 (2007): 42–63.

Cubilié, Anne. *Women Witnessing Terror: Testimony and the Cultural Politics of Human Rights*. New York: Fordham University Press, 2005.

Cumings, Bruce. *The Origins of the Korean War*, 2 vols. Princeton, N.J.: Princeton University Press, 1981.

Cvetkovich, Ann. *An Archive of Feelings: Trauma, Sexuality, and Lesbian Public Cultures*. Durham, N.C.: Duke University Press, 2003.

Dalton, Drew M. *Longing for the Other: Levinas and Metaphysical Desire*. Pittsburgh, Pa.: Duquesne University Press, 2009.

Das, Veena. *Life and Words: Violence and the Descent into the Ordinary.* Berkeley: University of California Press, 2007.

Daulatzai, Sohail. *Black Star, Crescent Moon: The Muslim International and Black Freedom beyond America.* Minneapolis: University of Minnesota Press, 2012.

Dawson, Ashley, and Malini Johar Schueller. "Introduction: Rethinking Imperialism Today." In *Exceptional State: Contemporary U.S. Culture and the New Imperialism,* edited by Ashley Dawson and Malini Johar Schueller, 1–33. Durham, N.C.: Duke University Press, 2007.

De Boever, Arne. *Narrative Care: Biopolitics and the Novel.* New York: Bloomsbury, 2013.

Deleuze, Gilles, and Félix Guattari. *Kafka: Toward a Minor Literature* (1975). Translated by Dana Polan. Minneapolis: University of Minnesota Press, 1986.

Delmendo, Sharon. *The Star-Entangled Banner: One Hundred Years of America in the Philippines.* New Brunswick, N.J.: Rutgers University Press, 2004.

Derrida, Jacques. "Force of Law: The 'Mystical Foundation' of Authority." In *Deconstruction and the Possibility of Justice,* edited by Drucilla Cornell, Michael Rosenfeld, and David Gray Carlson, 4–67. New York: Routledge, 1992.

Derrida, Jacques, and Anne Dufourmantelle. *Of Hospitality: Anne Dufourmantelle Invites Jacques Derrida to Respond.* Translated by Rachel Bowlby. Stanford, Calif.: Stanford University Press, 2000.

DeWitt, Larry. "The Decision to Exclude Agricultural and Domestic Workers from the 1935 Social Security Act." *Social Security Bulletin* 70, no. 4 (2010): 49–68.

Dimock, Wai Chee. *Through Other Continents: American Literature across Deep Time.* Princeton, N.J.: Princeton University Press, 2008.

Dingo, Rebecca. "Securing the Nation: Neoliberalism's U.S. Family Values in a Transnational Gendered Economy." *Journal of Women's History* 16, no. 3 (2004): 173–86.

Donnelly, Jack. *Universal Human Rights in Theory and Practice,* 2nd ed. Ithaca, N.Y.: Cornell University Press, 2003.

Douglass, Ana, and Thomas A. Vogler, eds. *Witness and Memory: The Discourse of Trauma.* New York: Routledge, 2003.

DuBois, Page. *Torture and Truth.* New York: Routledge, 1991.

Dudziak, Mary L. *Cold War Civil Rights: Race and the Image of American Democracy.* Princeton, N.J.: Princeton University Press, 2000.

Duggan, Lisa. *The Twilight of Equality? Neoliberalism, Cultural Politics, and the Attack on Democracy* Boston: Beacon Press, 2003.

Eckel, Jan. "Human Rights and Decolonization: New Perspectives and Open Questions." *Humanity: An International Journal of Human Rights, Humanitarianism, and Development* 1, no. 1 (2010): 111–35.

———. "The Rebirth of Politics from the Spirit of Morality: Explaining the Human Rights Revolution of the 1970s." In *The Breakthrough: Human Rights in the 1970s,* edited by Jan Eckel and Samuel Moyn, 227–59. Philadelphia: University of Pennsylvania Press, 2014.

Eckes, Alfred E. "The South and Economic Globalization, 1950 to the Future." In *Globalization and the American South,* edited by James C. Cobb and William Stueck, 36–65. Athens: University of Georgia Press, 2005.

Edkins, Jenny. "Humanitarianism, Humanity, Human." *Journal of Human Rights* 2, no. 2 (2003): 253–58.

———. *Missing: Persons and Politics.* Ithaca, N.Y.: Cornell University Press, 2011.

Edwards, Erica R. *Charisma and the Fictions of Black Leadership.* Minneapolis: University of Minnesota Press, 2012.

Eng, David L. *The Feeling of Kinship: Queer Liberalism and the Racialization of Intimacy.* Durham, N.C.: Duke University Press, 2010.

———. "Reparations and the Human." *Columbia Journal of Gender and Law* 21, no. 2 (2012): 159–81.

Escobar, Arturo. *Encountering Development: The Making and Unmaking of the Third World.* Princeton, N.J.: Princeton University Press, 1995.

Estes, David C., ed. *Critical Reflections on the Fiction of Ernest J. Gaines.* Athens: University of Georgia Press, 1994.

Evangelista, Susan. "Jessica Hagedorn and Manila Magic." *MELUS* 18, no. 4 (1993): 41–52.

Fanon, Frantz. *The Wretched of the Earth* (1963). Translated by Richard Philcox. New York: Grove Press, 2005.

Farrell, Amy, and Patrice McDermott. "Claiming Afghan Women: The Challenge of Human Rights Discourse for Transnational Feminism." In *Just Advocacy? Women's Human Rights, Transnational Feminisms, and the Politics of Representation,* edited by Wendy S. Hesford and Wendy Kozol, 33–55. New Brunswick, N.J.: Rutgers University Press, 2005.

Felice, William F. "The UN Committee on the Elimination of All Forms of Racial Discrimination: Race, and Economic and Social Human Rights." *Human Rights Quarterly* 24, no. 1 (2002): 205–36.

Flynn, Eilionóir. *From Rhetoric to Action: Implementing the UN Convention on the Rights of Persons with Disabilities.* Cambridge: Cambridge University Press, 2011.

Folks. Jeffrey J. *From Richard Wright to Toni Morrison: Ethics in Modern and Postmodern American Narrative.* New York: Peter Lang, 2001.

Forsythe, David P. "On Contested Concepts: Humanitarianism, Human Rights, and the Notion of Neutrality." *Journal of Human Rights* 12, no. 11 (2014): 59–68.

Foucault, Michel. *Society Must Be Defended: Lectures at the Collège de France, 1975–1976*. Edited by Mauro Bertani, Alessandro Fontana, and François Ewald. Translated by David Macey. New York: Picador, 2003.

Franco, Dean. "What We Talk About When We Talk About *Beloved*." *Modern Fiction Studies* 52, no. 2 (2006): 415–39.

Frasca, Timothy. "Transforming Practice through Activism." *Human Rights Dialogue* 6, no. 2 (2001): 11–12.

Freeman, Michael. *Human Rights: An Interdisciplinary Approach*. Cambridge: Polity Press, 2002.

Fujitani, T., Geoffrey M. White, and Lisa Yoneyama. Introduction to *Perilous Memories: The Asia-Pacific War(s)*, edited by T. Fujitani, Geoffrey M. White, and Lisa Yoneyama, 1–29. Durham, N.C.: Duke University Press, 2001.

Gaines, Ernest J. *A Gathering of Old Men*. New York: Vintage Books, 1983.

Gairola, Rahul K. "Deterritorialisations of Desire: 'Transgressive' Sexuality as Filipino Anti-Imperialist Resistance in Jessica Hagedorn's *Dogeaters*." *Philament* 30 (December 2005): 22–41.

Gardner, Lloyd C. "Korean Borderlands: Imaginary Frontiers of the Cold War." In *The Korean War in History*, edited by William Stueck, 126–44. Lexington: University of Kentucky Press, 2004.

Garland-Thomson, Rosemarie. "Disability and Representation." *PMLA* 120, no. 2 (2005): 522–27.

Gaudet, Marcia. "Gaines' Fifteen Narrators: Narrative Style and Storytelling Technique in *A Gathering of Old Men*." *Louisiana Folklore Miscellany* 6, no. 3 (1990): 15–22.

Gilmore, Ruth Wilson. *Golden Gulag: Prisons, Surplus, Crisis, and Opposition in Globalizing California*. Berkeley: University of California Press, 2007.

Go, Julian. "Modeling States and Sovereignty: Postcolonial Constitutions in Asia and Africa." In *Making a World after Empire: The Bandung Moment and Its Political Afterlives*, edited by Christopher J. Lee, 107–39. Athens: Ohio University Press, 2010.

Gonzaga, Elmo. *Globalization and Becoming-Nation: Subjectivity, Nationhood, and Narrative in the Period of Global Capitalism*. Quezon City: University of Philippines Press, 2009.

Gordon, Avery F. *Ghostly Matters: Haunting and the Sociological Imagination*. Minneapolis: University of Minnesota Press, 1997.

Grandin, Greg. *Empire's Workshop: Latin America, the United States, and the Rise of the New Imperialism*. New York: Metropolitan Books, 2006.

Grewal, Inderpal. "On the New Global Feminism and the Family of Nations: Dilemmas of Transnational Feminist Practice." In *Talking Voices: Multiculturalism in a Transnational Age*, edited by Ella Shohat, 501–30. New York: New Museum of Contemporary Art, 1998.

———. *Transnational America: Feminisms, Diasporas, Neoliberalisms.* Durham, N.C.: Duke University Press, 2005.

Grewal, Inderpal, and Caren Kaplan, eds. *Scattered Hegemonies: Postmodernity and Transnational Feminist Practices.* Minneapolis: University of Minnesota Press, 1994.

Griffin, Joseph. "Creole and Singaleese: Disruptive Caste in *Catherine Carmier* and *A Gathering of Old Men.*" In *Critical Reflections on the Fiction of Ernest J. Gaines,* edited by David C. Estes, 30–45. Athens: University of Georgia Press, 1994.

Grow, Michael. *U.S. Presidents and Latin American Interventions: Pursuing Regime Change in the Cold War.* Lawrence: University Press of Kansas, 2008.

Hagedorn, Jessica. *Dogeaters.* New York: Penguin, 1990.

Hairong, Yan, and Daniel Vukovich. "Introduction: What's Left of Asia." *positions* 15, no. 2 (2007): 211–24.

Harold, Christine, and Kevin Michael DeLuca. "Behold the Corpse: Violent Images and the Case of Emmett Till." *Rhetoric & Public Affairs* 8, no. 2 (2005): 263–86.

Harper, Mary T. "From Sons to Fathers: Ernest Gaines' *A Gathering of Old Men.*" *College Language Association Journal* 31, no. 3 (1988): 299–308.

Hartman, Saidiya V. *Scenes of Subjection: Terror, Slavery, and Self-Making in Nineteenth-Century America.* New York: Oxford University Press, 1997.

Hebert-Leiter, Maria. "A Breed Between: Racial Mediation in the Fiction of Ernest Gaines." *MELUS* 31, no. 2 (2006): 95–117.

Heerten, Lasse. "The Dystopia of Postcolonial Catastrophe: Self-Determination, the Biafran War of Secession, and the 1970s Human Rights Moment." In *The Breakthrough: Human Rights in the 1970s,* edited by Jan Eckel and Samuel Moyn, 15–32. Philadelphia: University of Pennsylvania Press, 2014.

Heglar, Charles J., and Annye L. Refoe. "'Survival with Dignity': The Elderly African Americans in the Novels of Ernest Gaines." *Crossroads* 3, no. 1 (1994): 57–68.

Heide, Markus. "The Postmodern 'We': Academia and Community in Ana Castillo's *So Far from God* and in Denise Chávez's *Face of an Angel.*" In *U.S. Latino Literatures and Cultures: Transnational Perspectives,* edited by Francisco A. Lomelí, 171–80. Heidelberg: Universitätsverlag C. Winter, 2000.

Hein, Laura. "Savage Irony: The Imaginative Power of the 'Military Comfort Women' in the 1990s." *Gender & History* 11, no. 2 (1999): 336–72.

Ho, Fred, and Bill V. Mullen, eds. *Afro Asia: Revolutionary Political and Cultural Connections between African Americans and Asian Americans.* Durham, N.C.: Duke University Press, 2008.

Holland, Sharon Patricia. *Raising the Dead: Readings of Death and (Black) Subjectivity.* Durham, N.C.: Duke University Press, 2000.

Holloway, Karla F.C. "*Beloved*: A Spiritual." *Callaloo* 13, no. 3 (1990): 516–25.

———. *Legal Fictions: Constituting Race, Composing Literature*. Durham, N.C.: Duke University Press, 2014.

Hong, Grace Kyungwon. *Ruptures of American Capital: Women of Color, Feminism and the Culture of Immigrant Labor.* Minneapolis: University of Minnesota Press, 2006.

Hunsaker, Steven. "Nation, Family and Language in Victor Perera's *Rites* and Maxine Hong Kingston's *The Woman Warrior.*" *Biography* 20, no. 4 (1997): 437–61.

Hunt, Lynn. *Inventing Human Rights: A History.* New York: W. W. Norton, 2007.

———. "The Paradoxical Origins of Human Rights." In *Human Rights and Revolutions,* edited by Jeffrey N. Wasserstrom, Greg Grandin, Lynn Hunt, and Marilyn B. Young, 3–17. Lanham, Md.: Rowman & Littlefield, 2000.

Ileto, Reynaldo C. "The Philippine–American War: Friendship and Forgetting." In *Vestiges of War: The Philippine-American War and the Aftermath of an Imperial Dream, 1899–1999,* edited by Angel Velasco Shaw and Luis H. Franca, 3–21. New York: New York University Press.

Ink, Lynn Chun. "Remaking Identity, Unmaking Nation: Historical Recovery and the Reconstruction of Community in *In the Time of the Butterflies* and *The Farming of Bones.*" *Callaloo* 27, no. 3 (2004): 788–807.

Irwin, Alec, Leonard Rubenstein, Anne Cooper, and Paul Farmer. "Fixing the U.S. Healthcare System: What Role for Human Rights?" In *Bringing Human Rights Home: A History of Human Rights in the United States,* vol. 3, edited by Cynthia Soohoo, Catherine Albisa, and Martha F. Davis, 173–207. Westport, Conn.: Praeger, 2008.

Isaac, Allan Punzalan. *American Tropics: Articulating Filipino America.* Minneapolis: University of Minnesota Press, 2006.

Ishay, Micheline R. *The History of Human Rights: From Ancient Times to the Globalization Era.* Berkeley: University of California Press, 2004.

James, Jennifer C., and Cynthia Wu. "Editors' Introduction: Race, Ethnicity, Disability, and Literature: Intersections and Interventions." *MELUS* 31, no. 3 (Fall 2006): 3–13.

JanMohamed, Abdul, and David Lloyd. *The Nature and Context of Minority Discourse.* New York: Oxford University Press, 1990.

Jensen, Steven L.B. "'Universality Should Govern the Small World of Today': The Cold War and UN Human Rights Diplomacy, 1960–1968." In *Human Rights in Europe during the Cold War,* edited by Rasmus Mariager, Karl Molin, and Kjersti Brathagen, 56–72. London: Routledge, 2014.

John, Mar. "Children's Rights in a Free-Market Culture." In *Children and the Politics of Culture,* edited by Sharon Stephens, 105–37. Princeton, N.J.: Princeton University, 1995.

Johnson, Kelli Lyon. "Violence in the Borderlands: Crossing to the Home Space in the Novels of Ana Castillo." *Frontiers: A Journal of Women Studies* 25, no. 1 (2004): 39–58.

Johnstone, Rachel. "Feminist Influences on the United Nations Human Rights Treaty Bodies." *Human Rights Quarterly* 28, no. 1 (2006): 148–85.

Jones, Suzanne W. "New Narratives of Southern Manhood: Race, Masculinity, and Closure in Ernest Gaines's Fiction." In *The World Is Our Home: Society and Culture in Contemporary Southern Writing*, edited by Jeffrey J. Folks and Nancy Summers Folks, 29–52. Lexington: University of Kentucky Press, 2000.

———. "Reconstructing Manhood: Race, Masculinity, and Narrative Closure in Ernest Gaines's *A Gathering of Old Men* and *A Lesson before Dying*." *Masculinities* 3, no. 2 (1995): 43–66.

Joseph, Miranda. *Against the Romance of Community*. Minneapolis: University of Minnesota Press, 2002.

Kang, Laura Hyun Yi. *Compositional Subjects: Enfiguring Asian/American Women*. Durham, N.C.: Duke University Press, 2002.

Kaplan, Amy. *The Anarchy of Empire in the Making of U.S. Culture*. Cambridge, Mass.: Harvard University Press, 2002.

Kayess, Rosemary, and Phillip French. "Out of Darkness into Light? Introducing the Convention on the Rights of Persons with Disabilities." *Human Rights Law Review* 8, no. 1 (2008): 1–34.

Keenan, Thomas. *Fables of Responsibility: Aberrations and Predicaments in Ethics and Politics*. Stanford, Calif.: Stanford University Press, 1997.

Keith, Joseph. *Unbecoming Americans: Writing Race and Nation from the Shadows of Citizenship, 1945–1960*. New Brunswick, N.J.: Rutgers University Press, 2013.

Keller, Nora Okja. *Comfort Woman*. New York: Penguin, 1997.

Kelley, Robin D. G. *Freedom Dreams: The Radical Imagination*. Boston: Beacon Press, 2002.

Kelly, John D., and Martha Kaplan. "'My Ambition Is Much Higher than Independence': US Power, the UN World, the Nation-State, and Their Critics." In *Decolonization: Perspectives from Now and Then*, edited by Prasenjit Duara, 131–51. London: Routledge, 2004.

Kelly, Patrick William. "'Magic Words': The Advent of Transnational Human Rights Activism in Latin America's Southern Cone in the Long 1970s." In *The Breakthrough: Human Rights in the 1970s*, edited by Jan Eckel and Samuel Moyn, 88–106. Philadelphia: University of Pennsylvania Press, 2014.

Kenny, Paul D. "The Meaning of Torture." *Polity* 42, no. 2 (April 2010): 131–55.

Kim, Daniel Y. "'Bled In, Letter by Letter': Translation, Postmemory, and the Subject of Korean War: History in Susan Choi's *The Foreign Student*." *American Literary History* 21, no. 3 (2009): 550–83.

———. "Do I, Too, Sing America? Vernacular Representations and Chang-rae Lee's *Native Speaker.*" *Journal of Asian American Studies* 6 (2003): 231–60.

Kim, Jodi. *Ends of Empire: Asian American Critique and the Cold War.* Minneapolis: University of Minnesota Press, 2010.

Kingston, Maxine Hong. *The Woman Warrior: Memoirs of a Girlhood among Ghosts.* New York: Vintage International, 1975.

Klein, Christina. *Cold War Orientalism: Asia in the Middlebrow Imagination, 1945–1961.* Berkeley: University of California Press, 2003.

Kolb, Robert. "The Relationship between International Humanitarian Law and Human Rights Law: A Brief History of the 1948 Universal Declaration of Human Rights and the 1949 Geneva Conventions." *International Review of the Red Cross* 38, no. 324 (1998): 409–19.

Kong, Belinda. "Beyond K's Specter: Chang-rae Lee's *A Gesture Life,* Comfort Women Testimonies, and Asian American Transnational Aesthetics." *Journal of Transnational American Studies* 3, no. 1 (2011): 1–29.

———. "Theorizing the Hyphen's Afterlife in Post-Tiananmen Asian-America." *Modern Fiction Studies* 56, no. 1 (2010): 136–59.

Koshy, Susan. "Minority Cosmopolitanism." *PMLA* 126, no. 3 (2011): 592–609.

———. "Neoliberal Family Matters." *American Literary History* 25, no. 2 (Summer 2013): 344–80.

Kristeva, Julia. *Powers of Horror: An Essay on Abjection.* Translated by Leon S. Roudiez. New York: Columbia University Press, 1982.

Kryzanek, Michael J., and Howard J. Wiarda. *The Politics of External Influence in the Dominican Republic.* New York: Praeger, 1988.

Kurasawa, Fuyuki. *The Work of Global Justice: Human Rights as Practices.* Cambridge: Cambridge University Press, 2007.

La Fountain-Stokes, Lawrence. "Translocas: Migration, Homosexuality, and Transvestism in Recent Puerto Rican Performance." *E-Misférica* 8, no. 1 (Fall 2011). http://hemi.nyu.edu/hemi/en/e-misferica-81/lafountain.

Lahiri, Jhumpa. *Unaccustomed Earth.* New York: Alfred A. Knopf, 2008.

Landé, Carl H. "Manila's Malaise." *Journal of Democracy* 2, no. 1 (1991): 45–57.

Lanza, Carmela Delia. "Hearing the Voices: Women and Home and Ana Castillo's *So Far from God.*" *MELUS* 23, no. 1 (Spring 1998): 65–79.

Latham, Michael E. *The Right Kind of Revolution: Modernization, Development and U.S. Foreign Policy from the Cold War to the Present.* Ithaca, N.Y.: Cornell University Press, 2010.

Lee, Chang-rae. *A Gesture Life.* New York: Riverhead Books, 1999.

Lee, Christopher J. "Between a Moment and an Era: The Origins and Afterlives of Bandung." In *Making a World after Empire: The Bandung Moment and Its Political Afterlives,* edited by Christopher J. Lee, 1–42. Athens: Ohio University Press, 2010.

Lee, Rachel. *The Americas of Asian American Literature: Gendered Fictions of Nation and Transnation.* Princeton, N.J.: Princeton University Press, 1999.

Levinas, Emmanuel. "Ethics as First Philosophy" (1984). Translated by Seán Hand and Michael Temple. In *The Levinas Reader,* edited by Seán Hand, 75–87. Oxford: Blackwell, 1989.

Lewis, Hope. "'New' Human Rights: U.S. Ambivalence toward the International Economic and Social Rights Framework." In *Bringing Human Rights Home: A History of Human Rights in the United States,* vol. 1, edited by Cynthia Soohoo, Catherine Albisa, and Martha F. Davis, 103–44. Westport, Conn.: Praeger, 2008.

Li, David Leiwei. *Imagining the Nation: Asian American Literature and Cultural Consent.* Stanford, Calif.: Stanford University Press, 1998.

Lionnet, Françoise, and Shu-mei Shih, eds. *Minor Transnationalism.* Durham, N.C.: Duke University Press, 2005.

Lipsitz, George. *The Possessive Investment in Whiteness: How White People Profit from Identity Politics.* Philadelphia: Temple University Press, 1998.

Longmire, Sylvia. "Should Migrants Fleeing Gang Violence in Central America Be Accorded Refugee Status?" *Small War Journal,* June 26, 2014. http://smallwarsjournal.com/jrnl/art/should-migrants-fleeing-gang-violence-in-central-america-be-accorded-refugee-status.

López, Haney Ian. *White by Law: The Legal Construction of Race.* New York: New York University Press, 1996.

Lord, Janet E. "Disability Rights and the Human Rights Mainstream: Reluctant Gate-Crashers?" In *The International Struggle for New Human Rights,* edited by Clifford Bob, 83–92. Philadelphia: University of Pennsylvania Press, 2010.

Louis, William Roger, and Ronald Robinson. "Empire Preserv'd: How the Americans Put Anti-Communism before Anti-Imperialism." In *Decolonization: Perspectives from Now and Then,* edited by Prasenjit Duara, 152–61. London: Routledge, 2004.

Lovelady, Stephanie. "Walking Backwards: Coming of Age in *My Ántonia* and *How the García Girls Lost Their Accents.*" *Modern Language Studies* 35, no. 1 (2005): 28–37.

Lowe, Lisa. *Immigrant Acts: On Asian American Cultural Politics.* Durham, N.C.: Duke University Press, 1996.

———. "The Intimacies of Four Continents." In *Haunted by Empires: Geographies of Intimacy in North American History,* edited by Ann Laura Stoler, 191–212. Durham, N.C.: Duke University Press, 2006.

Lubin, Alex. *Geographies of Liberation: The Making of an Afro-Arab Political Imaginary.* Chapel Hill: University of North Carolina Press, 2014.

Luibhèid, Eithne. *Entry Denied: Controlling Sexuality at the Border.* Minneapolis: University of Minnesota Press, 2002.

Lyotard, Jean-François. "The Other's Rights." In *The Politics of Human Rights*, edited by Obrad Savic, 181–88. London: Verso, 1999.

Macpherson, C. B. *The Political Theory of Possessive Individualism: Hobbes to Locke*. Oxford: Clarendon Press, 1962.

Maeda, Daryl J. *Chains of Babylon: The Rise of Asian America*. Minneapolis: University of Minnesota Press, 2009.

———. *Rethinking the Asian American Movement*. New York: Routledge, 2012.

Mallon, William T. "Voicing Manhood: Masculinity and Dialogue in Ernest J. Gaines's 'The Sky is Gray,' 'Three Men,' and *A Gathering of Old Men*." *Southern Studies* 5, nos. 3–4 (1994): 49–67.

Manela, Erez. *The Wilsonian Moment: Self-Determination and the International Origins of Anticolonial Nationalism*. Oxford: Oxford University Press, 2007.

Martin, Waldo E., Jr. *No Coward Soldiers: Black Cultural Politics in Postwar America*. Cambridge, Mass.: Harvard University Press, 2005.

Martînez, Daitzete. "Teaching Chicana/o Literature in Community College." *Rocky Mountain Review* 65, no. 2 (2001): 216–25.

Mason, Mary Ann. "The U.S. and the International Children's Rights Crusade: Leader or Laggard?" *Journal of Social History* 38, no. 4 (2005): 955–63.

McCallum, Shara. "Reclaiming Julia Alvarez: *In the Time of the Butterflies*." *Women's Studies* 29 (2000): 93–117.

McClintock, Anne. *Imperial Leather: Race, Gender and Sexuality in the Colonial Contest*. New York: Routledge, 1995.

McCoy, Alfred W. *Policing America's Empire: The United States, the Philippines, and the Rise of the Surveillance State*. Madison: University of Wisconsin Press, 2009.

McDougall, Gay J. "Toward a Meaningful International Regime: The Domestic Relevance of International Efforts to Eliminate All Forms of Racial Discrimination." *Howard Law Journal* 40, no. 3 (1997): 571–95.

McPherson, Tara. *Reconstructing Dixie: Race, Gender, and Nostalgia in the Imagined South*. Durham, N.C.: Duke University Press, 2003.

McRuer, Robert. *Crip Theory: Cultural Signs of Queerness and Disability*. New York: New York University Press, 2006.

———. "Disability Nationalism in Crip Times." *Journal of Literary & Cultural Disability Studies* 4, no. 2 (2010): 163–78.

Mégret, Frédéric. "The Disabilities Convention: Human Rights of Persons with Disabilities or Disability Rights?" *Human Rights Quarterly* 30, no. 2 (2008): 494–516.

Melamed, Jodi. *Represent and Destroy: Rationalizing Violence in the New Racial Capitalism*. Minneapolis: University of Minnesota Press, 2011.

Mendoza, Victor. "A Queer Nomadology of Jessica Hagedorn's *Dogeaters*." *American Literature* 77, no. 4 (2005): 816–45.

Meron, Theodor. "The Meaning and Reach of the International Convention on the Elimination of All Forms of Racial Discrimination." *American Journal of International Law* 79, no. 2 (1985): 283–318.

Metzel, Jonathan M. "Introduction: Why against Health?" In *Against Health: How Health Became the New Morality,* edited by Jonathan M. Metzl and Anna Kirkland, 1–11. New York: New York University Press, 2010.

Mills, Fiona. "Creating a Resistant Chicana Aesthetic: The Queer Performativity of Ana Castillo's *So Far from God.*" *CLA Journal* 46, no. 3 (March 2003): 312–36.

Minich, Julie Avril. *Accessible Citizenships: Disability, Nation, and the Cultural Politics of Greater Mexico.* Philadelphia: Temple University Press, 2013.

Mitchell, David T., and Sharon L. Snyder. "Compulsory Feral-ization: Institutionalizing Disability Studies." *PMLA* 120, no. 2 (2005): 627–34.

———. *Narrative Prosthesis: Disability and the Dependencies of Discourse.* Ann Arbor: University of Michigan Press, 2000.

Morrison, Toni. *Beloved.* New York: Penguin, 1987.

Morrow, Colette. "Queering Chicano/a Narratives: Lesbian as Healer, Saint and Warrior in Ana Castillo's *So Far from God.*" *Journal of the Midwest Modern Language Association* 30, no. 1/2 (1997): 63–80.

Moyn, Samuel. *The Last Utopia: Human Rights in History.* Cambridge, Mass.: Belknap Press of Harvard University Press, 2010.

———. "The Return of the Prodigal: The 1970s as a Turning Point in Human Rights History." In *The Breakthrough: Human Rights in the 1970s,* edited by Jan Eckel and Samuel Moyn, 1–14. Philadelphia: University of Pennsylvania Press, 2014.

Mullen, Bill V. "Du Bois, *Dark Princess,* and the Afro-Asian International." *positions* 11, no. 1 (2003): 217–38.

Mullen, Bill V., and James Smethurst. Introduction to *Left of the Color Line: Race, Radicalism, and Twentieth-Century Literature of the United States,* 1–12. Chapel Hill: University of North Carolina Press, 2003.

Nathans, Benjamin. "The Disenchantment of Socialism: Soviet Dissidents, Human Rights, and the New Global Morality." In *The Breakthrough: Human Rights in the 1970s,* edited by Jan Eckel and Samuel Moyn, 33–48. Philadelphia: University of Pennsylvania Press, 2014.

Nesaduri, Helen E. S. "Bandung and the Political Economy of North–South Relations: Sowing the Seed for Re-visioning International Society." In *Bandung Revisited: The Legacy of the 1955 Asian-African Conference for International Order,* edited by See Seng Tan and Amitav Acharya, 68–101. Singapore: National University of Singapore Press, 2008.

Ngai, Mae. *Impossible Subjects: Illegal Aliens and the Making of Modern America.* Princeton, N.J.: Princeton University Press, 1994.

Ngai, Sianne. *Ugly Feelings*. Cambridge, Mass.: Harvard University Press, 2005.

Nixon, Rob. *Slow Violence and the Environmentalism of the Poor.* Cambridge, Mass.: Harvard University Press, 2011.

Norman, Brian. *Dead Women Talking: Encounters with the Past in American Literature.* Baltimore, Md.: Johns Hopkins University Press, 2013.

Normand, Roger, and Sarah Zaidi. *Human Rights at the UN: The Political History of Universal Justice.* Bloomington: Indiana University Press, 2007.

Nowak, Manfred. "What Practices Constitute Torture? US and UN Standards." *Human Rights Quarterly* 28, no. 4 (2006): 809–41.

Oh, Bonnie B. C. "The Japanese Imperial System and the Korean 'Comfort Women' of World War II." In *Legacies of the Comfort Women of World War II,* edited by Margaret Stetz and Bonnie B. C. Oh, 3–25. New York: East Gate, 2001.

Omi, Michael, and Howard Winant. *Racial Formation in the United States: From the 1960s to the 1990s,* 2nd ed. New York: Routledge, 1994.

Ong, Aiwha. "The Gender and Labor Politics of Postmodernity." In *The Politics of Culture in the Shadow of Capital,* edited by Lisa Lowe and David Lloyd, 61–97. Durham, N.C.: Duke University Press, 1997.

———. *Neoliberalism as Exception: Mutations in Citizenship and Sovereignty.* Durham, N.C.: Duke University, 2006.

Painter, Joe. "The Rise of the Workfare State." In *Geographies of Global Change: Remapping the World,* 2nd ed., edited by R. J. Johnston, Peter J. Taylor, and Michael Watts, 158–73. Oxford: Blackwell, 2002.

Palumbo-Liu, David. *Asian/American: Historical Crossings of a Racial Frontier.* Stanford, Calif.: Stanford University Press, 1999.

Parikh, Crystal. *An Ethics of Betrayal: The Politics of Otherness in Emergent U.S. Literatures and Culture.* New York: Fordham University Press, 2009.

Parreñas, Rhacel Salazar. *Children of Global Migration: Transnational Families and Gendered Woes.* Stanford, Calif.: Stanford University Press, 2005.

Patten, Wendy. "The Impact of September 11 and the Struggle against Terrorism on the U.S. Domestic Human Rights Movement." In *Bringing Human Rights Home: A History of Human Rights in the United States,* vol. 2, edited by Cynthia Soohoo, Catherine Albisa, and Martha F. Davis, 153–86. Westport, Conn.: Praeger, 2008.

Pejic, Jelena. "Minority Rights in International Law." *Human Rights Quarterly* 19, no. 3 (1997): 666–85.

Perehudoff, S. Katrina. *Health, Essential Medicines, Human Rights & National Constitutions.* Geneva: World Health Organization, 2008.

Pérez, Emma. *The Decolonial Imaginary: Writing Chicanas into History.* Bloomington: Indiana University Press, 1999.

Phan, Aimee. *We Should Never Meet.* New York: St. Martin's Press, 2004.

Platt, Kamala. "Ecocritical Chicana Literature: Ana Castillo's 'Virtual Realism.'" In *Ecofeminist Literary Criticism: Theory, Interpretation, Pedagogy,* edited by Greta Gaard and Patrick D. Murphy, 139–57. Urbana: University of Illinois Press, 1998.

Poole, Mary. *The Segregated Origins of Social Security: African Americans and the Welfare State.* Chapel Hill: University of North Carolina Press, 2006.

Porsche, Michael. "*So Far from God*: Ana Castillo's Telenovelistic Xicanista Reassessment of the Paulinian Triad." In *U.S. Latino Literatures and Cultures: Transnational Perspectives,* edited by Francisco A. Lomelí, 171–280. Heidelberg: Universitätsverlag C. Winter, 2000.

Powell, Catherine. "Louis Henkin and Human Rights: A New Deal at Home and Abroad." In *Bringing Human Rights Home: A History of Human Rights in the United States,* vol. 1, edited by Cynthia Soohoo, Catherine Albisa, and Martha F. Davis, 57–73. Westport, Conn.: Praeger, 2008.

Power, Andrew, Janet Lord, and Allison DeFranco. *Active Citizenship and Disability: Implementing the Personalisation of Support.* Cambridge: Cambridge University Press, 2013.

Prashad, Vijay. *The Darker Nations: A People's History of the Third World.* New York: The New Press, 2007.

Pulido, Laura. *Black, Brown, Yellow, and Left: Radical Activism in Los Angeles.* Berkeley: University of California Press, 2006.

Rafael, Vicente L., ed. *Discrepant Histories: Translocal Essays on Filipino Cultures.* Philadelphia: Temple University Press, 1995.

———. *White Love and Other Events in Filipino History.* Durham, N.C.: Duke University Press, 2000.

Rancière, Jacques. *The Politics of Literature.* Cambridge: Polity Press, 2011.

———. "Who Is the Subject of the Rights of Man?" *South Atlantic Quarterly* 103, no. 2/3 (2004): 297–310.

Ray, Sangeeta. "Towards a Planetary Reading of Postcolonial and American Imaginative Eco-Graphies." In *A Companion to Comparative Literature,* edited by Ali Behdad and Dominic Thomas, 421–35. Malden, Mass.: Blackwell, 2011.

Reddy, Chandan. *Freedom with Violence: Race, Sexuality, and the U.S. State.* Durham, N.C.: Duke University Press, 2011.

Reimers, David M. "Asian Immigrants in the South." In *Globalization and the American South,* edited by James C. Cobb and William Stueck, 100–134. Athens: University of Georgia Press, 2005.

Ridda, Martha. "Thinking Global? Local Globalisms and Global Localisms in the Writing of Jhumpa Lahiri." *Postcolonial Text* 6, no. 2 (2011): 1–14.

Roberts, Dorothy. "The Social Immorality of Health in the Gene Age: Race, Disability, and Inequality." In *Against Health: How Health Became the New*

Morality, edited by Jonathan M. Metzl and Anna Kirkland, 61–71. New York: New York University Press, 2010.

Robertson, Geoffrey. *Crimes against Humanity: The Struggle for Global Justice.* London: Allen Lane, 1999.

Robinson, Cedric J. *Black Marxism: The Making of the Black Radical Tradition.* London: Zed Books, 1983.

Rodley, Sir Nigel. "*The United Nations Convention Against Torture: A Commentary* (review)." *Human Rights Quarterly* 31, no. 4 (2009): 1143–46.

Rodriguez, Dylan. "The Meaning of 'Disaster' under the Dominance of White Life." In *What Lies Beneath: Katrina, Race, and the State of the Nation,* edited by South End Press Collective, 133–56. Cambridge, Mass.: South End Press, 2007.

Rodriguez, Ralph E. "Chicana/o Fiction from Resistance to Contestation: The Role of Creation in Ana Castillo's *So Far from God.*" *MELUS* 25, no. 2 (2000): 63–82.

Romagnolo, Catherine. "Recessive Origins in Julia Alvarez's *García Girls:* A Feminist Exploration of Narrative Beginnings." In *Narrative Beginnings: Theories and Practices,* edited by Brian Richardson, 149–65. Lincoln: University of Nebraska Press, 2008.

Romero, Lora. *Home Fronts: Domesticity and Its Critics in the Antebellum United States.* Durham, N.C.: Duke University Press, 1997.

Roorda, Eric Paul. *The Dictator Next Door: The Good Neighbor Policy and the Trujillo Regime in the Dominican Republic, 1930–1945.* Durham, N.C.: Duke University Press, 1998.

Rorty, Richard. "Human Rights, Rationality, and Sentimentality." In *The Human Rights Reader: Major Political Writings, Essays, Speeches, and Documents from the Bible to the Present,* edited by Micheline R. Ishay, 263–67. New York: Routledge, 1997.

Routledge, Paul. "Resisting and Reshaping Destructive Development: Social Movements and Globalizing Networks." In *Geographies of Global Change: Remapping the World,* 2nd ed., edited by R. J. Johnston, Peter J. Taylor, and Michael Watts, 310–27. Oxford: Blackwell, 2002.

Sabatello, Maya. "A Short History of the International Disability Rights Movement." In *Human Rights and Disability Advocacy,* edited by Maya Sabatello and Marianne Schulze, 13–24. Philadelphia: University of Pennsylvania Press, 2014.

Sabatello, Maya, and Marianne Schulze, eds. *Human Rights and Disability Advocacy.* Philadelphia: University of Pennsylvania Press, 2014.

Sae-Saue, Jayson T. "The Inter-Ethnic Return: Racial and Cultural Multiplicity in Foundational Asian American and Chicana/o Literatures." *Comparative American Studies* 8, no. 4 (2010): 267–82.

Sáez, Ñacuñán. "Torture: A Discourse on Practice." In *Tattoo, Torture, Mutilation, and Adornment: The Denaturalization of the Body,* edited by Patricia Sharpe and Frances E. Mascia-Lees, 126–44. Albany: State University of New York Press, 1992.

Saldaña-Portillo, María Josefina. *The Revolutionary Imagination in the Americas and the Age of Development.* Durham, N.C.: Duke University Press, 2003.

Saldívar, José David. *Border Matters: Remapping American Cultural Studies.* Berkeley: University of California Press, 1997.

———. *The Dialectics of Our America: Genealogy, Cultural Critique, and Literary History.* Durham, N.C.: Duke University Press, 1991.

Sanders, Mark. *Ambiguities of Witnessing: Law and Literature in the Time of a Truth Commission.* Stanford, Calif.: Stanford University Press, 2007.

San Juan E., Jr. *After Postcolonialism: Remapping Philippines-United States Confrontations.* Lanham, Md.: Rowman & Littlefield, 2000.

Sargent, Daniel. "Oasis in the Desert? America's Human Rights Rediscovery." In *The Breakthrough: Human Rights in the 1970s,* edited by Jan Eckel and Samuel Moyn, 125–45. Philadelphia: University of Pennsylvania Press, 2014.

Scarry, Elaine. *The Body in Pain: The Making and Unmaking of the World.* New York: Oxford University Press, 1985.

Scheper-Hughes, Nancy, and Carolyn Sargent, eds. *Small Wars: The Cultural Politics of Childhood.* Berkeley: University of California Press, 1998.

Schmitt, Carl. *The Concept of the Political.* Translated by George Schwab. Chicago: University of Chicago Press, 1996.

Schmitz, David F. *Thank God They're on Our Side: The United States and Right-Wing Dictatorships, 1921–1965.* Chapel Hill: University of North Carolina Press, 1999.

Scott, James C. *Seeing Like a State: How Certain Schemes to Improve the Human Condition Have Failed.* New Haven, Conn.: Yale University Press, 1998.

Shapiro, Michael J. "Warring Bodies and Bodies Politic: Tribal versus State Societies." *Body & Society* 1, no. 1 (1995): 107–23.

Shelton, Frank W. "Of Machines and Men: Pastoralism in Gaines's Fiction." In *Critical Reflections on the Fiction of Ernest J. Gaines,* edited by David C. Estes, 12–29. Athens: University of Georgia Press, 1994.

Shimakawa, Karen. *National Abjection: The Asian American Body Onstage.* Durham, N.C.: Duke University Press, 2002.

Shiva, Vandana. *Staying Alive: Development, Ecology and Women* (1989). In *The Human Rights Reader: Major Political Essays, Speeches, and Documents from the Bible to the Present,* edited by Micheline R. Ishay, 253–62. New York: Routledge, 1997.

Shohat, Ella, ed. *Talking Visions: Multicultural Feminisms in a Transnational Age.* Cambridge, Mass.: MIT Press, 1998.

Siebers, Tobin. *Disability Theory.* Ann Arbor: University of Michigan Press, 2008.

Sifris, Ronli. *Reproductive Freedom, Torture and International Human Rights: Challenging the Masculinisation of Torture.* London: Routledge, 2014.

Silverio, Simeon G. "Nelia Sancho: The Beauty Queen Turned Activist Bats for Comfort Women." *Asian Journal,* November 19, 2005.

Singh, Nikhil Pal. *Black Is a Country: Race and the Unfinished Struggle for Democracy.* Cambridge, Mass.: Harvard University Press, 2004.

———. "Culture/Wars: Recoding Empire in an Age of Democracy." *American Quarterly* 50, no. 3 (1998): 471–522.

Slater, David. "Trajectories of Development Theory: Capitalism, Socialism, and Beyond." In *Geographies of Global Change: Remapping the World,* 2nd ed., edited by R. J. Johnston, Peter J. Taylor, and Michael Watts, 88–99. Oxford: Blackwell, 2002.

Slaughter, Joseph. *Human Rights, Inc.: The World Novel, Narrative Form, and International Law.* New York: Fordham University Press, 2007.

Smith, Valerie. *Toni Morrison: Writing the Moral Imagination.* Chichester: Wiley-Blackwell, 2012.

Socolovsky, Maya. "Patriotism, Nationalism, and the Fiction of History in Julia Álvarez's *In the Time of the Butterflies* and *In the Name of Salomé.*" *Latin American Literary Review* 34, no. 68 (2006): 5–24.

Soh, Chunghee Sarah. "Prostitutes versus Sex Slaves: The Politics of Representing the 'Comfort Women.'" In *Legacies of the Comfort Women of World War II,* edited by Margaret Stetz and Bonnie B. C. Oh, 69–87. New York: East Gate, 2001.

Song, Min Hyoung. *The Children of 1965: On Writing, and Not Writing, as an Asian American.* Durham, N.C.: Duke University Press, 2013.

Sonnie, Amy, and James Tracy. *Hillbilly Nationalists, Urban Race Rebels, and Black Power: Community Organizing in Radical Times.* Brooklyn, N.Y.: Melville House, 2011.

Soohoo, Cynthia. "Human Rights and the Transformation of the 'Civil Rights' and 'Civil Liberties' Lawyer." In *Bringing Human Rights Home: A History of Human Rights in the United States,* vol. 2, edited by Cynthia Soohoo, Catherine Albisa, and Martha F. Davis, 71–104. Westport, Conn.: Praeger, 2008.

Spivak, Gayatri Chakravorty. *Death of a Discipline.* New York: Columbia University Press, 2003.

Spurgeon, Sara L. *Exploding the Western: Myths of Empire on the Postmodern Frontier.* College Station: Texas A&M University Press, 2005.

Stacey, Judith. *In the Name of the Family: Rethinking Family Values in the Postmodern Age.* Boston: Beacon Press, 1996.

Stanton, Donna C. "Top-Down, Bottom-Up, Horizontally: Resignifying the Universal in the Human Rights Discourse." In *Theoretical Perspectives on*

Human Rights and Literature, edited by Elizabeth Swanson Goldberg and Alexandra Schultheis Moore, 65–86. New York: Routledge, 2011.

Stockton, Kathryn Bond. *The Queer Child, or Growing Sideways in the Twentieth Century.* Durham, N.C.: Duke University Press, 2009.

Stueck, William. *Rethinking the Korean War: A New Diplomatic and Strategic History.* Princeton, N.J.: Princeton University Press, 2002.

Suárez, Lucía M. "Julia Alvarez and the Anxiety of Latina Representation." *Meridians: feminism, race, transnationalism* 5, no. 1 (2004): 117–45.

Tadiar, Neferti Xina. "Manila's New Metropolitan Form." In *Discrepant Histories: Translocal Essays on Filipino Cultures,* edited by Vicente L. Rafael, 285–313. Philadelphia: Temple University Press, 1995.

Tan, See Seng, and Amitav Acharya, eds. *Bandung Revisited: The Legacy of the 1955 Asian-African Conference for International Order.* Singapore: National University of Singapore Press, 2008.

Taylor, Diana. *Disappearing Acts: Spectacles of Gender and Nationalism in Argentina's "Dirty War."* Durham, N.C.: Duke University Press, 1997.

Taylor, Peter J., Michael Watts, and R. J. Johnston. "Geography/Globalization." In *Geographies of Global Change: Remapping the World,* 2nd ed., edited by R. J. Johnston, Peter J. Taylor, and Michael Watts, 1–17. Oxford: Blackwell, 2002.

Thomas, Dorothy Q. "Against American Supremacy: Rebuilding Human Rights Culture in the United States." In *Bringing Human Rights Home: A History of Human Rights in the United States,* vol. 2, edited by Cynthia Soohoo, Catherine Albisa, and Martha F. Davis, 1–23. Westport Conn.: Praeger, 2008.

Thompson, Chad D. "Post-Colonialism, Post Socialism, and Multiple Remembrances." *Socialist Studies: The Journal of the Society for Socialist Studies* 6, no. 1 (Spring 2010): 1–10.

Toebes, Brigit. "Towards an Improved Understanding of the International Human Right to Health." *Human Rights Quarterly* 21, no. 3 (1999): 661–79.

Toribio, Helen C. "Dare to Struggle: The KDP and Filipino American Politics." In *Legacy to Liberation: Politics and Culture of Revolutionary Asian Pacific America,* edited by Fred Ho, 31–45. San Francisco: Big Red Media and AK Press, 2000.

Tucker, Terrence. "(Re)Claiming Legacy in the Post–Civil Rights South in Richard Wright's 'Down by the Riverside' and Ernest Gaines's *A Gathering of Old Men.*" *Southern Literary Journal* 43, no. 2 (2011): 105–24.

Tulinius, Torfi H. "Saga as a Myth: The Family Sagas and Social Reality in 13th-Century Iceland." *Old Norse Myths, Literature and Society* (2000): 35–43.

Turits, Richard Lee. *Foundations of Despotism: Peasants, the Trujillo Regime, and Modernity in Dominican History.* Stanford, Calif.: Stanford University Press, 2003.

Turner, Bryan S. *Vulnerability and Human Rights.* University Park: Pennsylvania State University Press, 2006.

Uehling, Greta Lynn. "The International Smuggling of Children: Coyotes, Snakeheads, and the Politics of Compassion." *Anthropological Quarterly* 81, no. 4 (2008): 833–71.

Van Bueren, Geraldine. "The International Protection of Family Members' Rights as the 21st Century Approaches." *Human Rights Quarterly* 17, no. 4 (1995): 732–65.

Volpp, Leti. "'Obnoxious to Their Very Nature': Asian Americans and Constitutional Citizenship." *Asian Law Journal* 8, no. 1 (2001): 71–87.

Von Eschen, Penny M. *Race against Empire: Black Americans and Anticolonialism 1937–1957.* Ithaca, N.Y.: Cornell University Press, 1997.

Wardi, Anissa J. "Inscriptions in the Dust: *A Gathering of Old Men* and *Beloved* as Ancestral Requiems." *African American Review* 36, no. 1 (2002): 35–53.

Warren, Kenneth W. *What Was African American Literature?* Cambridge, Mass.: Harvard University Press, 2011.

Weeks, Kathi. "Life within and against Work: Affective Labor, Feminist Critique, and Post-Fordist Politics. *ephemera* 7, no. 1 (2007): 233–49.

Weiner, Mark S. *Americans without Law: The Racial Boundaries of Citizenship.* New York: New York University Press, 2006.

Werrlein, Debra T. "Legacies of the 'Innocent' Frontier: Failed Memory and the Infantilized Filipina Expatriate in Jessica Hagedorn's *Dogeaters*." *Journal of Asian American Studies* 7, no. 1 (2004): 27–50.

Westad, Odd Arne. *The Global Cold War: Third World Interventions and the Making of Our Times.* Cambridge: Cambridge University Press, 2007.

Weston, Kath. *Families We Choose: Lesbians, Gays, Kinship.* New York: Columbia University Press, 1991.

White, Daniel. "'Haunted by the Idea': Fathers and Sons in *In My Father's House* and *A Gathering of Old Men*." In *Critical Reflections on the Fiction of Ernest J. Gaines,* edited by David C. Estes, 158–79. Athens: University of Georgia Press, 1994.

White, Hayden. *Metahistory: The Historical Imagination in Nineteenth-Century Europe.* Baltimore, Md.: Johns Hopkins University Press, 1973.

Williams, Randall. *The Divided World: Human Rights and Its Violence.* Minneapolis: University of Minnesota Press, 2010.

Wilson, Richard Ashby, and Richard D. Brown, eds. *Humanitarianism and Suffering: The Mobilization of Empathy.* Cambridge: Cambridge University Press, 2009.

Wright, Melissa W. *Disposable Women and Other Myths of Global Capitalism.* New York: Routledge, 2006.

Wyschogrod, Edith. "Towards a Postmodern Ethics: Corporeality and Alterity." In *The Ethical,* edited by Edith Wyschogrod and Gerald P. McKenny, 54–65. Malden, Mass.: Blackwell, 2003.

Xanthaki, Alexandra. "Multiculturalism and International Law: Discussing Universal Standards." *Human Rights Quarterly* 32, no. 1 (2010): 21–48.

Yamin, Alicia. "Embodying Shadows: Tracing the Contours of Women's Rights to Health." In *From the Margins of Globalization: Critical Perspectives on Human Rights,* edited by Neve Gordon, 223–58. Lanham, Md.: Lexington Books, 2004.

———. "The Right to Health under International Law and Its Relevance to the United States." *American Journal of Public Health* 95, no. 7 (2005): 1156–61.

Yoneyama, Lisa. "Traveling Memories, Contagious Justice: Americanization of Japanese War Crimes at the End of the Post–Cold War." *Journal of Asian American Studies* 6, no. 1 (2003): 57–93.

Young, Cynthia A. *Soul Power: Culture, Radicalism, and the Making of a U.S. Third World Left.* Durham, N.C.: Duke University Press, 2006.

Yuh, Ji-Yeon. "Moved by War: Migration, Diaspora and the Korean War." *Journal of Asian American Studies* 8, no. 3 (2005): 277–91.

Zaretsky, Natasha. *No Direction Home: The American Family and the Fear of National Decline, 1968–1980.* Chapel Hill: University of North Carolina Press, 2007.

Zuckert, Michael. "Natural Rights in the American Revolution: The American Amalgam." In *Human Rights and Revolutions,* edited by Jeffrey N. Wasserstrom, Greg Grandin, Lynn Hunt, and Marilyn B. Young, 59–76. Lanham, Md.: Rowman & Littlefield, 2000.

Index

CRYSTAL PARIKH is associate professor of English and social and cultural analysis at New York University. She is the author of *An Ethics of Betrayal: The Politics of Otherness in Emergent U.S. Literatures and Culture* and coeditor of *The Cambridge Companion to Asian American Literature.*